The Moral Psychology of Regret

Moral Psychology of the Emotions

Series Editor:

Mark Alfano, Associate Professor, Department of Philosophy, Delft University of Technology

How do our emotions influence our other mental states (perceptions, beliefs, motivations, intentions) and our behavior? How are they influenced by our other mental states, our environments, and our cultures? What is the moral value of a particular emotion in a particular context? This series explores the causes, consequences, and value of the emotions from an interdisciplinary perspective. Emotions are diverse, with components at various levels (biological, neural, psychological, social), so each book in this series is devoted to a distinct emotion. This focus allows the author and reader to delve into a specific mental state, rather than trying to sum up emotions en masse. Authors approach a particular emotion from their own disciplinary angle (e.g., conceptual analysis, feminist philosophy, critical race theory, phenomenology, social psychology, personality psychology, neuroscience) while connecting with other fields. In so doing, they build a mosaic for each emotion, evaluating both its nature and its moral properties.

Other titles in this series:

The Moral Psychology of Forgiveness
edited by Kathryn J. Norlock

The Moral Psychology of Pride
edited by Adam J. Carter and Emma C. Gordon

The Moral Psychology of Sadness
edited by Anna Gotlib

The Moral Psychology of Anger
edited by Myisha Cherry and Owen Flanagan

The Moral Psychology of Contempt
edited by Michelle Mason

The Moral Psychology of Compassion
edited by Justin Caouette and Carolyn Price

The Moral Psychology of Disgust
edited by Nina Strohminger and Victor Kumar

The Moral Psychology of Gratitude
edited by Robert Roberts and Daniel Telech

The Moral Psychology of Admiration
edited by Alfred Archer and André Grahle

The Moral Psychology of Regret
edited by Anna Gotlib

Forthcoming titles in the series:

The Moral Psychology of Hope
edited by Claudia Blöser and Titus Stahl

The Moral Psychology of Regret

Edited by Anna Gotlib

London • New York

Published by Rowman & Littlefield International Ltd.
6 Tinworth Street, London, SE11 5AL, UK
www.rowmaninternational.com

Rowman & Littlefield International Ltd. is an affiliate of Rowman & Littlefield
4501 Forbes Boulevard, Suite 200, Lanham, Maryland 20706, USA
With additional offices in Boulder, New York, Toronto (Canada), and Plymouth (UK)
www.rowman.com

Selection and editorial matter © 2020 by Anna Gotlib
Copyright in individual chapters is held by the respective chapter authors.

All rights reserved. No part of this book may be reproduced in any form or by any electronic or mechanical means, including information storage and retrieval systems, without written permission from the publisher, except by a reviewer who may quote passages in a review.

British Library Cataloguing in Publication Data
A catalogue record for this book is available from the British Library

ISBN: HB 978-1-78660-251-0

Library of Congress Cataloging-in-Publication Data Available

ISBN: 978-1-78660-251-0 (cloth : alk. paper)
ISBN: 978-1-78660-252-7 (pbk : alk. paper)
ISBN: 978-1-78660-253-4 (electronic)

To J. G. for making everything possible.

To my students at Brooklyn College
for reminding me to keep going.

Contents

List of Tables and Figures	xi
Acknowledgments	xiii
Backward Glances: An Introduction to *The Moral Psychology of Regret* Anna Gotlib	1

PART I: VARIETIES OF REGRET — 27

1. Cousins of Regret — 29
   Adam Morton

2. Regret as a Reactive Attitude: The Conditions of Responsibility and Revision — 45
   Audrey L. Anton

3. Regret as a Condition for Personhood — 76
   James F. DiGiovanna

4. Reasonable Regret — 98
   Maura Priest

PART II: REGRET AND THE SELF — 119

5. Remorse — 121
   David Batho

6. Narrative and Marital Regret — 144
   Sarah Richmond

7	Regret, Responsibility, and the Brain *Ben Timberlake, Giorgio Coricelli, and Nadège Bault*	165

PART III: WHETHER TO REGRET 185

8	"Bury Me in a Free Land": Regret for Slavery in Nineteenth-Century African American Philosophical Literature *Catherine Villanueva Gardner*	187
9	Regret: Considerations of Disability *Teresa Blankmeyer Burke*	203
10	Regret Aversion in Riskless Choice Contexts: A Formal Model of Choice Behavior and Morally Problematic Choice Architectures *Caspar Chorus*	221
11	Long-Term Regret, Perspective, and Fate *Christopher Cowley*	240

Index	259
About the Contributors	265

Tables and Figures

FIGURES

10.1 Attribute regret $\mu \cdot \left[ln\left(1+ exp\left[\frac{\beta_m}{\mu} \cdot \left(x_{jm} - x_{im}\right)\right]\right) - ln(2)\right]$,
for different values of μ, β 225
10.2 The RRM-LogSum—solid line—as a function of attribute performance (*Source*: Chorus, 2012)   231
10.3 Initial choice set   235
10.4 A choice architecture   236
10.5 A morally problematic choice architecture   236

TABLE

10.1 Illustration of attribute regret ($\mu = 1$) in the context of the housing choice example $ln\left(1+ exp\left[\beta \cdot \left(x_{jm} - x_{im}\right)\right]\right) - ln(2)$ 227

Acknowledgments

This collection has been in the making for quite a while—in part, because such projects just require the necessary time and space, and in part because for me, 2018 became a year unlike any other. In February of 2018, I found myself hospitalized with a sudden and frightening illness as my life became, without dramatizing the circumstances too greatly, simply a fight for survival. Even post-hospitalization, and perhaps not surprisingly, my projects, both personal and professional, had to play second fiddle to the slow process of recovery—physical, psychological, and emotional. Unfortunately, this volume became one of the casualties.

Returning to it months later was both a gift and a struggle. A gift due to the grace, kindness, and understanding that I received from the contributors, the general series editor Mark Alfano, as well as from Rowman & Littlefield International. A struggle, because reentering one's life after a lengthy absence is just that. Words cannot express how grateful I am not only for everyone's patience and generosity but also for the wonderfully diverse, fascinating contributions they sent my way, even as we ran much past the initial publication deadlines. Thank you, everyone—you are the best.

Of course, I also want to thank my constant friends, mentors, colleagues, and confessors: Hilde Lindemann and Larry Palmer, who, for many years now, are always there with what I need, rather than want, to hear. In my own academic and mentoring practices, you are everything to which I aspire.

I am also grateful to my amazing, supportive colleagues at the Philosophy Department, and elsewhere, in Brooklyn College CUNY, who not only granted me leave to finish the intimidating tonnage of work that has piled up over my lengthy absence but who were always there with encouragement and support. And to my students, who were so understanding and concerned when

I suddenly disappeared from classes on that horrible day in February—thank you, and see you soon!

Finally, this is a book about regret. My strongest regret right now is that I cannot put into words my love and gratitude for my partner in crime, Jeff Guevin, without whom this book, and so many other things, would not be possible.

Backward Glances:
An Introduction to
The Moral Psychology of Regret
Anna Gotlib

Make the most of your regrets; never smother your sorrow, but tend and cherish it till it comes to have a separate and integral interest. To regret deeply is to live afresh.[1]

—Henry David Thoreau

REGRETS, I'VE HAD A FEW[2]

When I thought about what a volume on regret might look like, I imagined a number of possibilities: one that addresses philosophy's ongoing debates about agent regret; a more interdisciplinary collection that focuses on current psychological, neurobiological, and other scientific research into emotions such as regret; or one that just takes a chance and leaves it open to see what kinds of contributions the topic of regret might attract. I am so very glad that I went with the third option.

Like most moral emotions, regret is psychologically and conceptually complex not only in its evolving understandings but also in its etymology. Its earlier usages suggested sorrow for the loss or absence of something or someone of great value. Thus, in *Sense and Sensibility*, Marianne mourns the last evening in her beloved home: "Dear, dear Norland! [. . .] when shall I cease to regret you?" (Austen 2016, 20). More recently, regret suggests disappointment over something that one has done, something that has come to pass (or not come to pass), and so on. Merely uttering the word elicits a number of reactions, from sadness and longing to nostalgia and even relief (of not having had to regret something, for example). But in the most general sense, when we regret, we might just wish that things were otherwise, regardless of whether they were outside, or within, our control. Yet regret can also be a powerful, motivating kind of mourning, a fervent desire that some event, some consequence, and some state of affairs had not taken place. It can be an experience of backward-looking pain that is formative of our present and of our future.

Regret forms a part of the psychology of how and why we justify (or fail to justify) what we do to ourselves, to others, and to the lives that flow forward following the relative success or failure of these justifications. It is, as R. Jay Wallace notes in *The View from Here: On Affirmation, Attachment, and the Limits of Regret*, "a kind of perspective" through which we affirm or reject "our choices, events, actions, etc. through retrospective thought" (Wallace 2013, 3). The things that we regret usually do not embrace or desire (although, as will be argued in some of the chapters in this volume, regret's absence can suggest a worrying social or psychological brokenness). And if we push away the regrettable, then its opposite is an embracing, an "affirmation" of something (Wallace 2013, 5). But herein lies a dilemma. I can regret a careless remark I made in a conversation. But ought I regret this remark if it prevented a worse eventuality from taking place—for example, if it kept my interlocutor safely in the room scolding me, rather than boarding a bus that later turned out to have crashed? Or, in a more complicated case, am I less likely to regret a whole series of professional and economic choices that provide comfort and security for my family if these choices, however indirectly, contribute to the social, economic, or other kinds of jeopardies for others? As committed as I am to my family's well-being, am I so attached to my past decisions that I am less likely to dwell on whatever harms to others made our present well-being possible? Perhaps—or so Wallace, with whom several contributors to this volume engage, seems to suggest (Wallace 2013).

But we are all invested in something—we all affirm some combination of choices, actions, and histories that, at least for us, are nonnegotiable. So perhaps it is in cases like this that we might consider that regret works as a moral check on our most deeply held commitments. In other words, regret might be something more than a negatively valenced emotional response to the failed, the unwanted, and the unrealized but a moral sense, a feeling that nudges us, sometimes with great force, toward a better version of ourselves. Regret asks us "at what cost?" and, importantly, "at whose cost?" In this light, regret can be constructive: its lack might suggest moral myopia, or, at worst, narcissism, or something quality darker yet, such as a sociopath might possess. Because there is always a past and always something in that past that follows us. As Faulkner reminds us, "The past isn't dead. It's not even past" (Faulkner 1951). Making way for regret can reveal to us a narrative, diachronic self that cares about its past, is morally responsive to it, and regards it as a source of self-knowledge. The other way lies an episodic self that cares little for such things, and that, like Galen Strawson insists, "has little or no sense that [. . .]

one was there in the (further) past and will be there in the future" (Strawson 2004).

But regret can also be destructive, both through its presence and through its absence. As an emotion, it can be fickle, irrational, and even damaging not only to others—as when we regret something that another remembers with great fondness—but also to ourselves. Indeed, regret can become neurotic, obsessive, and even damaging to our notions of who we are. We might regret helping another because we view the act as having deprived us of a possible opportunity for success. We might regret being kind, fearing that we might have been taken for fools. We can obsessively regret a mistake that we made out of naiveté, ignorance, or sloppiness—or due to a number of circumstances that were never under our control. And we can destroy our present and threaten our future through this self-destructive, neurotic regret. Thus, we can regret the wrong thing.

Moreover, since regret is (generally) about the past—and most people desire to recall the "good version" of the past (and be nostalgic, rather than regretful)—its lack can be just as harmful as its misplaced presence. Beyond moral myopia and narcissism, the absence of regret points to a broader worry about not merely one's refusal to honestly engage with one's past but also one's inability to do so. The lack of regret can thus suggest not only a failure of rationality, when one, for example, refuses to see patterns of repeated missteps that produce regrettable results, but moral failure itself, when the most unwelcome and indefensible outcomes of the past are either denied as such or pushed so far back into one's consciousness as to never surface as objects of deliberation or shame. Thus, we can fail to regret the right thing.

But these are mere preliminary remarks to begin the volume-long exploration of the moral psychology of regret. In this introduction, I hope to accomplish several objectives: First, I wish to examine what I am calling the "shape of regret"—its topographies, nuances, and significance for our moral lives. Second, I will offer brief summaries of the sections and contributions that comprise this volume. Finally, I will conclude with a few thoughts about regret as an emotion that has much to contribute to the meaning, and moral character, of our lives.

THE SHAPE OF REGRET

Guilt versus Regret

As the contributors to this volume argue, regret is many things: it is personal and public, agential and nonagential, appropriate and less so. It is somewhat like remorse in that it is backward-looking and unlike remorse in that it can be about acts and events in which one did not play any role at all. It can be about choices made and those not made—that is, one can regret not only what one has done but also what one has omitted to do. In this section, I would like to trace some outlines of the geographies of regret as a morally significant emotion that, among other things, differs from related, yet importantly different states—and specifically, from guilt.

Suppose that I have borrowed my friend's new, expensive car and, because I was in a hurry and not paying sufficient attention, backed it into a pole, ruining her bumper and glossy paint job. If I am a decent person, I feel guilt—and I regret my actions (my lack of care, my lack of awareness, my lack of consideration for another's property, and so on). My guilt pushes me to confess my lack of proper care and attention to my friend and to offer to pay for the damage. I deeply regret and abhor what I have done and resolve to never be this careless again. And no matter how much my very generous and understanding friend insists that all is forgiven and that the insurance company will take care of the expenses, I do not feel released from the bad feelings, the unsettling emotions of guilt and regret.

Thus far, we can say that both guilt and regret are unpleasant emotional states that involve feeling sorry for something that took place. They might also be similar in their relative lack of uptake of countervailing arguments—I regret my actions no matter how much my friend tries to reassure me that my carelessness is nothing major, and that its consequences are of the kind that will resolved by other parties. They might even be necessarily connected: In fact, some have argued that one cannot experience guilt without regret: after all, it seems that it would be odd for me not to regret something that has moved me to feel guilt, and that I might very well feel guilty about a regrettable action (Tannenbaum 2007).

But others suggest that important moral differences exist between them. Ben-Ze'ev noted that "we feel guilty after doing something which is forbidden; we feel regret after doing something which was basically a failure" (Ben-Ze'ev 2000, 498). For example, I feel guilty after my careless driving (something that is formally and informally forbidden). Yet, I can more likely feel regret (but not guilt) after plans for a surprise birthday party have failed—regardless of whether the failure might have been the result of my bad planning or simply due to the weather. These distinctions raise three possibilities about the differences between guilt and regret.

First, appropriate feelings of guilt might very well require an agential action—one's own or one for which one might be viewed as reasonably responsible—while regret can be either agential or nonagential. Landman describes this distinction in terms of conceptual differences: "In general, it seems impossible to imagine experiencing guilt without regret, but quite possible to imagine experiencing regret without guilt. Thus, regret is [. . .] the broader concept" (Landman 1993, 56). In other words, it is difficult to explain how one can reasonably feel guilty for one's lack of timeliness due to a train's late arrival (although there are some who might still claim to feel such guilt), while it is not a challenge to imagine feeling regret for one's lateness. And while it is agent-regret that has most occupied (mostly analytic, Anglophone) philosophers, regret that is not necessarily associated with agency opens up new and, important, moral geographies. Indeed, some contributions to this volume engage with issues of nonagential regret because, it seems to me, it matters that we address its possibility in cases that might not be the most obvious candidates for apt regret.

Second, guilt and regret also differ in how their appropriateness is assessed. A guilt-feeling agent focuses on herself and her emotional state. For her, guilt becomes a self-involved emotion, which can translate into wallowing—perhaps inappropriately so. If I am still consumed by guilt at damaging my friend's car, for example—even after significant time has passed, the car is fixed, and, importantly, long after my friend has assured me that she no longer thinks about what happened—and if I am simply unable (or unwilling) to stop my guilt-driven obsession about what I had done and how it makes me feel, then my actions are arguably self-regarding, selfish, and inappropriate. It would not be unreasonable for someone to suggest that perhaps I ought to get over my guilt and myself—at least to the extent that grants uptake to my friend's desire that the subject matter be concluded. And although guilt is often appropriate, necessary, and a sign of "emotional intelligence," there can also be this kind of excessive, solipsistic, and emotionally obtuse guilt.

The same might not be true of regret. We can appropriately regret that which we have done and that which might have been. We regret acts and omissions. And we even regret that which did not—could not—implicate our agency at all. What seems to be true of regret that is not also true of guilt is that regret does not appear to have a reasonable expiration date: that is, one is much less likely to be accused of wallowing, of self-obsessively ruminating, when regretting. But why? In part, perhaps because regret can be less inward than guilt and more other-directed: I regret something that had very little impact on me or that in which I did not participate or something that I did not cause. Indeed, I can just *feel regret* about those non-me-implicating things because they are unwelcome outcomes for someone else. If I am regretful about another's thoughtless and careless actions, my focus is not on myself and my guilty inner states but on another's lack of well-being. In part, because even if my regret focuses on my own actions, recent research suggests that rather than guilt-driven rumination, regret can lead to

behavior change aimed at remediation (Landman 1993; Roese and Summerville 2005; Zeelenberg 1999). In other words, information gleaned from regrets can guide future behavior aimed at achieving desired outcomes (Zeelenberg et al. 2001). Regret has been defined as a counterfactual emotion (Kahneman and Miller 1986), meaning that its basis rests on a counterfactual inference (i.e., that the past might have unfolded differently, particularly if a different decision had been made). Counterfactual thinking itself has been shown to bring benefits in terms of subsequent problem-solving and performance enhancement (Epstude and Roese in press; Markman et al. 2008; Roese 1994, 1997). Counterfactual inference, by identifying a cause of a problem, helps make sense of negative experience. (Saffrey, Summerville, and Roese 2008)

Thus, perhaps while guilt can amount to mere self-regarding, and sometimes circular, obsession and wallowing that do not necessarily lead to reevaluations of, and changes in, one's behavior, regret can be a powerful motivating force that opens up the moral spaces for change.

Third, guilt and regret differ in their scope. While guilt often corresponds to a reaction to wrongdoing to others, regret encompasses wrongs done to others *as well as to oneself*. In fact, Zeelenberg and Breugelmans have argued that

> interpersonal harm (negative outcomes for others) and intrapersonal harm (negative outcomes for self) is crucial in differentiating these two emotions. . . . We found that guilt is predominantly felt in situations of interpersonal harm, whereas regret is felt in both situations of interpersonal harm and intrapersonal harm. (Zeelenberg and Breugelmans 2008, 589)

Thus, since *interpersonal* harm for which one experiences guilt is not fully circumscribed by one's own feelings—after all, when I feel guilty about wronging another, it is in important ways about my stance toward *them*—its appropriateness has something to do with when and whether the victim has recovered after the wrongdoing. So, if my feelings of guilt are too brief, and do not take into account the wronged party's emotional state, then I am morally suspect, insensitive, and not fully mindful of what I have done. Similarly, if my inner-directed rumination has long passed the wronged party's focus on the offending action, then my reaction is also morally problematic, but this time, for being too solipsistic and myopic while my victim has managed to move beyond my misdeeds. The appropriate scope of the guilt, therefore, is limited by the offended party's feelings about, and views toward, the offense.

But because regret is also *intrapersonal*, the "negative outcomes for self" begin to matter, and the scope of how long, how deeply, and for what reasons one regrets widens. If I harm my friend and my own professional reputation by, say, forgetting or carelessly completing something for which I am responsible, I can regret my error in the sense that I can both feel horrible for my actions and make amends by resolving to do better. While the scope of my guilt associated with harming my friend has to correspond, at least in some minimal way, with her reaction to the harm, my self-directed regret might reasonably endure past the point of shared intelligibility. This is not to say, however, that one cannot regret inappropriately, for an excessive (or excessively short) length of time, or simply regret the wrong thing: My only point here is that regret can begin to be distinguished from guilt in ways that make a significant difference in the evaluation of their appropriateness, duration, scope, and consequences.

So far, so good—regret differs from guilt in several important ways. But even if we grant this claim for now, it alone does not explain why regret ought to be valued as a distinct moral emotion, why it often is not, and how it offers a curious and complex perspective on our moral lives. I turn to a brief consideration of the how and the why of valuing regret in the next few sections.

Valuing Regret

"Things without all remedy should be without regard; what's done is done," Lady Macbeth tells her husband (Shakespeare, *Macbeth*). Do not regret what cannot be changed—the past is past. But is it? And is there any value in looking backward, in ruminating on our past decisions, actions, and their outcomes? By "value," I do not simply mean the crude sense of the maximization of current and future benefits, derived from a careful analysis of past missteps, although I do not exclude that meaning entirely. What I have in mind is a broader sense of value: Might we become better people (which might, or might not, include "better-off people") if we set aside Lady Macbeth's desperately instrumental plea to not look back, to move forward, to never regret? In other words, how and why might we value regret?

Perhaps we already do, despite ourselves. Let us grant that regret can be a rather painful state that is both cognitive and emotional. Landman notes that

> it is an experience of felt-reason or reasoned-emotion. The regretted matters may be sins of commission as well as sins of omission; they may range from the voluntary to the uncontrollable and accidental; they may be actually executed deeds or entirely mental ones committed by oneself or by another person or group; they may be moral or legal transgressions or morally and legally neutral. (Landman 1993, 36)

Yet, regret is also one of the constants in our lives—in fact, it is the most commonly experienced "negative" emotion (Shimanoff 1984). But its emotional and cognitive breadth and ubiquity tell us relatively little about its value, except perhaps how often, and how powerfully, we experience it. Thus, because we cannot simply avoid it, or set it aside because it fails to offer us the pleasures of more positive emotional states, we ask: why regret? On the one hand, regret seems to function in opposition to affirmation of one's choices, one's projects—it appears to work against evidence of a life lived well. On the other hand, research tells us that people value regret "in both an absolute sense (the favorable aspects outweigh the unfavorable aspects) and in a relative sense (as compared to other commonly experienced negative emotions)" (Saffrey, Summerville, and Roese 2008). Indeed,

> recent depictions of the functional value of regret (e.g., Zeelenberg 1999; Zeelenberg and Pieters 2007) and the willingness of individuals to risk the experience of regret (van Dijk and Zeelenberg 2007) have been theoretically striking precisely because regret was previously assumed to be undesirable, both in terms of its biasing effect on rational decision-making and also its link to depression (Lecci et al. 1994; Markman and Weary 1998; Monroe et al. 2005). In the present research [. . .] [p]eople appear to value their regret experience, insofar as they retrospectively evaluate it in predominately positive terms. (Saffrey, Summerville, and Roese 2008)

So, a tentative response to the question of "why regret" has something to do with regret's role as a trigger not only for self-revision, reevaluation, and change but also for forward-looking meaning-making, for moral coherence itself. In fact, a study offered evidence that we rate regret favorably as it helps us navigate, make sense of, and remedy what went wrong (Saffrey, Summerville, and Roese 2008). But perhaps this should not be altogether surprising: Regardless of our tendencies to want to believe otherwise, we are not very good predictors of future risks, benefits, or outcomes. We can certainly try to reason why action x might, or might not, produce result y, but in order to do this with more certainty, we need something like precedent—we need proof beyond our most optimistic (or pessimistic) predictions. The reasons for this are many: We are naturally biased toward certain considerations, people, goals, and methodologies. We are too often self-serving, chaotic, and myopic in our calculus. We want something to be the case (or not to be the case), and thus we form our argument for or against a certain course of action, guided both consciously, but also often subconsciously, by those desires. And we simply tend to forget—our memories, far from accurate retrieval mechanisms, are plagued by bad recollection, fictionalizations, and outright lacunas.

Despite these decision-making flaws and weaknesses, we still need to not only move through the world but also to do so coherently, with at least a modicum of agential reason. And even though this requires us to focus on the present and the future, we also need to glance backward, and specifically, to look to the times where we failed. In other words, we need to be cognizant of that which we regret. While dwelling on past mistakes and unfortunate incidents as one's sole motivation for action carries its own dangers, paying attention to what, and why, one regrets might offer both a perspective of the "I have been here before" variety and force a more active engagement with one's evolving sense of self. That is, in recognizing that one already regrets, one might realize that current and future decisions have to grapple with, and be responsive to, this emotion; alternatively, one might view regret as a sign of past failure that one no longer desires to be constitutive of one's identity. In both cases, regret acts as a normative touchstone, as a check on our often rash, biased, and overenthusiastic selves. And while acknowledging and tangling with one's regret does not offer a panacea for our morally complicated lives, it gives us a fighting chance in confronting some of the consequences of agential moral failure—as well as in grappling with what is regretful yet outside of our control. Despite Lady Macbeth's urging, what's done is never quite done with us.

Philosophers on Regret as Human Predicament

In addition to the multidisciplinary psychological and behavioral research into regret, philosophers have also offered a few varied takes on its nature, function, and desirability. It is important to note that, as is evidenced by this volume alone, there is no consensus on what regret is, whether it is beneficial, when it is appropriate, how it is motivated, and so on. While a significant amount of philosophical analysis of regret has to do with exploring the nature and appropriateness of agent-regret, regret and decision theory, and the general rationality of regret, I will only note a few examples here. My intent is not to offer a full overview of philosophical approaches to regret as such but to examine a small sampling of the kinds of questions that have been raised in the course of numerous explorations.

If we begin with the worry that regret is somehow a negative, undesirable emotion that has to be explained—or explained away—and made more reasonable, more palatable, as a part of moral reasoning or practical action, then we need to either find ways to counteract it or else attempt to assimilate it into our daily lives in ways that seem less damaging and undermining of our sense of well-being. Given the prevalence of regret as human experience, casting it aside or explaining it away will simply not do. Yet if we decide that facing our regrets is the better path, we are presented with two worries: First, ought we focus on the morality and consequences of regretting singular agent-events or, alternatively, should we instead worry about the kinds of regrets whose intricate trajectories span lifetimes, threatening the moral grounding of our very lives? Second, should we view regret as a necessary, identity-constituting part of our moral universe—in the sense that its lack signals a serious moral, epistemic, or other kind of deficiency—or should we be more concerned with the potential destruction of this moral universe that regret itself represents? It depends on whom we ask.

In "Moral Luck" (and elsewhere), Bernard Williams focuses on regret for agential actions while answering the latter worry about the moral worth of regret in the affirmative. He famously argues for the moral importance of what he calls "agent-regret"—a sense of moral responsibility for the bad consequences of acts for which we are not morally, but causally, responsible (Williams 1981). His goal is to steer away from the juridical rigidity of (often ideal) moral theory and to replace it with a more nuanced, less black-and-white assessment of human agency (Williams 1981, 1985). Morality, Williams notes, is not at all what the leading moral theories insist it is—it is a not a zero-sum game, where we are either boundlessly guilty and remorseful or innocently regretful as sympathetic bystanders. Such a division is not only unrepresentative of actual lived human experience but also grants moral luck too much influence in how, and whether, we respond with regret (or other emotions) in a shared moral universe. By "moral luck" what Williams meant is the happenstance of a moral agent being blamed or praised for her action or its consequences regardless of her full control of either. Consider the following example: Person X and Person Y both attend a party. Person X, running to greet his friend, carelessly nudges another individual standing at the pool's edge into the water, where that individual drowns. Person Y, also running to greet her friend, carelessly nudges a different person into the same pool, but this time, the nudged person can swim and does not drown. The difference lies in something (the nudged individual's swimming ability) of which neither Person X nor Person Y had knowledge or control—Person X simply had bad moral luck, and person Y had good moral luck. Is this where our considerations of regret and moral responsibility ought to end?

Not quite. Moral value and regret cannot depend on mere luck, Williams writes. The consequences of leaving morality to the vagaries of luck produce some troubling results. Instead, he suggests that, distortions of ideal moral theory aside, our moral lives are just as immune to luck as they are to hierarchical system building (Williams 1993, 36). If moral systems tell us that we should either feel serious remorse only for the acts for which we are clearly responsible or else only experience some general, poorly defined regret for mere unfortunate events, then they fail to acknowledge any justifiable, and appropriate, agent-regret. And agent-regret, unlike remorse or general regret, is not about the assigning of blame for clear wrongdoing. Instead, it is a more subtle, and in some ways, a more difficult, assumption of responsibility as well as a desire to "make amends" (Sussman 2013, 1).

To illustrate the idea of agent-regret, Williams offers what is now a well-known example (Williams 1993, 43). Imagine an unimpaired, attentive truck driver who accidentally kills a child who ran out in the street in front of him.

This truck driver was simply unlucky—apparently blameless as a moral agent. Yet Williams argues that even though said truck driver is not blameworthy (and is thus not a candidate for full remorse), mere bystander-kind-of-regret is also insufficient—we ought to expect him to experience agent-regret, to blame himself for what took place, to apologize, and to try to make amends (Williams 1981). And before we argue that this would be an overreaction and a misreading of the moral geographies of the situation, Williams insists that "not just that the experience of agent-regret in such situations is psychologically normal, such that any half-decent agent will probably continue to feel guilty despite coming to know that she is not really culpable. In addition [. . .] these feelings and responses need not be confused or irrational in any way" (Sussman 2013, 2). Thus, our experiences of agent-regret, even in cases where we are not morally culpable, are neither extraordinary, nor supererogatory, nor really much more than the simply decent thing to feel—an essential part of our ethical lives. Indeed, it is worries about the rationality of this kind of regret that we ought to consider odd:

> It would be a kind of insanity never to experience sentiments of this kind towards anyone, and it would be an insane concept of rationality which insisted that a rational person never would. To insist on such a conception of rationality, moreover, would, apart from other kinds of absurdity, suggest a large falsehood: that we might, if we conducted ourselves clear-headedly enough, entirely detach ourselves from the unintentional aspects of our actions . . . and yet still retain our identity and character as agents. (Williams 1981, 29, cited in Sussman 2013, 2)

Is this view of regret reasonable, or is it a philosophical (indeed, perhaps even a psychological) error? After all, do we not want to say something like "that truck driver is mistaken, irrational, and perhaps over-emotional in his reactions to what was clearly an accident, a case of bad moral luck"? On the one hand, we might want to make a stronger case for *real* regret—the kind of regret that we clearly ought to feel when we have done something wrong on purpose or at least out of negligence or lack of proper attention. We want to say that the kind of regret an agent ought to feel when having done deliberate wrong is more justified both epistemically and morally, is more rational, and shows a fuller understanding of what it means to have failed in some important way. Yet on the other, we want the truck driver to appreciate that hitting the child (even negligently) is a moral horror from which he might not, and perhaps ought not, ever fully recover. We want him to feel something like agent-regret regardless of his blameworthiness, just because he is a part of a shared moral universe where we are often, due to bad moral luck or otherwise, not in control and where our sense of decency just might override a strictly juridical calculus of culpability. Rejecting this view of agent-regret, at least according to Williams, sells short the complexity, unpredictability, and actual lived experiences of our moral lives. But there are other approaches to regret, and I now turn to quite a different view.

Let's begin with the idea that often the things we can regret are not just individual events or accidents but are parts of long chains of experiences and circumstances that merge and twist in ways that come to constitute out lives. So, it is one thing to view regret as a response to a particular event or action, and it is quite another to imagine it as a challenge to the entirety of one's ongoing and valued life. This is where Wallace, with whom some of the contributors in this volume engage, begins his fascinating and much-discussed work, *The View from Here: On Affirmation, Attachment, and the Limits of Regret*. He focuses on the logic of regret, which, he argues, is grounded in our tendencies to attach, and to commit, ourselves to the course of events in our lived lives. From our perspective "from here," with the passage of time, we come to "affirm" or endorse actions and choices that made our lives possible but which, at the time of performance, we might have had strong reasons to regret or at least toward which we felt (and feel) ambivalent. Wallace suggests that reflecting on our lives from the perspective of the present, as we must invariably do, can lead to serious moral confusion. If we assume that our lives are the kind that we both enjoy and endorse as worth living, we might nevertheless look back on what made them possible and realize that some of our past choices were morally troubling, wrong, or difficult to defend. For example, perhaps Bill lied about the reasons he failed to finish a group work project on time—he claimed illness while really taking a "personal day" for no reason other than boredom at work. Because his excuse was trusted by his coworkers who finished the project without him, he still received a promotion, which led to a better job elsewhere, which led to his current professional and financial success. Bill realizes that what he did was wrong—that, in fact, there is no morally justifiable way of excusing his behavior—and yet, it was his lie that has led to, and was arguably necessary for, his deeply valued present. Because he values this life now, he affirms the old lie and everything that came after. Indeed, if his past choices were otherwise, they might have led to a less favorable outcome. In this sense, Bill cannot regret his lie, for to regret it is just to wish that his current life were otherwise. At the same time, he can also see the lie as a wrong. What now—how can any of this be a consistent moral position?

But this is where we find ourselves: While we are psychologically compelled to affirm our lives, we cannot seem to get rid of the sense that what we are attached to is made possible by that which might be regrettable or worse. This is a rather pessimistic conclusion—that to be committed to the value of our lives is at the same time to be explicitly committed to all of the historical atrocities, wrongdoing, and large and small regrettable actions that led us here. Or, to put it bluntly, to value our lives also means to negate any regret about their foundations. Might this seemingly inescapable conflict between the desirable and the morally regrettable lead to a kind of moral nihilism?

Perhaps. As an example, Wallace considers the case of complicity in injustice as a part of what he calls "the bourgeois predicament": Many of us in affluent societies live lives that we would like unconditionally to affirm yet are unable to do so as they seem to depend on morally troubling, and sometimes wholly indefensible, constellations of events, choices, and decisions. If what Wallace calls "unconditional affirmation" of one's life requires the nonregret of all that has preceded, the "we" of the present are left strangely othered from our past selves:

> The standpoint of retrospective assessment is constrained by this fact, such that "we can find ourselves unable to regret actions of ours that were unjustifiable at the time" and "committed to affirming features of our lives and of the world we inhabit that are objectively lamentable" (p. 3) [. . .] Hence the book's title: all such appraisal is "from here." (Wallace 2013, 3, cited in Thomas 2014)

Or, as Wallace suggests, there is "a rift between ourselves and the larger world in which we live" (Wallace 2013, 7). Surprisingly, Wallace does not assume the fully nihilist, despairing stance. Recall that he argues that even though our affirmation of our life necessitates an inability to regret all that led to its realization, we can still see the past event, choice, or circumstance as unjustified. We can thus be fully committed in terms of endorsing our lives as we know them while remaining "deeply ambivalent" about some of the choices that led us here (Wallace 2013, 185). But this kind of situation—one that most, if not all, of us are in—only supports what Wallace takes to be a modest nihilism: one where we can enjoy what are otherwise full and satisfactory lives while at the same time being aware of the objective badness of some of the events, choices, and actions that led us here.

But perhaps the psychological need to affirm our lives in this way is an absurdity—and not a "modest" one at that. Why not wholeheartedly regret our fortunate but "objectively lamentable" choices and circumstances, lessening our enthusiastic endorsement of our lives? Or else why not an embracing of a deep nihilism about any attempts to morally justify our lives altogether? And is Wallace correct that the ever-looming presence of regret leaves us existentially and morally unmoored in ways that we never considered?

The answers depend on several variables. There is the complexity of what one regrets. The simple case of regret nonproblematically coexisting with affirmation occurs when their objects are divisible and independent: For example, from here, I can regret having attended a particular school but affirm my performance while in attendance. My regret and affirmation, while both relating to my schooling, can be viewed as separate events that do not contradict each other, and that can coexist coherently without much ambivalence: Attending the school might not have been ideal, but it was also not a necessary condition of how I performed there.

The more difficult—and more common—version of events involves intersecting and complicated causal connections between the affirmable and the regrettable, where there simply is not the affirmable without the regrettable or, as Wallace puts it, "There is no psychological space for affirming the object while regretting on balance its necessary conditions, so long as one is clear that the conditions really are necessary for the thing that one affirms" (Wallace 2013, 73). I wish to conclude this section with a few questions and concerns about such a conclusion and perhaps offer another way to view regret and its place in our moral lives.

First, it seems that regret from here can place moral pressure on our past without undoing the present. That is, I can regret my actions insofar as they could have been otherwise because desiring to do better, to be better, or for things to have been other than they were does not necessarily annihilate my present commitments—it merely places them in the context of changing time, perspectives, interpretations, and valuations. Regretting the past tells us that we might have changed over time or that the moral valences of our various choices have shifted without creating a chasm between what is and what led us here. If I made a morally indefensible choice that led to my present success, I ought to regret—in fact, morally speaking, I *must* do so—but this does not invalidate my present, my life, or my identity. What it does is allow retrospection to play a crucial role in my evolving sense of who I am and of the choices and contingencies that led me here.

Second, if we regard regret as not merely an emotion, but as a normative stance toward the past, what results might very well fall short of affirmation of our lives yet grant us a better, broader perspective on some of our most dearly held pieties. In other words, what if regret is exactly what we need to figure out that, just maybe, some things are not worthy of being affirmed, regardless of their central roles in our lives? Indeed, what can truly invalidate my life might just be the *unacknowledged* badness of the past acts themselves—the silences and rationalizations and bargains struck with myself in order to be able to go on. Perhaps it is the fear of regret that denies us a necessary critical perspective on our identities and stymies the possibility of moral progress. Because as humans we will always morally fail in some way that matters (Tessman 2015), we need regret in order to try to understand why and how and to make amends. Stuck as we are in the "view from here," regret forces us to confront the existential limits of our moral, epistemic, and other blind spots that, when left unexamined, lead to atrocities. And so regret calls on us to proceed with more care.

Wallace's (even modest) moral nihilism about regret thus seems unnecessarily counterintuitive. I can value my life after having escaped the Soviet Union while at the same time regretting the many others who, perhaps via a causal chain that allowed my family to flee, were precluded from doing the same. And while, as Wallace notes, I am always valuing and judging "from here," I am in possession of more than one lens—my present commitments do not necessarily lessen, even when I express regret for the past, although I might see them in a less favorable, less affirmable, light. My point is that regret is not something that stands apart from, or contrary to, affirmation. Because regret is backward-looking, it can remind us why we value what we value and, perhaps, how we have gone wrong. And there is something else: Regret can point us in the direction of a deeper moral assessment of our current values—it can disturb us, distract us from our present projects, and remind us that there are some things that just might be more valuable than our immediate life course. We need regret not only because we could have done better in the past but also because we are so enthusiastically oriented toward the future—and perhaps a check on such enthusiasm is essential. From here, we can both endorse *and* regret, without losing ourselves in the process.

Regretting Regret

So far, we have seen that regret is complex, welcome, troublesome, contradictory, and, perhaps, utterly necessary for our understanding of ourselves as moral beings. But regret is also rather unpopular. Recall Faulkner's reminder that the past is always somehow with us (Faulkner 1951). But do we believe him? It turns out that regardless of Faulkner's claims, and despite any philosophically or psychologically grounded arguments for regret as a vital moral emotion, it is still more commonly viewed as something to be overcome, avoided, or explained away. The possibility of regret reminds us too clearly—and painfully—that we make mistakes, that we are nothing if not fallible. It also suggests that our focus on intent and agency can be myopic: No matter how much we try, we cannot deny that so much of our lives are comprised not by our agency but by the regrettable events that *simply happen* to us, regardless of what we desire, do, or believe. And all of this vulnerability and unpredictability can be quite unsettling.

Outside of academic discourses, the way (generally modern, Western) cultures have responded to the existential threats of regret has fallen somewhere between the defensive and the rejecting. Popular books, including *Woulda, Coulda, Shoulda: Overcoming Regrets, Mistakes, and Missed Opportunities* (1992); *No Regrets: A 10-Step Program for Living in the Present and*

Leaving the Past Behind (2004); *and Fearless Living: Live without Excuses and Love without Regret* (2001) offer easy-to-follow plans on how to eradicate it, like a virus or a muffin top. Regret isn't just seen as antithetical to reason, it's spiritually transgressive as well. Sayings such as "Everything happens for a reason" inherently condemn the sort of nihilist relativism that might experience regret as proof of the random meaninglessness of life. (Chocano 2013)

Even political leaders sometimes seem to view regret as evidence of failure and weakness: At a 2004 press conference, President George W. Bush was asked to name the biggest mistake he had made—something that, presumably, he regrets. After a few uncomfortable minutes, Bush stated that while he was sure that he had made such a mistake, none came to mind (Cooper 2004). Thus, no (admitted) mistakes—no regrets, and, presumably, no regret-indicated weakness. And even if there were any, then methods—such as counseling, self-help texts, and others—can assist one with nullifying this backward-looking, depressing, unhelpful, and generally harmful emotion. The past matters less, we are told—and has a much lesser hold on us—if we simply concentrate on the present and the future. Life has meaning, order, and, most importantly, happiness only if we focus on the right things, in the correct ways—and none of them include regret.

In *Regret: The Persistence of the Possible* (1993), Janet Landman argues that perhaps our overall approach to regret has a lot to do with how we view economic choice: Since decision theory takes the decision maker to be rational, informed, and able to make sensible, accurate decisions, the past, and thus the possibility of other choices, must be rejected. She notes that if we take our conflicts to be suitably resolved by cost-benefit analyses, then there is simply nothing to regret (Landman 1993). So, regret has to be excluded as a valid emotion, as an appropriate reaction to our behaviors, because its presence might signal our inability to optimize choices or to be in control—indeed, its presence might contradict the very definition of who we are as successful, rational, and calculating beings. As Landman tells us, denying regret is tantamount to denying that it is possible for us to be "losers" (Landman 1993):

> In a culture that believes winning is everything, that sees success as a totalising, absolute system, happiness and even basic worth are determined by winning. It's not surprising, then, that people feel they need to deny regret—deny failure—in order to stay in the game [. . .] Landman argues [that] the culture privileges a pragmatic, rationalist attitude toward regret that doesn't allow for emotion or counterfactual ideation, and then combines with it a heroic framework which equates anything that lands short of the platonic ideal with failure. In such an

environment, the denial of failure takes on magical powers. It becomes inoculation against failure itself. To express regret is nothing short of dangerous. It threatens to collapse the whole system. (Chocano 2013)

Examples of this regret-denial abound. Apart from the pop-psychological literature noted earlier, how many advertisements for items big and small—from shoes to cars to insurance to dating—are grounded in mining our fears of regretting, of missing out, of not making the single correct choice at the single correct moment? How often are we warned to get an education, to marry, to have children, to buy a home, and so on—lest we regret not doing so, doing so incorrectly, with the wrong person, at the wrong time, at the wrong interest rate? And how many times do we respond, sometimes before we are able to form our own views on the subject, with anxiety, with dread, with the desire to do something—*anything*—that would stave off, or prevent, regret altogether? We seem to have bought into Harry Truman's admonition to "never, never waste a minute on regret. It's a waste of time" (Landman 1993, 9).[3]

But, as Landman reminds us, regret is everywhere—everywhere that matters: in our inner thoughts, our wishes, our fears, in our greatest works of literature. From the youthful regret of John Knowles's *A Separate Peace*, to the regrettable hubris in Jane Austen's *Emma*, to the denial of regret in Virginia Woolf's *Mrs. Dalloway*, to the old-age regrets of Shakespeare's *King Lear*, regret is not only central to the immediate lives of individual characters but it also influences their broader worlds, their choices, their futures. And as generations engage with these (and numerous other) explorations of regret, it would seem both a misreading and shortsightedness to conclude that they do so only to learn to avoid it. The regret of others teaches us something about the human condition, about the meaning of choices and actions, about the role of emotions in our lives, about ourselves. Regret, these books remind us, is neither to be dismissed nor ignored—it is there to disturb us; to shake us out of complacency and self-satisfaction; to whisper to us that not everything is all right; to nudge us into a realization that change, or at least a reconsideration of a life, is needed. Regret is there to say that something, or someone—possibly ourselves—was, and perhaps is still, wrong. Outside of literature, it is there to remind us that most decisions are made with some ambivalence, some lack of knowledge, that their motivations and consequences can be ambiguous and requiring reconsideration—and that fundamentally, we are infinitely fallible, imperfectly rational, *regretting* selves.

Yet this is not what many of us wish to hear. We might prefer to embrace the myth of the rational decision maker who, with sufficient information, can maximize her choices such that regret would not enter the calculus. It is not that we do not want to learn from our mistakes once those mistakes are uncovered—I think that most of us, in fact, do—but it is that we would prefer to conceive of ourselves as creatures who can eventually move past the need to do so: That regret, like pain and debt, can, with enough effort, be eliminated.

But this idealized nonregretting self is neither possible nor preferable: Not possible because we are highly ambivalent, emotional, often-myopic beings, driven by motivations that are beyond our control and which strain our abilities to calculate consequences. Not preferable because we can be so wrong factually, insufficient rationally, ignorant empirically, unprepared emotionally. Simply put, we are not very good at reading our environments and each other. Because we so frequently morally fail, our regrets are there to let us know, despite ourselves, that other choices, other outcomes, and other paths are possible. And even after we think that we have taken all possibilities into account, unexpected, regrettable things just happen for no intelligible (to us) reasons. What then?

But this is why regret matters as a distinctly moral emotion: It both reminds us of our decision-making imperfections and of the complexity, seeming randomness, and uncontrollability of the world. In short, it keeps us humble while nudging us to do—to be—better. Perhaps avoiding regret is tantamount to shutting one's eyes and stopping up one's ears because one is unhappy with the scenery and the music—doing so neither removes the scenery nor silences the music in the long term. Denying regret as a valuable, albeit painful, experience can lock us in an airless *now*, where one's past, present, and future lack a common language. This volume is offered with the hope of centering regret epistemically, psychologically, and morally within the discourses about our selves, our motivations—and about how the past is never quite behind us.

THE SHAPE OF THIS VOLUME

As I noted earlier, this volume does not attempt to provide a singular definition of regret, whether psychological, philosophical, sociological, or any other. What it does offer is a variety of perspectives on the many understandings and functions of, and worries about, regret. The collection is organized into three parts: *Part I: Varieties of Regret*, which includes "Cousins of Regret" by Adam Morton, "Regret as a Reactive Attitude: The Conditions of Responsibility and Revision" by Audrey L. Anton, "Regret as a Condition for Personhood" by James F. DiGiovanna, and "Reasonable Regret" by Maura Priest; *Part II: Regret and the Self*, which includes "Remorse" by David Batho, "Narrative and Marital Regret" by Sarah Richmond, and "Regret, Responsibility, and the Brain" by Ben Timberlake,

Giorgio Coricelli, and Nadège Bault; and *Part III: Whether to Regret*, including "'Bury Me in a Free Land': Regret for Slavery in Nineteenth-Century African American Philosophical Literature" by Catherine Villanueva Gardner, "Regret: Considerations of Disability" by Teresa Blankmeyer Burke, "Regret Aversion in Riskless Choice Contexts: A Formal Model of Choice Behavior and Morally Problematic Choice Architectures" by Caspar Chorus, and "Long-Term Regret, Perspective, and Fate" by Christopher Cowley. I will now offer brief summaries of the contributions that constitute this book.

Adam Morton begins the conversation about the varieties of regret by arguing that regret, remorse, shame, and guilt are each distinct from one another. Indeed, while we can ascribe attitudes to our past less-than-admirable actions that fit into these categories, we can also describe distinctions between retrospective emotions that do not correspond to those between this particular list of English words. Morton then characterizes a range of emotions, which includes the emotions we apply these words to but in terms that do not presuppose that the distinctions between them are psychologically or morally very deep. In fact, he doesn't think they are. He concludes by describing an alternative set of distinctions that suggest that the line between moral and nonmoral is not well reflected in our attitudes to our past actions.

In "Regret as a Reactive Attitude: The Conditions of Responsibility and Revision," Audrey L. Anton attempts to define what regret might be—and what it is not. She argues that regret should be considered one of the *reactive emotions* insofar as it is a self-reactive attitude. First, she considers what it is for something to be a reactive attitude. She contends that reactive attitudes are emotions toward a subject concerning the subject's responsibility for something of normative import (but not necessarily of moral import). In the case of regret, she argues, the subject responds to herself as responsible for something suboptimal. In addition, regret is distinguished from other emotions like shame in that regret always involves some desire (even if only a faint one) to have behaved differently. The first condition is the condition of *responsibility*; the second is that of *revision*. Emotion theorists routinely exclude one or both of these conditions when describing regret. She thinks that this is a mistake. First, it is widely accepted that *remorse* is a reactive attitude whereby one feels responsible for some negative outcome of their actions and, as a result, wishes to right the wrong. In addition, remorse is often considered a species of the larger class, *regret*. If this is the case, and if regret is not itself a reactive attitude, the burden is on the opposition to explain how this can be the case. Second, she argues that the explanation cannot be simply that remorse involves responsibility and revision whereas regret does not, because all previous descriptions of regret absent these conditions are inadequate. She acknowledges that by adding the two criteria and considering regret a reactive attitude, there are some cases commonly referred to as "regret" that will be rightfully excluded, and that our reference to regret in such instances is metaphorical, hyperbolic, or simply mistaken. Finally, she reviews recent findings in neuroscience (mainly various instances of fMRI studies) that suggest regret does indeed involve some sense of responsibility and a desire for revision.

James F. DiGiovanna's "Regret as a Condition for Personhood" expands the evaluation of regret as a distinctly moral emotion by arguing that it is essential for nothing less than our personhood itself. He begins by construing regret as a cognitive emotion and argues that the capacity for regret is a necessary and sufficient condition for personhood. It fulfills standard personhood criteria as found in philosophy historically as well as in more contemporary theories: To be able to regret is to be self-conscious; it shows that one understands oneself as capable of blame; it shows that one has continuity of memory and mental content across time; it involves making moral judgments, at least about oneself; it reflects the presence of concern; and it involves a second-order volition in that one wills that one would will differently if similar circumstances arise. Further, regret is person-making and identity-securing in that it establishes a relation between past and present selves and an attitude toward future selves, creating both a narrative that is partly self-defining and an attitude that is future-directing. The analysis of regret further shows that, contrary to some leading theories of personhood, such as Dennett's and Frankfurt's, some emotional content is necessary for full personhood. An entity that was incapable of regret would be a person only in a reduced sense. He suggests that someone incapable of regret becomes unperson-like in that they lack a standard personal attitude that is central to social engagement and self-knowledge.

In "Reasonable Regret," Maura Priest explores cases of "questionable regret" and compares them to less controversial examples as a means to delineate when regret is both possible and reasonable. Priest first describes key features of uncontroversial regret. She then considers controversial examples and argues that the presence or absence of the aforementioned features speaks to regret's possibility and aptness. More specifically, she argues that in some cases, regret is not possible and therefore not reasonable. However, Priest claims that in other cases, regret is both possible and reasonable. What distinguishes these latter types of cases, however, is that regret is morally *obligatory* in some but *optional* in others.

David Batho begins the discussion about regret and the self with "Regret and Self-Knowledge," arguing that regret is often expressed in relation to states of affairs that one is somehow involved in having brought about. What Batho has in mind is what Bernard Williams expressed in his introduction of the notion of "agent-regret" in *Moral Luck*—the feeling that it would have been better if one had acted otherwise. Here, Batho focuses on the potential that regret can disclose not only alternative possibilities of action but also alternate possibilities of *selfhood*. In so doing, he draws on Max Scheler's analysis of the distinction between guilt (*Schuld*) and repentance (*Reue*), where guilt is the affective state in which one (1) perceives oneself to have done something wrong; (2) perceives the wrongdoing to be expressive of one's character; and (3) remains committed to the character of which the wrongdoing is expressive. Repentance, by contrast, involves surrendering one's character in light of the deed. These two forms of regret are not simply directed to particular actions; both involve understanding the relation between action and character as well as different possibilities of relating to one's character. By disclosing possibilities of relating to your character, regret can thus disclose ways of being a self that transcend any particular character formation. Thus, it is a consequence of Scheler's analysis that regret can disclose *what it is* to be a self over and above what it is to be the particular person you are. His contribution aims to add to the growing literature in the phenomenological analysis of what Matthew Ratcliffe has called "existential feelings." Drawing on Martin Heidegger's analysis of mood, studies in this field attempt to articulate the bodily affective states that are constitutive of being in a world. He claims that regret deserves consideration in these discussions and advances an initial analysis of the phenomenon.

Sarah Richmond begins "Narrative and Marital Regret" with an imaginary example of a regret which, she suspects, may be commonly experienced in life, and which has frequently figured in literature. Keith experiences marital regret, i.e. the regret one might feel in relation to ones choice of spouse. In the example, Keiths regret focuses on *inaction* rather than action, which already differentiates it from the action-focused research undertaken by most psychologists who have studied regret. Richmond argues that the nature and the phenomenology of Keith's regret speak in favour of a narrative framework, and she surveys some relevant contributions from anglophone philosophers, on the relationship between narrative structure and well-being. Richmond suggests that this work may suffer from an unnecessarily individualist focus; for marital regret, arguably, the notion of a *shared* narrative is required and the resources of psychoanalytical theory may also enrich our understanding.

Concluding the section on regret and the self, Giorgio Coricelli, Ben Timberlake, and Nadège Bault argue in "Regret, Responsibility and the Brain" that counterfactual emotions, such as regret, are elicited by the comparison between the outcome of our choice and the outcome of foregone alternatives. A sense of personal responsibility is the main signature of the emotion of regret. They suggest that results from a neuropsychological study show the role of the orbitofrontal cortex in the experience of regret, and neuroimaging data indicate that reactivation of activity within the orbitofrontal cortex and amygdala occurring during the phase of choice characterizes the anticipation of regret. In turn, these patterns reflect learning based on cumulative emotional experience. Moreover, they suggest that regret can induce specific mechanisms of cognitive control of the choice processes, involving avoidance of, for example, future episodes of the experienced behavior. This complex cognitive and neural architecture, they conclude, plays a fundamental role in adjusting our behavior after a feeling of personal responsibility for our wrong action.

Opening the section on whether to regret, Catherine Villanueva Gardner's "'Bury Me in a Free Land': Regret for Slavery in Nineteenth-Century African American Philosophical Literature" addresses the importance of perspective-dependent regret, arguing that regret is usually considered from the perspective of the individual agent: We feel regret about actions we have done as individuals, even if we believe we had no choice in the matter. However, she is interested in regret for actions done to a race, specifically to Americans racialized-as-black under slavery. She notes that, typically, discussions of regret for American slavery focus on reparations and formal declarations of regret by governing institutions, with regret understood as feelings of sadness and remorse. But this is regret issued on behalf of the *dominant group* who historically controlled and benefited from the institution of slavery. What of the direct descendants of slaves—their children and grandchildren? Does it make sense to say that they felt regret for the suffering and oppressions of their families? In other words, does it make sense to say that nineteenth-century Americans racialized-as-black could regret the institution of slavery? There is some reason to think that we should reject this question, for the standard model of "action-regret," with its accompanying notion of agency, implies that enslaved Americans can somehow be held responsible for their status and their lives. Alternatively, "regret" is not a strong enough emotion, either affectively or conceptually, to encompass the bitter feelings invoked by the past. However, when we look at nineteenth-century writings, especially the philosophical literature of African American women such as Frances Harper, we can see that regret is not simply understood in terms of passive sadness over slavery—regret is a complex emotion that can be both politicized and agentially empowering. She argues that if we do not allow this particular group of Americans participation in regret for slavery, then we have again consigned them to passivity and excluded them from moral and political citizenship.

Teresa Blankmeyer Burke continues the theme of the appropriateness of regret in "Regret: Considerations of Disability," arguing that the discussion about disability in the literature on regret focuses on two kinds of cases: the regret of the (presumably able-bodied) parent of a disabled child and the regret felt by people who have become disabled. Wallace introduces the concept of "the attitude of affirmation" as an explanation for how the phenomenon of regret is negotiated, with the attachment to the current situation (particularly attachment to the child) offered as part of the explanation for the absence or mitigation of regret. In the case of the disabled person who does not admit to regret, Wallace offers that this may emerge from a kind of confusion—whether about the objective value (or disvalue) of disability or affirmation of the person as the disabled individual she is. Burke examines the case of regret and disability more broadly, including such considerations as the possibility of regret for those experiences that might have been; the notion that one might not regret one's disability and not be confused or appealing to an affirmation of attachment; and the issue of what kinds of justification would be most cogent in such a move, appealing to the literature on the "transformative experience." She uses three cases to explicate her views: the case of hearing parents with a deaf child about to receive a cochlear implant; the case of parents making genetic selection for deafness through preimplantation genetic diagnosis and in vitro fertilization; and the case of the deaf adult contemplating a cochlear implant.

In "Regret Minimization as a Determinant of Riskless Decision Making; Overview, and Ethical Implications for Choice Set Engineering," Caspar Chorus expands the themes of regret's influence on decisional aptness and choices by claiming that minimization of anticipated regret is a well-known determinant of choice behavior under risk, having inspired a large number of studies in fields as diverse as consumer psychology, microeconomics, and neuroscience. This new conceptualization of regret postulates that even when there is no risk involved (i.e., when complete knowledge is available regarding all attributes of choice alternatives), regret aversion plays an important role in shaping choice behavior. This so-called random regret minimization (RRM) model hypothesizes that in many choice situations, individuals have to trade-off different attributes, which causes potential regret at the attribute level, even when the optimal alternative is chosen. The RRM model has been shown to perform well empirically in a variety of choice contexts, for example, by capturing a preference for so-called compromise alternatives with an average performance on each attribute. Chorus will review scholarly work on regret aversion as a determinant of choice behavior, culminating in an introduction and discussion of the recently proposed RRM framework. Although the emphasis will be on what he calls "consumer choices," he will also briefly refer to the role of regret in moral decision making. Subsequently, he will explain how different compositions of the set of choice alternatives may trigger very different levels of anticipated regret among decision makers. He will then argue that this creates important ethical implications for so-called choice set engineering, which is an increasingly popular nudging tool.

Indeed, some choice set architectures may be ethically problematic as they generate disproportionally high levels of regret.

Finally, in "Regret, Perspective and Fate," Christopher Cowley addresses how, and whether, regret fits into considerations of larger moral and epistemic notions, such as fate. He argues that regret is what one feels for having freely made the "wrong" decision. Here, he focuses on a special class of decisions, those that (1) one made a long time ago, for example, ten or twenty years; (2) have had a big impact on one's life during that time, for example, choice of career, spouse, or residence; and (3) lack the purely objective standard of value and comparability that money has. Such longer-term "life decisions" differ from short-term investment decisions by leading one down a certain path that changes one and brings one to contemplate one's life retrospectively, regretting the decisions from within a particular perspective. He suggests that not only is this perspective different from that of the past self that made the decision but also from the perspective of the person one imagines one would have become if one had chosen differently. Cowley claims that there is something deeply incoherent about this sort of long-term regret, and that a more honest approach is to accept one's path as "fated." While he certainly does not intend to suggest that one's life decisions were anything but free, and while working within a secular context, he nevertheless argues that the concept of fate, differently interpreted, can still play an epistemically useful role in challenging one's tendencies toward longer-term regret.

THE FUTURE OF REGRET[4]

So, what is regret, and why should we care? Perhaps it is neither a problem to solve nor a hurdle to overcome. On the one hand, regret can be a humanizing emotion—we ought to regret because we share a common moral universe where harm to each other, intentional or not, is a constant. On the other, regret can become overwhelming and, some would argue, largely ineffective, as we obsess over past acts and unforeseen events about which nothing can be done. Yet, it is such a familiar feeling, a universally recognizable emotion that points backward while casting shadows over our present and future. We have done, or witnessed, these things that move us to wish we had not, and regret becomes our memory's constant and dutiful partner. As such, regret ties our past inextricably to our present (and future) sense of personal identity, of our relationships with others and with the world—indeed, of our ideas of ourselves as moral beings. And it seems that we ought to care about such matters.

Regret, then, is a kind of attunement to past events of small and large consequence; to things we have, and have not, caused; to actions performed long ago; and to those the memory of which is all too fresh. And no matter how much we would prefer it to be otherwise, regretting will not change what was—it might, at times, only change the regretter. This brings to mind Kierkegaard's admonition that we do not change God when we pray—we only change ourselves (Kierkegaard 2009).

Would we wish to inhabit a moral universe where regret can be more easily dismissed, forgotten, or simply relegated permanently to the past and thus, in the parlance of so many self-help books, *overcome*? Or, should we prefer to regard regret as a kind of key to our moral navigations, at once slowing us down and motivating us to do better? Perhaps, it is this latter possibility that offers a way to understand, and engage with, regret in ways that neither rejects it as unwanted wallowing nor reduces it to concerns about intent and agency alone. Instead, we might begin to see openness to regret as a moral practice that creates epistemic spaces where we encounter ourselves without our usual self-serving defenses. It may be a kind of pause, a silence, where the past can speak to the present and inform the future, albeit rarely leaving us unscathed. And perhaps then, this less fearful engagement with regret might move us closer to embracing the inconvenient and messy nature of our humanity, fault lines and all, centering the necessity of a shared, yet fragile, moral universe.

ACKNOWLEDGMENTS

I would like to thank Mark Alfano for not only making this project possible but also for being encouraging, supportive, and patient throughout the process of conceptualizing, proposing, and completing this volume.

NOTES

1. See Thoreau (2005).
2. "My Way," Paul Anka, 1969.
3. Yet, interestingly enough, even Truman had reportedly expressed regret about the world's first atomic bombing. https://www.ctvnews.ca/world/truman-expressed-regret-over-loss-of-life-after-atomic-bombings-grandson-1.2919972.
4. A grateful reference to an influential work on memory, cultural history, and moral psychology (among other things), *The Future of Nostalgia*, by the late Svetlana Boym.

REFERENCES

Austen, Jane. 2016. *Sense and Sensibility*. April 24, 2019. Lulu.com.
Beazley, Hamilton. 2004. *No Regrets: A Ten-Step Program for Living in the Present and Leaving the Past Behind*. Hoboken, NJ: John Wiley & Sons.
Ben-Ze'ev, A. 2000. *The Subtlety of Emotions*. Cambridge: MIT Press.
Boym, Svetlana. 2002. *The Future of Nostalgia*. New York: Basic.

Britten, Rhonda. 2001. *Fearless Living: Live without Excuses and Love without Regret*. New York: Dutton.
Chocano, Carina. 2013. "Je Regrette." *Aeon*, October 16, 2013. https://aeon.co/essays/why-regret-is-essential-to-the-good-life.
Cooper, Matthew. 2004. "Sizing Up Bush's Press Conference." *Time*, April 13, 2004. http://content.time.com/time/nation/article/0,8599,610834,00.html.
Faulkner, William. 1951. *Requiem for a Nun*. New York: Random House.
Freeman, Arthur. 1992. *Woulda, Coulda, Shoulda: Overcoming Regrets, Mistakes, and Missed Opportunities*. New York: William Morrow.
Kierkegaard, Soren. 2009. *Upbuilding Discourses in Various Spirits*, Hong, ed. Princeton, New Jersey: Princeton University Press.
Landman, J. 1993. *Regret: The Persistence of the Possible*. New York: Oxford University Press.
Saffrey, C., A. Summerville, and N. J. Roese. 2008. "Praise for Regret: People Value Regret Above Other Negative Emotions." *Motivation and Emotion* 32 (1): 46–54. doi:10.1007/s11031-008-9082-4.
Shakespeare, William. *Macbeth*, Act 3, scene 2, 8–12. http://shakespeare.mit.edu/macbeth/full.html.
Shimanoff, S. B. 1984. "Commonly Named Emotions in Everyday Conversations." *Perceptual and Motor Skills* 58: 514.
Strawson, Galen. 2004. "Against Narrativity." *Ratio* 17, no. 4: 428–52.
Sussman, David. 2013. "Is Agent-Regret Rational?" The 47th Chapel Hill Colloquium in Philosophy. March 25, 2019. https://philosophy.unc.edu/event/47th-chapel-hill-colloquium-in-philosophy/.
Tannenbaum, J. 2007. "Emotional Expressions of Moral Value." *Philosophical Studies* 132: 43–57.
Tessman, Lisa. 2015. *Moral Failure: On the Impossible Demands of Morality*. New York: Oxford University Press.
Thomas, Alan. 2014. Review of *The View from Here: On Affirmation, Attachment, and the Limits of Regret*, by R. Jay Wallace. *Notre Dame Philosophical Review*, January 19, 2014. https://ndpr.nd.edu/news/the-view-from-here-on-affirmation-attachment-and-the-limits-of-regret/.
Thoreau, Henry David. 2005. *"Autumn." From the Journal of Henry D. Thoreau*, edited by H. G. O. Blake. New York: Adamant Media Corporation.
Wallace, R. Jay. 2013. *The View from Here: On Affirmation, Attachment, and the Limits of Regret*. New York: Oxford University Press.
Williams, Bernard. 1981. "Moral Luck." In *Moral Luck*, 20–40. Cambridge: Cambridge University Press.
Williams, Bernard. 1985. *Ethics and the Limits of Philosophy*. Cambridge, MA: Harvard University Press.
Williams, Bernard. 1993. "Moral Luck." In *Moral Luck*, ed. Daniel Statman, 35–55. Albany: State University of New York Press.
Zeelenberg, Marcel, and Seger M. Breugelmans. 2008. "The Role of Interpersonal Harm in Distinguishing Regret from Guilt." *Emotion* 8 (5): 589–96.

Part I

VARIETIES OF REGRET

Chapter 1

Cousins of Regret

Adam Morton

CLASSIFYING EMOTIONS

Regret is different from remorse is different from shame is different from guilt. At any rate, we can often make these distinctions. And we can often describe attitudes to our past less-than-admirable actions that do not fit easily into any of these categories. An essential preliminary question is how to individuate emotions. When someone says that one emotion is different from another, what does this mean? Rage is obviously different from sorrow, but rage and anger could be thought of as different intensities of the same emotion. Obviously, both are instances of some more general emotion, but then anger and excitement are also instances of a different more general emotion, which we might call arousal. There are many ways of subdividing any set of things.

The list that includes regret, remorse, shame, guilt, and potentially many other emotions is not hard to characterize in a preliminary way. It consists of affect-colored attitudes to past actions that one does not now endorse. The lack of endorsement is often moral: the emotion has an associated thought that one should not have done something. This is not always so, depending a bit on what one wants to include on the list. We tend to think of regret as a "moral" emotion, like remorse—more below on what this might mean—so it is interesting that there are uses of it that have little to do with morality. For example, one might regret not having learned to play the saxophone as a teenager, because in middle age one loves its sound. There are even cases of "immoral" regret. For example, one might regret having been so scrupulous in telling the whole truth in response to a question from a rival or regret not having responded to a romantic overture from someone in a dying relationship. More obviously, embarrassment often has nothing to do with morality. (In some languages, for example Spanish, the same word is used for shame and for embarrassment. So, if one is thinking in terms of such a language, one would be inclined to say that there can be nonmoral "shame.") But we need a rough characterization of this family of emotions in order to get started, so I shall take them all to be retrospective emotions of disapproval of oneself. Qualifications will follow, but pointing out how rough this description is should inject a note of warning about the ambiguities of what can be taken as morality.

There is an extensive discussion of these emotions in philosophy. My sense is that the contrasts between them are understood in roughly the same way by most writers, though different formulas are used to characterize them and the differences between them. Besides the writings of Bernard Williams, referred to below, important works are Taylor (1985), whose emphasis is on the contrasts between the emotions and their connections with emotions such as pride; Dilman (1999), whose emphasis is on the roles that ascribing of these emotions plays in social life; and Maibom (2010), whose psychologically well-informed account emphasizes developmental aspects of them. My contribution to the discussion is in Morton (2013), where my emphasis is on contrasts between regret, remorse, shame, and guilt, taken as morally relevant. A broad connection between emotion and morality is found in Prinz (2007). Prinz's discussion, in terms of emotional representations of situations that are then taken as constitutive of moral judgments, makes moral questions almost a matter of taste; one might want to inject more objectivity by making the retrospective emotions more central. I think one could do this by adapting the arguments in Zagzebski (2003), which interpret moral judgments as beliefs that situations are suitable objects of relevant emotions.

EMOTIONS AND THOUGHTS

Take two intuitively different members of the family, for example, regret and shame. How can we describe their differences? One way is in terms of associated thoughts. If you regret doing something, then you think that you should not have done it. To accommodate the arguments of Williams, Tessman (2015), and others, we must understand this so that one can regret decisions that one had no choice but to make, for example, because they were forced by overwhelming moral considerations and decisions made for nonmoral reasons when one realizes later that other decisions would have worked out better. If you feel shame about something, then you think that certain others will think badly of you in connection with it. (And typically, but not always, you think that they will be correct in thinking badly of you.) These are different thoughts. But there is a problem about individuating the emotions entirely in terms of the thoughts. A person can have the emotion and not have the thought as a belief or even as a thought that the person endorses at all. You can describe yourself as regretting having done something even though you realize on reflection that it was the right thing to do, but the regret just will not go away. Or you can describe yourself as feeling shame for something that in fact everyone praised you for. This point is sometimes made with the example of irrational fear: you can know that this tiny harmless spider is not going to hurt you but still be terrified of it. For spider-type examples, see Greenspan (1988) and Tappolet (2010).

Connecting emotion and thought makes it easier to talk about the rationality of emotion. For worked-out accounts, see Solomon (1993) and Nussbaum (2001). Solomon and Nussbaum put thoughts at the heart of emotion; Nussbaum associates the close connection between feeling and thinking with the Stoic account of emotion. Certainly, Solomon's and Nussbaum's accounts, like the Stoic account, reject a popular picture of emotion as inherently opposed to reason. So, if we identify reason with the formation of justified belief, we get a tendency to understand emotion in a way that makes it very close to belief. For all that, examples such as that of the harmless spider, which can be found for all emotions, prevent other thinkers from going down this route. So, the consensus now is that some emotions are reasonable and some unreasonable, given people's situations and their other states of mind, and that while there are connections between emotion and belief, neither is constitutive of the other. These threads are pulled together in Goldie (2000).

Some of the cases that interest Bernard Williams show a very complicated relation between emotion and belief. In these examples, a person regrets doing something because of the moral price but if given the same choice again would do the same thing again. (Typically, it is the lesser of two evils.) But not all situations where the thought does not characterize the emotion are like this. You can regret not having learned to play the saxophone as a teenager even though you realize that in developing your promising athletic skills rather than your inadequate musical skills, you made a good choice. (The thought is then "I wish I *had been able to* learn the instrument while also being an athlete.")

Williams uses the term "agent regret" with these cases in a way that I find rather confusing. As I read him, he does not distinguish between regret, remorse, guilt, and so on but wants to focus on emotions of any of these kinds that are directed at one's past actions and have a generally moral tone. (I think we can take this to include actions that affect others in ways to which principles that one subscribes to are relevant.) He is using this wide category to make a point about the inescapability of dilemmas in which all the options open to a person are problematic and the person knows in advance that they will regret whichever choice they make. I am convinced that such dilemmas exist, but I also think that the distinctions between the different retrospective emotions are important, and that it helps to grasp them if we want to look carefully at moral attitudes. I find his terminology to be at odds with a vague aim of many of his writings, that of distancing moral considerations from adherence to a determinate set of rules. This issue is very hard to make precise, and Williams is never explicit about it. Put imprecisely, the idea is that moral considerations, linked both to acting on principle and to emotions such as regret, are important features of human life but that we should not take them as giving precise rules about what people must do (Williams 1973a, 1973b, 1981, 1985, 1993). The same stimulating and ambiguous view on both retrospective emotions and the nature of morality is discernible in all of these. See also Rorty (1980). I have defended a position a little like one reading of Williams on morality in Morton (1996) and with a very different argument in Morton (2006). And in a recent self-consciously experimental paper, Morton (2017b), I have tried to connect the taxonomy of retrospective emotions to a position that is Williams-like but stronger and less careful.

Another problem about characterizing emotions in terms of thoughts is that the bare thought is possible without any emotion at all. An extreme example would be a very calculating psychopath who realizes that various important people would be appalled by an action that he really should not have done it but feels no shame about having performed it. (This is a way the opposite of the harmless spider problem.) Related to this is the fact that desires are as important as beliefs. Regret is connected to the desire to act differently in the future and shame to the desire not to be noticed or discovered. ("I could have sunk through the floor.") For emotions, we need thoughts, wants, and feelings to be unified and not simply to coincide.

My response to this need for unity will be to look for it in the various effects of an emotion. The strategy will be to get a formulation of what the effects of a particular emotion have in common, to find some psychological feature that is linked to them, and then to individuate emotions in terms of this feature.

POINTS OF VIEW

The articulating feature that I will make central is that of an imagined point of view. I'll get to it in several stages.

The thoughts that accompany retrospective emotions concern what it would have been better to do, although as already stated, the thoughts may not be fully endorsed by the person, and the sense in which it would have been better to do something other than what she did in fact do need not be moralized. These thoughts fit with corresponding desires, which may also be described as intentions or resolutions. (For a general connection with desire, see Tappolet 2010.) They are largely directed at doing things differently in the future. A regretful person vows not to make that mistake again; an ashamed person vows not to be in a position where they can be caught that way again; a remorseful person vows to change their character. As with the thoughts, these may not be fully endorsed by the person.

The combination of the thought and the desire motivate particular actions, though these may fail to be performed because other thoughts and desires are more dominant. (The connection between emotion and motivation is discussed in Tappolet [2000, 2016] and Brady [2015], with more emphasis on value-directed action in Tappolet and information-directed action in Brady.) A regretful person has some motivation to act differently in similar circumstances; an ashamed person has some motivation to avoid situations where their misdeeds or incompetences are visible, whether by not performing them or by performing them less visibly; a remorseful person has some motivation to take their life in hand and change some fundamental aspects of it. To repeat, the person may not do any of these actions, since the motivation may be weaker than the motivation to do incompatible actions. But there is a *pressure* to do them, which the person may choose to resist and often ought to resist. This is a difference between the motivations that stem from retrospective emotions and those that stem from nondominant beliefs and desires. In the latter case, it is usually not difficult to resist doing something when you really have a stronger motive to do something else. But emotions are always there, pressing, even when the pressure does not correspond to what you officially think.

This pressure is the affective side of the emotion. The influence on the person's actions and the general direction of their thinking is part of what it is like to be that person at that time. An irrational and disavowed fear of a tiny harmless spider makes you have fantasies of the spider attacking you and makes you identify possible routes of escape. Your heart rate increases and your breath comes short, just as it would if you were really planning a sudden exit. Similarly for the feeling of, say, remorse. You find plans for reforming your life occurring to you, and if you do not exercise some control, you will begin carrying them out; you find yourself weary as if from the deep self-examination this would require, even if you are not conscious of any such self-examination.

There is a way of representing the pressure in the special case of retrospective "moral" emotions that is quite revealing. Moral judgment is made by people arriving at verdicts about their own or other people's actions, but in the case of emotions, the attitude may not be self-endorsed in a straightforward way. It can be as if someone else was feeling it, someone else who can themselves be the object of a variety of the person's attitudes. Contrast the simple case where a person thinks *and feels* that she has done wrong and the subtler case where she thinks that someone of authority would disapprove of what she has done. In the subtler case, what she feels is a compound of her respect for the authority and her sense of the perhaps-imagined attitude of that authority. Thus, her emotion toward her past action is reflected through a series of other emotions. Even in the first case, inasmuch as the attitude represents itself as moral, it claims a certain objective authority: someone with sufficient knowledge or moral sense who had given the issue enough reflection would take the action to be wrong. There would be a very literal pressure in that this person would be trying to make one's acts or personality different.

A number of writers have made connections between emotions and imagined points of view. In dealing with another person, we have to imagine how the situation appears to that person. And in considering what to do, we have to imagine possible consequences of our actions and possible facts that might affect these consequences. Moreover, a responsible agent does not simply do one-person moral arithmetic but considers how others that she respects might react to her plans. See the essays in Nichols (2006), including Morton (2006). Gendler (2011) is a comprehensive account of imagination in philosophy, and Harris (2000) argues, with a lot of data about small children, for its fundamental role in psychology. There is a very general discussion of the role of imagination in moral epistemology in Gibert (2012).

This suggests a tidy formulation. The person considers or imagines a point of view from which the action would be condemned. She imagines a person to whom she has some sort of deference who has a negative attitude to the action. This is very general, as we can fill in the particular deference and the particular character of the negative attitude to fit the different retrospective emotions.

Standard labels for emotions in the retrospective spectrum can be interpreted in these terms. In shame, a person imagines an observer who finds the action less than admirable. The observer may represent a moral consensus, in which case the sense of appearing unworthy approaches the sense of actually being worthy. (Though one may think that the consensus is wrong.) Or the observer may represent a vivid attitude that the action is undignified or even comic. Then, shame fades into embarrassment. The person who feels ashamed may not agree with the imagined point of view, but inasmuch as she feels ashamed or embarrassed, she senses the pressure—the effect on her own plans and reactions—from this imagined attitude. (Try to imagine as vividly as possible someone being very angry with you: do you not feel tense and defensive?) In regret, the person imagines a knowledgeable and authoritative point of view from which an alternative action was preferable. The preferability may be moral, generating that particular variety of regret. Or it may be practical, representing what the person might have chosen if they had known then what they do now and had time to think over their options.

In remorse, when contrasted with other similar emotions, the person imagines a point of view that focuses on the effects of the action on some other person and bases a judgment on the situation of this victim. The "victim" may in fact not have disapproved of the action, but inasmuch as the emotion is of remorse, the emotion involves imagining how that person might have, or perhaps should have, disapproved. (You help a friend obtain a dose of an addictive drug. The friend is grateful. Later, he dies of an overdose and you feel remorse for having helped him.) And in guilt—the emotion of feeling guilty, not the state of being culpable—a person imagines an authority figure who condemns them for performing a particular action. The imagined figure need not exist, and even if they do exist they may not have the authority that imagination bestows on them: what is imagined is the respect that justified authority would confer.

The imagined points of view may not be those of any real people or collectives. The machinery can also individuate emotions that do not have tidy labels in English or for that matter emotions that are not acknowledged in the conventional repertoire. In the following two sections, I describe two of these.

REMORSE THAT DOES NOT PRESENT ITSELF AS MORAL

An emotion can have much of the force of a moral sentiment without the person having the thoughts that one might think would go with it. An example is given by Jonathan Bennett's famous case of Huckleberry Finn, in Bennett (1974). Huck, the central character of Twain (1885), has helped the slave Jim to escape and realizes that this goes against the moral code in which he was raised. He is depriving Jim's owner of her property. Bennett quotes Mark Twain as attributing the following thoughts to Huck:

(a) I couldn't get that out of my conscience, no how nor no way. . . . I tried to make out to myself that I warn't to blame, because I didn't run Jim off from his rightful owner; but it warn't no use, conscience up and say, every time: "But you knowed he was running for his freedom, and you could a paddled ashore and told somebody." That was so—I couldn't get around that, no way. That was where it pinched. (Twain 1885, chapter XVI)

(b) I knowed very well I had done wrong, and I see it warn't no use for me to try to learn to do right; a body that don't get started right when he's little, ain't got no show. . . . Then I thought a minute, and says to myself, hold on—s'pose you'd a done right and give Jim up; would you feel better than what you do now? No, says, I'd feel bad—I'd feel just the same way I do now. Well, then, says I, what's the use you learning to do right, when it's troublesome to do right and ain't no rouble to do wrong.... So I reckoned I wouldn't bother no more about it, but after this always do whichever come handiest at the time. (Twain 1885, chapter XVI)

In (a), Huck is telling himself that he has done wrong, violated conscience, and made himself blameworthy. Moreover, he feels a form of guilt: "that was where it pinched." In (b), he describes himself as incurably immoral and as taking the easiest and most self-centered course. He admits to himself that he would "feel bad" (meaning not "feel like a bad person" but "have a nasty feeling") if he were to do the right thing. So, he has a choice of retrospective emotions: the one that he identifies with morality and the one that corresponds to his deeper feelings. He is torn between them.

How to describe these two emotions? It is not extremely unusual to have simultaneous emotions that tend in opposite directions. (The normality of this is defended in Zimmerman [1993].) One can be attracted to and afraid of the same object, for example. Huck's first emotion is essentially shame: he feels how disapproving of what he has done the community of his upbringing, which he identifies with, would be. There is an element of remorse, also, because he can feel the potential condemnation of Jim's "owner." It is a special kind of shame, though, because at some level, he also imagines a point of view that would disapprove of frustrating the escape plans of slaves. This manifests itself in knowing that he would feel bad at turning Jim in. (And, in fact, he does feel bad just thinking about it.) But this point of view is not consciously available to him. It is potentially available, at most, as a reconstruction of a pattern of reactions that is more consistent than he realizes. So, he imagines a point of view that is appalled at his action, and he also imagines a point of view on that point of view, which is appalled at *it*. But this second imagining is unconscious and implicit. The essentials are that he has a meta-emotion of remorse directed at a first-order emotion of shame, and that the meta-emotion is less articulated and less available to his conception of himself. (Emotions about emotions are discussed in Mendonça [2013]. Very general connections between higher-order states and finding something valuable are found in Frankfurt [1971] and Lewis [1989].)

There is another striking feature of his shame. It is shame in that he is condemned from a conventional point of view, but his attitude to this point of view is very mixed. As explained, some of his other emotions undercut the authority of this point of view, although he realizes it is the attitude of parents and elders and other people he looks up to. So, it is in a way rather embarrassment-like. A similar emotion would be that of a moral philosopher who disapproves of an action as a result of thinking it through from the theories that she accepts, although it fits with her unreflective and unofficial intuitions about action. (Or the opposite, an action that she intellectually finds acceptable and even to be encouraged but which something in her recoils from.)

It would help to have a label for emotions like this. I shall refer to this one as "undermined shame." Undermined regret would also be possible, for example, in the case in which you think and correspondingly feel that your action was a mistake, but you are also glad that you did it. Perhaps you have married somebody and now realize that this will frustrate many of your plans and commitments, as this person will cost you a lot of money and come between you and some of your friends and mentors. So, you take it to be a mistake. But there is still real love, in spite of the quarrels over practical matters, and one of the reasons for the love is an attraction to this person's attitude to life, which is very different from the one that you think you have.

RETROSPECTION AND PSYCHOLOGICAL DAMAGE

We come now to an emotion that seems to me to belong in the retrospective family but which I have difficulty classifying as a form of shame, regret, or remorse.

People undergo various traumatic experiences that have long-term effects. Dramatic examples are abuse in childhood, rape, and violence, and less dramatic examples are demeaning parents, not being taken seriously because of one's gender or orientation, or being bullied. Years later, they can suffer many symptoms of damaged self-respect. The symptoms are from a narrowly rational point of view puzzling, because the experiences from which they stem do not provide anything like evidence that the person is incapable or unworthy. Among the effects of damaged self-respect is a tendency to feel that things are one's fault. This can focus on the experience in question, and notoriously children often do not report abuse by adults because they think that they had somehow been responsible themselves. And fantasies of guilt are quite common in long-term reactions to nasty experiences. But the scope can be much wider. The person can acquire a disposition to think that unrelated developments have occurred because of their faults. So, we are dealing with a disposition to retrospective self-critical emotions, whatever their objects. (There is an opposite pathology, also, of people who are immune to self-critical emotions. That is also not unknown but digresses from our topic, although I suppose there is a connection in the form of people who cannot allow themselves the tiniest bit of self-criticism for fear that it open the floodgates to an enormous sense of inadequacy.)

Assume that this happens. There is evidence for the phenomenon, although I take the unity of its causes still to be properly established, in Bernstein (2015), Kashdana et al. (2006), and Orth and Robins (2013). I make a connection with emotions of self-description in Morton (to appear) and Morton (2017a). The associated emotions do not have a particular action of the person as their target but rather the person's general value. So, in a way it is a disposition, a kind of standing mood or trait of character, always ready to interpret the person as being at fault. But, if you'll forgive the slight psychoanalytical tone, it also has a particular object, the traumatic event itself. Without identifying this as the focus of the emotion, the person has an attitude to it, that in some unspecified way it is her own fault, and this generates a sense of worthlessness that is at the root of the many occasions on which the person has a particular case of regret, remorse, or shame.

Consider this underlying emotion that one did wrong in causing the events that damaged one. Call it "self-accusatory retrospection." We can take it as shame or as remorse. Shame is pretty simple to apply here. The victim imagines an observer who sees her role in the events critically (the imagined perception is of course itself imagined). This imagination is painful, no doubt because it brings back the events themselves. So the victim wishes she was not so imaginable, that she should be invisible from any such point of view.

Remorse can also be applied, though it is rather peculiar. The victim imagines the perpetrator as harmed, as having their good character spoiled by the provocations of the victim. Thus, the victim has harmed the perpetrator, and the perpetrator judges the victim harshly but appropriately for this. Of course, this act of imagination has to remain unconscious, as it wouldn't survive the slightest examination.

Regret is hardest to apply. The victim would have to imagine a point of view that repeats her decisions and arrives at a better choice. Perhaps, there was a safer course of action, the thought would be, that would not have resulted in the catastrophe. Less encouraging, less vulnerable, more matter-of-fact or tougher: "It was my fault to have gotten into that situation in the first place."

However we decide to classify it, this self-directed accusatory emotion can generate regret, remorse, guilt, and other negative emotions toward the victim's acts on particular occasions. These can cover the range of such emotions: regret for this, remorse for that, guilt for a third thing. As I see it, we have a hard-to-classify core emotion that generates a disposition to a range of more tractable particular attitudes. These can be consciously held, although the core emotion almost never will be. Most dispositions are unconscious, in that a person's evidence for applying them to herself is the same as the evidence available to those who engage with her, namely her actions. Many emotions are not simply behavioral dispositions because people can attribute them to themselves on the basis of affect. It is significant that these attributions can confuse emotions with others that have similar affects. And it is interesting that among the likely confusions are those of one retrospective emotion for another: for example, a person who does not want to admit that she has done something wrong may label as regret what in fact is better described as remorse. (So why think that it exists? Well, the disposition is generated by an attitude to the crucial events. And it is a charged, feeling-laden, thing. If we are to take it as itself an emotion at all, it must be something like what I have described.)

FALSE REMORSE

One last example of an emotion of retrospective moral self-condemnation that does not fit into the standard list is feeling guilt for an action that one did not in fact commit. The background is in classic work on induced memory by Loftus and others, as in Loftus and Ketcham (1996). This shows that suitable, largely verbal intervention can cause people to have memories that do not correspond to real events. The objects of these false memories can be as varied as recent traffic accidents and long-ago sexual abuse. This should change our thinking on many topics. They include confessions in which accused people recall committing crimes that were in fact committed by others. A powerful journalistic account of one such case is in Aviv (2017). The central person in this case is relevant to our issues because while knowing that she is innocent, she still feels remorse for a murder that she was nowhere near and took no part in. Thoughts about it and images of her participation in it haunt her painfully. (A detailed psychological reconstruction of such real-world cases would be valuable. In this case, it would focus on details of her interrogation and on things she and others did and said during her years of prison. There is a suggestion that psychological damage earlier in life may make one more susceptible to such things, though no one is immune to them. This would make a connection with some of the other remorse-like cases.)

I said that she "feels remorse." Is she remorseful? In an obvious way she cannot be, because she knows that she did nothing wrong, inflicted no harm on the victim. But what other word could I have used? She has experiences that are like those of remorseful people and, at any rate, it seems likely that the psychological process has a lot in common with remorse. But there is a crucial difference, which we could describe as semantic: her crime does not exist. It is not hard to imagine cases with similar characteristics. Someone could feel remorse for hurtful behavior in a dream and could feel compelled to apologize for it. (The object of the harm might not exist, in which case the apology would have to be fantasy also.) Someone might feel shame for unuttered and out-of-character racist remarks. (Perhaps, they contained a very appealing pun. The most responsible humans have their infantile side.) And anyone could easily feel something subjectively like regret at not having given in to an impulse—to insult a powerful pompous leader, to commit a hopeless and immoral act of passion—that would have been catastrophic. It is plausible that states like each of these can really happen. Relatively inconsequential instances, such as the final regret case, are probably much more common than the tragic real remorse case I began this section with.

To smooth cases like these into the multidimensional continuum of retrospective emotions, I would suggest going back to the basic structure. One imagines a person to whom one has an attitude of a respectful kind—that's what makes the emotion moral—who has an attitude of a judgmental kind to one's performance of an action. The feeling of the emotion is a compound of the respect and the judgment. All the emotions I have discussed, and potentially others, can be fitted into this structure. In the cases in question—false remorse, false regret, and so on—the imagined judgmental person is themselves imagining an action (though they may not know that is what they are doing). This person may know that they did not perform any such action, but their imagination of it is still vivid and produces an affect that can be overwhelming. It can exert considerable pressure on the person's future thinking and action. Thus, it is subjectively and pragmatically of a kind with the other emotions of retrospective self-directed moral evaluation.

CONCLUSION

It is generally accepted that there are a number of retrospective morally colored emotions. The standard distinction between shame cultures and guilt cultures is evidence for a weak version of this, as is the fact that many languages have an extensive vocabulary for distinguishing between emotions in this family. I have been claiming that there are potentially very many retrospective emotions, perhaps even infinitely many. The argument for this has been that we can make a classification scheme that the standard labels in English fit into nicely and which also has room for many other types of these emotions. It is important here that the classification system comes with a way of individuating the emotions, to reassure us that items fitting into different boxes in the system are indeed different emotions.

These emotions are important because they have central roles in our principled behavior toward one another. The pressure that they put on our motivation leads us to change our plans, our attitudes, and, inasmuch as we are capable of it, our personalities. They do this in different ways, regret being focused particularly on change of plans, shame on change of manner, and remorse on change of personality. The novel labels that I introduced also connect to changes in motivation. Undermined shame may allow Huck one day to make the transition from his childish shame-based morality to a more complex one shaped by regret and remorse. And it will often allow people to play lip service to a conventional code while actually operating at a more nuanced level. Self-accusatory retrospection, the victim blaming herself, can be powerful in buttressing social cohesion and in maintaining traditional respectability, though from an enlightened perspective it is suspect. A milder version of it can also serve a more benign function, curbing the overconfidence of those who while rarely breaking any explicit rules, bring trouble repeatedly on themselves and others. (A very sharp remark that I once heard a wise person make of a well-known philosopher: "it's never his fault, but it is always someone else who gets hurt.") As for false remorse, and its cousins, they have an obvious function in ensuring that people are in a self-critical state when there is any suggestion that they have done harm. Useful as all these emotions are in maintaining good behavior, though, they have their perverse side. Self-criticism can be destructive.

The retrospective emotions are not the only ones playing similar roles. The family of disagreement, disapproval, and horror and the family of agreement, disapproval, and enthusiasm, among others, are also involved. No doubt there are parallels and connections between the families, and I would conjecture that these too have potentially more members than we have words for. There is a truly monstrous classification system lurking in the background.

The point I want to end the paper with, though, is that the variety of moral emotions has implications for the unity, or not, of morality. (The Bernard Williams papers already referred to are relevant here, as are Morton [1996] and Morton [2009].) In cases like the Huck Finn example, emotions in the same family conflict, as similar but more familiar emotions often do (Zimmerman [1993] again). It is, for instance, perfectly possible that someone feels shame about doing something that they would feel remorse about not doing. Standing up for their sexual identity in a homophobic culture would be an example. (The emotions could be distinct but consistent if whenever one applied the others did not. But it seems that the conflict is more direct than this. They are contradictories rather than simply contraries.) For instance, suppose that someone is avoiding situations that might lead to any such retrospective emotion (they are all negative in affect), avoiding actions of types that have led to these in the past, also avoiding actions of types that the person disapproves of in others, and so on. Is there a single coherent pattern of behavior, even by the standards current in a particular culture, that is the target of such emotions? Are they all moral emotions because there is a single topic that they all address? Do the emotional underpinnings of moral behavior determine a single style of action?

It seems unlikely, given what we have seen. There would have to be a gigantic coincidence, or some dominating extra factor, for all these forces to pull together coherently. Can Huck Finn be both a cooperative member of his society and a force for moral progress? Can you encourage biting remorse over wrongdoing without regretting the damage that clumsily widespread remorse can do? If the retrospective emotions play a large role in the psychology of moral behavior—whether or not they are as important in general abstract counts of what is right—then the best bet is that moral behavior, acting decently, is a diffuse bundle with many different aspects. We emphasize different tendencies in it depending on what matters to us at a particular moment.

REFERENCES

Aviv, Rachel. 2017. "Remembering the Murder You Didn't Commit." *New Yorker*, June 19, 2017. https://www.newyorker.com/magazine/2017/06/19/remembering-the-murder-you-didnt-commit
Bennett, Jonathan. 1974. "The Conscience of Huckleberry Finn." *Philosophy* 49: 123–34.
Bernstein, J. M. 2015. *Torture and Dignity: An Essay on Moral Injury*. Chicago, IL: University of Chicago Press.
Brady, Michael. 2015. *Emotional Insight: The Epistemic Role of Emotion*. Oxford: Oxford University Press.
Deonna, Julien, Raffaele Rodogno, and Fabrice Teroni. 2011. *In Defense of Shame: The Faces of an Emotion*. Oxford: Oxford University Press.
Dilman, Ilham. 1999. "Shame, guilt and remorse." *Philosophical Investigations* 22: 312–29.
Frankfurt, Harry. 1971. "Freedom of the Will and the Concept of a Person." *Journal of Philosophy* 68: 5–20.
Gendler, Tamar. 2011. "Imagination." In *The Stanford Encyclopedia of Philosophy*, ed. Edward N. Zalta (Fall Edition), http://plato.stanford.edu/archives/fall2011/entries/imagination/ (accessed January 7, 2013).
Gibert, Martin. 2012. *Emotion et imagination*. PhD thesis, Université de Montréal.
Goldie, Peter. 2000. *The Emotions: A Philosophical Exploration*. Oxford: Oxford University Press.
Greenspan, Patricia. 1988. *Emotions and Reasons*. London: Routledge.
Harris, Paul. 2000. *The Work of the Imagination*. Oxford: Blackwell.
Kashdana, Todd, et al. 2006. "Fragile self-Esteem and Affective Instability in Posttraumatic Stress Disorder." *Behaviour Research and Therapy* 44: 1609–19.
Lewis, David K. 1989. "Dispositional Theories of Value." *Proceedings of the Aristotelian Society*, 63: 113–37.
Loftus, Elizabeth, and Katherine Ketcham. 1996. *The Myth of Repressed Memory: False Memories and Allegations of Sexual Abuse*. Oxford: Oxford University Press.
Maibom, Heidi. 2010. "The Descent of Shame." *Philosophy and Phenomenological Research* 80 (3): 566–94.

Mendonça, Dina. 2013. "Emotions about Emotions." *Emotion Review* 5 (4): 390–6.
Morton, Adam. 1996. "The Disunity of the Moral." In *The Problematic Reality of Values*, ed. Jan Bransen and Marc Slors, 142–55. Amsterdam: Van Gorcum.
Morton, Adam. 2004. *Emotion and Imagination*. Cambridge: Polity.
Morton, Adam. 2006. "Imagination and Misimagination." In *The Architecture of the Imagination: New Essays on Pretense, Possibility, and Fiction*, ed. Shaun Nichols, 57–72. Oxford: Oxford University Press.
Morton, Adam. 2009. "Good Citizens and Moral Heroes." In *The Positive Function of Evil*, ed. Pedro Tabensky, 127–38. Basingstoke: Palgrave.
Morton, Adam. 2013. *Emotion and Imagination*. Cambridge: Polity Press.
Morton, Adam. (2017a). Post on Amy Kind's imagination blog. July 19, 2019. https://junkyardofthemind.com/blog/2017/5/1/damage-and-imagination.
Morton, Adam. 2017b. "Damage, Flourishing, and Two Sides of Morality." *Eshare: An Iranian Journal of Philosophy* 1 (1): 1–11.
Morton, Adam. 2017. "Pride *versus* Self-Respect." In *The Moral Psychology of Pride*, ed. Adam Carter and Emma Gordon. Lanham, MD: Rowman & Littlefield.
Nichols, S. 2006. *The Architecture of the Imagination: New Essays on Pretense, Possibility, and Fiction*. Oxford: Oxford University Press.
Nussbaum, Martha. 2001 *Upheavals of Thought: The Intelligence of Emotions*. Cambridge: Cambridge University Press.
Prinz, Jesse. 2007. *The Emotional Construction of Morals*. Oxford: Oxford University Press.
Orth, U., and R. Robins. 2013. "Understanding the Link between Low Self-Esteem and Depression." *Current Directions in Psychological Science* 22 (64): 55–460.
Rorty, Amelie Oksenberg. 1980. "Agent Regret." In *Explaining Emotions*, ed. Amelie Oksenberg Rorty, 489–506. Berkeley: University of California Press.
Solomon, Robert. 1993. *The Passions: Emotions and the Meaning of Life*. Indianapolis, IN: Hackett.
Tappolet, Christine. 2000. *Emotions et valeurs*. Paris: Presses Universitaires de France.
Tappolet, Christine. 2010. "Emotion, Motivation, and Action: The Case of Fear." In *The Oxford Companion to Philosophy of Emotion*, ed. Peter Goldie, 325–48. Oxford: Oxford University Press.
Tappolet, Christine. 2016. *Emotions, Values, and Agency*. Oxford: Oxford University Press.
Taylor, Gabriele. 1985. *Pride, Shame, and Guilt: Emotions of Self-Assessment*. Oxford: Oxford University Press.
Tessman, Lisa. 2015. *Moral Failure: On the Impossible Demands of Morality*. Oxford: Oxford University Press.
Twain, Mark (Samuel Clemens). 1885. *The Adventures of Huckleberry Finn*. New York: Webster.
Williams, Bernard. 1973a. "Ethical Consistency." In *Problems of the Self: Philosophical Papers 1956–1972*, ed. Bernard Williams, 166–86. Cambridge: Cambridge University Press.

Williams, Bernard with J. J. C. Smart. 1973b. *Utilitarianism: For and Against*. Cambridge: Cambridge University Press.
Williams, Bernard. 1981. "Moral Luck." In *Moral Luck*, ed. Bernard Williams, 20–39. Cambridge: Cambridge University Press.
Williams, Bernard. 1985. *Ethics and the Limits of Philosophy*. London: Fontana.
Williams, Bernard. 1993. *Shame and Necessity*. Berkeley: University of California Press.
Zagzebski, Linda. 2003. "Emotion and Moral Judgment." *Philosophy and Phenomenological Research* 66 (1): 104–24.
Zimmerman, Michael. 1993. "A Plea for Ambivalence." *Metaphilosophy* 24: 382–9.

Chapter 2

Regret as a Reactive Attitude: The Conditions of Responsibility and Revision

Audrey L. Anton

Since the first publication of P. F. Strawson's article, "Freedom and Resentment," a lot of philosophical attention has been paid to those emotions Strawson called *reactive attitudes*. These include resentment, gratitude, forgiveness, anger, guilt, remorse, approbation, and love. While Strawson explicitly denies that his list of reactive attitudes is exhaustive, it has served as the paradigmatic set of examples.[1] As a result, most of the attention paid to the reactive attitudes and their relationship to responsibility has been focused on interpersonal moral reactive attitudes. However, there is no reason the class of reactive attitudes is limited to interpersonal or moral ones. Emotions such as shame, guilt, and remorse are prime examples of how agents react to themselves, either as the object of assessment (e.g., one may be ashamed of one's appearance) or as an agent responsible for an outcome (e.g., one may feel remorse for stealing a friend's last dollar). In addition, instances like shame needn't be moral attitudes. For instance, one may be ashamed of one's appearance for purely aesthetic reasons. Nevertheless, shame is always evaluative and, therefore, normative. When we are ashamed, we feel that something about us is inadequate. Similarly, I contend, regret needn't be moral in content, but it is self-reactive and evaluative. In this chapter, I shall offer a conceptual analysis account of why regret is a self-reactive attitude involving a sense of responsibility and a desire for revision. In addition, I shall refer to some recent scientific evidence that supports my conceptual findings concerning regret.

REACTIVE ATTITUDES AND NORMATIVITY

Strawson focuses on a specific type of reactive attitude he calls *participant reactive attitudes*, which are attitudes that we are subject to by virtue of participating in ordinary interpersonal relationships.[2] He distinguishes three types of participant reactive attitudes. The first type Strawson calls *personal reactive attitudes*. These are attitudes a subject feels toward another in response to perceived good will, ill will, or indifference. For instance, person A may *resent* person B when person B appears to be indifferent to person A's rights. Imagine that B eats A's prepacked clearly labeled lunch, which A stored in the break room refrigerator of their workplace. Person A may resent B for B's lack of respect for A's property. The victim (A) reacts personally to the behavior of the wrongdoer (B), as the behavior suggests to the victim that the wrongdoer does not have the quality of will that one ought to show a colleague.

The second kind of participant reactive attitudes Strawson calls *general reactive attitudes*. Subjects react to others based on the quality of will those others appear to exhibit toward a third party. For example, a community might exhibit righteous indignation toward a murderer on behalf of the murder victim. The ill will was displayed by the murderer toward the victim. Yet, others react toward the murderer on behalf of the victim.

The third type of participant reactive attitude Strawson identifies is *self-reactive attitudes*. A subject of a self-reactive attitude reacts toward herself according to how she perceives herself to have met, failed to meet, or exceeded some standard. For example, a murderer may feel guilty for committing such a heinous crime. The subject reacts to herself as the object of her own evaluation of appropriate behavior toward others.

Expanding Strawson's View

While Strawson coined the term *reactive attitude*, the concept has evolved significantly. Strawson focused on reactive attitudes associated with moral responsibility between individuals, as this was the subject of his overall inquiry. However, others have noted that we react towards ourselves for other reasons. Most notably, Daniel E. Rossi-Keen identifies *self-reflexive reactive attitudes* as evaluative attitudes one has in response to how the subject herself meets (or fails to meet) self-imposed demands.[3]

Inspired by Strawson's *self-reactive attitudes*, Rossi-Keen expands the scope of reactive attitudes to include intrapersonal ones he calls *self-reflexive reactive attitudes*. This addition strikes me as most sensible. After all, we frequently reproach ourselves when we fail to honor commitments we make to ourselves (e.g., sticking to a diet) or when we fail to represent ourselves the way we believe is accurate (e.g., saying something "stupid" in front of a person we admire). There are also certainly instances of self-reflexive reactive attitudes that accompany self-reactive attitudes of the sort envisioned by Strawson. For instance, we don't always feel guilty for harming someone else exclusively because we are expected to treat others better; we may also feel guilty for allowing ourselves to be the kind of person who neglects to treat others with good will if *we* expect ourselves to be better. Imagine that Kara considers the development of virtue a worthwhile pursuit, and she commits to becoming the best version of herself possible. In a moral lapse, Kara disrespects a close friend, Cheryl; as a result, Kara is full of regret. She may feel guilty and regret exhibiting ill will toward Cheryl; but she may also be angry with herself and regret failing to meet her own standard. Even if Cheryl forgives Kara, points out her own share of blame in the altercation, and Kara comes to see herself as partially justified in her behavior, Kara may nevertheless regret her behavior for other reasons. After all, a virtuous person doesn't have to react with ill will every time it is justified. Kara may have expected she would be above such behavior regardless of whether Cheryl deserved it. Therefore, we can regret our behavior when it aims at others (self-reactive attitude) and we can regret our behavior in its own right (self-reflexive reactive attitude).

Regret, Remorse, and Responsibility

I suspect that regret's absence on Strawson's list stems from the fact that regret can be, but need not be, morally salient. We can regret harming our friends or we can regret eating too much. We often regret decisions solely on the basis that they do not turn out the way we had hoped: we might regret purchasing a losing lottery ticket, failing to call ahead when trying to visit a friend who is not home, or missing out on a sale. Nevertheless, regret's absence from Strawson's list is not indicative of its status as a reactive attitude. As previously noted, even Strawson admits that the list is not exhaustive.[4] Regret attends to instances when we find ourselves causally responsible for something suboptimal.

I have argued elsewhere that moral responsibility is a species of causal responsibility.[5] We are causally responsible for an outcome just in case we cause (either in part or in full) that outcome (with indirect causes qualifiedly included). If I stand in the sunlight at 3 pm, I cause my shadow. When I make certain movements with my mouth and vocal cords, I cause myself to speak. If I back up in a crowded china shop, I might cause a vase to fall and break. We are causally responsible for many things—some of which we do intentionally, others unintentionally. We are causally responsible for many things for which we are not morally responsible. I contend that we may feel regret for morally salient behaviors (as is the case with remorse) and we may also feel regret for behaviors (including omissions) of ours we take to have no moral import. We can regret mistreating a friend and we can regret our choice of checkout line at the grocery store.

In addition, we can regret our behavior regardless of whether we performed it voluntarily. As Bernard Williams famously pointed out, "The lorry driver who, through no fault of his, runs over a child, will feel differently from any spectator."[6] The fact that the driver ran over the child involuntarily is beside the point. It is only natural for him to feel deep regret. Indeed, Williams points out that we might have concerns about his character if he "too blandly or readily" got over the incident.[7] What all such instances share in common (and what I wish to show is the case for all instances of regret) is that the subject considers herself responsible in some way (even if only causally).[8]

Whether one feels regret or remorse is more sensitive to how the subject views herself and her moral obligations than whether a situation is morally salient. For example, imagine that two men explain how they feel about their recent robbery of a bank during their allocution before a court of law. Each has been asked to address the fact that a patron of the bank was shot and killed during the robbery. Imagine that the two were apprehended because the bullet in the victim led police back to one of them as the owner of the gun. The first bank robber (the owner of the gun, let us suppose) might express regret for having shot the person, but only because, had he remained cool, he could have gotten away with the robbery. The second bank robber might express remorse for having acted in such a way that put others in danger. Both bank robbers regret their actions. However, the callous nature of the first bank robber's regret precludes that attitude from constituting remorse, whereas the second's attention to moral aspects of the situation qualifies his regret as a specific type of regret. Let us call the first type of regret simple regret and the second type, remorse. Both types are negative reactions to the self stemming from perceived normative failures.

Normativity

Does the above distinction imply that the first bank robber's regret is not a reactive attitude? I contend that it does not. In fact, I suspect the impulse to deny that simple regret is a reactive attitude stems from being so entrenched in the idea that reactive attitudes are always moral attitudes. To my mind, all reactive attitudes are *normative* attitudes, since they are reactive in comparison to some standard. However, not all normative conditions are moral. For example, on arithmetical standards, $2+2=4$. One who claims that $2+2=5$ is wrong because mathematics is a normative enterprise. Still, we do not consider one who mistakenly believes the sum to be 5 morally deficient. The person might be seen as mathematically deficient in a sense relevant to our discussion.

The sense that I do not wish to invoke is that of a mere judgment or acknowledgment of a failure to meet a normative standard.[9] The class of mental states that I wish to consider is reactive; the agent experiencing them has some sense of attraction to or repulsion by a subject (depending on the polarity of the attitude). Therefore, let us make a note of excluding the detached "noticing" of a failed standard from our consideration. However, there are ways to fail to meet standards of nonmoral normativity that elicit reactive attitudes.

Consider the following example. My mother, an experienced high school English teacher, taught me about a specific sentence structure that requires the subjunctive mood. When, many years later, I foolishly uttered a sentence beginning with the phrase "If I was you," she rightfully exhibited a reactive attitude toward me. She was frustrated that I had forgotten her lesson, and she recognized that I failed to meet a standard of the English language. However, I think it is unlikely that such a failure is moral. If my error is an honest mistake (i.e., not made intentionally to irritate her), then it is hardly a moral indiscretion. However, I do think my mother was justified in reacting to my mistake, as she had patiently and explicitly reminded me of the grammatical rule on many separate occasions. It is for this reason that I consider all reactive attitudes to be *normative* attitudes but not necessarily *moral* attitudes. An attitude is normative just in case it evaluates its target in virtue of some standard. Sports fans who berate a player for botching a simple play display reactive attitudes that are normative but nonmoral. For example, imagine that a player in the NBA *should* be able to make a simple layup. If he fails, a fan may aptly exclaim "Awww, come on!" in reproach.

Such examples suggest that we react toward others in light of perceived nonmoral "obligations" to follow a certain standard and *get things right* regardless of the subject's awareness, willingness, or intentions.[10] In the example of my mother and the subjunctive mood, I should have known better (the fact that the rule slipped my mind is beside the point). In the example of our NBA player, let us assume, he knows how to make a layup and intends to do so but somehow fails (the fact that he tried is beside the point). If this analysis is correct, regret qualifies as a reactive emotion even if it is not, in every case, a moral attitude.

Reactive Attitudes

But how are we to understand reactive attitudes in this wider normative sense? Are there any felt qualities or phenomenal aspects shared by all reactive attitudes? I propose that we accept the following basic criteria for all reactive attitudes. First, the subject toward which the attitude aims is viewed by the person experiencing the attitude as somehow responsible for something relevant to the attitude. Such responsibility need not be moral; it can be merely causal. For example, one might feel guilty for accidentally knocking over a fragile, valuable vase.[11] Second, the reactive attitude would seem to involve, in at least some very weak sense, a judgment as to the appropriateness of the behavior or feature that warrants the reactive response.[12] For example, two art critics can react differently to an artist's controversial piece. One might praise the artist for her bold efforts whereas the other might criticize the artist for trying too hard or crossing some line. In each case, the artist is viewed as responsible for the piece. In the case of the first critic, the artist is responsible for something fitting or appropriate whereas in the second case, the artist is seen as responsible for something ill-suited.

These two criteria (responsibility and standard-based value) strike me as sufficiently general to encompass all reactive attitudes. However, many philosophers have explicitly denied some version of each of these criteria as being true of regret. Therefore, I shall argue that it is characteristic of all instances of regret that the agent takes herself to be responsible in some sense for that which is regrettable. In addition, I shall argue that there is some sincere sense in which regretful agents disapprove of their behavior and wish to have acted differently. By "wish," I do not mean to convey a sufficient desire such that, had the agent the ability to go back in time, the agent *would* act differently. The degree of desire need not be definitive. For instance, an addict might regret past behavior that the addict might nevertheless repeat. Similarly, one might regret a choice because one is not confident that one made the best choice. Therefore, while regret typically involves a desire to have done otherwise, the desire need not be the agent's strongest desire or the only desire motivating the agent.

In order to show that regret is properly described as a reactive attitude in virtue of its features of apparent responsibility and wish for revision, I shall first consider how other theorists have dealt with describing the nature of regret (some of whom explicitly deny the claims that I endorse). Then, I shall briefly describe my own account of regret. Third, I shall argue that my description of regret as a self-reactive attitude is superior to alternative descriptions that deny regret's self-reactivity by showing that all such descriptions are too broad. I shall argue that these descriptions allow emotions that are clearly distinct from regret to satisfy the conditions laid out. Fourth, I shall address the fact that my criteria, *prima facie*, appear to exclude certain cases frequently called "regret." In fact, I imagine that other theorists' reluctance to include the two criteria I propose might stem from a commitment to including these instances, which I shall argue are not genuine instances of regret. I shall argue that we are right to exclude such cases because the use of the term "regret" in such instances is metaphorical, hyperbolic, or mistaken. Finally, I shall point to recent scientific studies supporting my claims. I conclude that, since without the two proposed criteria, a description of regret is too broad, and since any cases excluded by the addition of the two criteria are rightfully excluded, we have more reason to include the criteria than to omit them. And because these two particular criteria are characteristic of reactive attitudes, not only will I have offered a more accurate description of the phenomenological content of regret, but I will also have shown that regret is a reactive attitude.

ACCOUNTS PROPOSED IN PHILOSOPHY OF EMOTION LITERATURE

Johann A. Klassen writes, "What is regret? It is another of the emotion terms which we toss about with great facility, assuming that what we mean by 'regret' is obvious."[13] Though this rather skeptical comment is somewhat uninformative as to the nature of regret, it is indicative of the present state of professional consensus; there seems to be little agreement among emotion theorists regarding the nature of regret.

Carla Bagnoli believes regret involves "valuable unchosen alternatives supported by reasons,"[14] while Marcel Zeelenberg feels that regret need not have any moral or reasonable content at all but is simply linked to unfavorable outcomes.[15] These views are not necessarily incompatible; however, the theorists' descriptions are not equivalent. There could be cases that one theorist considers to involve regret that another might not.

Janet Landman declares, "Regret is a more or less painful judgment and state of feeling sorry for misfortunes, limitations, losses, shortcomings, transgressions, or mistakes."[16] Landman's description is so general that it runs the risk of including all sorts of negative emotions that scholars like Bagnoli would exclude. Given Landman's description, one might appropriately regret world hunger, the natural death of a loved one, or even a lack of native athletic ability. Since Bagnoli focuses on the existence of valuable alternatives that were not chosen (but, by being alternatives, could have been chosen), she would probably exclude such cases; for, regardless of who the agent is, world hunger, natural death, and native weaknesses are paradigmatic examples of things about which individual agents have no choice.

Still, Bagnoli's description might be too broad for other scholars. For example, Amélie Rorty describes regret in virtue of the agent's role (and beliefs about that role) in precipitating that which is regrettable: "If an agent A regrets having done something, having brought about a state of affairs E, then he believes that he has contributed to the occurrence of E, and characteristically, he judges that E is harmful, bad, or undesirable . . . The objects of regret have two components, an event or state of affairs, and the agent's action in bringing about the state of affairs."[17] Here, Rorty explicitly evokes a notion of responsibility for bad outcomes. In contrast, Bagnoli's description does not require the agent judge the chosen alternative to be a bad alternative.

According to Bagnoli, regret simply requires that some unchosen options are viewed as valuable. For example, Jenna might be torn between ordering a mushroom soup or a sweet potato soup at a café. Let us assume that she has limited funds and appetite and therefore cannot have both options. She chooses the sweet potato soup and enjoys it. She does not regard her choice to have been a bad one. But, on Bagnoli's account, she might still regret choosing the sweet potato soup if the mushroom soup constitutes a valuable alternative, the taking of which would have been reasonable. For example, Jenna has never had a mushroom soup, which she considers a reason to order it since she likes trying new things. Strangely, it is possible that Jenna has the same reason supporting her actual choice. She had never had a sweet potato soup either and would find it reasonable to try it for that very same reason. In such cases (often called by free will theorists "Buridan's Ass" cases or "Chocolate/Vanilla" cases), there might be equally good reasons for choosing one of multiple options. According to Bagnoli, agents in such situations might regret their choices even if they also approve of them.

It seems that J. M. Joyce would agree with Bagnoli. According to Joyce, a lack of information can make it rational for one to know ahead of time that one will regret a choice and select that option nonetheless.[18] In the above example, Joyce would say that Jenna could reasonably know that she will regret either choice, as taking one excludes the other, and she will always wonder whether she would have preferred the unchosen option. Similarly, Caspar Hare argues that the discrepancy between what one ought to do objectively speaking and what one ought to do according to limited epistemic information causes us to doubt whether we did make the best choice and, if the outcome is deemed at all unfavorable, we might regret such a decision as a result. Additionally, Hare notes that the possibility of metaphysical indeterminacy can be reason to regret choices on the basis that having chosen the same option a different way (such as a second or two earlier or slightly more or less enthusiastically) could have changed the outcome significantly.[19]

To my mind, Bagnoli, Joyce, and Hare have accurately represented key phenomena among experiences of regret. Rorty, on the other hand, would seem to disagree (according to her definition noted above). In the above example, Rorty would only count Jenna as experiencing regret if she also viewed the purchase of the sweet potato soup as bad. However, I think it is more conservative to say that, if Jenna wonders whether the mushroom soup might have been more satisfying, she might both desire to have ordered that instead and find the taste of her actual choice quite pleasing. In other words, it is possible to regret what we take to be good choices insofar as we suspect that alternatives would have yielded even greater goods.

Rorty's description is also more specific than Landman's in that the agent recognizes some role she played in the regrettable outcome's actualization, and Rorty is not alone in this regard. Indeed, other theorists, such as Rüdiger

Bittner, concur with this need for an evaluation of one's role; Bittner defines regret as "a painful feeling about something we did which we think was bad."[20] But as we shall see, certain theorists want to include alleged cases of regret that do not satisfy this requirement.

More controversial than the claim that regret involves a sense of responsibility is the claim that one must wish that one had behaved differently. This second claim seems to require the first in that one cannot wish to have acted differently unless one sees oneself as responsible for (i.e., capable of) acting in the first place. However, even those who accept the first claim often deny the second. For example, in addition to the description above, Rorty later clarifies that a subject need not wish to undo her action, or even wish for the outcome to be different necessarily, so long as she simply wishes that it had not been her who had to do it.[21] Carla Bagnoli and Gabrielle Taylor agree with Rorty that wishing to choose differently is not necessarily an element of regret.[22] While the denial of the second new criterion is common, it is not universal. Robert Sugden considers regret "the painful sensation of recognizing that 'what is' compares unfavorably with 'what might have been' . . . regret, we have suggested, is wishing you had chosen differently."[23] While Sugden's position is representative of a minority, I hope to show that the position is, nonetheless, the right one.

While there is much disagreement between these theorists, it would be misleading to suggest that their accounts are so diverse that they have nothing in common. On the contrary, all of these definitions imply what Landman calls a "counterfactual element," which she describes as "ways the world might be or might have been."[24] When we regret, we fixate on whether and how alternative behavior might have initiated a different causal chain of events (in particular, whether the consequences of those events would have been preferable to the actual consequences we now face). The counterfactual element would seem to require the object of regret consists of at least two propositions: the first evaluating the actual state of affairs and the second considering the possible desirable state of affairs. In addition, all theorists showcased here seem comfortable acknowledging that, despite any opportunities to remedy the situation, the opportunity to cause a different outcome has passed. In short, all accounts of regret thus far include an evaluative (it is bad/suboptimal), a counterfactual (if it weren't for X, perhaps Y), and a retrospective (in the past) aspect. While I concur with these three aspects of any account of regret, I contend that they are not jointly sufficient to pick out regret exclusively.

THE PROPOSED VIEW

I agree with Rorty and Williams that regret must entail an agent's sense of responsibility. However, I consider Sugden's contribution equally helpful; one who regrets wishes to undo one's actions (or wishes to undo one's role[25]) that led to the actual consequences. Given these contributions, the definition of *regret* that I shall endorse is the following:

> A negative emotion associated with considering oneself responsible for some unfavorable or possibly sub-optimal outcome of a situation that presented alternatives the agent believes could have been selected in the past, and in some sense, the agent wishes that she had selected instead.

From this definition, we can make several inferences concerning the types of conditions that obtain when an agent feels regret: (1) That the outcome of the situation is one judged by the agent as somehow unfavorable or, at least, possibly suboptimal; (2) the emotion has a counterfactual element in that it focuses not only on how things are but also in comparison to how things could have been;[26] (3) the opportunity for things to be different has, in a way, passed (simply because the regretted event is in the past—even if one can redeem oneself, that does not change the fact that the regrettable act or consequence happened and this cannot be reversed); (4) that the agent considers herself responsible for the outcome in some way; and (5) the agent feels that had she the chance to choose again (theoretically, a do-over), she might want to choose differently.[27]

All of the theorists discussed thus far hold at least one of these conditions as part of their definitions of regret. However, while I contend that each is necessary, I also hold that none is sufficient by itself, and only if the phenomenological content of the emotion includes all of these elements can the emotion properly be called *regret*. Failure to include all conditions may result in misidentifying an emotion that, though similar to regret, is, in fact, something else. Since this chapter directly addresses those theorists who discount the fourth and fifth criteria, I shall attempt to provide counterexamples by way of other distinct emotions that could satisfy the first three criteria listed above, indicating that these three criteria are jointly insufficient for distinguishing regret.

WHY ADD TO THE CRITERIA?

Let us consider four distinct emotion types that are obviously different from regret but manage to satisfy criteria 1–3 nonetheless. Since defining these alternative emotions philosophically might require writing four additional chapters similar to this one, we shall rely on the common notions of these emotions as they are defined by the *Oxford English Dictionary* (OED).[28] Demonstrating that these emotions satisfy this subset of our criteria will show that criteria 1–3, though perhaps necessary, are not sufficient for distinguishing cases of regret from instances of other emotions.

The first emotion we shall consider is anger. The OED defines anger as "a strong feeling of annoyance, displeasure, or hostility." Let us imagine a situation that is capable of yielding regret (even given the criteria above) but, in one instance, fails to incorporate the fourth and fifth criteria. Betting is an activity commonly discussed when examining regret. Imagine Saul is a powerful mobster. While at a racetrack, Saul gives Jimmy, one of his younger associates, $100 and tells Jimmy to go place a bet on any horse he wants. After the bet is placed, the horses race and Saul's horse loses. Immediately, Saul turns to Jimmy, slaps him across the face, and yells, "You putz! You blew my money!" In this instance, Saul clearly judges the outcome to be unfavorable. He also wishes that the situation weren't what it was (that the horse his money was on had won or that his money had been placed on the winning horse). In addition, the opportunity to do anything to remedy this situation has passed. Saul's emotion satisfies criteria 1–3; however, most of us would consider Saul angry and not regretful. We doubt Saul's reaction is regret since the responsibility, in Saul's mind, was Jimmy's (therefore, Saul clearly fails to satisfy the fourth criteria).[29] Interestingly, it is possible that Saul could have felt regret. Instead of being angry, Saul could have felt responsible for giving the money to Jimmy or for failing to specify a horse. He might feel responsible for betting at all and wish that he had simply saved his money and watched the race. Nonetheless, if he had felt any of these things, he would certainly have felt a desire to have acted differently. However, since Saul did not feel these things, his emotion is something else.

A second example is pity, which the OED defines as "a feeling of sorrow and compassion caused by the sufferings of others." Most would say that pity and regret are distinct. However, pity does satisfy the first three criteria. For example, one would not pity someone for something one thought was favorable. One's pity would be inspired by a desire that the circumstances or situation were different. One who pities does so since the situation in question seems like it cannot be helped, either because the opportunity has passed or there never was an opportunity to alter the situation. Consider Malcolm. Malcolm pities his college roommate, Billy, who is intellectually deficient in many ways. Billy studies diligently and cannot seem to remember anything. Billy is having a terrible time in school, failing exams often. Malcolm wishes it weren't the case that Billy had such difficulties. He considers Billy's struggle and misfortunes unpleasant. It would also seem that there is nothing one can do to help Billy. Malcolm is not responsible for Billy's predicament and therefore does not wish to undo any decisions.[30] Malcolm does not seem to regret Billy's misfortune, but rather he seems to pity or sympathize with Billy.

Our third example is grief. Grief is defined as "intense sorrow, especially caused by someone's death." A mother may feel grief over the loss of a son without feeling responsible for the loss and without wishing to have acted differently. For example, Peggy and her son, Jonathan, are both extremely patriotic. She has always been very proud of Jonathan for joining the army. Jonathan has always wanted to die for his country. Though Jonathan has no desire to die soon, he is not particularly concerned with dying old either; indeed, he hopes that when his day comes, he will be on the battlefield. When she hears the news of her son's death, Peggy is immediately grief-stricken. Though she is truly proud of her son and happy that he got his wish, it does not change the fact that she considers his death unfavorable (even if inevitable), wishes the situation to be different (perhaps that he could die in a battle twenty years from now and after she passes away), and considers the outcome irreversible. Here, she need not feel responsible and need not wish that she had acted in any way to prevent him from joining the army. Had she also felt these things though, her grief might have been accompanied by regret.

The final counterexample to the claim that criteria 1–3 are sufficient for regret is displeasure, which the OED defines as "feeling of annoyance or dissatisfaction." One can certainly feel displeased in a way that satisfies the first three criteria but does not satisfy the final two. For example, Tommy is thirsty and spends his last dollar in an attempt to buy a can of Sprite. Much to his dismay, the machine dispenses a Coke instead. Tommy dislikes the taste of Coke and is unable to stomach quenching his thirst with this lesser option. Tommy finds the outcome unfavorable, wishes he had received a Sprite instead of a Coke, and feels that the chance for the situation to be different has passed. Tommy is displeased with the result and might feel annoyed that the delivery person failed to stock the machine properly. Without criteria four and five, Tommy is simply displeased. However, if he felt responsible for choosing that machine, and wished that he had walked down the hall to another vending machine that might have been properly stocked, his feeling might have amounted to regret.[31]

Responsibility

Though we have seen that without the fourth and fifth criteria, descriptions of regret can be too broad and admit counterexamples, some theorists still hold that genuine instances of regret occur without satisfying these two criteria. For example, Bagnoli, Williams,[32] and Landman hold that regret may ensue when the agent is well aware of her impotence in the situation. One might object that being aware of one's impotence precludes judging oneself to be responsible (our fourth criterion). However, this is not the case. We must remember that the scope of the term 'responsible' is broader than the very specific species of responsibility we call *moral*. While it may be the case that an agent felt powerless regarding his or her role in the situation, the agent might also feel responsible nonetheless. I suspect that several theorists disregard the element of responsibility because they confuse it with culpability. There are many examples of regret where the agent was the impetus of an unfavorable outcome but need not consider herself morally accountable for that outcome. For example, if Tim were to open a door that happened to have someone else on the other side of it inspecting the doorknob (say, his colleague Joe), and he inadvertently broke Joe's nose, though Tim could not be considered morally culpable, he might still view himself as causally responsible and regret opening the door in that exact moment. But such examples are not counterexamples to our fourth criterion of regret. The fact that one is not *morally* responsible for a dreadful outcome does not alone entail that the same agent isn't responsible in some other relevant sense (e.g., Tim is causally responsible). Tim can still regret opening the door even though he knows he's not blameworthy for breaking Joe's nose. He's not blameworthy because he could not have known that Joe's nose was in danger. However, that he broke Joe's nose is indisputable. Tim might wish that he had known about Joe (and his nose) because, had he known, he would not have opened the door. He might even wish that he had opened the door more slowly, which could have given Joe time to react and announce his presence. If Tim regrets breaking Joe's nose (and we have stipulated that he does), then he considers himself responsible and wishes he had done something different.

Revision

A sense of responsibility is necessary for one to satisfy the fifth criterion. If one does not feel responsible for the suboptimal outcome, how could one wish to choose differently? Surely, one could still wish that the world were other than it is. But one could not consistently wish to behave differently while denying that she behaved at all in the first place.

Finally, the fifth criterion—that the agent wish to have behaved differently—follows naturally from the fact that regret is a *negative* emotion concerning one's responsibility for an outcome. This criterion is what distinguishes regret from nostalgic wondering. If I wonder what my life would be like had I chosen a different career, lived in different places, and made different choices, I can do so without regret. The exercise could be purely cognitive. However, if I regret my choices, I think I ought to have made better ones.

The fifth criterion is more than a mere consequence of the fourth (that we are responsible for something possibly suboptimal). It does not follow that believing one ought to have acted better means one wishes one had acted differently. While it does follow analytically that if I think doing X is bad, I think that *my* doing X is bad, it is not the case that believing *my* doing X is bad entails wishing that I had not done X. For example, one might acknowledge that long-term (perhaps unforeseen) consequences make an error worthwhile, as is often the case for parents whose children were conceived accidentally. Perhaps engaging in unprotected sexual intercourse is not something one ought to do if one does not want to conceive; nevertheless, a parent might maintain that very belief while experiencing no desire to have acted otherwise. In such instances, the lack of a counterfactual wish or desire is precisely what precludes an agent from experiencing regret. If one does not wish to have acted otherwise—even when the agent acknowledges the hardships that came with the original decision—one does not *regret*.

Be that as it may, I do not believe that the counterfactual desire constitutive of regret must be effective. As mentioned above, Jenna may regret ordering sweet potato soup insofar as part of her wishes she had tried the mushroom soup instead. She wonders whether she would have liked that even more. She was ambivalent as to which soup ought to be tasted first. In fact, it is possible that Jenna was bound to experience regret regardless of her choice. After all, in choosing one, she has forfeited the other (at least, for the time being). The mystery of whether the choice made was the best possible choice renders regret possible.

While the counterfactual wish or desire needn't be compelling, its existence seems to be necessary for an emotion to qualify as regret. Otherwise, we leave ourselves open to a slippery slope complaint that we regret the vast majority of our decisions (from the trivial to the significant). For instance, imagine that Milly desires some milk to go with her brownie. Let us also imagine that whenever Milly is able, she prefers to acquire goods for free rather than for purchase. It just so happens that all available milk in Milly's proximity costs money. Suppose that she deems the milk important enough to part with a very small portion of her personal disposable funds. Imagine she is perfectly content with the outcome, experiencing no doubt that she made the right choice. Are we to concede that Milly may regret purchasing the milk? After all, she would have preferred to get the milk for free. In fact, I imagine most people would prefer not to pay for things they want that happen to have a price tag. Without the fifth criteria, we cannot explain why Milly does not regret her decision. Milly knows that she caused herself to acquire milk (responsibility) *and* as she would have preferred to have acquired the milk for free (counterfactual), she viewed having to pay for the milk as suboptimal. However, once purchased, Milly cannot recuperate those funds. Still, if she has no desire to have acted differently, is it fair to say Milly regrets? I think it is not. Acknowledging that some other imaginary arrangement would be preferable to the actual situation is insufficient for regret. Without a desire to have acted otherwise, Milly's example merely illustrates the ubiquitous exchange we call *compromise*. If lack of satisfaction with reality suffices for regret, we might regret having to pay for anything, needing to sleep, and having obligations of any kind. To weaken our notion of *regret* this much is to wash it of its meaning. Surely, the experience of regret is more acute and complex than the acknowledgment of most mundane disappointing facts.

COUNTEREXAMPLES TO THE PROPOSED VIEW

By adding the descriptors of a sense of responsibility and a counterfactual desire for revision, we can now distinguish regret from emotions such as anger, pity, grief, and displeasure. However, we must also consider whether these additions narrow the scope of regret too much, thus excluding instances of genuine regret. I have classified four types of instances when an agent is spoken of as if in the throes of regret; yet, such instances fail to meet all the criteria listed in my account. I shall argue that we ought to exclude such instances, as they do not describe genuine experiences of regret.

The examples are as follows: R1 is "regret" due to other people's actions; R2 is "regret" of situations; R3 is "regret" of having to perform acts that will result in outcomes that other people will judge unacceptable; and R4 is regret as a result of having made a choice in the midst of a moral dilemma. This list may not be exhaustive; however, I do think that it includes the most common types of examples that might challenge the addition of our fourth and fifth criteria of regret.

For an example of R1, imagine a young man (call him Raul) expressing regret that Adolph Hitler (among others) perpetrated the Holocaust. While it might seem that this example satisfies each of the criteria, a closer look will show that the person about whom one considers each criterion changes. For example, the chance to act differently has passed for Hitler. Hitler is responsible for the outcome. Raul, the person judging Hitler and the one claiming to express regret, is not responsible in any way. It is the case that Raul judges the outcome to be unfavorable (and, in fact, immoral). However, this is not truly experiencing regret. In this example, Raul is expressing the opinion that the agent about whom he speaks ought to feel regret. One might argue that Raul might truly wish it weren't the case that Hitler committed this atrocity. While this may be true, the counterfactual element of Raul's desire is not sufficient to call it regret. For many other emotions can be equally counterfactual and require that the agent not be responsible. For example, an agent might be sad that someone else did X action. He might also be angry with someone else for committing Y crime.[33] Raul might lament the fact that anyone could commit such heinous acts. He might bemoan human weakness. Though one may feel sympathy for victims of others' acts, and one may passionately wish that it had not been the case that others behaved in such ways, what one expresses in these situations is not regret.

To illustrate this point, imagine the following conversation between Rick and Raul. Raul states that he regrets the Holocaust. Rick playfully responds, "You should!" Raul would certainly be taken aback by such a comment. Raul is too young to have witnessed (let alone caused) the Holocaust. Therefore, while regret is a reactive attitude, it seems to be exclusively a self-reactive attitude. That is to say, unlike personal reactive attitudes, which address another directly (e.g., I am angry at you for stomping on my toe) and general reactive attitudes we have empathically for a third party (e.g., we may resent a violent criminal's lack of respect for her victims even if we are not among them), regret targets its own subject every time. This is not to say that we cannot resent Hitler for the Holocaust. On the contrary! That is a salient example of a general reactive attitude (*resentment*, one of Strawson's favorite to discuss, it seems). What we do not do is *regret* what we believe we did not perpetrate.

Examples of R2 include cases where an agent is allegedly regretful that negative events happen; however, the agent knows that no one is responsible for said events. Imagine Pauline proclaims to regret that Indonesia has suffered so many devastating tsunamis in recent years. Clearly, Pauline may experience strong feelings indicating a desire that it were not the case that Indonesia suffer tsunamis. However, there is no element of self-assessment or any desire to choose differently since, in order to choose differently, one must have chosen initially. This example is even less likely to be an example of regret than the previous one since, with R1, someone ought to regret something (even if it is not the subject experiencing the feeling). Presumably, no one had any role in this unfortunate outcome. This example ought to be labeled pity or sympathy for others or even displeasure with nature. However, it is not regret.

When one says that one "regrets" the Holocaust or a tsunami, that person either misspeaks or is speaking hyperbolically or metaphorically.[34] If the locutor means *regret* literally, she is mistakenly labeling what is more likely resentment (in the case of agent perpetrators) or lamentation (in cases when no one is at fault). If she wishes to exaggerate her sensitivity to the matter, or convey extreme empathy, she may use the word "regret" figuratively. Much like how one might say, "I would kill for such an opportunity!" to convey extreme value of some blessing (i.e., nobody understands such a phrase to be a literal threat), or how one might proclaim, "I love ice cream!" to express a strong preference for the dessert (i.e., we do not presume the speaker imagines herself to have a deep personal relationship with ice cream), we sometimes say that we regret heinous historical events because it personalizes our respect for their gravity.

Hyperbolic and metaphorical uses of the term "regret" abound in our third type of example. In these instances, a subject expresses regret in having to carry out some kind of obligation, such as informing some applicant of her rejection, but the person does not experience conflict and would not actually wish for a different outcome. It is my contention that such examples do not constitute regret but have an element that feigns regret out of hyperbole or politeness. In order to explain this claim further, I will introduce a distinction made by Ronald De Sousa.[35]

De Sousa notes "the motivational role of emotions defines their characteristic *aims*"[36] or what the emotion motivates us to do. For example, regret can motivate us to revise our decision-making practices, and fear motivates us to flee danger. De Sousa warns us not to confuse the natural aim of an emotion with "the aim that someone might have in expressing or feeling one."[37] Someone might express an emotion (e.g., *sympathy*) because that person wants to come off as a certain type of person (*sympathetic, caring*), whereas the subject does not actually feel that emotion. For instance, even if Jan is very depressed one day, she will feign joy in response to a friend's good news because she wants to appear attentive and supportive (and, perhaps she is naturally so, under normal circumstances).

De Sousa adds, "In other cases the aim is vestigial—only some form of expression, perhaps even only an inclination to some utterance."[38] Imagine Miriam is drafting a rejection letter to Sue, a job applicant. Miriam writes that she "regrets to inform" Sue that she was not selected for the job. De Sousa might say that Miriam is trying to convey sympathy or appear sensitive and caring. Perhaps, Miriam simply wants to sound professional (after all, most rejection letters follow this convention). Regardless of what Miriam is feeling, she is probably not feeling regret; at most, she must be trying to appear to feel regret because, in our culture, expressing such sentiments is a matter of etiquette.

Even if we are to entertain that the subject is not feigning anything, we still have difficulty classifying this example as regret. For example, Miriam might recognize that someone had to be rejected from the job. Even if she knew Sue personally and truly did wish for the outcome to be different, this would fall under those instances when the subject is displeased but not regretful. Surely Miriam might feel uncomfortable being the bearer of bad news, but does she regret doing it? She would not, if given the chance, change her mind and *not* inform people of their acceptance status. This is a traditional form of politeness. However, it does indicate something of what we expect from regret. It is possible that, though regret is not necessarily moral, we view it as morally required after doing wrong. A rejected applicant might feel that some injustice had occurred. Perhaps this bit of etiquette developed to assuage the anger of applicants. After all, if the employer truly does feel bad about what she has chosen to do, it is easier to forgive her for her actions.[39]

R4 is when an agent supposedly feels regret for an action that the agent knew at the time would bring about an unpleasant consequence but nonetheless is wholeheartedly confident in the correctness of her behavior.[40] One salient type of example is a moral dilemma.[41] Bagnoli brings up the example of Agamemnon, who decides to sacrifice Iphigenia, his daughter, so that he may please the gods.[42] If he does not please them, his fleet won't make its journey. Clearly, Agamemnon would rather not sacrifice his daughter if he could avoid it. However, in this situation, he is convinced that if he does not, he fails to fulfill another moral obligation.

In such examples of moral dilemmas, we are to assume that the agent would not choose differently if given the opportunity to choose again. Agamemnon, for example, seems to believe that he did the right thing. Still, some might protest, Agamemnon regrets (and *ought to regret*) killing Iphigenia. Mark Strasser offers the following commentary on the problem:

> Those who argue that an agent ought to feel compunction for having done [the morally correct thing], thereby seem to be claiming that one deserves to feel badly for having performed the morally right action. Those who argue that an agent ought not feel compunction in such a situation thereby seem to be claiming that one ought not feel badly even though, for instance, one may have severely disappointed many people's hopes or expectations . . . when we have acted rightly, we don't deserve to feel it but, rather, ought to feel moral distress in these types of situations.[43]

Strasser recognizes the problem in considering agents who behave morally deserving of regret. Paradoxically, however, one might argue that feeling something in the face of tragedy is morally required. While I agree with both of these claims, I disagree that *the something* in question must be regret. "Moral distress," as Strasser puts it, is a better label for what an agent such as Agamemnon would be feeling. He may even feel shame for being the one to do her in. However, if he does not wish to have done otherwise in any sense, he does not feel regret about his decision. Though he laments the loss of his daughter, and certainly feels responsible for initiating her death, I argue that his feeling is not properly described as regret. It is true that his feeling is in relation to an unfavorable consequence. As Bagnoli holds, his feelings indicate a value of his that could not be realized. However, if he did not desire to have acted differently, I propose that something else is afoot.

When an agent feels terrible as a result of a moral dilemma, either she regrets her choice or she laments her situation. If an agent does actually feel that she failed to choose the most important morally obligatory option, then she certainly might feel regret. If the agent in no way wishes to have chosen differently, either because she feels she has chosen the best option or that no option was better than any other, the situation can be explained as "regretting" having been put in such a situation, which can be reduced to R2 (which we have already established is not an example of genuine regret but rather sympathy, sadness, or even disdain for how the world is). Bagnoli is aware of this interpretation; when considering Agamemnon's dilemma, she writes, "If the world were not ruled by such tyrannical gods, his repugnant action would not be required. The moral agent regrets not the action undertaken but having had to undertake such an action."[44] The "having had to undertake such an action" is another way of saying *being put in such a position*, which can be boiled down to situations and circumstances for which the subject bears no responsibility.

R4 is surely the most difficult to eliminate given that it is clearly a form of an agent-related emotion. However, R4 illuminates why we need the revision requirement. Take the quintessential moral dilemma—*Sophie's Choice*. Sophie is instructed by a Nazi official to choose one of her two children to be spared. The alternative is to spare neither, which is hardly an alternative. Naturally, Sophie loves both children equally and can see no reason to spare one over the other. When she chooses child A over child B, her selection is completely random. Some might suggest that Sophie will regret her choice regardless of whom she chooses. However, this description is mistaken. For if it were true that Sophie regretted not choosing child B, she would thereby also regret having chosen child A. But does she? Does she wish that she had instead condemned the other child? Certainly not. She wishes she didn't have to condemn either (i.e., that she could save both). Now, let us consider a modified scenario. Let us imagine that Sophie chooses child A and, that very night, child A dies in her sleep of an aneurism. In this instance, we can imagine Sophie regretting her choice. Sophie could regret having chosen child A on the basis that child A had no chance of survival and the assumption that child B may have lived a full life. But in the modified scenario, Sophie's regret makes sense only because she has come to believe her choice was suboptimal. She regrets her choice, in part, *because* she wishes she had chosen differently. And wishing we had chosen differently is precisely the desire for revision at issue.

SCIENTIFIC CONFIRMATION

Regret and Disappointment

The distinction between regret and disappointment is essential to the argument of this chapter. I contend that many instances of supposed regret that fail to meet our fourth (and sometimes fifth) criteria are, in fact, instances of disappointment mislabeled. Such a mistake is easy to make, as both emotions surely share phenomenological content. However, some scientific research suggests that, despite the phenomenological similarities between regret and disappointment, the experiential differences are (1) pronounced, (2) directly related to a sense of responsibility and a desire for revision, and (3) seem to be caused by slightly different processes of the brain.

Statistically significant results concerning the experiential differences of responsibility between regret and disappointment can be found in earlier studies on similar questions. For instance, Frijda, Kuipers, and ter Schure asked participants a series of questions concerning how they felt about specific instances of regret or disappointment. They found the emotions differed significantly concerning the appraisal item, *self-agency*. They measured this appraisal item by asking, "Were you responsible for what happened or had happened?" Regret scored significantly higher than did disappointment.[45] In 1994, Gilovich and Medvec asked participants to make a list of their "biggest regrets." Less than 5 percent of regrets reported were determined to concern factors beyond the respondent's control (10 out of 213), leading Gilovich ad Medvec to conclude that "a sense of personal responsibility is central to the experience of regret."[46]

Zeelenberg, van Dijk, Manstead, and van der Pligt researched the experiential differences between regret and disappointment insofar as they relate to responsibility directly. They randomly distributed questionnaires to 313 participants between the ages of eighteen and forty-six (with twenty the median age) that asked subjects to visualize a moment in their lives when they experienced either intense regret or intense disappointment (each questionnaire asked about one or the other). Participants were then asked to rank on a nine-point scale (with 1 being *not at all* and 9, *to a very great extent*) the extent to which they felt, thought about, or did certain things as a result of the emotional experience. Interestingly, those who drew a survey concerning regret scored significantly higher on questions concerning a feeling that the participant should have known better, thoughts about having made a mistake, self-reproach (literally, "the tendency to kick yourself"), attempts to correct a mistake, and a desire for a second chance than did participants asked about an experience of disappointment.[47]

These last two items on the list suggest not only a sense of responsibility (our fourth criterion) but also a desire for revision (our fifth). Indeed, in their concluding discussion, Zeelenberg et al. write, "Our findings concerning the *experience of disappointment* show that this experience, more than that of regret, involves feeling powerless, feeling a tendency to do nothing and to get away from the situation, actually turning away from the event, and wanting to do nothing."[48]

It is possible that the similarities between regret and disappointment stem from a relationship between the two experiences. For instance, Landman suggested, "Regret is a superordinate concept that subsumes certain defining features of disappointment."[49] In other words, it might be that regret is a specific type of disappointment (the type where we also feel a sense of responsibility and a desire to revise that for which we are responsible). The complications that these additional aspects of regret create sometimes amplify the depth of the experience of lamentation. While this possibility is too rich to explore in this chapter, if true, it would help explain why some might use the word "regret" to describe that which is, in fact, extreme disappointment. For our purposes, this possibility provides the interesting consequence that, while all instances of regret might be (accompanied by) instances of disappointment, the converse is not the case. Therefore, our fourth and fifth criteria would still remain necessary to distinguish experiences of regret from those of general disappointment.

Responsibility Studies

Recently, psychologists and neuroscientists have been reporting evidence suggesting that regret involves some feeling of responsibility. For instance, Neal J. Roese and Amy Summerville analyzed several distinct studies concerning comparative regret. Roese and Summerville found that the degree to which a person reports to have (and appears to have via fMRI evidence) regrets depends upon the degree of perceived opportunity: "People's biggest regrets are a reflection of where in life they see their largest opportunities; that is, where they see tangible prospects for change."[50] Antinette Nicolle, Dominik R. Bach, Chris Frith, and Raymond J. Dolan found that subjective ratings of regret depend on a higher subjective sense of responsibility as well as a more objective sense of responsibility. In a series of gambling games, subjects are led to believe, on some occasions, that they are the sole cause of a poor outcome, one of several sources of a poor outcome, or not a source at all of a poor outcome (i.e., their choice or gamble was outweighed by a democratic majority. Had their selection been played, the outcome would have been favorable). Nicolle et al. found that the more responsible subjects felt, the greater the reported self-blame regret. In a related study reported in the same article, Nicolle et al. discuss fMRI results indicating an enhanced amygdala response to regret-related outcomes when the subjects believe to have high levels of responsibility (this, in comparison to similar subject exhibiting lower such levels).

Nathalie Camille, Giorgio Coricelli, Jerome Sallet, Pascale Pradat-diehl, Jean-René Duhamel, and Angela Sirigu discovered further evidence suggesting that a sense of responsibility is constitutive of regret and, without it, one's experience resembles more closely that of mere disappointment.[51] In this series of experiments, subjects played several rounds of gambling games, whereby a random computer generator calculated the outcome (much like how slot machines operate). Subjects are given two choices: one with a low probability of winning but a high reward and the other with a moderate probability of winning but also a moderate reward. In addition, losing entailed a specified point deduction. For example, a subject might be presented with one option, the high yield of which is +200 and the loss of which is −50 (Camille et al. used French Francs), and a second option, whereby the yield is +50 and the loss is −50. The subject is informed that the first option has a 20 percent chance of winning, and the second option has a 50 percent chance of winning. In other words, the odds are worse in the first option; however, the yield is better (if one were to win). The result of losing is the same; however, one is *more likely* to lose if one chooses the first option. Camille et al. also arranged the outcomes such that the options with the lower odds *did in fact* lose more than those with the higher odds of success.

In the first round, subjects view only the outcome of the game they select. In other words, they learn whether they win or not (and, of course, how much). They do not learn whether the unchosen option came out positive or negative.[52] In these games, Camille et al. found that, on average, subjects who won were pleased and subjects who lost reported disappointment. This round of games set a baseline for joy and disappointment induced by winning and losing (respectively). Then, the same subjects played another series of games similar to the first, only this time, both results are revealed. Consider the options described above. On average, Camille et al. found that if one were to have chosen the more conservative option and lost, one's reaction depended on whether the unchosen option came up positive or negative. If both options lost (each yielding −50), subjects tended to be indifferent. However, if the unchosen option won, players reported significant disappointment (substantially more than they had earlier when they lost similar amounts). Camille et al. concluded from this information, "Contrary to mere disappointment, which is experienced when a negative outcome happens independently of our own decision, regret is an emotion strongly associated with a feeling of responsibility."[53]

Revision

Research supports the revision criterion as well. While many have postulated and observed that regret motivates revision in future decision processes, Davide Marchiori and Massimo Warglien found that regret operates as a better revisionary regulator than does social pressure, previously presumed in economic models to be highly motivating. Through observing subjects' participation in individual and interactive games as well as imaging of responses of neural networks, Marchiori and Warglien discovered that regret-based models were found to be more accurate predictors of behavior and learning than economic models were.[54] While many forms of learning and decision-making adjustments come from a social context and interactive exchange, the fact that regret serves as an intrapersonal feedback loop supports two aspects of the present account: (1) regret is closely (if not essentially) associated with a desire for counterfactual scenarios or opportunities for revision and (2) regret serves as a self-reactive attitude.

Camille et al. (see above) also studied our propensity to revise when regret is induced. They did this by comparing the outcomes of the second round of games (what they labeled *complete feedback*) to the outcomes of a similar round played exclusively by subjects known to have lesions in their orbitofrontal cortex (OFC). As the consensus among neuroscientists suggests that the OFC (in conjunction with the dorsolateral prefrontal regions of the brain known to be active in reasoning and planning, to which the OFC is connected) is active in reward evaluations and comparisons, Camille et al. suspected that persons with injuries to that part of the brain would revise their strategy less. The results support this hypothesis. First, the neurotypical subjects overwhelmingly demonstrated a shift in strategy to the more conservative gambles over time when both outcomes were revealed. In other words, as the higher reward options lost more often, subjects who chose them initially soon after ceased selecting those options. Camille et al. suggest that the regret these subjects felt inspired a change of course. If this conclusion is correct, it stands to reason that if a subject changes her strategy after experiencing regret, something about the experience of regret contributes a desire to revise behavior.

One might protest that this outcome could be explained by mere disappointment as well. Perhaps the disappointment of losing is sufficient to generate a desire (albeit a separate and otherwise unrelated mental state) to avoid such feelings in the future. However, this objection seems to fail. Camille et al. found that the subjects with damage to the OFC registered their experiences differently. First, there was no statistical difference between the reports of degrees of sadness in the partial and complete feedback sessions. Whether a subject knew that, had she chosen otherwise, she would have won, had no effect on her subjective rating of disappointment after losing. Recall that neurotypical subjects reported feeling significantly more disappointment when they learned that they could have won (had they chosen differently) than they reported after losing without knowing the outcome of the unchosen option. In addition, recall that the experience of loss and disappointment was muted when neurotypical subjects learned that, regardless of their choice, they were determined to lose the exact same amount (in our scenario above, −50). These results suggest that the feeling of responsibility for the outcome cuts both ways; if it is our fault that we lost, we feel strong regret, but if we know that it was not up to us to win, we do not feel as badly as we did when we were uncertain of whether the unchosen option was better. Interestingly, this result was not present in the group with OFC damage.[55]

Perhaps more interesting still is the way that the neurologically atypical subjects continued to play subsequent games without altering their strategy. Camille et al. found that subjects with OFC damage who chose the riskier options and lost early on continued to choose the riskier option in subsequent games—regardless of the fact that they have witnessed this to be a losing strategy. Camille et al. believe these data suggest that persons with OFC damage are less likely to feel responsible for the outcome of their choices and, therefore, less likely to desire to change their behavior when they dislike the consequences of their choices. While these data are not entirely conclusive, and more work needs to be done testing these emotional responses, they could help explain the relationship between the sense of responsibility and the desire for revision characteristic of regret.[56]

Research also supports my hypothesis that, without any subjective sense of responsibility and counterfactual desires for revision, the experience a subject has cannot be regret, properly described. While the OFC is thought to be essential to both the experience of regret and mediating the experience of regret, Nicolle et al. found that "regret-related neuronal activity in the amygdala was enhanced by increased responsibility,"[57] whereas the OFC is implicated in similar emotions that do not involve self-evaluation of responsibility. For example, they observed activity in the OFC of participants who were disappointed by an outcome of a gamble but felt no responsibility for the outcome since it was not congruent with their personal vote. The participants' reports of feeling no responsibility were corroborated by muted-to-no activity in the amygdala. They write, "It is surprising that we find lateral OFC involvement in negatively discrepant outcomes without responsibility. It is possible that this lateral OFC response reflects anger, frustration, or loss of control in the participant."[58] In other words, Nicolle et al.'s fMRI studies showed that while OFC is integral to both the experience of regret and some negative, non-self-reactive attitudes, additional activity in the amygdala (indicative of a sense of responsibility) is expected when a subject experiences regret specifically.[59]

CONCLUSION

The above evidence suggests that a sense of responsibility and a desire for revision is essential to the experience of regret. When neuroimaging is not possible, pragmatic, or decisive, we must turn to the phenomenology of experiencing regret for clues about how to make clear and fitting judgments. There too we find ample reason to include these criteria of *responsibility* and *revision*, as any conceptual framework lacking these is too broad to distinguish *regret* from other decidedly distinct emotion concepts and experiences.

Alleged counterexamples that diverge from the agent's self-assessment can be explained as other negative emotions that do not involve self-assessment and may not even involve a reaction to any other person, such as disappointment and sorrow. That regret does involve a sense of responsibility and a desire for revision explains its inclusion in the class of emotions called *reactive attitudes*. She who regrets reacts to herself as one who is responsible for something bad or suboptimal, and this reaction fosters a desire to have done something differently. Therefore, regret is a *self-reactive attitude* given its normative content coupled with the fact that the object and possessor of the attitude are identical. The normative content is sensitive to the agent's sense of responsibility, which informs the agent's wish that she had behaved differently.

NOTES

1. See Strawson (1997), Section III, esp. 124.
2. Ibid., 130–2.
3. See Rossi-Keen (2007), 54–5.
4. One might protest that regret's absence is conspicuous since a similar emotion, *remorse,* does make the cut. After all, one might argue that remorse just is a species of regret—the only species relevant to moral responsibility. Even if that were true (though I do not suggest that it is), the possibility remains that *simple regret* (what I shall call regret without moral import) involves responsibility of a different kind.
5. See Anton (2015), Chapter 5. Though, we can be blameworthy in virtue of moral attitudes even when we do not cause harm *and* even if we did not choose the moral attitude.
6. See Williams (1982), 28.
7. Ibid.
8. Researchers have discovered that intuitions behind the famed "trolley" problems (where one must either flip a switch [rerouting a runaway trolley over a single victim] or shove a man to his death [to stop the runaway trolley] in order to save five potential victims) are more sensitive to our sense of personal causation via touch than it is to the previously believed do/allow distinction. That is to say, we feel like we cause the man's death more (and we feel more responsible) when we personally physically put him in the way of the train than when we move the train in the direction of his path. See Greene (2013), 211–45.
9. These sorts of attitudes were termed by Strawson, *detached attitudes.* Strawson's own example is that of the consequentialist who justifies punishment not because the punished *deserve* such treatment but for other objective and external reasons (Strawson 1997, 122). Similarly, I take detached attitudes to be judgments about what does or does not meet a standard minus any particular emotional inclination toward expressing such judgments or altering one's behavior toward those who are judged. Like Strawson, I exclude these attitudes from my discussion.

10. I follow those such as George Sher who hold that one can be blameworthy for failing to know something if there is an obligation to acquire and/or utilize such knowledge. The fact that the person was unaware of the obligation, or "slipped" in fulfilling it, does not render them ill-suited for reactive attitudes. For example, a rapist who defends himself by saying that he didn't *know* that his victim was sincere when his victim protested his advances is blameworthy in part simply based on the fact that he *should have known*. See Sher (2009).

11. Indeed, Aristotle famously claimed that all involuntary actions are painful—such agents regret what they did due to ignorance as soon as one realizes what one has accidentally done (1999, III. 1–5).

12. I qualify this claim as being in some "weak sense" because I recognize that issues concerning self-awareness might interfere with the transparency of such a judgment. For example, imagine that Chloe is in college and is angry with her parents for moving away from her hometown. Perhaps Chloe is not aware of *why* she is angry. She might be confused about the source of her feelings. She might not be self-aware enough to recognize that she wants to visit her childhood home or that she thinks her parents should facilitate her visiting her family and friends simultaneously during school vacations. Nonetheless, we can say that there is an obvious weak judgment embedded in the attitude—Chloe's attitude is indicative of the fact that she views her parents as responsible for *something* that violates *some* standard to which Chloe subscribes.

13. See Klassen (1998), 238.

14. See Bagnoli (2000), 169.

15. See Zeelenberg (1999), 325–40.

16. See Landman (1993), 4.

17. See Rorty (1980), 489–90.

18. See Joyce (2012), 123–45.

19. See Hare (2011), 190–206.

20. See Bittner (1992), 262. See Bittner's paper for a position that ultimately argues (using both Spinoza and Nietzsche) that regret is never reasonable.

21. See Rorty (1980, 495).

22. See Bagnoli (1985, 99).

23. See Sugden (1985, 77–9).

24. See Landman (1987, 138).

25. I mention this aside since, it is possible that one might not feel capable of preventing an unpleasant outcome but still wish that one hadn't gone to work that day or had luckily chosen to take a different road so that one not be put in the position where one could feel regret.

26. Though I do not discuss it here in this chapter, this feature would seem to suggest a stronger characteristic: namely, that the counterfactual element involves some steadfast consideration for the fact that one cannot literally undo what one has done. Even if one could redeem oneself by rectifying the situation, one can still regret having done whatever one did to require redemption. That is, even if one harms a loved one and rectifies the situation some way, that person can still regret the initial transgression. While regret can be assuaged, there is some element concerning the fact that

one cannot undo the past that allows regret to linger even when circumstances have been rectified.

27. This is due to the emotion being counterfactual. The agent feels that choosing differently could bring about the state of affairs that is contrary to the present reality, thus extinguishing the possibility of her feeling regret.

28. Henceforth noted as OED, www.askoxford.com.

29. It should be noted that we may feel emotions (such as anger and regret) based on conscious evaluations of responsibility even when those evaluations contradict subconscious ones (and possibly vice versa). For example, Saul might *know* deep down that he is the one responsible for his loss, but his subconscious desire to appear flawless inspires an alternative assessment of responsibility that manifests in his conscious (and public) experience of anger.

30. Some theorists would say it is possible that Malcolm regrets Billy's lack of intelligence, but it is likely that they would also say that *pity* and *regret* are not synonyms and express different emotions. For this reason, I later consider similar situations as examples of emotions mislabeled as regret.

31. One way to alter this situation where Tommy would not be able to embody criteria four and five would be if there had been no Sprite available and the machine indicated this by flashing the words "Sold Out" across the screen. In this scenario, Tommy buys a Coke instead. Now he is displeased with what he has but saw no other options. He does not feel responsible but, nonetheless, dislikes an outcome he wishes were different that he cannot affect now (or perhaps, at all).

32. See Williams (1982, 20–39).

33. Some might object that it is possible to be angry with oneself. I concur. However, I also contend that such examples are likely instances of mixed emotions in that the agent is experiencing multiple emotions. Therefore, I believe that such instances are constitutive of anger and regret. Another way to consider such an example could be that one is angry with oneself for giving oneself reason to regret. Nonetheless, regret in such instances would seem to be associated with being angry with oneself. For that reason, I will continue to treat anger in general as most often projected outward toward others.

34. See Sabini and Silver (2005, 1–10) for more on how pragmatic contexts of words can affect how they are used to pick out certain emotional states such as envy, embarrassment, and regret.

35. See De Sousa (1987, 120–1, 282, 294).

36. Ibid., 121.

37. Ibid.

38. Ibid.

39. The above example also relates to the temporality of the emotion *regret*. As I have argued above, I hold that regret is regarding some lost opportunity that one had in the past. In this example, Miriam is presumably regretting what she is doing at that very moment. She regrets to inform. As she is typing this expression, she is informing. For an interesting article on anticipation of regret related to positive outcomes, see Sorensen (1998, 528–37). According to Sorensen, it might be impossible to feel regret about future outcomes you know will ensue. In his article, he proposes offering

subjects either $1 or $10, and if they regret their choice they are given an additional $100. Sorensen cleverly proves that it is impossible to regret something you think will have a positive outcome. For example, if I were to choose the $1 in hopes of regretting it and receiving the $100, I would instantly be rendered incapable of feeling regret. I would be too pleased with acquiring the $100. See also Humberstone (1980, 175–6).

40. Already, one must note that presumably, the agent knows that the agent will regret the action about to be performed. The previous discussion concerning the temporality of regret ought to be kept in mind when reading this section.

41. The possibility of moral dilemmas is taken for granted in this chapter. For arguments for the existence of moral dilemmas (including the impossibility of acting correctly, see Tessman 2015). For an interesting discussion of the idea that there is no such thing as a moral dilemma, see Conee (1989, 133–41).

42. See Bagnoli (2000, 170).

43. See Strasser (1987, 133). It is important to note that while I am using Strasser's insight on this issue, he ultimately does not conclude the position for which I am advocating in this chapter. Instead, he distinguishes between two types of compunction, one an agent deserves to feel and another an agent does not deserve to feel but nonetheless will feel if the agent is moral.

44. See Bagnoli (2000, 173).

45. See Frijda, Kuipers, and Schure (1989, 212–28).

46. See Gilovich and Medvec (1994, 359).

47. See Zeelenberg et al. (1998, 224–6).

48. Ibid., 228. Italics in the original. Zeelenberg et al.'s results were challenged by T. Connoly, L. D. Ordonez, and R. Coughlan in 1997. This prompted an exchange between the teams, whereby Zeelenberg et al. provide ample clarification and argumentation defending their claim that "regret is partly determined by perceived responsibility for the regretted outcome" (1998a, 254). See Connolly, Ordonez, and Coughlan (1997, 73–85); Zeelenberg, van Dijk, and Manstead (1998, 254–72); Zeelenberg et al. (1998, 117–41); Ordóñez and Connolly (2000, 132–42); and Zeelenberg, van Dijk, and Manstead (2000, 143–54).

49. See Landman (1993, 56).

50. See Roese and Summerville (2005, 1273).

51. See Camille (2004, 1167–70).

52. In fact, it is not clear as to whether subjects know that both games were run, or if they are led to believe that the only gamble played was the one that they chose.

53. See Camille et al. (2004, 1167).

54. Marchiori and Warglien (2008, 1111–3).

55. More recently, Funayama et al. found that guilt—another emotion typically associated with a sense of responsibility—is also affected by impairments of the OFC. See Funayama et al. (April 2018).

56. Coricelli et al. repeated a similar series of experiments in 2005, adding the observation of subjects' brain activity via fMRI. They report, "Increasing regret enhanced activity in the medial orbitofrontal region, the anterior cingulate cortex and the hippocampus. Notably, across the experiment, subjects became increasingly regret-aversive, a cumulative effect reflected in enhanced activity within medial

orbitofrontal cortex and amygdala. This pattern of activity reoccurred just before making a choice, suggesting that the same neural circuitry mediates direct experience of regret and its anticipation" (see Coricelli et al. 2005, 1255). In 2009, Chua et al. conducted a similar study, whereby they concluded that regret and disappointment share a general neural network, but regret seems to demonstrate greater magnitude and intensity in certain areas. See Chua et al. (2009, 2031–40).

57. See Nicolle et al. (2011, 187).

58. Ibid.

59. It is worth noting that Canessa et al. report that understanding the regret of others can inspire activation in the exact same neuronal networks in the brain of observers. In other words, if one is watching a movie and a character is portrayed as being in the throws of great regret, moviegoers might, for lack of better terms, *feel the actor's pain*. As interesting as this is, I dismiss it on the basis that the observers do, in a sense, feel the regret of the actor because they are empathizing with the actor. In other words, it does not surprise me that empathy involves mimicking perceived genuine emotions of others *even though* the empathic agent does not necessarily satisfy the conceptual and cognitive requirements for experiencing the emotion. Empathy, by way of imagination, brings one to a similar mental and emotional state as the object of imagination. In that way, we are imagining being in the position that warrants regret. So, while the audience member does not actually believe herself to be responsible and desire to have acted differently when she empathically feels the regret of another, via imagination, she is entertaining the idea that she could believe such things. The imagination's ability to conjure mirrored emotional experiences should not discount the standard conditions of an organic and sincere experience of an emotion. See Canessa et al. (2009, e7402).

REFERENCES

Anton, Audrey L. 2015. *Moral Responsibility and Desert of Praise and Blame*. Lanham, MD: Lexington.

Aristotle. 1999. *Nicomachean Ethics*, 2nd ed. Edited and translated by Terrence Irwin. Indianapolis, IN: Hackett.

Bagnoli, Carla. 2000. "Value in the Guise of Regret." *Philosophical Explorations* 3 (2): 169–87.

Bittner, Rudiger. 1992. "Is It Reasonable to Regret Things One Did?" *Journal of Philosophy* 89 (5): 262–73.

Camille, Nathalie, Giorgio Coricelli, Jerome Sallet, Pascale Pradat-Diehl, Jean-René Duhamel, and Angela Sirigu. 2004. "The Involvement of the Orbitofrontal Cortex in the Experience of Regret." *Science* 304: 1167–70.

Canessa, Nicola, Matteo Motterlini, Cinzia Di Dio, Daniela Perani, Paola Scifo, Stefano F. Cappa, and Giacomo Rizzolatti. 2009. "Understanding Others' Regret: A fMRI Study." *PLoS ONE* 4 (10): e7402. doi: 10.1371/journal.pone.ooo7402.

Chua, Hanna Faye, Richard Gonzalez, Stephan F. Taylor, Robert C. Welsh, and Israel Liberzon. 2009. "Decision-Related Loss: Regret and Disappointment." *Neuroimage* 47 (4): 2031–40.

Conee, Earl. 1989. "Why Moral Dilemmas Are Impossible." *American Philosophical Quarterly* 26 (2): 133–41.
Connolly, T., L. D. Ordonez, and R. Coughlan, "Regret and Responsibility in the Evaluation of Decision Outcomes." *Organizational Behavior and Human Decision Processes* 70 (1997): 73–85.
Coricelli, Giorgio, Hugo D. Critchley, Mateus Joffily, John P. O'Doherty, Angela Sirigu and Raymond J. Dolan. 2005. "Regret and Its Avoidance: A Neuroimaging Study of Choice Behavior." *Nature Neuroscience* 8 (9): 1255–62.
De Sousa, Ronald. 2001. *The Rationality of Emotion*. Cambridge: MIT Press, 2001.
Frijda, N. H., P. Kuipers, and E. ter Schure. 1989. "Relations among Emotion, Appraisal and Emotional Action Readiness." *Journal of Personality and Social Psychology* 57: 212–28.
Funayama, Michitaka, Akihiro Koreki, Taro Muramatsu, Masaru Mimura, Motoichiro Kato, and Takayuki Abe. April 2018. "Impairment in Judgement of the Moral Emotion Guilt Following Orbitofrontal Cortex Damage." *Journal of Neuropsychology*. doi: 10.1111/jnp.12158.
Gilovich, T., and V. H. Medvec. 1994. "The Temporal Pattern to the Experience of Regret." *Journal of Personality and Social Psychology* 67: 357–65.
Greene, Joshua. 2013. *Moral Tribes: Emotion, Reason, and the Gap between Us and Them*. New York: Penguin, 2013.
Hare, Caspar. 2011. "Obligation and Regret When There Is No Fact of the Matter about What Would Have Happened If You Had Not Done What You Did." *Noûs* 45 (1): 190–206.
Humberstone, I. L. 1980. "You'll Regret It." *Analysis* 40: 175–6.
Joyce, James M. 2012. "Regret and Instability in Causal Decision Theory." *Synthese* 187: 123–45.
Klassen, Johann A. 1998. "Guilt, Shame, and Regret in the World of T. S. Garp: Moral Taint and a Modern Novel." In *Technology, Morality, and Social Policy*, ed. Yeager Hudson, 227–47. Lewiston: Mellen Press.
Landman, Janet. 1987. "Regret: A Theoretical and Conceptual Analysis." *Journal for the Theory of Social Behavior* 17: 135–60.
Landman, Janet. 1993. *Regret: The Persistence of the Possible*. New York: Oxford University Press.
Marchiori, Davide, and Massimo Warglien. 2008. "Predicting Human Interactive Learning by Regret-Driven Neural Networks." *Science* 319: 1111–13. doi: 10.1126/science.1151185.
Nicolle, Antinette, Dominik R. Bach, Chris Frith, and Raymond J. Dolan. 2011. "Amygdala Involvement in Self-Blame Regret." *Social Neuroscience* 6 (2): 178–89. doi: 10.1080/17470919.2010.506128.
Ordóñez, Lisa D., and Terry Connolly. 1998. "Regret and Responsibility: A Reply to Zeelenberg et al. (1998)." *Organizational Behavior and Human Decision Processes* 81 (1): 132–42.
Roese, Neal J., and Amy Summerville. 2005. "What We Regret Most and Why." *Perspectives of Social Psychology Bulletin* 31 (9): 1273–85. doi:10.1177/0146167205274693.

Rorty, Amélie O. 1980. "Agent Regret." In *Explaining Emotions*, ed. Amélie O. Rorty, 489–506. Berkeley: University of California Press.
Rossi-Keen, Daniel E. 2007. "Explaining and Expanding the Scope of Strawson's Reactive Attitudes: An Examination and Application of Freedom and Resentment." *Kriterion—Journal of Philosophy* 21: 46–63.
Sabini, John, and Maury Silver. 2005. "Why Emotion Names and Experiences Don't Neatly Pair." *Psychological Inquiry* 16 (1): 1–10.
Sher, George. 2009. *Who Knew? Responsibility without Awareness*. New York: Oxford University Press.
Sorensen, Roy A. 1998. "Rewarding Regret." *Ethics* 108 (3): 528–37.
Strasser, Mark. 1987. "Guilt, Regret and 'Prima Facie' Duties." *Southern Journal of Philosophy* 25: 133–46.
Strawson, P. F. 1997. "Freedom and Resentment." In *Free Will*, ed. Derk Pereboom, 119–42. Indianapolis, IN: Hackett.
Sugden, Robert. 1985. "Regret, Recrimination and Rationality." *Theory and Decision* 19: 77–99.
Taylor, Gabriele. 1985. "Guilt and Remorse." In *Pride, Shame, and Guilt: Emotions of Self-Assessment*, ed. Gabriele Taylor, 85–107. New York: Oxford University Press.
Tessman, Lisa. 2015. *Moral Failure: On the Impossible Demands of Morality*. New York: Oxford University Press.
Williams, Bernard. 1982. "Moral Luck." In *Moral Luck*, 20–39. New York: Cambridge University Press.
Zeelenberg, Marcel. 1999. "The Use of Crying over Spilled Milk: A Note on the Rationality and Functionality of Regret." *Philosophical Psychology* 12 (3): 325–40.
Zeelenberg, Marcel, Wilco W. van Dijk, Joop van der Pligt, Antony S. R. Manstead, Pepijn van Empelen, and Dimitri Reinderman. 1998. "Emotional Reactions to the Outcomes of Decisions: The Role of Counterfactual Thought in the Experience of Regret and Disappointment." *Organizational Behavior and Human Decision Processes* 75 (2): 117–41.
Zeelenberg, Marcel, Wilco W. van Dijk, and Antony S. R. Manstead. 1998. "Reconsidering the Relation between Regret and Responsibility." *Organizational Behavior and Human Decision Processes* 74 (3): 254–72.
Zeelenberg, Marcel, Wilco W. van Dijk, and Antony S. R. Manstead. 2000. "Regret and Responsibility Resolved? Evaluating Ordóñez and Connolly's (2000) Conclusions." *Organizational Behavior and Human Decision Processes* 81 (1): 143–54.
Zeelenberg, Marcel, Wilco W. van Dijk, Antony S. R. Manstead, and Joopvan der Pligt. 1998. "The Experience of Regret and Disappointment." *Cognition and Emotion* 12 (2): 221–30.

Chapter 3

Regret as a Condition for Personhood

James F. DiGiovanna

Beginning with Burks' "Laws of Nature and the Reasonableness of Regret," and picking up force with the popularity of decision theories, much, and perhaps most, of the work on regret in Anglo-American philosophy since the forties has asked whether regret is rational (Burks 1946; Egan 2007; Hurka 1996; Joyce 2012; Sorensen 1998; Zeelenberg 1999;), whereas the centrality of regret to personhood has barely been considered (though see Rorty 1980; Wallace 2013; Williams 1981, and in psychology, Landman's foundational text *Regret: The Persistence of the Possible*, 1993).

While Anglo-American philosophy in particular, and philosophy generally, has been preoccupied with rationality, emotions needn't be rational to be justified. As humans, we are subject to emotion, and to remove emotion, even if irrational emotion, is to make us something other than persons. The emotionless being is the science-fiction stereotype of the nonperson and with good reason. So, judging emotional states on their rationality misses the point of our emotions and our feelings generally. If we could move forward with our lives without regret, we might be happier, but we would be less personlike: our self-awareness would be a collection of facts and not a feeling of being one with ourselves, nor a feeling of being connected, positively or negatively, with others. Emotions provide meaning, motivation, variety, and connection in our lives. They are person-making.

Regret is a sufficient condition for personhood: if you experience regret, you are a person. Contrapositively, if you are not a person, then you do not experience regret. The capacity for regret is a necessary condition for being a person: If you are a person, then you *should be able to* or *have the capacity to* experience regret. Contrapositively, if you are constitutionally incapable of experiencing regret, then you are either not a person or are a person who is in some way deficient. Finally, regret is *person-making*. The process of regretting involves taking account of our past, owning it as ours, evaluating our actions and values, and thinking of ways we should be different in the future. All of this ties us together across time and marks a striving towards integrity (in a sense I'll discuss below) of character that is crucial for full personhood.

DEFINITION OF REGRET

Regret is a *cognitive emotion*. That is, it is an emotional state that includes thought. To regret is to wish that things had been different and to experience distress at that thought. I'll be analyzing *personal regret*, which falls into two categories: If your regret focuses on a wish to have *done something different*, you are experiencing *agent regret*. If you are regretting that you *are not* different, that is, if you wish you were a different sort of person, then you are experiencing *character regret*. Personal regret can be (and often is) of both kinds at once: we can wish that we were not the sort of person who had done this thing we wish we hadn't done.

Regret can also be *impersonal*, about things beyond one's control or character, as in *I regret that that happened to you*. I won't focus on this kind of regret, but it also includes many person-making features. I'm uninterested in what Landman (1993, 14) calls "phony regret," as in "I regret that I cannot attend your party," when it is uttered as a formality, or "we regret to inform you that your phone service will be terminated due to not-payment," where I doubt there is any corresponding emotion.

Persons

Locke writes, "Person is a forensic concept" (1689). This is more a constraint on what counts as a person than a full definition: to be a person is to be the sort of thing to which we attach praise, blame, and responsibility. Further, persons are said to be thinking things (Descartes 1641/2006), rational (Kant 1785/2004), to have intentional states and be able to attach intentional states to others (Dennett 1976), to have second-order intentional states (Frankfurt 1971), to be relations that relate themselves to themselves (Kierkegaard 1980b), to be beings that assess their preferences and endeavor to act accordingly (Friedman 1989), and to be beings that relate themselves to their own pasts and futures in a narrative (Korsgaard 1989; Lindemann 2014; Ricoeur 1984; Schechtman 2007; Williams 1970). Among the necessary but insufficient conditions for person, there is the tendency to form emotional attachments (Wallace 2013), to have emotions (Damasio 1999; Locke 1689), to be conscious (just about everybody with a few rare exceptions), and to have a capacity for memory (Locke 1689; Parfit 1984; Shoemaker 1970).

I'll argue below that regret satisfies all of these conditions. When we regret, we attach blame, usually to ourselves. To regret, we must think that things should have been otherwise. Regret shows rational thought in that we weigh choices and outcomes, though generally retroactively, with at least some thought that we would not follow the same path given the same conditions in the future. Regret necessarily includes intentional states and, in agent regret, the ability to attach intentional states to our past selves. Further, these are generally second-order intentional states in that they refer to our own, previous intentional states. Regret is quintessentially relating ourselves to ourselves: we judge ourselves and simultaneously feel the negative force of that judgment. It is clearly an assessment of preferences in that we see ourselves as having chosen not just wrongly but badly. It is the most narrative of emotions: we cannot have regret without a story about how we were and how we came to be in the state of regret. These are importantly *self-defining* stories: we understand ourselves to be flawed when we have character regrets and as agents who failed in agent regret. To regret is to have an emotional attachment: if we did not feel attached to ourselves, our self-image, and the effects of the choices we made, we would not regret. We regret especially when we harm that which we value, whether it is another person, or ourselves, or merely our sense of ourselves. And clearly, all of the above implies that in regret we have emotion, consciousness, and memory.

Thus, regret is sufficient for just about every condition for personhood. Still, many states are sufficient without being necessary. It is uninterestingly sufficient for personhood that I be, for example, serving a jail sentence (as only persons are jailed) or that I have a marriage license, and so on. Regret, though, is interestingly sufficient in that it's a state that a person can be in that noncontingently fulfills personhood conditions; we could imagine a society where dogs have marriage licenses and horses are imprisoned, but if dogs and horses began to express regret, they would undergo a category change that would force us to treat them as persons.

Still, regret could be an unnecessary condition for personhood. Here, I'll argue not only that regret makes one a person but also that being incapable of regret makes one either a nonperson or a seriously deficient person.

Williams makes a claim for the necessity of regret in "Moral Luck" (28), when he notes that if a truck driver struck and killed a child, even though he was not at fault legally or morally, we would be very disturbed if he did not personally *regret* (which is to say, personally feel bad about his own contribution to) what had happened. (Williams, in delightful understatement, says that "some doubt would be felt" about the driver.) But even more so: if someone is doing something that is a net good, even a great net good, and yet must cause the death of an innocent, we would "feel some doubt" about the person were he or she not to have at least some regret about the innocent's death – even if, overall, he or she would do the same thing again.

For day-to-day regrets, someone who never once thought they could have done better, or wished they had made some other choice, would seem to lack the sorts of emotional attachments (Wallace 2013) that make life meaningful. If you found that someone had never for one moment felt bad about a failing or misdeed, and had no backward-looking thoughts about what they should have done differently, you'd be dealing at best with what Frankfurt (1971, 11) calls a "wanton." Wantons never evaluate themselves. They do not care about the content of their will. It's hard to imagine such a being could exist without also lacking something like mature consciousness. And even if they did exist, they would be demi-persons. We would have trouble attaching full blame or praise to them, as their actions are things that happen to them, not things that they can claim as their own. They drift from moment to moment, unable to do and to feel much of what it is that makes us persons, because they never undergo the kind of necessary reflection.

Other Emotions That May Be Necessary and/or Sufficient

There are many emotions that could be necessary for personhood. For example, it is hard to imagine that a being without the capacity for sorrow would truly be a person. Commonly, in science fiction, this absence is used to mark the nonpersonhood of intelligent robots. Such beings would lack a certain capacity to be injured that we count as essential in assigning rights and protections.[1] Further, we could not converse with it about something that we take as central and essential to our definitions of ourselves.

However, sorrow is insufficient for personhood: dogs might feel sorrow at times, say, upon being bereft of their companions for extended periods, but this would not make them persons. But certain emotions contain so much cognitive content, and are of such a specific sort, that they alone would allow for the satisfaction of most, and perhaps all, accepted and proposed conditions of personhood. I would grant that some beings that currently feel no regrets, and by happenstance will not feel any regrets in the future, are indeed persons—if only they have the capacity to regret. Very young children might not count as persons on this account, as regret might be impossible for them, but I do not think that is a terrible flaw with the proposal, as very young children fail to meet personhood criteria on many accounts: we do not charge them with crimes, for example.

Some other emotions that might also serve this purpose, though I won't argue for them here, are grief, anxiety (cf. Kierkegaard's *Concept of Anxiety* [1980a] and the tradition moving through Heidegger and the twentieth-century existentialists), hopefulness, and the happiness that we take in the success or joy of others.[2] I've chosen regret both because it fulfills conditions of personhood and because it's a particularly undervalued emotion. This is in part because it is one of the more difficult emotions one can experience: it's a form of grief for a life not lived, with blame directed at oneself. It's the subject of countless movies and is presented as something to overcome. Americans often take pride in saying they have no regrets, though I think they're probably lying about the absence of all regrets (or, at the moment they make this claim, they are not aware that it's false). And if they really had no regrets at any point in their lives, then they missed out on an essential and singular experience, an experience that adds importantly to the richness of life by building moral character and connecting us to past selves that we would wish to disown. That is, they have missed out on negative self-evaluation, whether of character or action. If we have no regrets, we think we have always been good and done well. And if we think that, we are not in a particularly good state to grow and learn and to become better people. Further, we place ourselves outside the vast majority of humans who do feel regret and who, in communicating with others, expect that those others have a capacity to empathetically understand what it is to feel bad about oneself.

THE SORT OF THING THAT REGRET IS

Regret as an Emotion

I do not wish to take a strong stance on the dispute between cognitivist and affectivist theories of emotion. However, regret, as I understand it here, must have cognitive content. Thus, I won't be following the "James-Lange" theory that reduces emotions to bodily feelings (James 1884). If this is an accurate account of emotions, then regret is not an emotion or not *just* an emotion. Further, regret will not be understood simply as a passing feeling/cognitive state but rather as something that is importantly recurrent and perhaps active even when not experienced. (I'm agnostic on the later point.) It is like what Aaron Ben-Ze'ev (2009, 55) calls a "sentiment": while it has a specific intentional object, it endures, like grief or love, and needn't be emergent, like rage, for it to be said to exist. Perhaps better would be to describe regret in Roddy Cowie's terms as an "established emotion" (2009, 3520). That is, one like grief or shame in that it may form a background to experience, make repeated appearances in conscious life, and include an intentional object that is, to some extent, narrative. Cowie later calls this sort of emotion a "condition" as opposed to a "state" and refers to the period during which the emotion persists as an "emotional era" (2010, 74).

Cowie's terminology is probably most helpful in discussing the sort of thing regret is; it is clearly not necessary for someone to be presently having an emergent emotional state in order to say that he or she regrets something. Nonetheless, it is necessary that there be associated cognitive content regardless of the somatic content. Still, at some point, there must be a feeling attached to regret, or it is merely Landman's "phony regret" (1993, 14). Without endorsing the entire cognitivist program, regret will fall in line with cognitivist views insofar as it contains propositional attitudes.

While I accept that Eric Schwitzgebel is correct in that we may have very poor cognizance of our emotions, I don't think this impedes the value of regret as a marker of personhood. As Schwitzgebel notes, citing a study by Russ Hurlburt, "A person might very frequently have angry thoughts about his children, as he reports when sampled at random moments, and yet he might sincerely deny that it is so in the general case" (Schwitzgebel 2012). Similarly, a person could have recurrent regretful thoughts but not be able to access these when asked; the fact that the thoughts *are* recurrent and that they then color his or her outlook, and that they have an intentional object, is all that's needed for them to do the work required here. Just as with the angry thoughts about one's children, regretful thoughts will reference earlier regretful thoughts and have strong cognitive and emotional content.

Recently, questions have been raised about the universality of emotions, and it has been suggested that emotions are all culturally specific, or at least the interpretation of emotions is culturally specific (Tanaka et al 2010; Tsai 2007; Tsai, Knutson and Fung 2006). Regardless, regret points to general human capacities: the ability to form a personal narrative, to have a negative reaction to what one has done, and to feel responsibility for a prior act or omission. Whether this set of capacities, when experienced collectively, has a name in some language or not, it would at least be odd if it never occurred in some large sample of people. I await some evidence that this is the case but meanwhile will accept, to at least a limited degree, Ekman's (1971, 1999) claims about the universality of at least some emotional content.

So, in short, I will understand regret to be a (usually) recurrent affective state, accompanied by a negative judgment toward a past action, or failure of action, on the part of the agent having the state. It will thus have a reasonably consistent object. While there may be a sense of "regret" that includes a nonrecurrent state, insofar as one can briefly regret something, I'll be more interested in the form of regret that is longer lasting, like grief or love, and which, while not always present to consciousness, forms an element of the lasting psychological content of the agent and is identifiable in part by having a consistent object. As such, it constitutively includes memory and an intentional state toward those memories. Again, I'm speaking here largely of "personal regret," which is the combination of what Bernard Williams (1976;

reprinted in Williams 1981, 27) calls *agent regret* (regret about what I did) and what Amelie Rorty (1980, 490) calls *character regret* (regret about the sort of person I am).

Regret's Cognitive Content: Memory and Imagination

The cognitive content of regret is a memory. But one could argue that memory can't be part of regretting certain *failures to act*. However, in the case of regret, one regrets both the decision and the conditions that follow from this decision. One could regret not going to college, for example. This could be a regret about an active decision to not go to college or about decisions one made that precluded going to college, but even if it were not, there would still be an accompanying set of memories: all of the things one did that were not the things that college graduates do, in one's own estimation. Such regrets are often in the form, "If I had done X, I wouldn't have Y," where Y involves something one underwent. Perhaps some such regrets never address memories, only present moments: "if I had gone to college, I wouldn't be here now." This would still involve an attitude towards one's past, which, if not strictly a memory, shares with memory that it is personal and backward-directed and requires at least that one have a narrative memory sufficient to know that one didn't go to college. In this case, we might talk of *counterfactual memories:* that is, a sense of the narrative of oneself that includes what might have been had one done differently. These counterfactual accounts of oneself are important in developing our moral and evaluative consciousness.

For this reason, regret demands *imagination*. To regret is, often, to think of what is not and what might have been. It is strange that this counterfactual ability is rarely counted as one of the conditions of personhood but it probably should be. Counterfactual narrative thought is, at this time, known to exist only in humans and only in those humans who are not infants, comatose, seriously mentally impaired, and so on. It's a uniquely personal ability and sums up much of what separates persons from nonpersons. Looking at regret as person-constituting and person-building in this way sheds important light on both the value of regret and the value of imagination.

Why Persons?

Personhood is one of a handful of fundamental moral concepts, along with good, right, and virtue. It may be the most fundamental as persons are the beings who are subject to moral evaluation. It is wrong for a person to torture an animal that is not a person. We shouldn't vivisect bears purely for amusement. But it is not *morally* wrong for a bear to torture a person, even if it is tragic and horrible. The bear simply cannot be held to moral account, even if we denounce and hate it for what it did. So without persons, there may be good and bad but no right and wrong and no morals or ethics.

Frankfurt, coherently with the concerns of the existentialists and the ancients, claims that "person," as a philosophical term, is "designed to capture those attributes which are the subject of our most humane concern with ourselves and the source of what we regard as most important and most problematical in our lives" (1971, 6). Locke, and many following, held that accounts of personhood need to explain what those beings are that can be praised, blamed, and held responsible. Dennett divides accounts into the metaphysical, which focus on the importance of consciousness, and the moral, which focus on accounts of persons as entities that can properly be praised and blamed. Personhood, on almost all accounts, includes rationality and, on many accounts, sociability. *Accountability, rationality,* and *sociability* are each meant to be necessary conditions for personhood, and in some cases, the first two are given as necessary and sufficient. For example, Kant, Descartes, Aristotle, and Plato's accounts emphasize the rational. Aristotle notably holds that the social is a necessary condition as well. Locke, Rawls, Korsgaard, and a number of medieval figures, including Aquinas,[3] place strong emphasis on justice, morality, and accountability. Social, or relational, accounts are found in Aristotle,[4] Plato,[5] Schechtman (2010), Marilyn Friedman (1989), and a number of feminist writers.[6] Here, "person" is a sort of entity that enters into meaningful relations with others. Some who do not regret appropriately or enough ("I hurt your feelings? So what? I'm just being me!") would wind up socially excluded and have diminished personhood on these accounts. This is not to say that a regretless human should receive less political representation or voice. But to be incapable of regret is to be incapable of taking a negative emotional attitude toward oneself when one has done wrong. And if one could judge right and wrong without any emotional content, it's not clear how such judgments would matter for the meaning of a person's life. Even the meaning of moral wrong seems tied to an idea of negative emotional reactions. We do not simply judge the murderer wrong: we abhor the murder. That is part of what it is to understand that the act was wrong: it is repellent. Personhood, understood forensically, implies at least the capacity to understand that one was wrong. Sociopaths, for example, might have diminished personhood on this account. It's not that we can't judge and punish them, but they are incapable of understanding that it might be *just* to do so, because, even if they understood that there was a system of rules governing the use of "right" and "wrong," they wouldn't understand why a wrong act is, regardless of social rules or the possibility of punishment, something that one should not engage in.

Because "person" has a legal sense, definitions of "person" need to be sufficient for picking out those beings to whom one attributes responsibility and blame for actions. There are, though, a minority of philosophers who reject this. Some reject praise and blame entirely, as in some hard determinist and behaviorist accounts. It's unclear if there are persons, as we commonly think of them, in these accounts. Animalist accounts of personhood, that is, those that claim a person is merely a living human body, are unable to account for relations of praise and blame. The best known of these is Eric Olson's (1997, 1999) account, where he claims that personal identity simply cannot be used to track legal or moral responsibility. For Olson, the aspect of human beings that is of interest in legal and moral cases is simply not their personhood. But an account that doesn't include moral selfhood both fails to account for most of what we care about when we wonder about our future selves and is out of touch with what most people mean when they speak about their own identity. In fact, Strohminger and Nichols (2014) found that people identified more strongly with their moral character than with either their bodies or their memories.

Further, while Olson's account is about a person across time, it's insensitive to the subjective experience of that person. It lies, then, outside of most accounts of personhood, which require some kind of self-awareness and is limited to tracking the living, animal body of a person.

Because of this, I would object to those philosophical definitions of person, found among hard-core behaviorist and determinist conceptions, that do not meet this condition. Still, if the entity described is one to whom most would ascribe responsibility and blame, even if described in behaviorist/determinist terms, then it probably meets this constraint for definitions of "person." Recent research by Eddy Nahmias, for example, has found that certain wordings of determinist cases still elicited blame toward the characters described in experiments with naïve subjects (Nahmias and Murray, 2011).

EARLY DEVELOPMENT OF THE CONCEPT OF THE PERSON

"Person," when not used as a species term, is a constructed concept answering to both social and individual needs and practices. The term serves to pick out the sorts of beings we allow into our societies, bestow with rights, hold responsible for bad actions, befriend, marry, elevate to official positions, obey, and respect and whose opinions matter.

The term is found in medieval religious thought to describe the "persons" of the trinity, and before that, in classical Roman theater, it referred to the masks worn and, indirectly, the characters played by stage actors. But it gets its contemporary sense in the late medieval and early modern period when it acquires its legal sense. The Magna Carta uses "persons" to refer to those having specific legal duties and rights, for example, and Hobbes devotes an entire chapter of Leviathan to "persons, authors, and things personated," where he gives persons the sole authority to make covenants. "Children, Fooles, and Mad-men, that have no use of Reason, may be Personated [that is, represented legally] by Guardians or Curator, but can be no Authors (during that time) of any action done by them" (Hobbes 1651/2013, VXI).

Right at the start, we see that personhood is tied to some understanding of right and wrong or at least of duty and failure. While this minimal sense includes no necessity of regret, it establishes the place that regret will hold in personhood: to be able to see where one has failed and repent of it.

While Hobbes makes it clear what the *use* of "person" is—that is, the standing of persons as legal entities—he only notes that they must have reason. Others in philosophy, seeing the need for a fuller elaboration, began a long tradition of picking out persons from nonpersons by sets of essential attributes.

Descartes gives a similarly minimal definition of himself as "nothing but a thinking thing." Here, regret would be a sufficient condition, though hardly a necessary one. But then, Descartes' definition of himself is clearly not sufficient for personhood: That crows can think seems clear: they solve puzzles and do simple math. But we do not (yet) treat them as persons.

Kant's approach to personhood is similar to Descartes' in that he includes only rationality, but he fleshes it out more fully:

> Rational beings . . . are called persons, because their very nature points them out as ends in themselves, that is as something which must not be used merely as means, and so far therefore restricts freedom of action (and is an object of respect) . . . rational nature exists as an end in itself. (Kant 2004/2016, section ii)

Since Kant uses "rationality" to mean thinking of oneself as an end in oneself, he at least includes in his definition an implication of time and a goal. This establishes the conditions for regret, because it establishes conditions for failure. Further, one could at least argue that the capacity for regret is a necessary element of this: if I couldn't think of myself as falling short of a moral ideal just in case I did fall short, and view this retroactively as something in need of atonement, I would fail to have the proper kind of agency, which involves comparing one's actions to a moral standard.

But it is with Locke that we get the most thorough and influential definition of "person" and one that is cited in nearly every later philosophical work on the subject: "we must consider what PERSON stands for;—which, I think, is a thinking intelligent being, that has reason and reflection, and can consider itself as itself, the same thinking thing, in different times and places; which it does only by that consciousness which is inseparable from thinking, and, as it seems to me, essential to it" (1689, Book II, Ch. XXVII, section 11). Locke notes the prevailing legal constraints on the use of "person": "Person is a forensic term . . . appropriating actions and their merit; and so belongs only to intelligent agents, capable of a law, and happiness, and misery. This personality extends itself beyond present existence to what is past, only by consciousness, whereby it becomes concerned and accountable; owns and imputes to itself past actions" (1689, Book II, Ch. XXVII, section 26.) This account is well-addressed by regret.

A regretting being is a Lockean person. To regret, one must be intelligent, capable of language, and of conceiving not only what is present and simple but also what is past and under a description. It is to see that past in relation to a judgment, a law, and to judge it wanting. Most importantly, it is to identify that past as one's own and to see oneself as extended across time and responsible for what one has done. Regret shows concern about one's actions and character. Further, regret answers to Locke's emotional condition, because it is a form of misery, and as Locke notes, misery is an essential part of the nature of persons: It would be very hard for us to accept as fully human a being who could in no way relate to our tales of distress.

While it is possible to be a Lockean person without regretting, one could not be one without the *capacity* to regret, because if one were incapable of ever seeing one's own actions as regrettable, were those actions to be wrong, one would either lack identification with past actions or be unable to compare them to a law—or simply be unconcerned about them.

CONTEMPORARY ACCOUNTS OF THE CONCEPT OF THE PERSON

Frankfurt and Dennett: Sets of Conditions

The Lockean approach of making a list of conditions is taken up by Dennett, who, following from Frankfurt, looks to define persons in terms of particular features of consciousness. Since Dennett and Frankfurt's work is so influential, and shapes much of the modern discussion of personhood, they're worth a detailed look. Both, strangely, fail to include emotion as a necessary condition of personhood.

Dennett (1976) lists the following conditions: (1) rationality, (2) that intentional predicates apply, (3) that a stance is taken toward that entity such that it is treated as an entity capable of action (in the sense of the work of an agent), (4) that it can reciprocate the stance, (5) that it can communicate verbally, and (6) that it is self-conscious or aware of itself. One could conceivably be a person on Dennett's account without ever having been sad, angry, or wistful, although it seems on short reflection that emotion should be an added condition, lest we run into the science fiction robot problem: X-37 would be a person, if only he could love. Dennett holds that "the concept of a person is inescapably normative. Human beings or other entities can only aspire to be approximations of the ideal" (1976, 193). That is, one may be more or less a person or more or less successfully achieve personhood. Regret can then play an important role in helping us achieve personhood. It is person-making because it brings together conditions 3 (intentional predicates) and 6 (self-awareness) that involve understanding oneself to be a being that has intentional states. When we regret, we regard ourselves (if only perhaps our past selves) as persons, because we regard those selves as agents, and since we regard ourselves as having intentions, we are capable of being judged.

Further, when we regret our past actions, we are applying intentional predicates to ourselves (condition 2); otherwise, they wouldn't be actions but merely movements. So, regret is sufficient for condition 2. Condition 4, reciprocation, is met, because the entity attributes intentionality to a temporal other, its prior self, which both marks that self as other, as an object of thought, and brings it into narrative continuity with the subject of thought. The reciprocity, difference, and sameness are described in Kierkegaard's definition of the self as "that relation that relates itself to itself" (1980b).

Regret's sentential, and generally subjunctive character ("I wish I hadn't"), certainly implies verbal capacity, condition 5. Since there's a weighing of choices, insofar as we look at some choice and compare it to another, noninstantiated choice, and judgment between them, regret clearly involves rationality, condition 1, in a minimal sense.

So while regret is sufficient for Dennett's account, he seems to allow for emotionless persons. But, since the capacity for regret is necessary for accounts of persons as moral agents, (i.e., one must be capable, just in case one fails to live up to a moral standard, of judging one's past actions negatively, attributing those actions to oneself, wishing one had done otherwise, and hoping or intending to act differently in the future) and these accounts are central to the forensic notion of person, this may be more a problem for Dennett than for the status of regret. However, in discussing Frankfurt's definition of person, which Dennett claims is contained in his own account, Dennett writes that part of Frankfurt's notion of personhood is that "one schools oneself; one offers oneself threats, persuasions, arguments, bribes . . . only if one can say, can become aware of one's desires, can one be in a position to induce oneself to change" (1976, 193). Clearly, regret applies here: all of this "schooling" of oneself to be better implies that one is not one's best, that one has at least character regret, and perhaps some specific agent regret, that moves one to change. And emotion is indeed implicated; otherwise, there would be no point to the threats and no desire to mold oneself to be better.

Frankfurt's account helps us here by defining persons as beings that have second-order volitions (1971, 10): they have a will about their will, or they would that they willed differently (I wish I didn't want to eat that ice cream). This is precisely what personal regret is: I wish I hadn't willed that, or I wish I wasn't the sort of person who did that.

The life that contains regret necessarily and inherently includes the capacity for self-evaluation, something Frankfurt thinks is characteristic of personhood (1971, 7–13). Regret involves thinking that one could have been (character regret) or done (agent regret) *better*. So, even a person holding a reprehensible moral position must be capable of regret: if Joe regrets not killing Charlie when he had the chance, he at least is using a higher-order reflection upon some desire. In making a judgment while being moved by regret, we make ourselves coherent in a larger sense: we hold that we have specific ideals, that we have at least one value that should be used in determining our moral worth across time, and insofar as we have failed to evince that value, we believe we should have done otherwise. We self-evaluate. Marylin Friedman calls this "whole moral personhood": "My thesis is that one essential constituent of whole moral personhood is the ongoing tendency both to critically assess those preferences which one acts to satisfy, and to endeavor to act accordingly . . . To the extent that an individual omits to evaluate her preferences, and simply acts uncritically to satisfy them, to that extent, she fails to achieve whole moral personhood" (1989, 147).

Narratives as Person-Making

Unlike the list of conditional accounts, narrative accounts of personhood argue that persons are created by self-narrative or, sometimes, a combination of self-narrative and other-narrative. Narrativists like Schechtman (2005b), Goldie (2012), Wallace (2013), and Taylor (1989), while varying enormously, accept that persons are essentially, in nondamaged cases, beings that see themselves as living out stories. Regret includes a self-narrative: I wish that I (in the past) had not done something, and I regret it because the action/inaction is causally related, through my life story, to my present circumstances. Regret is, in this way, *person-making*. That is, in regretting, I create myself as a person by tying myself together across time, evaluating my actions and aiming at greater integrity. This is coherent with Charles Taylor's (1985) narrative account, which includes the criterion that we hold our actions to be significant. Obviously, we wouldn't regret if there were no significance, for ourselves at least, to our actions. And once we hold our actions to be significant, it is necessary that we be capable of regret, because we may find ourselves failing in what we hold significant, in what we care about. In this caring lies the possibility of remorse.

In this mode, R. Jay Wallace says that meaningful human lives are marked by attachment, which are "the main sources of meaning for us" (2013, 29) and which "constitutively involves a susceptibility to regret" (2013, 12). While he never clearly claims that those who cannot regret are nonpersons, he does claim they are deficient: "If you aren't able to be pained by contemplation of serious misfortune in the recent past that you yourself were directly involved in, then it seems there is probably something wrong with you" (2013, 18). He later removes the "it seems" and "probably," stating, "There is something amiss about people who are never subject to feelings of retrospective assessment" (2013, 29).

Attachments are part of what makes life meaningful because they give focus to our life stories and provide our lives with purpose. This is coherent with Rawls' claim (drawn from Royce) that "a person may be regarded as human life lived according to a plan . . . an individual says who he is by describing his purposes and causes, and what he intends to do with his life" (Rawls 1971, 408), that is, "his" attachment, plans, and potential life narrative. As Korsgaard puts it, "Some of the things we do are intelligible only in the context of projects that extend over long periods" (1989, 113). Understanding life as a *project* or *plan* constitutively incudes, as Wallace (2013) says, "a susceptibility to regret," whenever we neglect our purposes, do not do justice to our causes, and fail to follow through with our plans.

Accounts Where Regret Would Be Neither Necessary Nor Sufficient

While most of the contemporary accounts follow Locke's in allowing for regret to be a sufficient and necessary condition for personhood, a handful do not and, to make my claim, these need to be addressed. For example, Schechtman has a special, second type of person: those who have no self-narrative because of extreme mental disability. But she only allows that they are persons insofar as *other persons* claim them as such: "Mother in the late stages of dementia may no longer be the feisty, independent, and quick-witted woman I remember, but she is still Mother, the woman who sacrificed so much to raise me" (Schechtman 2010, 276). If we grant this (and it's problematic as it lacks cross-cultural consistency), we can just add that the sorts of persons discussed here meet the forensic criterion: they are agents, and they can be held accountable for their actions. It's not clear how that applies to those in vegetative states, so I'd hold that they fail to meet the standard sense of "person."

Similarly, I do not address "animalist" and purely bodily accounts of personhood such as Wiggins (1967, 22–5), Olson (1997, 1999), and Williams (1970), which claim that identity persists after total and permanent loss of all psychological content. On these accounts, persons are merely bodies of a certain type, and while the body may have consciousness, moral thought, and so on, these are not necessary for personhood. These do not pick out forensic persons, and they do not help us to decide if some newly discovered species, say, intelligent space aliens, should count as persons. These accounts also don't cohere with the common sense of the word "person," as in studies by Nichols (2010) and Strohminger and Nichols (2014), where surveys showed that persons were identified with their moral character and psychological content much more so than with their bodies. It seems that the animalist or bodily accounts circulate mostly among philosophers and do not cohere with natural language or legal senses of "person." Further, as Christine Korsgaard notes in adopting a bodily account of identity, "*given the technology we have now*, the unit of action is the human body ... the basic unit of action might be different if technology were different" (1989, 115.) Korsgaard, unlike others in this camp, holds that persons are fundamentally actors of a certain sort, and if it were possible for actors to switch bodies, such that one might regret what one had done in a different form, then a person would not be tied to a body. The point Korsgaard makes is important for our analysis: it is not the body but the agent that is the person, because the agent is the unity of actions across time because of its capacity to address its prior actions as its own. We must be able to look at some past event and say, "I did that," or even, if memory fails us, "that could have been me," for us to count as persons. It is this temporal sense of personhood, combined with our need to see ourselves as capable of doing well or poorly, that establishes us as regretting beings.

Identity across Time: Regret, Memory, and Narrative

An entity with no transtemporal sense of self would be a person in a highly limited sense. Such an entity may, as Mary Midgley (1985) notes, deserve moral consideration; it may have or be a self, according to Galen Strawson (1999). But we'd be hard-pressed to say that it would really count as a *person*. If it cannot see itself in the past and future, then moral blame and accountability would make little sense. We might quarantine such a being, but we cannot ask it to hold itself responsible. Perhaps this is why the position that persons must be temporal is widely held (Frankfurt 1971; Korsgaard 1989; Locke 1689; Schechtman 2005b, 2007): it's a necessary corollary of the forensic, narrative, and plan-based accounts of personhood.

Regret is available only to beings with personal memory and transtemporal personal identity. We only personally regret things we ourselves (think to) have done, and in so doing, we create a story about ourselves. This is why regret is identity-making, understanding identity in the common sense of one's distinctness[7] (as opposed to the bare or strict sense of identity in pure metaphysics), in the sense of what makes us ourselves as opposed to someone else. Part of our identity, our unique self-identification, is derived from our recurring thoughts and our attitudes toward what we believe ourselves to be. Such thoughts *constitute* who we are and *make* us who we are by their repetition and by the impetus they give to our future actions. They color how we interpret ourselves and our world in that they form an aspect of what is most uniquely our own: our perspective. In regret, we establish a take on some entity that we take to be ourselves, and we return to and rehearse that take, repeatedly reconnecting and making coherent that self and our attitude toward it. This makes the story of who we are and shapes how we, and others, see ourselves in the world.

It's important to note that this does not mean that the things we regret are things we actually did; rather, regret is identity making because we *believe* ourselves to have done certain things, and we define ourselves in relation to those events and our emotional and moral responses to them. If I believed I was Chamberlain, I might spend a great deal of time regretting the Munich Treaty. Then, much of what makes me who I am, both in my private moments of reflection and in my interactions with others, would come with and from this recurrent regret. Maybe I worry when I appease someone. Perhaps, I resolve not to compromise. My person, my personality, and the content of my consciousness are shaped by this regret, even if *in fact* I did not do the thing I regret having done.

Narrativists hold that persons are those who conceptualize their lives as stories, with themselves as the main characters. Part of the purpose of this move is to tie personhood in to the continuity that grants identity. Regret is sufficient for at least a partial self-narrative, and it's a self-narrative that carries with it agency, responsibility, and a sense of oneself as the active center of the narrative.

Regret does something additional that Schechtman (2005) notes as essential to narrative. It unites the story by means of *emotional* content. Since I can only feel my feelings, the feelings I have in my narrative are essential to making it mine and to marking elements in the narrative as things I value and am attached to. While Schechtman (2003) rightly emphasizes empathic and sympathetic connections to my past self in order for me to be the same person, this is clearly not a sufficient condition. One can have empathic and sympathetic access to a narrative that is not the narrative of one's own life; otherwise, as Marcia Eaton (1982) notes, I wouldn't become sad when reading about fictional characters. So, it isn't simply an emotional connection that makes a story into my story but the right kind of emotional connection. I don't personally *regret* the actions of Jane Eyre. I can only personally regret what I take as my own actions. This is not merely a circular point: personal regret is a unique emotion, containing a different valence from impersonal regret. The pain of my self failing has an inner orientation and a sharp directness. I can escape from others whose behavior I regret, but I cannot escape from myself. I can see others as worthy of scorn, without feeling the pain of self-hatred. So personal regret is, significantly, a particular emotional state, like my dread or my joy. I must judge myself negatively and take the consequences of that judgment.

REGRET, IDENTIFICATION, ALIENATION, AND COLLECTIVE IDENTITY

A key feature of personal regret is the feeling of self-blame. We understand ourselves to have offended against ourselves, and this is what makes it so essential to selfhood: It's a confrontation with oneself that both establishes a connection to the past and sets us at odds against ourselves. In this way, it answers to both intuitions that we *are*, and that we are *not*, our past selves. This gets at something that distinguishes persons from nonpersons: the ability to separate oneself as the judge from oneself as the object of judgment. It does this splitting while maintaining the connection between the two through our affective states: I condemn myself, and the condemner feels the pain of being condemned.

It is this pain of self-condemnation that makes it clear that my past self is indeed me. If I could de-identify with my past self, I wouldn't feel pain. I might feel the redemption of being born again or of spiritual release from self. But in regret, I get a moment of moral clarity: I realize that I am not living up to the values I most strongly identify with, and am alienated, and cannot escape from, myself.[8]

It is also possible to have regret toward actions taken by a group of which one was a part, even if one would not have authorized such actions nor was directly responsible. For instance, U.S. citizens can, under the right emotional description, personally regret the invasion of Iraq, even if those citizens had protested against the invasion, because a U.S. citizen *identifies* with his or her country. This identification allows people to feel regret for actions taken on their behalf or in their names. What many Germans felt after World War II was perhaps like this: even if an individual could have done nothing to stop the atrocities, these atrocities were done in that individual's name. In other words, our actions are not always under our direct control, but it's their role in the entirety of our agential narrative that makes them ours. The narrative of who we are is thus also a collective one. If one identifies as a member of a family, tribe, religion, or nation, then one's identity is in important ways defined by group membership, and the kind of deep personal pain felt in personal regret can be experienced over actions of the collective.

One might imagine that a German fighting in the resistance against the Nazis could be somewhat immunized from personal regret about the atrocities (no doubt he or she would feel horror, revulsion, etc.), because such a person would have identified very strongly *against* the Nazi regime. She or he would thus not feel that a "we" that included him or her had engaged in the atrocities. All of this points to the deep connection between identity and regret.

CONCLUSION

Regret is person-making: it provides us with the material to become Frankfurtian persons, narrative persons, self-reflective persons, and entities that understand blame and praise. It includes emotion as a necessary element. It demands an existential self-relation. It includes the capacity to evaluate, to make higher-order judgments, and to direct those judgments toward behavior. It is self-shaping in that it instills a desire to be different than we are, and it ties us to a sense of self, a self-story, with which we cannot help but identify.

Regret can serve to pick out nonhumans who are persons. If we could determine that our computers had begun to feel regret, we would have to take them seriously as person candidates. Signs of regret in nonhuman animals would point to a need to reconsider their rights and, potentially, their duties. Further, unlike dread or anxiety, which had been the standard emotional condition for personhood given by the existentialists, regret requires less abstract, more evaluative and narrative sense of self.

Commonly, insufficient social value is placed on regret. We hear positive talk of "living without regrets," and people saying, proudly, "I have no regrets." Philosophers have also been notoriously weak on valuing emotions and especially on valuing negative emotions. But without emotions, including negative ones, we are left with, at best, a diminished personhood. Indeed, we tend to share a common intuition about emotions and about regret in particular: The intelligent beings of science fiction, robots, and supercomputers are often depicted as emotionless and without regret—as nonpersons. Nonpersons, because we suspect that living without regrets is living without an interesting and complicated relationship to one's history. Having no regrets reflects a failure to reflect: surely in the examined life, there must be at least something we would have done differently, and if we fail to see that, we fail to prepare for the future. This ability to look back wistfully and to not just wonder, but to wish that things had been otherwise, makes life richer. It increases the variety of the ways one views oneself, it demands the entertainment of alternate possibilities, and, unlike mere fanciful imagination, it imbues our imaginings with an emotional and evaluative connection to who we are, were, and could have been.

NOTES

1. One problem in saying what counts as a condition of personhood is that the process is in part one of defining personhood, so there's the risk of circularity or at least of having no clear standard to appeal to. I'd note, though, that the standard claim that persons are those who are protected by laws and accorded rights provides a decent heuristic: if an entity could not feel pain, grief, sorrow, or any negative emotion, it's hard to see how it could be harmed, at least from its own perspective, and since much of law is concerned with protection from harm, there is at least a question of how to apply law in regard to such a being. On the other hand, a being of this sort might well have consciousness and the ability to reason, so we could conceivably hold it responsible for actions that would harm others. As such, it would have an interesting status, a kind of partial personhood. We ascribe partial personhood in a legal sense to children or the extremely mentally impaired, though in the inverse manner: we often don't hold them responsible for the actions but do protect them from harm. So, an emotionless being would be a sort of inverse child.
2. There's no separate name for this emotion in English, but it is distinct in its cognitive and affective qualities. In Buddhism and Hinduism, the term "mudita," often translated as "unselfish joy," is used.
3. "The equality of distributive justice consists in allotting various things to various persons in proportion to their personal dignity," *Summa Theologica*, Q.63.
4. "Man is by nature a political animal," *Politics*, 12–53a.
5. "We have many wants, and many persons are needed to supply them," *Republic*, 369c.
6. For an overview, see the SEP article, "Feminist Perspectives on the Self," section 3.1, "The nature of the self as dynamic and relational" (Willett, Anderson, and Myers 2015).
7. See, for example, Vignoles, Chryssochoou, and Breakwell (2000) for a discussion of the "distinctness principle" as a necessary element of identity.
8. There is, of course, a long tradition of analysis of self-alienation from Hegel through Marx, Kierkegaard, Nietzsche, and Sartre that could be plumbed for a deeper look at the person-making and person-unmaking character of regret.

REFERENCES

Aristotle. 1984. *Sense and Sensibilia*, IV, 441a1–2, in *The Complete Works of Aristotle*, vol. 1, ed. Jonathan Barnes, trans. J. I. Beare. Princeton, NJ: Princeton University.
Aristotle. 1994–2009. *Nichomachean Ethics*, Book I, section 13, Trans. W. D. Ross. Retrieved December 2016 from classics.mit.edu.
Ben-Ze'ev, Aaron. 2009. "The Thing Called Emotion." In *The Oxford Handbook of Philosophy of Emotion*, ed. Goldie, Peter, 41–61. Oxford: Oxford University Press.
Burks, A. W. 1946. "Laws of Nature and Reasonableness of Regret." *Mind* 55 (218): 170–2.

Cowie, R. 2009. "Perceiving Emotion: Towards a Realistic Understanding of the Task." *Philos Trans R Soc Lond B Biol Sci.* 364 (1535): 3515–25. doi:10.1098/rstb.2009.0139.

Cowie, R. 2010. "Describing the Forms of Coloring That Pervade Everyday Life." In *Oxford Handbook of Philosophy of Emotion*, 63–94.

Damasio, A. R. 1999. *The Feeling of What Happens: Body and Emotion in the Making of Consciousness*. New York: Harcourt Brace.

Dennett, D. C. 1976. "Conditions of Personhood." In *The Identities of Persons*, ed. A. O. Rorty, 175–96. Berkeley: University of California Press.

Descartes, René. 1641/2006. *Meditations, Objections, and Replies*, trans. Roger Ariew and Donald A. Cress. Indianapolis, IN: Hackett.

Descartes, René, 1989. *Passions of the Soul*, trans. Stephen Voss. Indianapolis, IN: Hackett Publishing.

Eaton, M. M. 1982. "A Strange Kind of Sadness." *Journal of Aesthetics & Art Criticism* 41 (1): 51–63.

Egan, A. 2007. "Some Counterexamples to Causal Decision Theory." *Philosophical Review* 116 (1): 93–114.

Ekman, Paul. 1971. "Universals and Cultural Differences in Facial Expressions of Emotion." *Nebraska Symposium on Motivation* 19: 207–83.

Ekman, Paul. 1999. "Basic Emotions," in *Handbook of Cognition and Emotion*, ed. T. Dalgleish and M. Power, 45–60. Sussex: John Wiley.

Frankfurt, H. G. 1971. "Freedom of the Will and the Concept of a Person." *Journal of Philosophy* 68 (1): 5–20.

Friedman, M. 1989. "Friendship and Moral Growth." *Journal of Value Inquiry* 23 (1): 3–13.

Goldie, Peter. 2012. *The Mess Inside*. Oxford: Oxford University Press.

Hurka, T. 1996. "Monism, Pluralism, and Rational Regret." *Ethics* 106 (3): 555–75.

Hillman, J. 1979. *The Dream and the Underworld*. New York: Harper & Row.

Hobbes, T. 1651/2013. *Leviathan*. Retrieved from Project Gutenberg, December 2017. https://www.gutenberg.org/files/3207/3207-h/3207-h.htm.

James, William. 1884. "What Is an Emotion?" *Mind* 9: 188–205.

Joyce, J. M. 2012. "Regret and Instability in Causal Decision Theory." *Synthese* 187 (1): 123–45.

Kant, Immanuel. 1785/2004. *Groundwork for the Metaphysics of Morals*, Section 2, trans. Thomas Kingsmill Abbott. Retrieved November 2016 from Gutenberg.org.

Kierkegaard, S. 1980a. *The Concept of Anxiety: A Simple Psychologically Orienting Deliberation on the Dogmatic Issue of Hereditary Sin*. Princeton, NJ: Princeton University Press.

Kierkegaard, S. 1980b. *The Sickness unto Death: A Christian Psychological Exposition for Upbuilding and Awakening*. Princeton, NJ: Princeton University Press.

Korsgaard, Christine. 1989. "Personal Identity and the Unity of Agency." *Philosophy and Public Affairs* 18 (2): 101–32.

Landman, J. 1993. *Regret: The Persistence of the Possible*. Oxford: Oxford University Press.

Lindemann, Hilde. 2014. *Holding and Letting Go: The Social Practice of Personal Identities*. New York: Oxford University Press
Locke, John. 1689. *Essay Concerning Human* Understanding, Book II, Ch. XXVII, section 11. July 19, 2019. Retrieved from http://oll.libertyfund.org/titles/locke-the-works-vol-1-an-essay-concerning-human-understanding-part-1.
Mesquita, B., and N. H. Frijda. 1992. "Cultural Variations in Emotions: A Review." *Psychological Bulletin* 112 (2): 179–204.
Midgley, M. 1985. "Persons and Non-Persons." In *In Defense of Animals*, ed. P. Singer, 52–62. Malden: Blackwell.
Nietzsche, Friedrich. 1974. *Gay Science*, trans. Walter Kaufmann. New York: Vintage.
Nichols, Shaun. 2010. "Intuitions about Personal Identity: An Empirical Study." *Philosophical Psychology* 23 (3): 293–312.
Nahmias, Eddy, and Dylan Murray. 2011. "Experimental Philosophy on Free Will: An Error Theory for Incompatibilist Intuitions." In *New Waves in Philosophy of Action*, eds. J. Aguilar, A. Buckareff, K. Frankish, 189–216. Basingstoke: Palgrave Macmillan.
Olson, Eric T. 1997. "Was I Ever a Fetus." *Philosophy and Phenomenological Research* LVII (1): 95–110.
Olson, Eric T. 1999. *The Human Animal: Personal Identity without Psychology*. New York: Oxford University Press.
Parfit, D. 1984. *Reasons and Persons*. Oxford: Oxford University Press.
Plato. 1914. *Euthyphro. Apology. Crito. Phaedo. Phaedrus*. The Loeb classical library 36. Cambridge, MA: Harvard University Press.
Rawls, John. 1971. *A Theory of Justice*. Cambridge, MA: Harvard University Press.
Ricoeur, Paul. 1984. *Time and narrative. Vol. 1*, trans. Kathleen McLaughlin and David Pellauer. Chicago, IL: University of Chicago Press.
Rorty, Amelie. 1980. "Agent Regret." In *Explaining Emotions*, ed. Amelie Rorty, 489–506. Berkeley: University of California Press.
Schechtman, M. 2003. "Empathic Access: The Missing Ingredient in Personal Identity." In *Personal* identity, ed. R. Martin and J. Barresi, 238–59. Malden, MA: Blackwell.
Schechtman, M. 2005a. "Self-Expression and Self-Control." In *The Self?*, ed. G. Strawson, 45–62. Malden, MA: Blackwell.
Schechtman, M., 2005b. "Personal Identity and the Past." *Philosophy, Psychiatry, & Psychology* 12: 9–22.
Schechtman, M. 2007. "Stories, Lives, and Basic Survival: A Refinement and Defense of the Narrative View." *Royal Institute of Philosophy Supplement* 60: 155–78.
Schechtman, M. 2010. "Personhood and the Practical." *Theoretical Medicine and Bioethics* 31 (4): 271–83.
Schechtman, M. 2011. "Memory and Identity." *Philosophical Studies* 153 (1): 65–79.
Schwitzgebel, Eric. 2012. "Self-Ignorance." In *Consciousness and the Self*, ed. Jee-Loo Liu and John Perry, 184–97. Cambridge: Cambridge University Press.
Shoemaker, S. 1970. "Persons and Their Pasts." *American Philosophical Quarterly* 7 (4): 269–85.
Sorensen, R. 1998. "Rewarding Regret." *Ethics* 108 (3): 528–37.

Strawson, G. 1999. "The Self and the SESMET." *Journal of Consciousness Studies* 6 (4): 99–135.
Strohminger, N., and S. Nichols. 2014. "The Essential Moral Self." *Cognition* 131 (1): 159–71.
Tanaka A., A. Koizumi, H. Imai, S. Hiramatsu, E. Hiramoto, and B. de Gelder. September 2010. "I Feel Your Voice. Cultural Differences in the Multisensory Perception of Emotion." *Psychological Science* 21 (9): 1259–62.
Taylor, Charles. 1985. "The Concept of a Person." In *Philosophical Papers. Volume 1*, 98–102. Cambridge: Cambridge University Press.
Taylor, Charles. 1989. *Sources of the Self: The Making of Modern Identity*. Cambridge, MA: Harvard University Press.
Tsai, Jeanne. September 2007. "Ideal Affect: Cultural Causes and Behavioral Consequences." *Perspectives on Psychological Science* 2 (3): 242–59.
Tsai, Jeanne, Brian Knutson, and Helene Fung. 2006. "Cultural Variation in Affect Valuation." *Journal of Personality and Social Psychology* 90 (2): 288–307.
Vignoles, V. L., X. Chryssochoou, and G. M. Breakwell. 2000. "The Distinctiveness Principle: Identity, Meaning, and the Bounds of Cultural Relativity." *Personality and Social Psychology Review* 4: 337–54.
Wallace, R. Jay. 2013. *The View from Here: On Affirmation, Attachment, and the Limits of Regret*. Oxford: Oxford University Press.
Wiggins, David. 1967. *Identity and Spatio-Temporal Continuity*. Hoboken, NJ: Blackwell.
Williams, Bernard. 1970. "The Self and the Future." *Philosophical Review* 79 (2): 161–80.
Williams, B. 1981. "Moral luck." In *Moral Luck: Philosophical Papers, 1973–1980*, 20–39. Cambridge: Cambridge University Press.
Willett, Cynthia, Ellie Anderson, and Diana Meyers. 1999/2015. "Feminist Perspectives on the Self." *Stanford Encyclopedia of Philosophy*. July 19, 2019. https://plato.stanford.edu/entries/feminism-self/.
Zeelenberg, M. 1999. "The Use of Crying over Spilled Milk: A Note on the Rationality and Functionality of Regret." *Philosophical Psychology* 12: 3.

Chapter 4

Reasonable Regret

Maura Priest

INTRODUCTION

I have frequently run into people who claim that they "live life with no regrets." I have always found this puzzling, for I live a life filled with regrets. Perhaps, though, I have too many. There might be times during which I feel regret unreasonably, or perhaps I would be behaving both more reasonably and ethically if I refrained from regretting. On the other hand, I suspect that those who truly live their lives with no regrets are skipping over those that they ought to have. There are likely instances in which these individuals would be behaving both more reasonably and ethically if they did feel regret for things they currently do not.

This chapter is a philosophical investigation into the abovementioned issues. I believe that both common moral intuitions and reflected reasoning suggest that not all regret is created equally. Indeed, there are instances in which ethical persons with properly functioning emotions *should* feel regret. But there are other instances in which those same individuals *should not* feel it. Hence, both the presence and absence of regret can be reasonable or unreasonable, moral or immoral.[1] This chapter aims to distinguish between these instances in systematic ways. Although this is a philosophical investigation, I rely heavily on the scholarship of psychologists. Morality is ultimately inseparable from our psychology (i.e., our thoughts and attitudes), and thus philosophy is improved when it is grounded in the empirical science of psychology and cognition.

My chapter proceeds as follows. The section "What Is Regret?" analyzes the emotion of regret and subsequently describes its identifying features. I explain how guilt differs from regret and how some seeming cases of regret are only pseudo-regret. This definition will serve as a point of conceptual reference for the discussion that follows. In the section "What Is Reasonable Regret?" I start with basic intuitive cases where most people would likely agree on the reasonableness of regret. This is followed by a discussion of their opposite: instances in which regret is intuitively unreasonable. The aim is to compare these cases so that we might glean some features of regret that are reasonable and moral making and other features that are unreasonable and immoral making.

To delve a bit further into what has already been said, throughout this chapter I will refer back to the aforementioned terms: reasonable, unreasonable, moral, and immoral. Philosophically, I wish to refrain from taking a contentious theoretical position on what I mean by them. Rather, I hope to work with a broad intuitive notion that latches on to how we use these terms in common conversation. A reasonable action is one that most adults can make sense of (if they really tried) and also an action that can be understood and "approved of" in the sense that it falls in line with the way an informed, intelligent, and consistent person might act. To be unreasonable, then, is to be the opposite of this. An unreasonable action is one that does not seem to make sense in the situation and would cause people to wonder whether or not the agent was uninformed, lacked intelligence, or was perhaps under the influence of mind-altering substances. A key part of the definitions just offered is "if they really tried." Because all of us have a lot going on in our lives, and because we often lack pertinent information about others, we may pay little attention to unreasonable acts and not even recognize them as such. However, if we were to take the time to sit and think deeply about the acts of another, and if we had full information about a given situation, then we would recognize the agent as being unreasonable.

I take a moral action to be one that most community members (given a community of informed and intelligent persons) would deem as either praiseworthy or morally neutral (i.e., an action that is at least morally acceptable given community standards of ethical behavior).[2] An immoral action is one that breaks these community standards and makes one worthy of blame and perhaps punishment. I will assume that the overwhelming majority of immoral acts are ones that do wrong to others. If an action wrongs another, then it is appropriate for the wronged individual to make a complaint against the wrongdoer and demand that the person cease to behave immorally. Sometimes, it may even be appropriate to demand that the wrongdoer compensate the wronged party. At the very least, individuals who behave immorally are worthy of negative judgment from fellow members of the community (members who together uphold the commonly accepted moral standard). Extrapolating from this, a feature of an act is moral making if it contributes to upholding ethical standards of the community, and it is immoral making if it does the opposite. Last, as is the case with reasonable and unreasonable acts, the average person often lacks both the time and information to aptly judge an act as moral or immoral (even if it really does warrant such a label).

Identifying these features provides a framework when trying to understand less intuitive categories of regret. The section "The Hard Cases: Membership and Interpersonal Regret" will discuss the more difficult cases, that is, *membership regret* and *interpersonal regret*. These cases are controversial because both types of regret involve actions that the regret holder herself did not commit. *Membership regret* occurs when a person who is a member of a group regrets the group's action despite the member having no direct involvement. *Interpersonal regret* occurs when an agent regrets the actions of another individual with whom she holds a close relation. I will argue that while something may seem initially strange about both membership and interpersonal regret, both types can be reasonable given the right circumstances.

WHAT IS REGRET?

Regret as a Cluster Concept

In the introduction, I hinted at an understanding of regret when I called it an emotion. It might not be obvious to all that regret is an emotion rather than a judgment. And while I will argue that regret involves a judgment, the concept of concern is more than just a form of rational recognition. We frequently, in common parlance, use the phrase "feeling regret." Consider, for instance, a headline from the *Washington Post*: "Bully *feels* regret for lashing out at tormentor" (Hax 2017; emphasis added). A brief survey of contemporary publications will show that regret is frequently treated as something that is *felt*. This chapter takes such cases of regret as the standard.

In defining the emotion of regret, I am not attempting a conceptual analysis that gets at the one true answer of what regret really is. I doubt there is an answer. I suspect there are a variety of cluster concepts used across languages and cultures. Instead, I am going to offer a definition of one of these cluster concepts while admitting that there are probably others. I am satisfied if what I loosely define as regret matches many (rather than all) instances of the way we use the term in common parlance. Most importantly, I aim to identify an emotional state/affective attitude that can be more or less reasonable and moral in a variety of circumstances.

Defining Regret (casually, loosely, broadly, etc.)

Like many emotions, what I am calling regret involves both a phenomenological "feel" and a cognitive judgment. I will refer to these as the feel aspect and the cognitive aspect throughout the chapter.[3] An individual who has a purely rational judgment with no emotional component is not experiencing what I am calling regret. For instance, imagine a very well-designed robot who has been programmed to learn what behaviors are socially acceptable and what are not. Suppose further that this robot knows hurting others is considered wrong and then accidently hurts someone via its robot arms hitting the person on the head. This robot may have a computational reaction that judges its movement as wrong and calculates data to avoid such movement in the future. But however close this robot regret might be to human regret, it is *not* human regret because it lacks the necessary emotional component.

While there are notable limitations to the extent to which we can describe the phenomenology of emotions, one thing we can do is reference them in comparison to other emotions and descriptive terms. For instance, regret is neither a feeling of happiness nor sadness, yet we can say that it is closer to the latter. Similarly, regret is closer to a negative emotion than a positive one. A reasonable word to describe the feeling of regret is *discomfort*. The idea that regret consists of a negative, uncomfortable, emotional experience is indeed supported by psychological science. According to one recent study, the "signature" of regret is "an *unpleasant* emotion triggered by knowledge of the rejected alternative's outcome" (Camille et al. 2004, 1168; emphasis added). Understanding the *reasons* for the discomfort associated with regret will be central to understanding the *cognitive* component of the emotion. For now, let us focus on the "unpleasant" feeling. From the philosophical side of scholarship, Rorty (1980, 496) has described regret as "a particular type of painful feeling, a pang, a stab, waves of stabs."

With all this in mind, let us offer a general definition of *regret's emotional phenomenology*: Regret is a negative and uncomfortable feeling that is specially directed at a past occurrence.

In addition to an uncomfortable feeling of sorts, regret has a cognitive (or rational) component that is more specific than many other emotions. As Gilovich and Medvec (1995, 379) has noted, "Judgement is more central to the experience of regret than . . . the experience of jealousy or anger." For example, whatever rational judgment (if any) accompanies the phenomenological feeling of happiness, it is not as specific as regret. Regret involves not only a judgment but also a judgment of a certain kind.[4] Take ten happy persons: each can have reasons for happiness that are entirely unique. Regret is a thicker concept, and if two persons are feeling regretful, the rational content of that feeling must share important conceptual features. "Thick" and "thin" are terms often used in the virtue ethics literature. Thin concepts are vague ones and their definitions lack specificity. For instance, the term "good" is generally considered a thin concept because its definition is quite vague. A thick concept would be "jealousy" because describing jealousy is not a vague task. It requires mentioning a specific emotional mind-set. Hence, there could be great variation in two persons who are both described as good but less variation in two persons who are described as being jealous. Similarly, because regret is also a thick concept, two persons who are described as regretful will have quite a lot in common (likely more in common than two persons described as being happy).

Let us now make a first attempt at describing the content that unifies regret across time and people. Regardless of who is feeling regret or when and where that person is feeling it, such instances of regret seem to share the important similarity of *regret's rational content*: The desire that some past occurrence with which the agent identifies had turned out differently than it in fact did.

Looking at the above statement, two unique features of regret are salient. First, some emotions, such as excitement, fear, and dread, are primarily focused on the future. Regret is the opposite of these, and its primary focus is the past. Only from this perspective does the emotion look toward the present or future. For instance, because Tom regrets what he has done, he might commit to future states of affairs being different. Although he has a set attitude regarding the future, a separate attitude inspired by regret and directed at the past was foundational to its inspiration.

In addition to looking toward the past, regret's cognitive content is *identifying*. Here is what I understand an *identifying emotion* to be: an emotion whose cognitive content relates to self-perception and personal character assessment.

Identification (as I am understanding it) incorporates responsibility. As psychologists Camille et al. (2004, 11687) noted in their study, "Contrary to mere disappointment . . . regret is an emotion strongly associated with a feeling of responsibility." The identification I describe is a specific sense of responsibility. It is feeling responsible for something because your sense of self is tangled together with the object of your responsibility. For example, if I regret failing to make the basketball team, my identification as an athlete explains why (in my eyes) I should have done better and made the team. If I did not identify as an athlete, I might be sad *sans* regret if I didn't make the team. While most emotions can be identifying given the right circumstances, unlike regret, most emotions are not of necessity identifying. For instance, consider happiness. Jane might feel happiness when watching a random act of kindness between two strangers. This type of happiness has nothing to do with how Jane views her own character. Simply by virtue of having regret, however, we are making a judgment concerning our own behavior and character (viz., that some past occurrence does not fit well with our view of ourselves). An emotion just like regret but without the identifying feature is not in actuality regret at all and would be better described as disappointment or sadness.[5]

The way I have been describing regret thus far is importantly similar to Williams' brief but famous description of *agent regret*.[6] But despite the similarities, I will argue (in contrast to Williams) that we can feel regret even when we have had no direct involvement in the action. Hence my biggest disagreement with Williams (2002, 27), which will influence my account of reasonable regret, is with his claim that "a person can feel [agent regret] only towards his own past actions (or, at most, actions in which he regards himself as a participant)" (parentheses in the original). Contrary to Williams, I argue that what matters is not participation in the relevant act but *identification with the act*. Because we can identify with groups and their actions, it is both possible and reasonable to feel a deep type of personal regret (Williams' agent regret) for actions in which you were not a participant at all. This collective regret directed at occurrences in which you were not directly involved is more than a "I wish that hadn't happened" feeling and instead is a feeling associated with deep responsibility and self-blame.[7]

Impossible Regret

Having just described regret in general terms, let us turn to some examples that can illuminate instances when regret is possible and when it is not. Here is a first test case:

> Tom is reading a book about Timothy McVeigh and immediately regrets McVeigh's decision to murder so many innocents.

Let us assume that Tom is just a regular guy: a fifty-year-old African American dentist. While there might not be anything *immoral* about Tom's feeling of regret, something about his response just seems off. Upon reflection, it is easy to understand what is so unfitting about Tom's response: Tom had nothing to do with the bombing—he did not do the action himself, and he bears no connection whatsoever to those who did. Regret is an emotion that has an object. When we feel regret, we feel regret *toward something*. The something in Tom's case is the bombing by McVeigh. But this makes little sense because the second criterion of regret has not been met in Tom's case: Tom lacks identification with McVeigh's evil deed.[8] Hence, it seems safe to say that regret is not merely unreasonable in this case but *impossible*.

Now, Tom might be having a phenomenological experience identical to regret, but this is not enough. Regret is a thick emotion that requires both a phenomenological feel and cognitive content. Because Tom lacks the proper cognitive content, including identification, what he is feeling is at best pseudo-regret. Pseudo-regret occurs when one has an emotional (phenomenological) experience identical to an emotion but lacks the cognitive content of that emotion. Suppose, for instance, that jealousy involves a specific feel. In other words, there is a characteristic feeling involved in "feeling jealous." Imagine that after getting hit in the head, Toby suddenly feels a strong pang of jealousy. Yet, he has no idea why he feels this way. (It has something to do with his injury.) Because there is no sense in which Toby is really jealous of something, what he is feeling is pseudo-jealousy. Likewise, when one has the feel of regret while lacking the matching cognitive content, one is experiencing pseudo-regret.

Before moving on from the above example, however, let us consider a twist to our story. Suppose that for whatever strange reason, Tom does identify with McVeigh. Perhaps he has been fascinated with the Oklahoma City bombing story since childhood, and this fascination has bred a strong sense of identity. If Tom did have this identification, his regret would be possible; but his regret would also be unreasonable. Even though Tom identifies with McVeigh, his reasons for identification are themselves unreasonable, which makes his regret unreasonable. We can identify with all sorts of people and groups for unreasonable reasons, and when we do, the regret that follows from such identification is itself unreasonable. This is similar to feeling deep grief over the death of a celebrity with whom we bear no actual relation. Such grief is clearly possible, but because the relationship is entirely contrived, the emotion is unreasonable: Grief is fitting when it is directed toward those who we really knew and loved, not those we only wish we had known. Likewise, regret is fitting when it is directed at events with which we bear some real identifying connection (i.e., not a mere psychologically fabricated identification).

I do not mean to suggest that we can never feel reasonable regret nor grief over someone we have never met. However, the identification must be both real and appropriate. For instance, if Sam is a musician who was greatly influenced by a professional musician's work, not only might he feel real grief at the celebrity's death but he might feel regret over being profoundly influenced by a musician who was later revealed to have stolen all of his music. Identification is not a cut-and-dry concept but a spectrum, and the reasonableness of certain cases will fall on the border of apt and inapt. What swings something toward the apt side is both the existence of identification and the fact that such identification is founded on a meaningful connection.

Guilt versus Regret

Guilt and regret are very closely related moral emotions, perhaps as close as empathy and sympathy or kindness and beneficence. I agree with the psychologists Gilovich and Medvec (1995, 393) that when an individual feels regret, such an experience is "likely to be tinged with guilt." This chapter is focused on regret, but because it is a moral emotion so similar to guilt, it makes sense to say a few words about how they relate. As mentioned, I am not trying to get at the one true definition of regret, nor do I believe one exists. Thus, I will say the same about guilt. What exists is a class of cluster concepts and, speaking generally, we can delineate the conceptual differences between the concepts labeled as guilt and regret. Both emotions involve a negative feeling focused on a past event with which the agent can identify. Regret, however, is a broader concept.[9] I can regret forgetting to pick up cornflakes at the grocery store, but guilt for doing the same would be unreasonable. In usual circumstances, forgetting cornflakes is not a moral failing, yet insofar as I love eating them for breakfast, *it is* a personal failing. The first difference between guilt and regret is that the latter concept is broader. Regret can be directed at personal failings that have little to do with morality. The very feeling of guilt, on the other hand, seems to have moral connotations.

There is a second difference between guilt and regret worth mentioning: Guilt seems more about personal inadequacy than about the past occurrence itself. If I feel guilty for failing to donate money to the homeless, my main focus seems to be my own moral shortcoming. If I regret failing to donate money to the homeless, my focus seems directed at the fact that the homeless were not helped. To take words from Zeelenberg et al. (2000, 532), "Regret is associated with a tendency to blame oneself for having made the wrong decision, a focus *on the regretted event* with a view to undoing it or preventing it from happening again in the future" (emphasis added). This focus on "undoing [an event] and preventing it from happening in the future" seems more central to regret than guilt. While guilt might lead to a person behaving differently, the emphasis on taking steps toward making things different is more salient in the case of regret.

Although different emotions, the similarities between regret and guilt are significant, and because of this we should keep in mind that we can likely learn a lot about one by studying the other.

WHAT IS REASONABLE REGRET?

The Easy Case of Moral Regret

Emotions can be reasonable or unreasonable, moral or immoral. Although some might find this controversial, this line of thinking goes as far back as Aristotle, who argued that we can be too angry or not angry enough or be angry at the wrong time or for the wrong things.[10] Emotions impact our behavior and are an important part of our moral life; emotions say a lot about our character—or so I will assume and many agree.[11] If we want to be good people, we should take care to feel the right emotions in the right circumstances to the right degrees.

It is hard to create an exact formula for ethical behavior. Philosophers have been arguing with one another over morality for upward of three thousand years. Ethics, morality, right and wrong, virtue, good and bad: This is difficult stuff. Due to the nature of the subject, then, I want to start out with "easy" cases: instances in which regret is *clearly* reasonable and other instances in which it is *clearly not*. By beginning with a point on which many people can agree, I hope to glean insights to help us analyze more difficult cases where opinions are initially less unified. The goal is for us to know that, speaking generally, circumstances that have feature F are those in which regret is reasonable and circumstances that lack F are cases in which regret is unreasonable.

Let us start with an example of the former: Tom promised his sister he would watch his nephew. However, Tom is invited to go golfing and decides to leave his nephew (four years old) home alone. His nephew trips into the pool and nearly drowns while Tom is gone. Tom thinks back on what he has done and feels deep regret.

In this instance, we have a clean case of regret that seems to be the moral emotion to have in such a circumstance. It would say something negative about Tom as a person, if, having learned about what had happened to his nephew, he felt no twinge of regret. An example such as this brings out what is wrong with those who proclaim they live life with no regrets, namely, at times we do things that are *worthy* of regret. If Tom's bumper-sticker life motto stopped him from feeling regret, it would be a sign of selfish disregard for his sister and his nephew. When we do something that is a wrong against others, or harms them in some way, it is disrespectful to go on as if nothing has happened. Regret is a form of showing respect, insofar as regret owns up to a wrongdoing. Regret is a way of suggesting, "I had no right to treat you that way." Because regret need not be expressed, it does not always "show" respect. Yet silent regret is a private expression of respect. Much like, for example, how unexpressed admiration is still admiration. Lacking regret altogether suggests callous disregard toward the possibility of doing a harmful thing in the future. Indeed, the inability to feel regret is associated with antisocial behavior. In the words of psychologists Baskin-Sommers, Stuppy-Sullivan, and Buckholtz (2016, 14438), "Psychopathy is associated with persistent antisocial behavior and a striking lack of regret for the consequences of that behavior." This addresses the perception. However, the truth might be a bit more complicated, and the aforementioned authors argue that while psychopaths are able to experience the phenomenological discomfort of regret, for them it provides no motivating force. Notwithstanding, there remains a strong link between antisocial behavior and a nontypical regret experience.

Why is regret a sign of respect? Looking at the lose definition offered earlier, we can spell out the why of what seems fairly intuitive, that is, lacking regret sometimes is disrespectful while the presence of regret can be the opposite. The first part of regret we described is its uncomfortable feel. Let us think of that feel in respect to our example with Tom. Tom did something that endangered his nephew. When he reflected upon the danger that he had inflicted, it makes sense that he felt uncomfortable. Indeed, discomfort is an apt response to putting his nephew in danger. It is respectful to his nephew, for it is his nephew's worth as a person that merits the feeling of discomfort. *Perhaps* Tom would be able to judge what he did negatively and make a commitment never to do it again *absent* the emotional feel of regret, but such a situation still seems to fall short of the best response. Humans are emotional creatures, and our emotions influence our actions.[12] The emotional experience of regret is a sign of respect toward those we have wronged and also a motivational component of avoiding future bad behavior. To return to the study of Camille et al. (2004, 1167), "Regret has a profound impact in decision making . . . and is a powerful predictor of behavior because people's choices are often made to avoid this highly unpleasant emotion."[13] From the above examples, then, we can come away with two features that speak in favor of regret's reasonableness and morality. The presence of these features might not *always* mean regret is moral, all things considered. However, because they are in themselves morally valuable features, they speak strongly in favor of it. The relevant features associated with moral regret are the following:

- It is directed toward a behavior that should be avoided in the future.
- Its presence displays respect toward any persons wronged or harmed by the regrettable occurrence.

The first condition above speaks to the relevance of regret and control: The more control we had over our past actions, the more likely regret is reasonable. Indeed, Zeelenberg et al. (2000) confirmed in a series of experiments that the more control an agent had over an outcome, the greater her regret.[14] Now, it need not follow that regret is never reasonable in instances where we lack control. The claim is only for the converse: When we do have control over a "bad" action of sorts, this fact speaks in favor of regret's reasonableness. Regret is a psychological sticky note reminding us not to do the same thing in the future. Just like real-life sticky notes, regret is not always a successful reminder, and we may again do the thing that was regrettable. Nonetheless, regret is morally advisable because making an effort to avoid immoral action (even if such effort fails) is morally superior to taking no such action at all. Moreover, this motivational aspect of regret is an additional way in which it manifests respect: An effort to change behavior that harmed S is a sign of respect toward S.

When Regret Goes Wrong

Let us move on to examples where regret seems clearly unreasonable or immoral. When we compare these cases to the previous ones, we can glean some information about regret's reasonable-making features. The consequent challenge is to then apply them to more difficult cases involving membership and interpersonal regret.

- **Case 1:** Jenny's father beats her whenever she does not please him. Eventually, Jenny finds the courage to move out and move on. However, she feels constant regret that she was unable to please her father.
- **Case 2:** Jack stands up for a female coworker who was sexually harassed. He puts himself on the line and testifies to witnessing the harassing actions. Since doing so, Jack has suffered serious career and social consequences and hence regrets helping his coworker.

Both of the cases above are instances where many would agree that regret is not the best response.[15] Let us try to analyze each in turn.

- **Case 1:** The object of the agent's regret (Jenny not pleasing her father) is *not* a moral failing.
  - There are no morally important changes to be made in the future. (Jenny is under no moral obligation to change her behavior.)
- **Case 2:** The object of the agent's regret (standing up for a coworker) is *not* a moral failing.
  - There are no morally important changes to be made in the future. (Jack is under no moral obligation to change his behavior.)

It should be noted that in both cases, the regret is directed toward a morally admirable action.

Earlier we identified morally worthy traits of regret, such as displaying respect toward wronged agents and serving as a motivational impetus for change. What the above cases of regret have in common is that their features are nearly the opposite of these. Rather than show respect, regret in these instances shows *disrespect*. Jenny's regret shows disrespect toward herself and her own self-worth. If Jenny had proper self-confidence, she would not regret her inability to please an overdemanding and immoral father. Jack's regret is disrespectful toward his female coworkers. Regret in this instance is a sign that he values his own career goals more than the proper treatment of his female colleagues.

Neither Jack nor Jenny is experiencing moral regret, and there is a common consequence to this similarity. Both of their types of regret *inhibit cooperative life with others*. Jenny's lack of self-respect, if a consistent problem, will make it harder for her to navigate life in a social community. She is unlikely to stand up for herself when the situation demands it, and because of this, she gives those with antisocial habits a willing victim. In Jack's case, it is even more obvious how his regret inhibits cooperative social life: Disrespecting your fellow community members is a detriment to a well-functioning communal life. All things considered, we can say this: *Reasonable regret promotes cooperative life, and unreasonable regret inhibits it.*

As long as we are understanding regret as a moral emotion, the above statement is not at all surprising. Moral psychology concerns how our emotions, attitudes, and mental states influence our moral lives, and under most understandings of morality, interactions with others are an important part of them. Cases of unreasonable or immoral regret seem to stem from two ways in which regret might serve to do nearly the *opposite* of moral regret. These cases can be identified by the following features:

- Regret does *not* display respect toward ourselves nor anyone else deserving.
- The object of regret is neither a moral nor a personal failing.

When we look at our exemplar cases, each has at least one of the above features. Jenny's regret, if it displays respect at all, displays it toward her undeserving father. This inability to please her father is not an objective failing of any sort. Her regret is hence not moral regret, although it is not necessarily immoral either.[16] Most people would probably look upon Jenny with sympathy. Even though her regret is not reasonable, it seems most of us would not blame her for feeling that way. We can contrast our hesitancy to blame Jenny with the much different attitude we may intuitively hold toward Jack. It appears that Jack *is* morally blameworthy and that his regret goes past the "not moral" line and into the *immoral* classification.

Both Jack and Jenny lack the moral-making features of regret, so we will have to dig deeper to understand why Jack's regret seems so much worse than Jenny's. One important distinction between them is that Jack's regret is directed not toward a morally neutral occasion but rather something that is either morally required or morally admirable. Jack not only gets things wrong: He gets things *completely backward*. The act he regrets is one that shows respect toward his female colleagues, and to regret showing respect is itself disrespectful in the most salient of ways. Jack's selfish motives show that he cares more about his own career than the safety of his female colleagues.

THE HARD CASES: MEMBERSHIP AND INTERPERSONAL REGRET

Regret via Proxy

From looking at the paradigm cases (both the good and the bad), we were able to glean a few key features of regret that contribute to its moral reasonableness:

- Moral regret is directed at a past moral wrong. Via regret, the agent acknowledges that a wrong was committed and that the person wronged was undeserving of this offense. This acknowledgment displays respect toward the wronged individual. (It is similar to saying, "You did not deserve to be treated that way.")
- Unreasonable or immoral regret is directed at a past event that is morally admirable or at least morally neutral. Via regretting something morally admirable, the agent is suggesting the moral act normatively should not have occurred.

Given the moral-making (and -unmaking) features now identified, we can turn to the tough cases involving group (membership) and relationship (interpersonal) regret. It might seem odd for people to regret the actions of a group because regret connotes responsibility and a group member might have had no involvement with the group's actions. Thus, if the member had no involvement, how could the individual in question be responsible? And if the member is not responsible, why would the person feel regret? Psychologists, however, have long recognized that group members can feel *guilt* for actions in which they had no part.[17] Because regret is similar to guilt, it should not be surprising that membership regret functions in a similar way as membership guilt. Let us return to our discussion earlier where I explained that *identification* allows for the ascription of personal responsibility. Regret is an emotion in which agents feel responsible not because (or not essentially because) they performed or took part in the regrettable action but because they identify with it in some way. For example, Mary might deeply regret that her university discriminated against women even if she herself has not experienced such discrimination.

Something similar to group regret occurs concerning individuals with whom we bear a close relationship. For example, if Jack's husband insults his friend, Jack might feel regret even though Jack was not the one who did the insulting. Because Jack's own identity is wrapped up in his husband's, he feels responsibility, and then regret, for something he did not do. Although membership regret and interpersonal regret are similar, I will discuss each in turn to emphasize the distinctions.

Membership Regret

Let us consider two different cases of membership regret and see how they fare when judged according to the moral-making features articulated earlier. Each example is a token of a type of group regret.

1. Jamie has been working at her university for over twenty years and deeply regrets its recent decision to deny admission to atheists.
2. Jack is an openly gay accountant and regrets that many in the gay community organize parades. He believes parades distract from the important truth that gay persons are just like everybody else.

Let us stipulate that the above agents experience the necessary phenomenology of regret. The cognitive component of regret is also met because we can suppose that each agent personally identifies with the relevant group. In the words of one social-psychological study, "The behaviors and attributes of other group members have implications for the self" (Lickel et al. 2005, 147). The strong way in which human beings connect to other members of the same group makes it possible for us to identify with group actions we have not been directly involved with. However, simply because regret is possible, it does not follow that regret is morally reasonable. To answer that question, let us recall regret's moral-making features:

- Regret displays respect toward the persons who were harmed or wronged.
- Regret serves as recognition that a past circumstance should not have occurred.

Jamie's regret seems straightforward and easily meets the demands of moral regret. She believes that the university's decision is a mistake, and her regret displays that recognition and is a sign of respect toward atheists. Her display of respect (via regret) is a small way of mitigating the disrespect displayed by the university. Her regret is also a recognition that the university should have acted differently. Hence, her regret includes both moral-making features.

The second example is perhaps more contentious. Whether Jack's regret is moral depends on whether his belief that pride events harm the gay community is reasonable, thereby representing a situation worthy of moral concern.

If his belief is not reasonable, Jack has real regret that is unreasonable and immoral. And there is an additional factor that makes this example controversial. For regret to be "real," an agent must identify with the party responsible for the object of the regret. Yet, sometimes people identify with a group that does not identify with them. This mismatch of identification does not change regret into another emotion. For instance, Max can be sad when his favorite professional athlete is injured even if Max really bears no actual relationship with the athlete. Perhaps his sadness is built on a psychological fabrication of a relationship, but it is still sadness. Likewise, Jack can feel regret over the gay community's behavior whether or not the community accepts him. However, if Jack is not part of the relevant gay community, his regret is likely unreasonable insofar as it is founded upon an unreasonable sense of identification.

Interpersonal Regret

We can regret the actions of an individual distinct from ourselves in a way similar to the way we regret the actions of a group. In both cases, identification makes the regret possible. While with group regret, identification comes via membership, with interpersonal regret, there is no membership but merely a sense of an interpersonal connection. We can turn back to social psychology to help us with this conceptual discussion. In the above case of membership regret, the identity involved is what social psychologists call a *shared identity*. Shared identity occurs when several persons share at least one common feature that each considers a deep part of their personal identities (Lickel et al. 2005). Catholics, for instance, share common features, and members of the Catholic church deeply identify with them. Interpersonal regret, on the other hand, does not involve a shared identity but rather *interpersonal independence*. Let me quote the work of Lickel et al. (2005, 148) to describe this unique type of collective identity:

> The degree to which individuals are perceived to have high levels of social interaction, possess joint goals, and have shared norms of behavior (e.g. Gaertner & Shopler, 1998; Hinsz, Tindale, & Vollrath, 1997; Lewin, 1948; Lickel et al., 2000; Rabbie & Horwitz, 1988; Wilder & Simon, 1998). An important aspect of interdependent associations is that the associated persons have the opportunity for shared communication and influence over one another's thoughts and behaviors.

With the above in mind, and having analyzed regret, perhaps we can now understand why what initially seems strange (regretting the actions of others) actually makes sense. Because we identify with those especially close to us (i.e., friends, family, etc.), we feel a sense of responsibility for their actions. When we are in very close communication with another, as Lickel et al. (2005, 148) note, we have "influence over one another's thoughts and behaviors."

It makes sense then that awareness of an interpersonal relation will cause us to regret another person's behavior: We know there is mutual influence between thoughts and actions, and hence we cannot help but identify with the regrettable act of a person with whom we share interpersonal interdependence. This is noticeable insofar as we express responsibility through apologies, the emotion of pride, and various social practices such as imposing blame and bestowing awards. People sometimes apologize for the actions of their children, their spouses, and even their parents. We also impose social blame on the parents, spouses, and children of "badly" behaving members of society. Moreover, it is common for a close relation to accept an award for an individual who is unable to do so. In such circumstances, there is social recognition that persons with close relationships can act on behalf of one another.[18] Regret for the actions of another falls under the same category of social practice. Consider, for instance, the following instances of regret:

- Janice regrets that her husband has evaded taxes.
- Eddie regrets that his best friend was rude to his mother.
- Amy regrets that her (adult) daughter has been arrested for shoplifting.

We can judge the reasonableness and morality of these instances of regret in the same fashion that we have judged group regret. The cases above qualify as actual regret as long as the agent (1) genuinely identifies with a relevant individual and (2) experiences the cognitive and emotional components of regret. Whether the regret is reasonable will depend on (1) whether it makes sense that the agent identifies with the relevant person and (2) whether the regret serves the purpose of displaying respect.

The reasonableness of regret can be seen as a spectrum where some cases clearly fall into the "okay" range and others hit a murky area. Whether Janice ought to identify with her husband depends on the nature of their relationship. If he tricked Janice into marriage and thus their relationship was established under false pretenses, identification makes less sense than if she went into the situation with eyes wide open.[19] Provided that identification does make sense, there is an obvious way in which regret for her husband's actions displays respect toward her fellow taxpayers. In such a situation, Janice recognizes that someone with whom she identifies has acted disrespectfully toward the community. She wishes that her husband had acted differently, that he had not shown such disrespect, and she recognizes that she has failed to influence him in the right sort of way. This form of recognition (wishing that her husband had acted respectfully and feeling regret over the situation) is itself a sign of respect toward those he has wronged. The role of regret is similar to an apology. In both cases (of apologizing and regretting), a certain act and/or expression serves to recognize a wrong and therein mitigate it. It makes sense for *me* to apologize when I wrong someone. It is not quite as reasonable, but it still makes sense, for my close relations to apologize on my behalf.[20] It is entirely unreasonable and makes little sense for strangers to apologize for me. (They do not bear the right type of relationship to the wrongdoer.) Similarly, the psychological experience of regret by a stranger (as opposed to a close relation) is unreasonable for the same reasons.

CONCLUSION

In this chapter, I have discussed the moral and normative implications of the emotion of regret. I started with two key assumptions. First, regret is an emotion with both psychological and cognitive content. Second, emotions can be both reasonable or unreasonable, moral or immoral. A key part of uncovering the normative content of regret is gaining an understanding of regret itself. Hence, this chapter began with such investigation. My aim was to arrive at a definition broad enough to fit the varied situations in which we use the term and garner the agreement of a wide class of individuals. Regret that is reasonable must be directed at past events that violated personal or moral norms; moreover, regret must display respect toward the persons wronged by such violations. While it is easier to observe these features in cases of regret that are intuitively reasonable, I showed how these moral-making features can be applied to more difficult cases involving membership regret and interpersonal regret. Indeed, in certain circumstances, it is both possible and reasonable for an agent to feel regret due to the actions of a group or an individual distinct from the agent herself.

NOTES

1. I will proceed as though all regret that is moral is reasonable, and because of this reasoning, I will often use the terms interchangeably. However, it is important to note that not all reasonable regret is moral or even fits that category. We can feel regret over failing to meet our personal goals (e.g., by failing to maintain a diet or publish a paper). Such regret could be reasonable without fitting into the category of morality. This chapter is mostly focused on moral regret, and the assumption will be I am discussing moral regret (which falls under the broader category of "reasonable") unless otherwise noted.

2. But what about moral disagreement among community members? A great deal of moral disagreement concerns dissent about factual issues. For instance, two

persons who disagree about abortion likely also disagree about whether the fetus is a person or the mother has other plausible alternatives. While there might remain some disagreement if all factual issues were resolved, there would be far less disagreement than we see today. In other words, there would be enough agreement to have clearer community standards than we see in many modern societies. When I talk about what is moral, I assume a community in which members are in epistemic alignment.

3. In the literature on the philosophy of emotions, many theorists divide themselves between cognitivist and noncognitivist lines. It seems uncontroversial to me, however, to conclude that those who believe emotions are primarily one or the other are off base and to assert that emotions involve both a cognitive (judgment) and noncognitive (phenomenological "feel") component. For my purposes, it is simply not necessary to delve into the discussion of which feature (cognitive or noncognitive) is more primary or whether one is the result of the other. For those interested in this debate, a good starting point is Johnson (2017).

4. Hampshire (1960) also emphasizes regret's demanding cognitive content when compared to other emotions (see especially pp. 240–2).

5. The series of experiment conducted by Zeelenberg et al. (2000) show that when an agent believed she had control over an outcome, she felt regret, but when she lacked this control, the emotion was closer to disappointment.

6. See Williams (2002, 27–33).

7. In the beginning of his discussion of regret, Williams describes a very lose sense of the emotion, stating that "states of affairs, (that) can be regretted, in principle, by anyone who knows of them." I think what Williams describes here is just the sad recognition that a past event was a misfortune; this does not seem like regret at all.

8. It is possible to describe a scenario in which Tom's regret is not unreasonable. For instance, if Tom felt regret for what McVeigh did specifically because both Tom and McVeigh are "Americans." In such a situation, Tom is identifying as an American and also identifies McVeigh as an American. There is hence a common link between them. However, in the scenario I provided, Tom is simply regretting McVeigh's actions as such, not as part of a group. Personal regret over the action of another is only reasonable when one bears a personal connection to the agent.

9. Gilovich and Medvec (1995) draw a nice picture of how guilt is morally laden in a way that regret is not. The psychological experiments of Zeelenberg, van der Pligt, and Manstead (1998) focused largely on *moral* regret and the role it plays in social interaction. The authors show that regret can motivate pro-social behaviors such as apologizing and harm mitigation. Considered together, these studies confirm my suggestion that guilt is of necessity concerned with morality, while regret can be a moral emotion but need not be.

10. See Aristotle (Book IV, chapters 5–14).

11. There are thousands of citations I might give to support the two claims I casually mentioned above (i.e., that emotions influence our behavior and are a part of moral life). Here, I offer just a sampling. For a general overview of the psychology of emotions and behavior, see Johnston and Olson (2015). For an overview of the role of emotions in philosophy, see Goldie (2014). For a more specific focus on emotions and *morality* in the psychological discipline, see Parrott (2001), and for the discipline of philosophy, see Bagnoli (2015). For the philosophy of moral psychology, see

Alfano (2016) and Nadelhoffer, Nahmias, and Nichols (2010). An informative book covering morality and the emotions from the combined perspective of neuroscience, psychology, and philosophy can be found in Sinnott-Armstrong (2008).

12. For a great introduction to the philosophy of emotions, see Johnson (2017).

13. There have been studies about the motivational import of regret in respect to rational choice theory going back to the 1980s. See, for example, Bell (1981, 1983, 1985) and Loome and Sugden (1987). More modern work on regret's impact on motivation includes Zeelenberg and Beattie (1997); Connolly and Zeelenberg (2002); Coricelli et al. (2005); Hayashi (2008); Khan Dhar, and Wertenbroch (2005); and Zinkevich et al. (2008). All these studies confirm (in various ways) that regret serves as a motivational impetus to change one's behavior in the future so as to avoid future regret.

14. Interestingly, the reverse appeared to be true with disappointment, that is, the *less* control an agent had over an outcome, the greater her disappointment (Zeelenberg et al. 2000, 12254). The authors note that the correlation between regret and control has been confirmed in studies by Frijda et al. (1989) and Van Dijk (1999).

15. Of course, not *everyone* will agree. My argument is meant for those who do agree. From this agreement, we can move forward and identify the features of each that explain these moral problems.

16. By "not moral," I mean something like "not morally admirable" or "not morally advisable." One might argue that it is "moral" in the sense that *she herself* believes she did something wrong. However, this is a moral mistake and so is not something that would be "morally advised."

17. To cite only a sample of scholarly work by psychologists on membership guilt, see Branscombe and Doosje (2004); Doosje et al. (2006), Lickel et al. (2005, 2011); and Wohl, Branscombe, and Klar (2006). On the philosophical side of things, Gilbert (1997, 2002) has written about a distinct but related phenomenon. However, Gilbert focuses on how the group itself feels guilty as opposed to group members. Nonetheless, guilt felt by individual group members is discussed.

18. See Priest (2016).

19. It depends, of course, on what the pretense is. Persons working in the Central Intelligence Agency could tell a lot of lies to protect their identities while still "being themselves." It is only when people truly hide who they are as individuals that identification becomes a pretense.

20. Again, see Priest (2016).

REFERENCES

Alfano, Mark. 2016. *Moral Psychology: An Introduction*. Cambridge: Polity.
Bagnoli, Carla. 2015. *Morality and the Emotions*. Oxford: Oxford University Press.
Baskin-Sommers, Arielle, Allison M. Stuppy-Sullivan, and Joshua W. Buckholtz. 2016. "Psychopathic Individuals Exhibit but Do Not Avoid Regret during Counterfactual Decision Making." *Proceedings of the National Academy of Sciences* 113 (50): 14438–43. doi: 10.1073/pnas.1609985113.

Bell, David E. 1981. "Components of Risk Aversion." In *Operational Research*, ed. J-P Brans, vol. 8, 371–78. Amsterdam: North-Holland.
Bell, David E. 1982. "Regret in Decision Making under Uncertainty." *Operations Research* 30 (5): 961–81. doi: 10.1287/opre.30.5.961.
Bell, David E. 1983. "Risk Premiums for Decision Regret." *Management Science* 29 (10): 1156–66. doi: 10.1287/mnsc.29.10.1156.
Bell, David E. 1985. "Putting a Premium on Regret," *Management Science* 31: 117–20.
Branscombe, Nyla R., and Bertjan Doosje. 2004. *Collective Guilt: International Perspectives*. Cambridge: Cambridge University Press.
Camille, Nathalie, Giorgio Coricelli, Jerome Sallet, Pascale Pradat-Diehl, Jean-René Duhamel, and Angela Sirigu. 2004. "The Involvement of the Orbitofrontal Cortex in the Experience of Regret." *Science* 304 (5674): 1167–70.
Connolly, Terry, and Marcel Zeelenberg. 2002. "Regret in Decision Making." *Current Directions in Psychological Science* 11 (6): 212–16.
Coricelli, Giorgio, Hugo D. Critchley, Mateus Joffily, John P. O'Doherty, Angela Sirigu, and Raymond J. Dolan. 2005. "Regret and Its Avoidance: A Neuroimaging Study of Choice Behavior." *Nature Neuroscience* 8 (9): 1255–62.
Doosje, Bertjan E. J., Nyla R. Branscombe, Russell Spears, and Antony S. R. Manstead. 2006. "Antecedents and Consequences of Group-Based Guilt: The Effects of Ingroup Identification." *Group Processes & Intergroup Relations* 9 (3): 325–38.
Frijda, Nico H., Peter Kuipers, and Elisabeth Ter Schure. 1989. "Relations among Emotion, Appraisal, and Emotional Action Readiness." *Journal of Personality and Social Psychology* 57 (2): 212.
Frijda, Nico H., Peter Kuipers, and Elisabeth Ter Schure. 2002. "Collective Guilt and Collective Guilt Feelings." *Journal of Ethics* 6 (2): 115–43.
Gilbert, Margaret. 1997. "Group Wrongs and Guilt Feelings." *Journal of Ethics* 1 (1): 65–84.
Gilbert, M. 2002. "Collective Guilt and Collective Guilt Feelings." *Journal of Ethics: An International Philosophical Review* 6 (2): 115–43.
Gilovich, Thomas, and Victoria Husted Medvec. 1995. "The Experience of Regret: What, When, and Why." *Psychological Review* 102 (2): 379.
Goldie, Peter. 2014. *The Oxford Handbook of Philosophy of Emotion*. Oxford: Oxford University Press.
Hampshire, Stuart. 1960. *Thought and Action*. London: Chatto-Windus.
Hax, Carolyn. 2017. "Advice." *Washington Post*, June 3. Accessed June 19, 2017. https://www.washingtonpost.com/lifestyle/style/carolyn-hax-bully-feels-regret-for-lashing-out-at-tormentor/2017/05/31/d38cbaf8-4261-11e7-adba-394ee67a7582_story.html?utm_term=.23876818959b.
Hayashi, Takashi. 2008. "Regret Aversion and Opportunity Dependence." *Journal of Economic Theory* 139 (1): 242–68.
Johnson, Gregory. n.d. "Theories of Emotion." Internet Encyclopedia of Philosophy. Accessed June 27, 2017, from http://www.iep.utm.edu/emotion/#H3.
Johnston, Elizabeth, and Leah Olson. 2015. *The Feeling Brain: The Biology and Psychology of Emotions*. New York: W. W. Norton.

Khan, Uzma, Ravi Dhar, and Klaus Wertenbroch. 2005. "A Behavioral Decision Theory Perspective on Hedonic and Utilitarian Choice." *Inside Consumption: Frontiers of Research on Consumer Motives, Goals, and Desires*, 144–65.
Lickel, Brian, Rachel R. Steele, and Toni Schmader. 2011. "Group-Based Shame and Guilt: Emerging Directions in Research." *Social and Personality Psychology Compass* 5 (3): 153–63.
Lickel, Brian, Toni Schmader, Mathew Curtis, Marchelle Scarnier, and Daniel R. Ames. 2005. "Vicarious Shame and Guilt." *Group Processes & Intergroup Relations* 8 (2): 145–57.
Nadelhoffer, Thomas, Eddy A. Nahmias, and Shaun Nichols. 2010. *Moral Psychology: Historical and Contemporary Readings*. Malden, MA: Wiley-Blackwell.
Parrott, W. Gerrod. 2001. *Emotions in Social Psychology: Essential Readings*. Philadelphia, PA: Psychology Press.
Priest, Maura. 2016. "Blame after Forgiveness." *Ethical Theory and Moral Practice* 19 (3): 619–33.
Rorty, Amelie. 1980. "Agent Regret." In *Explaining Emotions*, ed. Amelie Rorty, 489–506. Berkeley: University of California Press.
Schechtman, M. 1996. *The Constitution of Selves*. Ithaca, NY: Cornell University Press.
Sinnott-Armstrong, Walter. 2008. *Moral Psychology: Emotion, Brain Disorders, and Development*. Cambridge: MIT Press.
Van Dijk, W. 1999. "Dashed Hopes and Shattered Dreams: On the Psychology of Disappointment." PhD diss., University of Amsterdam.
Williams, Bernard. 2002. *Moral Luck: Philosophical Papers, 1973–1980*. Cambridge: Cambridge University Press.
Wohl, Michael J. A., Nyla R. Branscombe, and Yechiel Klar. 2006. "Collective Guilt: Emotional Reactions When One's Group Has Done Wrong or Been Wronged." *European Review of Social Psychology* 17 (1): 1–37.
Zeelenberg, Marcel, and Jane Beattie. 1997. "Consequences of Regret Aversion 2: Additional Evidence for Effects of Feedback on Decision Making." *Organizational Behavior and Human Decision Processes* 72 (1): 63–78.
Zeelenberg, Marcel, Joop van der Pligt, and Antony S. R. Manstead. 1998. "Undoing Regret on Dutch Television: Apologizing for Interpersonal Regrets Involving Actions or Inactions." *Personality and Social Psychology Bulletin* 24 (10): 1113–19.
Zeelenberg, Marcel, Wilco W. van Dijk, Antony S. R. Manstead, and Joop van der Pligt. 2000. "On Bad Decisions and Disconfirmed Expectancies: The Psychology of Regret and Disappointment." *Cognition & Emotion* 14 (4): 521–41.
Zinkevich, Martin, Michael Johanson, Michael H. Bowling, and Carmelo Piccione. "Regret Minimization in Games with Incomplete Information." In: *Advances in Neural Information Processing Systems 20, Proceedings of the Twenty-First Annual Conference on Neural Information Processing Systems*, Vancouver, British Columbia, Canada, December 3–6, 2007. 2007, pp. 1729–36. http://papers.nips.cc/paper/3306-regret-minimization-in-gameswith-incomplete-information.

Part II

REGRET AND THE SELF

Chapter 5

Remorse

David Batho

REMORSE AND REPARATION

How do we live with the things we have done? For many regrets, consolation can be reached through acts of reparation. If I regret spending too much money last year, I might be consoled by the amount of money I was able to save this year, having learned my lesson. If you feel guilty for having broken my jug, you might feel better for having bought me a replacement. It is difficult to figure out how exactly to make amends. It could also be that reparation is out of reach. My lost investment may never be recovered; you might never come to find a suitable jug. Nevertheless, the possibility of reparation is at least conceivable for many regrets, by which we should expect to ease the pain.

This point is sometimes taken as obvious. In a recent article, for example, Byron Williston argues that before you ask for forgiveness, you owe it to those you have wronged to forswear "self-directed negative attitudes like contempt, anger, and hatred, attitudes generated by an agent's belief in her own moral failing" (Williston 2012, 67). To do so, Williston argues, you must submit to a thorough overhaul of your capacity for right action, so as to repair the fault that generates these attitudes. To be sure, this is not plain sailing. But he holds that reformation of character is part of making amends. And he claims that in this way we can get over the pain of what we have done. He therefore presumes that self-directed negative attitudes can be consoled through acts of reparation, however hard the slog. What about remorse?

It is sometimes taken for granted that remorse and reparation are closely connected. Writing in a volume entitled *Remorse and Reparation*, for example, Douglas Cairns claims that remorse is "a species of regret over actions . . . whose damage one would undo if one could. It thus has a natural association with the desire to make reparation" (Cairns 1999, 172). A similar intuition is also at play in many jurisdictions, where the absence of remorse can be taken as an aggravating factor in sentencing. Consider the following representative case, reported in the *Financial Times*:

> In the autumn of 2000, Robert Bierenbaum sat motionless and silent at his trial for the murder of his wife, Gail Katz-Bierenbaum. She had disappeared from the couple's New York apartment in the summer of 1985, though no body has ever been recovered. [. . .] [In] 2000, Bierenbaum was convicted of murder. [. . .] "I can only look at the defendant's cold-blooded behaviour after the fact," the judge said. "He is not rehabilitated—which means accepting, admitting and expressing remorse. Only then can one expiate guilt." (Apostle 2010)

We might interpret the judge's rationale as follows. The offender should seek to heal the social wound caused by his wrongdoing by attempting rehabilitation. Remorse is part of this process. By failing to express remorse, the judge surmises, Bierenbaum showed that he had not begun rehabilitation and so deserved a harsher sentence. Here, as with Cairns, remorse is held to have a close relationship with making amends.

But rehabilitation is one thing and consolation quite another. Our question is not whether the expression of remorse is necessary for reparation but whether remorse can be consoled through acts of reparation. The judge's sentence leaves the question unanswered. Perhaps remorse can *expiate* guilt, where that means paying dues. But that tells us nothing about how the offender will feel after all is said and done. Similarly, perhaps Cairns is right that remorse constitutively involves a *desire* for reparation, but that tells us nothing about how remorse will be affected, if at all, by the satisfaction of that desire. Should we expect the pain of remorse to be lifted by making amends?[1]

There is some prima facie etymological evidence to suggest not. Remorse derives from the Classical Latin *remordēre*, which could be literally translated as to bite (*mordēre*) again (*re-*). The OED suggests "to vex persistently" as a gloss. The image invoked, of a figure biting over and again, chimes with Adam Smith's treatment of this "moral sentiment":

> The thought of [the remorseful person's actions] perpetually haunts him, and fills him with terror and amazement. He dares no longer look society in the face, but imagines himself as it were rejected, and thrown out from the affections of all mankind. He cannot hope for the consolation of sympathy in this his greatest and most dreadful distress. The remembrance of his crimes has shut out all fellow-feeling with him from the hearts of his fellow-creatures. The sentiments which they entertain with regard to him, are the very thing which he is most afraid of. Everything seems hostile, and he would be glad to fly to some inhospitable desert, where he might never more behold the face of a human creature, nor read in the countenance of mankind the condemnation of his crimes. But

solitude is still more dreadful than society. His own thoughts can present him with nothing but what is black, unfortunate, and disastrous, the melancholy forebodings of incomprehensible misery and ruin. The horror of solitude drives him back into society, and he comes again into the presence of mankind, astonished to appear before them, loaded with shame and distracted with fear, in order to supplicate some little protection from the countenance of those very judges, who he knows have already all unanimously condemned him. Such is the nature of that sentiment, which is properly called remorse; of all the sentiments which can enter the human breast the most dreadful. (Smith 1999/1759, 99)

As Smith has it, then, the person who suffers remorse is *perpetually* haunted by what he has done. The pain of being with others whips the agent into solitude, whereupon he finds himself alone with his unremittingly dark thoughts and in response to which he is driven back to society. Since society appears to him no less hostile than before, however, he is once more pushed into solitude. And so the cycle continues.

Smith thus presents remorse as something of an interminable oscillation between pain before others and pain before oneself. On this view, we have reason to doubt whether remorse is the sort of thing that could be consoled through acts of reparation. Indeed, we might even doubt whether remorse can be consoled at all, irrespective of the means. For, on Smith's view, the remorseful agent understands himself to be *ruined*, that is, fallen beyond repair. In this connection, Raimond Gaita remarks, "We are perfectly familiar with the fact that a person might commit suicide because she became a murderer" (Gaita 2004, 51).

How, then, do we live with the things we have done if they are of the sort to occasion remorse? In what follows I shall be arguing that remorse cannot be overcome through acts of reparation. That may seem a rather depressing conclusion, but I shall not offer counsel of despair. If remorse cannot be overcome by acts of reparation, it does not follow that there is no other way in which it might be consoled. Rather, the distinctive character of remorse invites reflection on whether there is a distinctive form of consolation attached to it. In closing, I shall sound out a proposal for just this sort of consolation, though I leave it for another occasion to thrash out the details.

I proceed as follows. In §II–IV, I develop an account of remorse. I take my orientation from Raimond Gaita's rich discussion of the phenomenon. I draw out some problems with his account and suggest some ways beyond them. I argue that remorse is the pained acknowledgment of something as irreducibly valuable through the shock of having violated it and the pained acknowledgment of having become a wrongdoer through this action. In §V, I ask whether remorse is consolable through reparation. I argue that since each aspect of remorse involves acknowledgment of an irreparable harm as such, it cannot be overcome through acts of reparation. This raises the question of whether remorse might be consoled in any other way. In §VI I turn to Kierkegaard to sketch a possible alternative, which I shall call *palliative* consolation.

RAIMOND GAITA

Remorse has been subject to relatively little discussion in Anglophone philosophy. This is striking, especially considering how much attention has been paid to guilt and shame. Besides the few articles scattered across journals and decades apart, the most sustained treatment of the phenomenon is to be found in Raimond Gaita's *Good and Evil: An Absolute Conception*.[2] Since Gaita's account is the most developed on offer and at any rate of great interest, I take my orientation from his remarks.

Gaita argues that remorse has two faces, one directed toward the wrong done, the other directed toward the wrongdoer. More specifically, he argues that remorse is the pained acknowledgment of the preciousness of another person through the shock of having wronged her and the pained acknowledgement of what one has suffered through having acted in this way (Gaita 2004, 52). He develops his analysis around the testimony of a woman interviewed in the documentary series *The World at War*:

> A Dutch woman was interviewed in an episode on the Nazi concentration camps. She had given shelter to three Jews fleeing the Nazis, but after some days she asked them to leave because she was involved in a plot to assassinate Hitler and judged that it would be at risk if she were caught sheltering Jews. Within days of leaving her house the three were murdered in a concentration camp. She said Hitler had made a murderess of her, that she hated him for many things but most of all for that. (Gaita 2004, 43)

Gaita takes the Dutch woman's testimony to be authoritative; he finds her to be unsentimental.[3] For this reason, he supposes that we can learn a great deal from her expressions of remorse. In particular, he supposes that in understanding remorse we would do well to make sense of her claim to have hated Hitler most of all for having made a murderess of her. How are we to understand this claim?

On one way of looking at it, the Dutch woman might appear to be claiming to find no difference between her actions and those of an SS guard. After all, she claims to have been made into a murderess. If this is what she meant, however, then we would have reason to doubt the authority of her testimony. There is plainly a great deal of difference between her actions and those of an executioner. No court of law would hold her to account for the crimes committed by those who rounded up and murdered the family she turned away.

If we are to hold on to the authority of her testimony, we shall have to find some other way of understanding her remarks.

Gaita claims that it is rather too literal-minded to think that the Dutch woman was claiming to be no different from a Nazi executioner (Gaita 2004, 43). He has a point. I might describe myself as child, without meaning that I see no difference between myself and a child. I might only mean to convey that I acted immaturely. You might describe yourself as a criminal in full knowledge that you are guilty of no actual crime, if only to put across your sense of guilt. Similarly, Gaita argues, we should not suppose that the Dutch woman is claiming that her actions are morally equivalent to those of a murderer. Rather, we should take her to be conveying her sense of the seriousness of her actions.

It is important for Gaita that in conveying her sense of the seriousness of her actions the woman need not take herself to be blameworthy. "We can say that *a person is morally responsible for what may claim her and us in one of the many forms of serious and lucid moral response*" (Gaita 2004, 45). To be sure, a guilty sense of one's own culpability is a sort of "lucid moral response." But so is remorse, which Gaita argues need not involve a sense of one's own blameworthiness. We can imagine the Dutch woman grimly accepting that she acted just as she should have done in the given circumstances, while nonetheless feeling remorse over her actions. In this respect, her case is close to another. Sophie Zawistowska, the eponymous protagonist of William Styron's (1979) *Sophie's Choice*, finds herself forced to choose which of her two children is to be taken from her and murdered. She is told that if she refuses to choose between them, both children will be killed. Panicked, she hands her daughter away. It would obviously be inappropriate to blame Sophie, as though the fault lay with her. We might even suppose that Sophie would not blame herself, as if she could conceive of a better way of acting in the given circumstances. But we find it readily intelligible that she would be haunted by remorse for the rest of her life in light of what she has done.[4]

According to Gaita, then, the Dutch woman is expressing her sense of the severity of her action but not that she is blameworthy for what she has done. What exactly is she acknowledging, then, in expressing her remorse? Gaita holds that in remorse we acknowledge the reality of another person through the shock of having wronged her as well as who we have become through acting in this way (Gaita 2004, 52). Let us take each aspect in turn.

Suppose that you are walking down the street in a horrible mood. A homeless person approaches you, asking for money. Unthinkingly, you reach out your arm as though to bat his attention aside. But you accidentally strike the man, knocking him to the ground, which causes a fatal head injury. You did not intend to kill this man; you did not even intend to hit him. And yet the action is liable to occasion remorse. In this example, remorse *dispels* the mood that masked the reality of the other person, of which you are newly aware through having caused his death.[5] This point is made vivid in Coleridge's (1999/1798) *Rime of the Ancient Mariner*. Having shot dead an albatross that had accompanied his crew on its voyage, the mariner cannot escape the reality of the bird: the crew hang its corpse around his neck in place of a crucifix.[6] In this connection, we might also think of Ilya Repin's *Ivan the Terrible and His Son Ivan*. In a fit of rage, the elder Ivan has killed the younger. In light of what he has done, his eyes are now wide, newly open to reality, as he clings to the body of his son.

But why should the acknowledgment of the *reality* of another person occasion remorse? We acknowledge the reality of bacteria in and through the act of taking antibiotics, but no one feels remorse for taking their medication. Gaita argues that it is not simply the reality of others that is acknowledged in remorse but rather the irreducible *preciousness* of human beings (Gaita 2013, 4). He is a little embarrassed about the use of this word; at times, he reverts to the sterner Kantian language of duty and dignity when that seems more appropriate (Gaita 2013, p. xxii). His point, however, is that human beings are valuable in and of themselves, unconditionally, which value we can lose sight of but which we can come to recognize in remorse.

It is important for Gaita that the recognition of the preciousness of the other person is retrospective. Since it is *through* wrongdoing that one comes to realize the significance of one's action, the awareness of their preciousness comes too late.[7] Gaita is not the first to have claimed that remorse is a form of recollective acknowledgment. Laurel Fulkerson uses "remorse" to translate Aristotle's term "metameleia," which might be more literally translated as "after-care" (Fulkerson 2004, 2013).[8] In his discussion of remorse, Vladimir Jankélévitch notes that "the sinner did not know, at the moment of *doing*, that there were so many riches, and just as many adventures, in his decision, he did not suspect that the most massive works are born, so to speak, from such a simple seed" (Jankélévitch 2015/1933, 104). In this, Jankélévitch is self-consciously following the psychologist Vigilius Haufniensis, who draws out a similar point in his discussion of the Genesis narrative.[9] Adam's fall is precipitated by eating the forbidden fruit of the Tree of Knowledge, by which act he gains knowledge of good and evil. Haufniensis points out that since the ability to understand the significance of God's prohibition presupposes knowledge of good and evil, Adam could only understand what he was doing after he had done it (see Kierkegaard 1980/1844, 25ff). The Genesis narrative thus presents a primeval form of the structure that Gaita finds in remorse: the consciousness of the significance of the act is acknowledged in hindsight as a result of the action.[10]

Gaita argues, then, that in her remorse the Dutch woman is recollectively acknowledging the preciousness of those she has wronged, through the shock of having wronged them. This is only half of the story, however, since he also claims that remorse involves acknowledging who one has become. He does not say much about this; he claims that remorse involves acknowledging oneself to have become a wrongdoer (Gaita 2004, 50) and thus to have suffered evil (Gaita 2004, 65). He is, however, not alone in having noted this aspect of remorse. Max Scheler approvingly quotes Schopenhauer making this point:

> Schopenhauer in particular used to stress that the deepest state of repentance is not expressed in the formula "Alas! what have I done?" but in the more radical "Alas! what kind of a person I am!" (Scheler 1987/1954, 101–2)

We have already seen that Adam Smith agrees. According to him, the remorseful person finds himself in a state of "incomprehensible misery and ruin."

The experience of having become a wrongdoer, so presented, is somewhat different to experiencing oneself to have done something wrong. I might experience a minor moral wobble on recounting a misdemeanor. I might even take a sort of spicy pride in my predilection for misbehavior. The experience of having become a wrongdoer that Smith and Scheler have in view and to which Gaita is referring, however, lends itself to language of ruin, destitution, and to-the-roots corruption. The remorseful experience of having become a wrongdoer, as Smith and others present it, is the experience of having somehow destroyed yourself by your own hand rather than merely cognizing that you have done something wrong. Much more could be said to draw into view the self-directed aspect of remorse. I shall develop an account of this below. For now, however, it is sufficient to note that for Gaita—along with Schopenhauer, Scheler, and Smith—remorse also involves understanding oneself to have become a wrongdoer in the severe sense just outlined.

In sum, then, Gaita argues that remorse is a lucid moral response in which the agent is confronted with the severity of her actions, both regarding the nature of the violation and the consequences for herself. Remorse should not be confused with a guilty sense of culpability. According to Gaita's account, remorse may involve guilt—if one is blameworthy—but it need not, since blameworthiness is not the only form of complicity in evil. Rather, Gaita argues that remorse involves the recollective acknowledgment of the preciousness of another person through having wronged her and the acknowledgment of having become a wrongdoer, having ruined oneself, through having acted in this way. But need we accept Gaita's position? In the next section, I raise some issues with the account we have just sketched.

ST. AUGUSTINE

Borrowing Arendt's phrase, Gaita thinks that remorse shows us that there is "goodness beyond virtue" (Gaita 2004, 200). By this he means that remorse discloses the real preciousness of other human beings, which preciousness cannot be accounted for in terms of their relative worth. In remorse, Gaita argues, we find ourselves confronted by the preciousness of a particular human being. This claim is tendentious. Where Gaita sees the perception of human preciousness that transcends comparable worth, others may find a case of an obviously Christian moral interpretation of an unchristian amoral reality in need of a timely debunking.[11,12]

In this chapter, I aim to describe remorse as it is experienced. I do not intend to take sides on the question of its value. For this reason, I shall "bracket" the question of whether things are as remorse presents them to be; I am concerned to elaborate how the individual and her world appear to person who experiences remorse, not to assess its credentials. The account I develop below should be insulated from the more contentious aspects of Gaita's position, then, since I leave it open that remorse is ripe for revaluation. With that in mind, might we find any other reason to challenge Gaita's account, irrespective of whether he is right to think that remorse is a way of encountering goodness beyond virtue?

As we have seen, Gaita develops his position around the analysis of what he takes to be the authoritative testimony of the Dutch woman. To put pressure on Gaita's account, I follow suit and call upon further testimony. The following passage is taken from Augustine's *Confessions*, in which he describes an incident from his youth:

> There was a pear tree near our vineyard laden with fruit, though attractive in neither colour nor taste. To shake the fruit off the tree and carry off the pears, I and a gang of naughty adolescents set off late at night [. . .]. We carried off a huge load of pears. But they were not for our feasts but merely to throw to the pigs. Even if we ate a few, nevertheless our pleasure lay in doing what was not allowed.
>
> Such was my heart, O God, such was my heart. You had pity on it when it was at the bottom of the abyss. Now let my heart tell you what it was seeking there in that I became evil for no reason. I had no motive for my wickedness except wickedness itself. It was foul, and I loved it. I loved the self-destruction, I loved my fall, not the object for which I had fallen but my fall itself. My depraved soul leaped down from your firmament to ruin. I was seeking not to gain anything by shameful means, but shame for its own sake. (Augustine 1998, 123–4)

Augustine, I submit, felt remorse over scrumping. He felt compelled to repent his action before God, which action he found to be wicked and expressive of a heart that lay "at the bottom of the abyss." Moreover, Augustine claims that he suffered from a "lack of any sense of, or feeling for, justice" such that the wickedness of the act was only acknowledged in hindsight. Although he was capable of recognizing that theft was prohibited, since he lacked any sense for justice at the time of the theft, he was in no position to recognize the significance of transgressing the prohibition. Finally, Augustine acknowledges having become evil through his action, through which deed he hurled himself from "firmament to ruin."

It is not difficult to see the uncanny similarity between Augustine's story and the Genesis narrative. In both cases, the consciousness of sin is precipitated by the consumption of forbidden fruit. And in both cases, the significance of the act is acknowledged only in recollection. In these respects, Augustine's testimony also parallels Gaita's remarks. Given Gaita's analysis, we should expect authoritative testimony of remorse to express pained acknowledgment of the significance of a misdeed, whose acknowledgment is achieved in hindsight. We should also expect to find an acknowledgment of having become a wrongdoer. This is just what we find in *Confessions*: Augustine says, "I became to myself a region of destitution" (1998, 135). To that degree, Augustine's testimony lends support to most of the central claims of Gaita's analysis. Augustine's confession also takes us beyond Gaita's account, however, since Augustine makes no direct reference to having wronged another person.

If we take Augustine's word for it—and we should do so, if we are taking his testimony as at least as authoritative as the Dutch woman's—then he is pained because he acted out of desire to do what was not allowed.[13] To be sure, we can imagine that someone was wronged by Augustine's action. Perhaps the owner of the pears could not make enough money at the market to buy enough food to feed his family. We can also imagine that someone might have felt remorse about that, perhaps upon the discovery of the consequences of his actions. We would not, however, be imagining Augustine. If Augustine's remorse had been occasioned by the recognition of having wronged the orchard owner, we should expect to find some reference to it in his confession.

In light of Gaita's account of remorse, this is something of a mystery. For we have a putative example of remorse presented in authoritative testimony that does not appear to involve the disclosure of the reality of another person through the shock of having wronged her. Where Gaita even finds it absurd that someone might feel remorse over having violated the moral law (Gaita 2013, 32), Augustine is apparently declaring just that: he recognizes that he did what was not allowed and took pleasure in it.

Augustine, then, expresses remorse without claiming to have wronged another person and seemingly in acknowledgment of having violated the moral law. But read on. For it is not just a formal moral law of the Kantian sort that Augustine realizes he has violated, it is *God's* law, handed down as an act of love. In light of that fact, it is not so much the transgression of a law that Augustine is responding to but his refusal of God's love:

> Yet sin is committed [...] when, in consequence of an immoderate urge towards those things which are at the bottom end of the scale of good, we abandon the higher and supreme goods, that is you, Lord God, and your truth and your law (Ps. 118: 142). These inferior goods have their delights, but not comparable to my God who has made them all. It is in him that the just person takes delight; he is the joy of those who are true of heart (Ps. 63: 11). (Augustine 1998, 125)

Augustine acknowledges that his sin was a consequence of having abandoned God, the highest and supreme good, whose love is the source of value: "I went astray from you (Ps. 118: 76), my God" (1998, 135). What should we make of this?

We have seen that there is substantial overlap between Augustine's testimony and Gaita's account. This gives us some motivation to see how much we can preserve of the latter in accounting for the former. But there is also a significant disagreement. This gives us motivation to further develop Gaita's account, so as to explain the discrepancy. Gaita claims that remorse involves the acknowledgment of the preciousness of another human being through the shock of having wronged her. Augustine's confession makes at most only indirect reference to having wronged another human being. Whatever drives his remorse, it is not in the first instance the recognition of having harmed another person. He does, however, express pain over having abandoned God, the irreducibly valuable source of all value whose law is a gift of love to those in need of it. That suggests that Gaita is simply too specific in claiming that remorse is a response to having harmed other human beings. It would have been better if he had said, more broadly, that remorse is an acknowledgment of something as irreducibly valuable through the act of having violated it.

If we hold that remorse is the recollective acknowledgment of something as irreducibly valuable, then we have an account that is neutral enough to allow for wide variation between irreducibly valuable beings—encompassing the Dutch woman's remorse over having turned away the family, Augustine's remorse over having abandoned God, and indeed the mariner's remorse over having shot and killed an albatross—but not so broad as to allow for remorse over having taken your medicine (*ceteris paribus*). Bacteria is rarely, if ever, acknowledged as irreducibly valuable and for that reason hardly, if at all, experienced as an object of remorse. We have, then, a way of extending Gaita's account so as to make sense of Augustine's testimony. The suggestion is modest enough but nonetheless significant: it is not only humans who can be experienced as irreducibly valuable, so remorse is not necessarily a response to having wronged another person.

So far, I have suggested a way to develop Gaita's account of the other-facing side of remorse: it is the acknowledgment of something as irreducibly valuable through the shock of having violated it. But what of the self-facing side of remorse? To recall, Gaita claims that in feeling remorse we acknowledge ourselves to have become wrongdoers. Scheler, Schopenhauer, and Smith agree and suggest a gloss: to acknowledge yourself to have become a wrongdoer is to acknowledge yourself to have ruined yourself. Augustine's testimony also falls in line: in his confession, he acknowledges that he has become evil. This contention is further supported by Jankélévitch, who has a similar sense of the severity of the evil suffered. According to him, the remorseful person is liable to exclaim "how will [. . .] our will ever be forgiven? When will we learn again to say Amen?" (Jankélévitch 2015/1933, 108). For Jankélévitch, the remorseful person experiences herself to have suffered a catastrophe, akin to losing the capacity to pray, from which it is unclear how she might recover. For our purposes, this need be all we emphasize for now: remorse involves understanding oneself to have become a wrongdoer. I shall not challenge that point. This leaves us with a rather thin conception of this important aspect of remorse, however. In the next section, I will develop an account of this side of remorse, so as to draw the phenomenon more fully into view. Since all we need to accept is that remorse involves having ruined oneself, no matter how we spell this out, I emphasize that when it comes to our primary aim, nothing rides on whether we accept the description I develop below.

RUINATION

To begin with, we can note that the experience of having become a wrongdoer is more temporally complex than the experience of simply being a wrongdoer. If you experience yourself to be a wrongdoer, you might also experience yourself to have always been a wrongdoer. To experience yourself to have *become* a wrongdoer, however, you must experience yourself not always to have been a wrongdoer. The experience of having become a wrongdoer, then, is an experience of having made a transition. It thus involves understanding oneself to be located in time in a particular way.

Jankélévitch describes this transition as follows: "to have remorse is [. . .] to have been able to do it or not do it [. . .] we were able to do all, and we have debased everything" (Jankélévitch 2015/1933, 108). Granted that no one is determined to become a wrongdoer, however unlikely it is to avoid the possibility, it follows that it was once possible to not become a wrongdoer.

To experience yourself to have become a wrongdoer, Jankélévitch is claiming, is to experience yourself to have lost the possibility of not becoming a wrongdoer. Rather, as the death of a friend leaves the world as a whole seeming as though it has been stripped of a layer, similarly the loss of the possibility of not becoming a wrongdoer transforms the appearance of the world as a whole. *Everything* is changed, according to Jankélévitch, because *nothing* offers a way of retrieving the possibility that has been lost.[14] If this is right, however, then as well as relating the individual to the present and past in a particular way, remorse also distinctly orients the individual toward the future: the future is understood to lack a possibility that was open in the past. On this account, then, the self-facing side of remorse is temporally complex, since the individual finds herself in a present heading toward a future that lacks a possibility that was open in the past but cannot be retrieved.

But there are wrongdoers and then there are wrongdoers. By this, I mean to emphasize that remorse does not involve the awareness of being simply a wrongdoer but also being a wrongdoer of a certain sort. Lady Macbeth, for example, acknowledged having become a *murderer*, as did the Dutch woman. Others might acknowledge having become cheats, liars, drunks, and so on. To acknowledge oneself to have become a wrongdoer, then, is to acknowledge oneself to have lost *two* possibilities: first, to have lost the ability to avoid becoming a wrongdoer *simpliciter*; second, to have lost the ability to avoid becoming the specific sort of wrongdoer that you have become.

This has an important implication. If the subject-facing side of remorse were nothing more than the acknowledgment of having become a wrongdoer simpliciter, there would be no future possibility of becoming a wrongdoer again. Having already become a wrongdoer, you would experience your future as lacking the possibilities of both avoiding and becoming a wrongdoer. But since the acknowledgment of having become a wrongdoer also involves the awareness of having become a specific sort of wrongdoer, it also involves an intimation of the possibility of realizing indefinitely many different wrongdoings and thereby becoming indefinitely many different sorts of wrongdoer. The future of the remorseful individual is not only experienced as lacking a possibility for innocence, then, but as containing a *minefield* of further possibilities for evil, the realization of which might occasion remorse. To recall, however, remorse involves acknowledging the significance of a wrongdoing through having done it. It therefore involves the awareness of having been blind to what you were doing until after the fact. The metaphor of the minefield is doubly apt, then, since you are aware not only of the possibility of further ruin but the possibility that you might stumble into it through a kind of moral somnambulism.

Consideration of Schopenhauer and Scheler's presentation of the distinctive expressions of remorse suggests a further complication. As we have seen, Scheler quotes Schopenhauer as claiming that remorse is liable to be expressed in a statement such as "Alas! what kind of a person am I?"' Other characteristic expressions of remorse include "who have I become?" or "how could I have done this?" In each case, the individual is expressing that she has become opaque to herself. Somehow, the experience of having lost the possibility of not becoming a wrongdoer unsettles the individual's self-understanding, leaving her wondering who she must be to have been capable of such a thing. Why should this be?

The experience of the transition to having become a wrongdoer simpliciter, as it is experienced in remorse, is rather different from the experience of more mundane transitions. An individual might move from being an undergraduate through to being a graduate without at any stage becoming alien to herself. This is because it is part and parcel of understanding what it is to be an undergraduate that you project yourself toward a future articulated in terms of precisely these transitions. This is not the case with the experience of having become a wrongdoer, as experienced in remorse. As we have seen, remorse involves a retrospective acknowledgment of the significance of what one has done; in remorse, one becomes aware of what one has done through having done it. This applies to both sides of remorse: just as the agent becomes aware of something as irreducibly valuable through the shock of having violated it, so too she becomes aware of the possibility of becoming a wrongdoer through the shock of having become one. This places severe difficulties on the remorseful person's ability to straightforwardly recognize herself as the agent of the wrongdoing. And this explains why remorse involves a sense of having become alien to oneself, as I shall now argue.

Prior to having become a wrongdoer, the agent was not aware of what she was about to become, since it is just this awareness that she gains through crossing the threshold. Before becoming a wrongdoer, then, the agent could not have conceived of herself as lacking awareness of the possibility of being about to become a wrongdoer, since to be aware of *that* she would have had to have been aware of precisely the possibility of which she lacked awareness. Having become aware of having become a wrongdoer, however, the agent is now able to understand herself as having once been unaware of what she was about to become. But she will struggle, to say the least, to *imaginatively occupy* the perspective of being unaware of being about to become a wrongdoer, since to imagine herself as such would be to imagine herself in terms of a possibility of which she is supposed to be unaware! To be sure, she might imaginatively *observe* her past self, as it were third-personally. But since the perspective she occupied prior to having become a wrongdoer is only intelligible as such after having become a wrongdoer, her prior perspective is imaginatively inaccessible from the perspective in which it has become intelligible. It is no wonder that those who experience remorse become alien to themselves; it is as if they have been asked to imagine how the world appears to a person without the capacity for imagination. Not only have they lost their innocence, their innocence is lost from view.[15]

There is more that could be said here.[16] I shall restrict myself to emphasizing the following points. First, the self-facing side of remorse is temporally complex. It involves understanding yourself to be facing a future marked by the absence of a possibility that was open in the past (you are no longer able to not become a wrongdoer) as well as containing indefinitely many possibilities of which you had been unaware (you might yet become indefinitely many sorts of wrongdoer) and into which you may yet stumble blindly (you are susceptible to moral sleepwalking). Second, in remorse the experience of becoming a wrongdoer is not experienced as a straightforward transition but a transformation by which you have become aware of the possibility of becoming a wrongdoer (*simpliciter* and specific) through having realized that possibility. From this perspective, your past is experienced as both yours, as the state you have left behind, and not yours, as a perspective you cannot imaginatively project yourself into. Since you are aware of indefinitely many future occasions for remorse, however, you are also aware of yourself as open to the possibility of further experiences of such self-alienation, on the occasion of having sleepwalked into having become another specific sort of wrongdoer. To reiterate, nothing hangs on this description of the self-facing side of remorse, so we can leave it to one side. All that matters for our purposes is that we accept that remorse involves the pained acknowledgment of having ruined oneself, however we spell that out. For now, however, let me briefly sum up before moving on.

In §II, we saw that Gaita argues that remorse is the pained, recollective acknowledgment of the preciousness of a human being through having wronged her and the pained acknowledgment of having become a wrongdoer. On his view, remorse is a double-faced form of acknowledgment: it acknowledges the significance of object of the wrongdoing, and it acknowledges the significance of what the subject has suffered. In §III, I responded to Gaita's account by way of Augustine's *Confessions*. Augustine's expression of remorse parallels Gaita's discussion closely. On Gaita's account, we should expect to find the authoritative expression of remorse to involve an acknowledgment of the severity of the wrongdoing in hindsight. We should also expect to find an acknowledgment of what has become of the wrongdoer, also in hindsight. This is just what we find in Augustine's confession of having stolen pears. To this degree, Augustine's testimony lends further support to Gaita's position. But Augustine takes us beyond Gaita's account, since his testimony makes no direct acknowledgment of the preciousness of other human beings. To make sense of this disparity, I suggested that we understand remorse to involve the acknowledgment of something as irreducibly valuable through the shock of having wronged it. This gives us a sufficiently broad account to make sense of the various examples we have encountered. In §IV, I developed an account of the self-facing side of remorse, although that can fall by the wayside as far as our argument is concerned. We are now in a position to ask whether remorse, so understood, is consolable through acts of reparation.

RETURNING TO REMORSE AND REPARATION

In the opening page of this chapter, I described Byron Williston's discussion of reparation and consolation. He has a particular form of consolation in mind: through repairing your damaged ethical agency, you are able to "forswear" self-directed negative attitudes better suited for the person you once were, rather than who you have now become. By this, he means that we can justifiably seek to resist and even expunge attitudes such as self-contempt, perhaps through reminding ourselves of our moral progress. On this view, consolation is directed toward overcoming negative attitudes, either by batting them aside or altogether removing them from the agent's psychological economy. For this reason, I shall call this a *remedial* conception of consolation. Remedial forms of consolation aim to eliminate painful feelings, rather as remedial medicine aims at a cure. On Williston's account, then, reparation is a remedial form of consolation for many negative attitudes, since he holds that by making amends, we can repair the damage that generates our painful feelings. Is reparation also a way of remedially consoling remorse?

According to Williston, we can justifiably forswear negative attitudes if we repair our ethical agency. This form of consolation, then, targets reparable harms and sets to work repairing them, so as to undermine the source of the negative attitudes. Consequently, if remorse is to be consolable in this way, it must be a response to a reparable harm. I have argued that remorse involves the recollective acknowledgment of something as irreducibly valuable through having violated it and the acknowledgment of having become a wrongdoer. It is, then, a responsive "negative attitude." Is either the other-facing or subject-facing side of remorse a response to a reparable harm?

The other-facing side of remorse acknowledges having violated something irreducibly valuable. The self-facing side of remorse acknowledges having become a wrongdoer. Neither *having* violated something nor *having* become someone is a reparable harm. Suppose that I gave you deliberately misleading information and thereby put you in harm's way. I might feel remorse about that. So long as there is still time, I may seek to undo the damage done by pulling you out of danger.[17] In this way, I might make amends. But what I cannot do is undo *having* put you in harm's way in the first place. Nor can I undo *having* become one who acted in that way. The future necessarily holds out no way of not having done something or not having become someone.[18] When Lady Macbeth states that what's done cannot be undone, she is not merely lamenting her inability to reanimate Duncan's corpse. Even if she were an able necromancer, we should still imagine her to be haunted by remorse. As Robert Rosthal notes, "Remorse is associated primarily with the *irrevocability* of the past" (Rosthal 1967, 578, my emphasis). It is for this reason that reparation *cannot* offer remedial consolation; the harms that are acknowledged in remorse cannot be healed, even if reparations for the wrongdoing can be made.

This may seem like a rather depressing conclusion. St. Mark the Ascetic sharpens the point by claiming that the person who suffers from remorse faces a severe practical dilemma:

> To recall past sins in detail inflicts injury on the man who hopes in God. For when such recollection brings remorse it deprives him of hope; but if he pictures the sins to himself without remorse, they pollute him again with the old defilement. (St. Mark the Ascetic 2010, 138)[19]

Simplified and stated in secular terms, St. Mark's point is as follows: either we are transparent to having violated something of irreducible value and having become a wrongdoer, in which case we feel remorse and are hopeless before the irrevocability of the past, or we are opaque to the significance of what we have done, in which case we are blind to ourselves. Jankélévitch also draws attention to the distinctive practical difficulty of living with remorse, in light of its resistance to remedial medication:

> Bad conscience has appeared to us as an inconsolable sadness. [. . .] The bad conscience [. . .] suffers from a misdeed that does not make up its mind either to escape it completely or belong to it unreservedly. From two things the one: either it will go until the extreme of objectivity or else it will succeed in undoing its work; it will destroy the misfortune of irreversibility either in coming back to the past or in forgetting this past as much as possible, in making it so that pain heals itself with a homeopathic cure. (Jankélévitch 2015/1933, 109)

As with St. Mark the Ascetic, then, Jankélévitch claims that the irreparability of the harms acknowledged in remorse leaves the individual having to navigate between two pitfalls. On the one hand, she might find herself dealing with the irreversibility of the past by refusing to turn away from it. In this way, she accepts irreversibility by making the past a permanent feature of her present. It is not hard to imagine that such a person may lose hope, as St. Mark suggests. Alternatively, she might find herself trying to forget all about it, and thereby commit to living her life as a fugitive from the past, so as to enact a

"homeopathic" (read: ineffective) remedy. Neither route seems easy to recommend. Where the first is self-lacerating, the second is self-occluding.
How, then, are we to live with the things we have done if they are the sort to occasion remorse, granted that remorse is the acknowledgment of irreparable harms? Is there no consolation available to the remorseful agent, besides full flight from the past? Only if consolation must be remedial. In closing, I shall briefly sketch Kierkegaard's account of remorse, since with it he offers a solution to this dilemma by presenting what I shall call a *palliative* form of consolation.

KIERKEGAARD AND PALLIATIVE CONSOLATION

A Providence watches over each man's wandering through life. It provides him with two guides. [The] one beckons forward to the Good, the other calls man back from evil. [. . .] [In] order to make the journey secure, they must look both forward and backward. Alas, there was perhaps many a one who went astray [. . .] [for] his course was along a false way, and he pressed on so continuously that remorse could not call him back onto the old way. There was perhaps someone who went astray because, in the exhaustion of repentance, he could go no further, so that the guide could not help him to find the way forward. [. . .] The two guides call out to a man early and late, and when he listens to their call, then he finds his way, then he can know where he is, on the way. [. . .] Of these two, the call of remorse is perhaps the best. For the eager traveller who travels lightly along the way does not, in this fashion, learn to know it as well as a wayfarer with a heavy burden. (Kierkegaard 2008, 26–7)

This is a very rich passage, but let me focus on just a few points. The guide in front calls the individual towards the good, showing her that there is a way forward and giving her a sense of its direction. The guide behind the individual warns her away from the bad, issuing reminders of the past. Neither guide is within visual range, although each is within earshot. In moving ahead, as Kierkegaard imagines her, then, the individual is not simply following the leader. She is, rather, making her own way while listening out for the call from the front or the call from the back, each of which offers correctives and inducements to her path.

According to Kierkegaard, then, remorse can be accepted; indeed, remorse can be a "sincere and faithful friend" (Kierkegaard 2008, 23). In accepting remorse, however, the individual does not have to hold her gaze on what she has done. On this view, remorse follows behind her, out of view. This is not the same as being totally forgetful of the past, since she acknowledges that remorse may return. More specifically, she proceeds in such a way that she is ready to hear the warnings issued by remorse, when they might emerge. Kierkegaard thus sees remorse as having a positive value when its return is accepted as a welcome possibility, rather than a persistent actuality, where its reemergence serves to reorient oneself away from going astray. We might imagine remorse serving this role in a number of ways. It could emerge to ward one away from specific actions similar in kind to that which previously occasioned remorse. Alternatively, remorse might serve as an aid to general wakefulness, holding one from nodding off into the kind of moral somnambulism that led one into trouble.

While this sketch of Kierkegaard's view is certainly brief, we can at least see how he indicates a way in which the individual may be able to navigate the pitfalls of overwhelming overattention, on the one hand, and underwhelming inattention, on the other. Since the agent comports herself towards the possibility of the return of *remorse*, she acknowledges the reality of what she has done, rather than seeking the "homeopathic" remedy of full flight. In this way, she is not willfully blind to the past. But since she comports herself toward the *possibility* of the return of remorse by harkening for its call, she does not dwell in the fact of what she has done. In this way, she avoids the kind of self-punishing torment of someone who cannot turn away from their past. Kierkegaard thus sketches a way of skirting the traps identified by St. Mark and Jankélévitch and thereby presents us with an alternative to remedial forms of consolation. Consolation from remorse, as he presents it, is achieved through trying to live as well as possible in light of a past that cannot be undone and a harm that cannot be repaired. The sort of consoling comportment that Kierkegaard describes does not involve trying to remove remorse from your psychological economy, far from it: remorse is to be accepted as a permanent possibility that one is powerless to heal but that nonetheless has a positive role in keeping the agent on the straight and narrow. For this reason, I shall call this a palliative conception of consolation.

My aim here is not to defend Kierkegaard's recommendation. In this chapter, I have argued that remorse places a specific burden on the person who suffers from it, since it cannot be overcome through reparative consolation. I have appealed to Kierkegaard only so as to highlight a possibility where we might have thought there was none. Kierkegaard points to the possibility of a palliative mode of consolation, even if we think that such a response is inappropriate for remorse. I leave it open that there are other, better ways of consoling remorse. Indeed, since I have left it open that remorse is ripe for a revaluation in light of a secular moral psychology, I have left space for an altogether different response. If remorse should be debunked, then we do not need the palliative consolation that Kierkegaard describes: we need psychotherapy. Nonetheless, I hope to have shown that we need not think that the problem raised by remorse is hopeless, since there are conceivable ways forward. Let me conclude by briefly summing up.

CONCLUSION

In this chapter, I have argued that while remorse cannot be remedially consoled through acts of reparation, this need not lead us to conclude that remorse cannot be consoled at all, since we might think of other ways in which the pain of remorse might be assuaged. I first developed an account of remorse by raising some problems with Raimond Gaita's discussion and suggesting a way beyond them. I argued that remorse is the pained acknowledgment of something as irreducibly valuable through the shock of having violated it and the pained acknowledgement of having become a wrongdoer. I then argued that since neither aspect of remorse acknowledges a reparable harm, remorse cannot be overcome through acts of reparation. In closing, I sketched another way in which remorse might be consoled, drawn from Kierkegaard. By comporting oneself in readiness for remorse, one accepts the positive value of remorse in diverting one either from specific bad actions or more general moral somnambulism. In this way, the agent can bear in mind what she has done without dwelling in the past, thereby treading a path between the two pitfalls of overwhelming awareness, on the one hand, and self-occlusion, on the other. Kierkegaard thus helps us see the possibility of a *palliative* form of consolation, by which we are relieved of pain through accepting our powerlessness to mend what is beyond repair.

NOTES

1. John Deigh (1982) claims that remorse may be inconsolable by reparation, just in case the evil done leaves no way in which the wrong might be remedied (Deigh 1982, 401). He grants, however, that remorse *can* be consoled through reparation, just in case there is some material means of doing so. Our question is whether there could possibly be material means of consoling remorse through acts of reparation.

2. In the 1960s, Ivan Thalberg and Robert Rosthal had a short debate over the connection between remorse and weakness of the will. See Thalberg (1963, 1968) and Rosthal (1967). In the same decade, D. Z. Philips and H. S. Price argued that remorse need not entail repudiation (Philips and Price 1967). Their argument was effectively rebutted by L. N. Zoch (1986) nearly two decades later. Besides these scattered contributions, remorse has received most attention in the field of jurisprudence, where the question concerns the rationale for holding the presence of remorse to be a mitigating (and its absence an aggravating) factor in sentencing. See, for example, Tudor (2008).

Jurisprudential discussions of remorse, however, tend to assume an account, rather than developing a rich analysis, and so I shall not discuss them further here. It is worth noting that this is a problem, however, since in the absence of any well-defined judicial sense of remorse, there is a danger that the mitigation/aggravation of sentencing on the basis of the presence/absence of remorse is likely to be arbitrary.

3. How are we to determine which testimony is authoritative except by appeal to the quality of the presentation of the phenomenon they afford? And how are we to determine the quality of the presentation of the phenomenon without already being familiar with exemplary cases? It would appear that our identification of exemplary cases would depend on our capacity to identify authoritative testimony, which capacity is dependent on our ability to identify exemplary cases. Gaita may accept that the authority of testimony cannot be justified independently of the understanding of the phenomenon that the testimony affords. Since that understanding can only be developed through having taken the testimony as authoritative, the justification for the authority of the testimony can only be in the offing at the time of its introduction. This would only be a problem if the authoritative status of testimony needed to be granted by appeal to some independent standard, by which we compare and contrast alternatives and come to a decision. But this is not what it is like to respond to authoritative testimony. We find ourselves *claimed* by the authority of the testimony. Moreover, we find ourselves claimed by the authority of the testimony even if we do not understand what the testimony has shown us. Indeed, we might even accept the testimony begrudgingly, since it shows us how little we understand, which is liable to sting our pride. It is, perhaps, for this reason that we can learn from such authorities, since they present us with compelling testimony that we need to come to understand.

4. For an extensive and illuminating discussion of examples of tragic moral failure, see Lisa Tessman's *Moral Failure: On the Impossible Demands of Morality* and *When Doing the Right Thing Is Impossible*.

5. This is a variation of an example deployed by Gaita. See Gaita (2013, 30).

6. This point may help to distinguish between Gaita's account of remorse and Bernard Williams' account of "agent-regret" (Williams 1981, 27ff). In introducing this latter notion, Williams argues that any satisfactory moral psychology will have to allow for the rationality of regrets over events for which one is causally responsible but not blameworthy. He does not aim to give a rich phenomenological distinction of a particular affect, so much as to draw attention to a category of affects that had been neglected. His example is of a truck driver who accidentally and blamelessly knocks over a pedestrian. If agent-regret is just regret over one's actions irrespective of blameworthiness, then remorse is a sort of agent-regret. Remorse is different from the sort of regret the truck driver would feel, however. On Gaita's account, the remorseful person feels as though she had not been sensitive to the reality of others. The truck driver in Williams' example would not feel this way; we can at least imagine a version of the story in which the pedestrian leaped out before the truck before the driver had a chance to be sensitive to her reality or not.

7. One might resist Gaita's suggestion that remorse must involve a retrospective shock, as though we could only feel remorse over actions whose significance we were not aware of before acting. We might imagine someone terrified in view of what they are *about* to do, perhaps under duress. Another interesting potential counterexample is presented by the Milgram Experiment. We can easily imagine that a person who

followed the order to administer a fatal electric shock would feel remorse, even after he discovered that the whole thing was an experiment in which no one was actually harmed. Here, it seems, remorse need not have to involve wronging anyone *at all*. On the account of remorse I develop below, we can make sense of both of these examples in the following way: remorse involves the acknowledging something as irreducibly valuable through the shock of having violated it and having become a wrongdoer through having done so. These conditions are fulfilled even in the example of a Milgram Experiment and prospective shock, because you can violate a human being by demonstrating your readiness to harm them.

8. I am indebted to David McNeill for drawing this term to my attention.

9. Vigilius Haufniensis is the pseudonymous author of Kierkegaard's (1980/1844) *The Concept of Anxiety*.

10. There is a question as to whether the Genesis narrative presents Adam as feeling remorse. There is some reason to think not: Adam and Eve's immediate reaction is to cover themselves with fig leaves. J. David Velleman develops his account of shame to accommodate this point (Velleman 2001). As far as I am concerned, however, that is by the by: even granted Adam did not feel remorse, that does not imply that remorse does not share a recollective structure with something like shame. The claim is that remorse has this structure, not that the structure is unique to remorse.

11. For an account of the structure of a Nietzschean moral psychology, see Williams (1993). For an attempt to debunk regret wholesale, see Bittner (1992).

12. Gaita is inspired by Simone Weil. Weil's insistence on the ethical significance of the reality of other people is explicitly grounded in her interpretation of the commandment to love the neighbor: "The love of our neighbour in all its fullness simply means being able to say to him: 'What are you going through?' It is a recognition that the sufferer exists, not only as a unit in a collection, or a specimen from the social category labeled 'unfortunate,' but as a man, exactly like us, who was one day stamped with a special mark by affliction [*malheur*]" (Weil 2009, 64).

13. Gaita also has some reason to take Augustine's word for it, since he elsewhere admits his testimony as authoritative. See Gaita (2013, 30). Nonetheless, he may wish to deny that this is an example of remorse. It is unclear, however, on what grounds he could make such a denial. As part of his inheritance from Wittgenstein, Gaita holds that we should allow our understanding of phenomena to be developed through an honest, unsentimental look at the phenomena themselves, rather than imposing constraints on what features *must* be present in order for something to count as an example of the phenomenon in question.

14. F. Scott Fitzgerald echoes this insight in his expression of remorse, experienced during sleepless night:

> —Waste and horror—what I might have been and done that is lost, spent, gone, dissipated, unrecapturable. I could have acted thus, refrained from this, been bold where I was timid, cautious where I was rash.
> I need not have hurt her like that.
> Nor said this to him.
> Nor broken myself trying to break what was unbreakable.

The horror has come now like a storm—what if this night prefigured the night after death—what if all thereafter was an eternal quivering on the edge of an abyss, with everything base and vicious in oneself urging one forward and the baseness and viciousness of the world just ahead. No choice, no road, no hope—only the endless repetition of the sordid and the semi-tragic. Or to stand forever, perhaps, on the threshold of life unable to pass it and return to it. I am a ghost now as the clock strikes four. (Fitzgerald 1993, 67)

15. For an account of a similar difficulty (namely, in finding ourselves akin with Adam), see Martin (2011, 131–2).

16. See Kierkegaard (1980, 25–40), from which I have drawn extensively in this section.

17. This suggests the following explanation of the supposedly "natural" connection between remorse and reparation. If I feel remorse over what I have done to you, then I newly acknowledge you as irreducibly valuable. Seeing you *as* irreducibly valuable provides me with motivation to treat you as such. If there is possibility of reparation, then I am likely to be motivated to pursue it out of my acknowledgment of your value and my consequent desire to help you. This is not to deny that I *may* be motivated toward acts of reparation by a desire to undo what I have done and thus to seek remedial consolation. The point is just that I need not be motivated by a desire for my own consolation in seeking to make amends upon the occasion of remorse.

18. Even if the experience of remorse were to lead to a kind of moral rebirth, it will remain the case that you *had become* a wrongdoer, no matter who you go on to become.

19. I am obliged to Dan Watts for this reference.

REFERENCES

Apostle, Julia. 2010. "The Role of Remorse in Court Convictions," in *Financial Times*, accessed online August 3, 2017 from https://www.ft.com/content/10a583da-9ab1-11df-87e6-00144feab49a.
Bittner, Rüdiger. 1992. "Is It Reasonable to Regret Things One Did?" *Journal of Philosophy* 89 (5): 262.
Cairns, Douglas. 1999. "Representations of Remorse and Reparation in Classical Greece." In *Remorse and Reparation*, ed. Murray Cox. London: Jessica Kingsley.
Coleridge, Samuel Taylor. 1999. *The Rime of the Ancient Mariner*, ed. Paul Fry. (pp. 171–8) London: Macmillan.
Deigh, John. 1982. "Love, Guilt, and the Sense of Justice." *Inquiry* 25 (4): 391–416.
Fitzgerald, F. Scott. 1993. "Sleeping and Waking." In *The Crack-Up*, ed. Edmund Wilson. New York: New Direction.
Fulkerson, Laurel. 2004. "*Metameleia* and Friends: Remorse and Repentance in 5th and 4th Century Athenian Oratory." *Phoenix* 58: 241–59.
Fulkerson, Laurel. 2013. *No Regrets: Remorse in Classical Antiquity*. Oxford: Oxford University Press.
Gaita, Raimond. 2004. *Good and Evil: An Absolute Conception*, 2nd ed. London: Routledge.
Gaita, Raimond. 2013. *A Common Humanity: Thinking about Love and Truth and Justice*. London: Routledge

Jankélévitch, Vladimir. 2015. *The Bad Conscience*. London: University of Chicago Press.
Kierkegaard, Soren. 1980. *The Concept of Anxiety*. Princeton, NJ: Princeton University Press.
Kierkegaard, Soren. 2008. *Purity of the Heart Is to Will One Thing*. London: HarperCollins.
Martin, Wayne. 2011. "The Judgment of Adam: Self-Consciousness and Normative Orientation in Lucas Cranach's Eden." In *Art and Phenomenology*, ed. Joseph D. Parry. London: Routledge.
Philips, D. Z., and H. S. Price. 1967. "Remorse without Repudiation." *Analysis* 28 (1): 18–20.
Rosthal, Robert. 1967. "Moral Weakness and Remorse." *Mind* 76: 576–9.
Scheler, Max. 1987. *Person and Self-Value*. Dordrecht: Martinus Nijhoff.
Smith, Adam. 1999/1759. *The Theory of Moral Sentiments*. Cambridge: Cambridge University Press.
St. Augustine. 1998. *Confessions*. Oxford: Oxford University Press.
St. Mark the Ascetic. 2010. "On Those Who Think That They Are Made Righteous by Works: 226 Texts." In *The Philokalia vol.1*. London: Faber and Faber.
Styron, William. 1979. *Sophie's Choice*. London: Jonathan Cape.
Tessman, Lisa. 2015. *Moral Failure: On the Impossible Demands of Morality*. Oxford: Oxford University Press.
Tessman, Lisa. 2017. *When Doing the Right Thing Is Impossible*. Oxford: Oxford University Press.
Thalberg, Ivan. 1963. "Remorse." *Mind* 72: 545–55.
Thalberg, Ivan. 1968. "Rosthal's Notion of Remorse and Irrevocability." *Mind* 77: 288–9.
Tudor, Steven Keith. 2008. "Why Should Remorse Be a Mitigating Factor in Sentencing?" *Criminal Law and Philosophy* 2: 241–57.
Velleman, J. David. 2001. "The Genesis of Shame." *Philosophy and Public Affairs* 30 (1): 27–52.
Weil, Simone. 2009. *Waiting for God*. London: Harper Perennial.
Williams, Bernard. 1981. *Moral Luck*. Cambridge: Cambridge University Press.
Williams, Bernard. 1993. "Nietzsche's Minimalist Moral Psychology." *European Journal of Philosophy* 1 (1): 4–14.
Williston, Byron. 2012. "The Importance of Self-Forgiveness." *American Philosophical Quarterly* 49 (1): 67–80.
Zoch, L. N. 1986, "Remorse and Regret: A Reply to Philips and Price" *Analysis* 46 (1): 54–7.

Chapter 6

Narrative and Marital Regret

Sarah Richmond

I, *Name*, take thee, *Name*, to be my wedded Wife/Husband,
to have and to hold from this day forward,
for better for worse, for richer for poorer,
in sickness and in health,
to love and to cherish,
till death us do part.
The Book of Common Prayer

There is a type of regret that, I suspect, is quite widespread, although it is probably experienced more often than it is discussed, at least outside a personal journal or the psychotherapist's consulting room. The regret concerns the major life decision of choosing a permanent or quasi-permanent partner in life, a spouse for example, and its content is (or implies) that one would have been better off had one married someone else.[1] This scenario appears often in literature and especially in novels: for example, Edith Wharton's *The Age of Innocence*, Anthony Trollope's *The Small House at Allington*, and Gustave Flaubert's *Madame Bovary*.[2] For convenience, I refer to it as "marital regret."

Perhaps its recurrence in literature already constitutes evidence for the real-life existence of marital regret, but there are also several "real-life" reasons to predict it. Marriage is an intimidating undertaking and our choice of spouse, therefore, appears to be one of the most important "life choices" we can make. ("Appears," because that choice may make less difference to the success of the marriage than we think; defenders of arranged marriages often press this thought.) Given our susceptibility to regret in general, it would be odd if we never doubted our marital decisions or wondered how a different marriage might have gone (and of course the high rates of divorce and remarriage suggest that these thoughts do indeed occur to many people).[3]

For a particular example of marital regret, we could borrow from a novel. But I want to present a relatively generic situation that anyone can imagine without difficulty and to avoid any interference that might be introduced by a reader's previous acquaintance, through literature, with my characters. The example I will consider is, therefore, the product of my own imagination; any resemblance to actual persons, living or dead, or to actual events is coincidental.

Here are the basic features: a married man in his forties (call him Keith) experiences marital regret, insofar as he entertains counterfactual thoughts about how wonderful things might have been had he married someone else. He has a particular person in mind, a close friend at university (call her Carey). Keith believes that there was once a real possibility of romantic entanglement with Carey: they were *very* close; they loved spending time together; there were several ambiguous moments. Now Carey and Keith are separately married, and Carey has moved to a far-off country. Keith's marriage to Liz is for the most part harmonious: they behave well toward each other; they celebrate their wedding anniversary. Keith is only rarely in touch with Carey (they occasionally meet at college reunions or exchange Christmas cards) but, unbeknownst to Liz, she is often in his thoughts.

The term "regret" can correctly encompass a range of psychological states and in a wide range of circumstances (an advantage of exploring just one type is that it protects against false generalizations). Bernard Williams' well-known formulation of regret's "constitutive thought"—*how much better if it had been otherwise*—cleverly captures the breadth of the range (Williams 1981, 27).[4] Within this range, we can distinguish between moral and nonmoral cases, noting also the gray area between. In moral cases, the subject will typically regard herself as morally blameworthy; her state of mind will be close to, or identical with, *remorse*. Remorse is typically felt in connection with one's past actions and toward people whom the agent believes he has *wronged*. Keith's regret is not remorseful in that sense, but (as we will see) that does not necessarily exempt it from moral assessment. The psychological literature on regret also distinguishes between regrets whose object is an *action* and regrets about *inaction*; we will also return to this distinction.

As readers of this volume will know, the phenomenon of regret in general has been researched in a number of disciplines. In the following sections, I consider some relevant discussion in social and cognitive psychology and Anglophone philosophy. In each of these two sections, I survey a body of work that is either (in the case of psychology) explicitly about regret or within which (in the case of philosophy) regret ought easily to find a place, and I consider the extent to which these approaches may, or may not, satisfactorily account for our example of marital regret. In "Marital Regret: Evaluation and Explanation," I offer some additional thoughts about the ways in which we might evaluate and explain this example.

In the last half-century, the two most influential discussions of regret in Anglophone philosophy have been initiated first by Bernard Williams and, more recently, by R. Jay Wallace. Readers who are familiar with this literature may therefore be surprised that I do not pursue either of these debates. The reason is that neither debate, in my view, is especially applicable to the phenomenon I wish to explore. In papers that were first published in the 1960s and 1970s, Williams invoked moral agents' experiences of regret for two main purposes: to emphasize the role of "moral luck" and to argue against moral realism (Williams 1973, 1981). Wallace's book (2013) focuses especially on some problems with the "logic" of regret, problems that arise especially from our propensity to change our attitudes toward events in our lives, as those lives progress. With the passing of time, we often come to "affirm" actions that, when we performed them, we had strong reasons to regret.

In these discussions, the object of regret is typically an *action*, performed at a specific and identifiable point of time. Many regrets are like this: "If only I had not placed all my money on that horse," and so on. Keith's regret, however, is different and more diffuse; it is not focused on an action or an event but, on the contrary, encompasses his current marriage and perhaps even his current life (we will return to this). The philosophical debate that seems more relevant here is about *narrative*, and especially life narratives, in which a person's marriage (if she marries) is typically a central structure. Keith's marital regret is, we have seen, simultaneously couched within a wider "alternative" narrative: the counterfactual story of his and Carey's perfect marriage.

SOCIAL AND COGNITIVE PSYCHOLOGY

A great deal of psychological research has been influenced by decision theory, which has also played a central role in economics. Within this tradition, attention to the phenomenon of regret (and to emotional states more generally) tends to focus on the effects of emotional experience on one's behavior, and especially on decision-making behavior, with a view to determining whether these effects make the experience "rational" or "functional."[5] Several studies in the 1990s, for example, established that *anticipated* regret influences people's choices in a number of domains (Inman and McAlister 1994; Simonson 1992; Zeelenberg and Beattie 1997) and that anticipated regret can in some cases play a functional role; for example, where someone's predictions are accurate, prospective thoughts about the regret she expects to feel can help her to avoid choices that would incur that emotional cost. Within this approach, it may be harder to find a functional role for *experienced* regret, since "sunk costs" frequently have no rational bearing on decisions about the future. Nonetheless, psychologists have pointed out that in some cases it *may* yet be good to "cry over spilled milk" (Zeelenberg 1999) and have pointed to at least two types of beneficial consequences. First, some of these regrets may relate to actions that can be "undone": if, for example, I regret my choice of a recent purchase, it may be possible to return it to the shop for an exchange, in which case my regret has led me to own a more satisfactory product. Second, in cases where the regretted action cannot be "undone," the experience of regret may enable us to "learn from our mistakes," by making relevant features of our decisions salient to us in the future. If we learn, by eating them, that the egg sandwiches in a café are disappointing, we will know not to order them on our next visit.

Neither of these functional advantages seems applicable to our case of marital regret. Keith recognizes the real benefits of his marriage to Liz and does not want to "undo" it by divorcing her. Moreover, even if he *were* to be free to remarry, Carey is unavailable and it is unlikely that Keith could "learn from his mistakes," in choosing a different new spouse, by bearing in mind the properties that he noticed in Carey when they were young.[6]

A fascinating paper, published in 1995 by Gilovich and Medvec, is more applicable to our case. In it, the authors draw attention to an apparent contradiction between the findings of various empirical investigations into the ways human beings (in modern Western societies) tend to experience retrospective regret. On the one hand, there is evidence that people tend to feel more regret in relation to their actions (or commissions) than in relation to their inactions (or omissions). A famous "scenario" devised by Kahneman and Tversky (1982) compares two investors:

> Paul owns shares in Company A. During the past year he considered switching to stock in Company B, but he decided against it. He now finds that he would have been better off by $1200 if he had switched to the stock of Company B. George owned shares in Company B. During the past year he switched to stock in Company A. He now finds that he would have been better off by $1200 if he had kept his stock in Company B. (Kahneman and Tversky 1982, 173)

The scenario was designed to test the hypothesis that George, whose *action* led him away from the profits, will feel more regret than Paul, who merely *failed to act*, and a survey of respondents confirmed this. Around 92 percent replied that George would feel more regret, while only 8 percent said that Paul would. Other studies (e.g., Landman 1987) have replicated this so-called actor effect, in which actions are regretted more than inactions.

On the other hand, it is also commonly believed that what people regret most when they look back on their lives are things they did *not* do, that is, inactions and missed opportunities, and there is evidence to support this. In 1986, surviving members of the cohort of "geniuses," who were the subjects of a famous longitudinal study by Lewis Terman and colleagues, were asked (when most of them were in their seventies) what they would do differently if they could live their lives over again: the analysis of their responses revealed that there were many more references to inaction (50 percent) than to action (12 percent).[7] Further studies have confirmed this finding: retrospective "real-life" regrets focus more frequently on inaction rather than action.[8]

Gilovich and Medvec sought to reconcile these apparently conflicting findings by hypothesizing a "temporal pattern" to regret: in the *short term*, they suggest, people regret their *actions* more intensely while in the *longer term* people come to have stronger regrets about their *inactions*. Gilovich and Medvec also suggest a number of psychological mechanisms that might explain this temporal pattern. As we have noted, regretted actions may be amenable to rectification. As Gilovich and Medvec put it, "A person who regrets marrying Mr. Wrong will likely get divorced; someone who regrets passing up Mr. Right typically must cope with the fact that he is no longer available" (Gilovich and Medvec 1995, 385). We can surmise that, where "rectification" is possible, it has the effect of purging the initial regret.[9] Another helpful mechanism for regretted actions may be the consoling force of "silver linings" that, once perceived, diminish the intensity of regret. In the case of inaction, on the other hand, the "feedback" over time is quite different, as Gilovich and Medvec explain,

> What is troubling about a regrettable action is the set of bad things that actually happened as a consequence of the action taken. Thus, the consequences of regrettable actions are often finite: *They are bounded by what actually happened.* In contrast, what is troublesome about a regrettable inaction is the set of good things that would have happened had one acted. The consequences of inactions are therefore potentially infinite: *They are bounded only by one's imagination.* (Gilovich and Medvec 1995, 390; my emphases)

How robust is the distinction made in this research between "action" and "inaction?" Although Gilovich and Medvec acknowledge the potential difficulty in determining, with respect to a reported regret, whether it *does* actually turn on an action or an inaction, they are inclined to downplay it (1995, 381). To address it, they appointed eight judges, unaware of the research hypothesis, to determine whether the reported regrets concerned actions, or inactions, or were "indeterminate" (the missing reports [34 percent]) from the figures mentioned above were missing precisely because they fell into this third category).[10]

If we were obliged to apply this distinction to Keith's regret, we would probably judge that, insofar as he sees Carey as a "missed opportunity," it is a regret about inaction. However, we can easily add a detail, which would allow us to reframe it in terms of action; perhaps Keith remembers one ambiguous moment whose possibilities, he believes, *he* closed down: at the end of an evening together, Carey was standing invitingly close and smiling affectionately when Keith took action by saying "see you in the lecture tomorrow" and walking away. But this reclassification does not make any fundamental difference to the character of Keith's regret, as I conceive it, precisely because the essential shape of his regret is that of a *story*; Keith's regret concerns a "path not taken," and within that regret, musings about particular moments are mere details. This suggests that for some kinds of regret, Gilovic's and Medvec's action/inaction distinction is contrived and, therefore, their suggestion about the difference in the regretful experience does not apply.

A qualification is also needed to the passage (just quoted) in which Gilovich and Medvec suggest that the consequences of concern to an agent who regrets her inaction are imagined ("bounded only by one's imagination") rather than real. Although this may often be true, there are counterexamples. For example, in the case of *preventative* inaction, the agent may focus on an unfortunate event whose *actual* consequences she failed to prevent.

Despite these caveats, the same passage contains an important insight: a distinctive feature of *many* regrets about past inaction is their imaginatively rich elaboration such that the counterfactual material extends far beyond a mere thought of the "how much better" variety. It is worth making one further observation, arising from this body of research, about the "unrealistic" quality of many regrets about inaction. The missed opportunities regretted by respondents in the studies are often expressed in quantitative terms: they regret not having spent *more* time in education, or with family and friends, or not having made *more* effort with their career, and so on.[11] But as time and energy are finite resources, it is likely that these wishes could not have been fulfilled without incurring costs elsewhere. Our finite days may not allow us to spend the "right" amount of time on all of our concerns.[12]

There are some important ways, then, in which retrospective regret about inaction may be distinctively unrealistic. Daniel Kahneman's response to the research by Gilovich and Medvec, which offers "a somewhat different interpretation" of their data, develops this thought (Kahneman 1995, 390).[13] Kahneman rejects Gilovich's and Medvec's hypothesis about the temporal patterns of action and inaction regrets and suggests instead that regrets about actions are *qualitatively* different from regrets about inaction and, therefore, that we should recognize a new *type* of regret. According to Kahneman, short-term regrets are often *hot*; the everyday expression we often use—"I am kicking myself"—conveys this heat. The regretful evaluations made by Terman's respondents, on the other hand, are formulated from a long-term standpoint and, where they concern inaction, the regrets have a *wistful* quality associated, Kahneman says, with *"pleasantly sad fantasies* of what might have been" (Kahneman 1995, 391; my emphasis).

Note that, for Kahneman, *wistful* regrets come into existence late in the day. Against Gilovich and Medvec, he does not believe that this type of long-term regret about inaction typically begins at the time of the regretted inaction and then "grows" in intensity. The "regret curves" do not cross (Kahneman 1995, 391). Instead, "What grows over time, on [Kahneman's] view, is not the regret associated with a particular consequence but the recognition that there is a large consequence to be regretted" (Gilovich, Medvec, and Kahneman 1998, 603).

Wistful regret, as Kahneman characterizes it, may well be what Keith is feeling. In particular, it makes little sense to attribute Keith's "might have been" regrets about Carey to him at the time when they were co-students since he could, at that time, have courted her. It seems likely, too, that Keith's imaginings about the life he would have led with Carey are pleasant. It needs to be noted, however, that if Kahneman account of "wistful" regret is correct, the way that regret is almost always defined (and especially in the psychological literature) needs to be revised.[14] In most discussions, the experience of regret is *negative*. For Janet Landman, regret "can be briefly defined as the feeling of distress when one is sorry about something that one judges to have gone awry" (Landman 1995, 246). Gilovich and Medvec refer to regret (quite generally) as an "unpleasant emotional experience," while Zeelenberg characterizes its phenomenology as follows:

> It is accompanied by feelings that one should have known better and by having a sinking feeling, by thoughts about the mistake one has made and the opportunities lost, by feeling a tendency to kick oneself and to correct one's mistake, and wanting to undo the event and to get a second chance. (Zeelenberg 1999, 326)

Kahneman's "wistful" regret, on the other hand, involves "pleasantly sad" fantasies and/or nostalgia (Gilovich, Medvec, and Kahneman 1998, 612). If it is indeed pleasant to indulge this type of regret, then perhaps no (further) functional justification for it is needed.

Some people might reject Kahneman's suggestion on the grounds that, once we allow that this mental process (to give it a neutral description) *is* often pleasurable, we should classify it as a wish or a fantasy, rather than as a regret.[15] Although I think this is too strong, and that Kahneman's classification is defensible, the objection directs us nonetheless to an important point, which theorists frequently overlook: in our actual mental lives, our emotions are not only often intermingled at a time but also liable to being ousted by other emotions (e.g., as an inner narrative unfolds) such that the boundaries between an emotion and its putative successor may be quite indeterminate.

Keith believes that his friendship with Carey could have taken a romantic turn and, given the information that he holds, we can judge this belief to be reasonable. In addition, he tells himself, "I should have married Carey," and believes (or imagines?) that their marriage would have been wonderful. Perhaps he never formulates Williams' "constitutive thought" explicitly—it may be that, psychologically, he holds back from thinking, comparatively, that Carey would have been *a better wife than Liz*. But his thought processes (in conjunction, perhaps, with some tacitly held premises) do seem to point to that conclusion. There is surely enough here to warrant description of Keith's emotional state as "regret."[16] On the other hand, if we now stipulate that Keith moves on to envisage, in rich and imaginative detail, the blissful life he would have led with Carey, we might want to say that at this point a train of thought that *began* with regret has indeed *become* a wishful fantasy, a type of *mental activity*, to use Wollheim's helpful term (Wollheim 1984, 34–5). And, precisely because it builds on actual events in the past and a real possibility, it may be difficult for Keith to recognize it as fantasy.[17]

The word "fantasy" is meant here in its ordinary, everyday use, more or less synonymous with "daydream," and without controversial theoretical baggage (such as the psychoanalytic belief in the unconscious).[18] A fantasy has temporal extension (a fleeting image is not a fantasy) and it typically has a narrative structure. Indeed, fantasy's material is frequently borrowed from preexisting narratives, with more or less awareness of the borrowing. Western culture supplies us with a vast library of images suitable for romantic fantasies. Emma Bovary, wishing to arouse a more intense love for her husband, gets herself to recite, "By moonlight in the garden . . . all the passionate verses that she knew and sing to him with a sigh many a melancholy adagio" (Flaubert 2003, 41). Think too of the way in which we often imagine ourselves in the place of the characters in a film.

NARRATIVE IN ANGLOPHONE PHILOSOPHY[19]

In English-speaking philosophy, attention has been focused in recent decades on the phenomenon of *narrative* and has affected several domains of the discipline.[20] One founding text is Alasdair's MacIntyre's *After Virtue* (first published in 1981), an original and wide-ranging analysis of the "moral culture of advanced modernity," in which the concept of the "narrative unity" of human life plays a central role.[21] A second canonical discussion, Charles Taylor's *Sources of the Self*, appeared in 1989.

More locally, claims about the role of narrative have now been introduced into theories of the conscious self (Dennett 1992), personal identity (Lindemann 2014; Schechtman 1996), emotion (Goldie 2000; Wollheim 1999), and value (specifically, in relation to the values of personal well-being or the "goodness" of a person's life) (Rosati 2013; Velleman 1991). In this section, I want to consider these last accounts, in particular, and to examine the claims made by David Velleman and Connie Rosati about the interaction between narrative conceptions of our lives and our judgments about the value of those lives.

In his 1991 paper, "Well-Being and Time," David Velleman argues that "narrative relations" make a difference to the determination of the welfare value of a person's life. In consequence, as Velleman points out, "well-being" isn't (necessarily) additive: it is a mistake to believe that the welfare value of an extended period within a life (or a life as a whole) can generally be computed by adding the welfare values of the temporal parts within it.[22] Narrative enters in because different *orderings* of the same events can render our lives better or worse (this claim belongs in the so-called shape of the life debate). Velleman illustrates this by asking his reader, "Consider two different lives that you might live" (Velleman 1991, 49). The first life begins with a miserable childhood, followed by numerous struggles in youth; in middle age, however, the person succeeds in achieving his most important goals and he goes on to enjoy a fulfilling retirement. In the second life, the ups and downs are reordered so that a happy childhood and "precocious triumphs" are followed by setbacks in middle age and a wretched retirement (Velleman 1991, 49–50). In Velleman's view, "most people" will deem the first life to be more valuable, just because it is a "story of improvement" rather than "a story of deterioration" (Velleman 1991, 50). Thus, the *narrative arc* of the events in a life may be one determinant of that life's value.

In relation to this example, Velleman notes that he is not defending this *particular* value judgment (or "evaluative intuition") but simply drawing attention to the possibility and legitimacy of a certain *type* of judgment, in order to discredit an additive conception of well-being (Velleman 1991, 50). This is, of course, fine as far as it goes, but it leaves many interesting questions unanswered.

Some of these relate to the metaphysics and epistemology of narratives. *Which* narrative relations between a life's parts genuinely confer value on the life as a whole, and how objective are the judgments to which they give rise? Is Velleman's appeal to what "most people" would say about the "story of improvement" supposed to suggest that the correct judgment of a life's value is fixed by a majority intuition about which stories are best?[23] Or is the *subject* of a life the authority, in relation to judgments about the narrative relations that contribute to its value? There seem to be good reasons to think so: it seems odd to claim, about someone to whom marital constancy means nothing, that her life is nonetheless narratively "marred" by the collapse of her first marriage.[24] Indeed, do we have to *care* about narrative relations at all, for them to affect the value of our lives? Galen Strawson claims (citing himself as an example) that, as a matter of psychological fact, there are people who have no tendency to consider their lives or their ongoing experience in narrative terms, and he also rejects normative claims about the value of such an outlook: "It's just not true that there is only one good way for human beings to experience their being in time. There are deeply non-Narrative people and there are good ways to live that are deeply non-Narrative" (Strawson 2004, 429).

We might also ask whether a "unified" life is necessarily more valuable. In Velleman's examples, continuity and interconnections seem, objectively, to add value: if one becomes wealthy *as a result of one's efforts*, he suggests, our life may be better than one in which our later well-being derives from mere luck. Similarly, the right sort of link between an earlier and a later episode can "redeem" the misfortune of the earlier episode: this underpins our "interest in learning from misfortunes" (Velleman 1991, 74). But does a good life *need* to include these retrospective continuities?[25,26]

Two further questions about Velleman's account are especially relevant to our case of marital regret. First: Does Velleman's conception of narrative value have any normative implications? If we can enhance the value of our life by lending it the right kind of narrative structure, ought we (self-consciously) to do that? Against this suggestion, there is a familiar "order-of-explanation" objection: surely we ought to aim primarily to lead good lives rather than to generate good stories? (Call this the 'Life Imitating Art' objection.) Second: Does each narrative belong to just one person? Although Velleman is not explicit on this point, his examples are all individualist in this way. We will return to the question of whether we should accept this individualism.

Connie Rosati's "The Story of a Life" accepts Velleman's claim 'that narrative contributes to a person's good or enhances the welfare value of her life": she calls this the "Narrativity Thesis" (Rosati 2013, 24). The additional question which Rosati considers is the following: *How does narrative enhance our good or the value of our life?* Her answer to this question resolves one of the indeterminacies noted in Velleman's account, since Rosati explicitly requires that any narrative that enhances the value of a person's life must be one that she is willing to take up; in other words, the perspective of the person living the life is essential.

Rosati claims that "if narrative makes a distinctive contribution to personal good, it is not because our lives have distinctively narrative features or structures. . . . Rather, it is because we can, and often do, *recount* our lives as narratives" (Rosati 2013, 24). And *recounting* our own lives can enhance our good, by securing or supporting "a sense of who we are" and "a sense of ourselves as controlling authority over our selves and our lives" (Rosati 2013, 45).[27]

Rosati points out that although we are the "subject" of these narratives, we do not have to be their only—or even principal—*source*, for them to have this beneficial power. An effective psychotherapist may help her client precisely by developing for her (and, obviously, from information provided by her) an "empowering" narrative of her life that the client had not hitherto considered (Rosati 2013, 47). Although there may be a number of possible stories that someone could recount, all of which were life-enhancing for her, they can fulfill this function only if they remain reasonably faithful to the facts: stories that excessively distort reality may invite contradiction, and they will not be able to provide a stable basis from which she can move forward.

Note that by shifting the site of narrative value to the *recounting* of narratives of our lives (an activity that is conceived as the construction of a helpful interpretation of the life), Rosati avoids the Life Imitates Art problem. Like Velleman, Rosati does not explicitly address the question of individualism, although her reference to the potential contribution of a psychotherapist does allow for some coauthoring of one's narrative (which seems to belong, nonetheless, to just one person).[28] Rosati's reference to the psychotherapeutic role also makes space for the idea (which she does not pursue) that some people's life narratives are *dysfunctional*, a quality that is salient to the clinical point of view.

It is a pity that Velleman and Rosati do not relate their claims about the value-conferring aspects of narrative to the ideas about narrative that have been developed within clinical psychology, as the clinical literature is obviously relevant to the topic of well-being and has many additional insights to offer. Systemic family therapists, for example, explicitly believe that narratives (or "scripts") are typically *collectively* owned by a family, which means they are operative at an interpersonal level, not just intrapersonally. Each person in the family, then, may be working to develop their particular role within the play, while "simultaneously playing roles in everyone else's scripts" (Byng-Hall 1986, 3). This step away from narrative individualism (a move that, of course, does not require that the other participants and contributors always be *family*) is, I think, necessary for a full understanding of marital regret.[29]

MARITAL REGRET: EVALUATION AND EXPLANATION

In this section, I will offer some thoughts about these two aspects of marital regret—its evaluation and its explanation—in turn.

First, evaluation: Keith's regretful attitude naturally invites assessment, but how should it be assessed? Is it susceptible to moral assessment, or cognitive assessment, or both of these, or neither? (Here I seek to avoid the subtle distinctions—e.g., between an emotion's "rationality," "justification," "warrant," or "fittingness"—which a greater degree of precision might require.)

One difficulty (as we have observed) relates to the individuation of regret, which seems to be a precondition for its assessment. Keith's regret, we noted, may be an "outlier" case if it is pleasurable. But in addition, it forms part of a sequential mental *activity* that is narratively structured and which, as it develops, becomes increasingly an exercise of the creative imagination, rather than a realistic appraisal of what is regretted.[30] All of us have experienced, I suppose, these *enchaînements* in mental life; their ubiquity limits the usefulness of many philosophical discussions of emotion, which confine themselves to the synchronic. The prevalence of mental activity also vindicates, I think, the claim made by recent moral philosophers that novels (as well as other forms of fictional discourse) can provide us with a useful source of information— for example, by granting access to characters' streams of consciousness— about what it is *actually* like, experientially, to be a person who is trying to lead a good life, ethically and/or prudentially.[31]

A different problem concerns the assessment of the "cognitive" component of regret, that is, its counterfactual content. A comparison with the case of anger (which is often cited to illustrate an emotion's "cognitive core") makes this clear: expressed roughly, my anger with X is rational/warranted/justified, and so on, if my belief that X has wronged me is correct. But Keith, we have seen, regretfully thinks, "I should have married Carey." The representational adequacy of *that* belief is far more difficult to assess (and most people, I think, would not seek to criticize Keith's regret primarily on those cognitive grounds.)[32]

Fortunately, Thomas Hurka has developed a philosophical account of the requirements of "rational regret," which we can consider in relation to Keith's case (Hurka 1996). Hurka considers the rationality of regret in situations where one has to choose between two goods, one of which is greater than another. Invoking a principle of *proportionality*, Hurka argues that rational regret is proportionate to the good that has been foregone; for this reason, it may be rational to feel some (mild) regret about the choice one did not make, even if one believes one made the correct choice (i.e., of the greater good) and, in consequence, feels "predominantly" satisfied (Hurka 1996, 556). Hurka illustrates this claim with the example of someone choosing between various possible holidays.

Hurka's holiday example, however, is far simpler than ours, especially if we suppose that the person choosing her holiday has ample information about the alternatives. Perhaps Holiday A, at an inland location, is inexpensive and has few tourists, while Holiday B is expensive but has beaches: if the person dislikes tourists and high prices, she may feel confident that A is the "greater good." Since Keith, on the other hand, lacks reliable information about what marriage to Carey would have been like, the proportionality principle is of little help here.

However, Hurka does not leave the proportionality principle unqualified. In his view, there is an additional constraint on rational regret, a "modal condition," whereby the rationality of regret is also determined by the degree of "remoteness from actuality" of what is regretted. Pursuing his holiday example, Hurka says that while it may be rational, *immediately* after choosing holiday A, to feel regret about the unchosen holiday B, once holiday A has begun, the rationality diminishes: "as you reach your destination and accumulate experiences there, the possibility of being somewhere else becomes progressively more remote and progressively less an object of rational concern" (Hurka 1996, 560).

I think Hurka is right in thinking that the distance between the "good foregone" and actuality is often central to our assessment of regret, although his way of expressing the modal condition (in terms of "objects of rational concern") is unsatisfactory.[33] Hurka seems to overlook the possibility that holiday A may, as one's experiences of it accumulate, turn out to have unforeseen flaws.[34] If it rains every day, surely it *is* rational to reflect that holiday B, in a sunnier spot, might have been a better choice, at least in terms of the weather? Even if one does not regret one's choice overall, this thought puts one in a position to make a better-informed choice in the future by taking into account the meteorological probabilities.

Perhaps the intuition that underpins some kind of modal constraint on regret can be expressed only in general terms; in any case, it is extremely familiar. The basic idea is that we should generally—and especially from the viewpoint of rational agency—be more concerned with what *is* the case, and thereby with circumstances on which we may be able to act, than with unrealizable "paths not taken." (Possibilities for the future, especially those that we aim to actualize, are quite different.) This piece of folk wisdom is expressed in numerous idiomatic phrases in English, for example, "counting one's blessings" and, of course, "it's no use crying over spilled milk" (as the Poland manager said after his team lost 1–2 to Senegal in its first game in the 2018 World Cup).[35] And this critical thought does seem applicable to Keith, who might be charged with "pointlessly" musing about Carey and encouraged to concentrate instead on the life that he has. We will return to this after examining two further types of reason provided by Hurka for limiting one's regret.

Given the assumption that regret is a painful emotion, Hurka points out, we may have an intrinsic reason (based on pain's intrinsic badness) to limit or "restrain" our experience of it. That seems correct in general, although, as we have seen, Kahneman rejects that assumption and we have allowed that Keith may enjoy thinking about Carey. Hurka also cites a further *instrumental* reason, which might apply, "If the good to be had from your holiday is pleasure, and intense regret would interfere with this pleasure" (Hurka 1996, 559). Again, if Keith's regret is a *source* of pleasure, this does not apply to him.

However, as we noted two paragraphs ago, there is a different instrumental reason available to Keith for restraining his regret—which does not concern the pleasure/pain economy but, instead, Keith's *focus*. Keith's regret is a distraction from the life he is in fact living and, in addition, it diverts his attention away from his actual spouse, Liz. While Hurka's account of regret does not consider its significance for, or its impact on, any of the agent's interpersonal relations, this dimension seems important in Keith's case. Are there grounds for saying that Keith's regret is ethically discreditable, perhaps because it is unfair or disrespectful to Liz?

Some of the obvious objections one might raise to this charge (citing, e.g., the spontaneous nature of Keith's regret and the fact that, because he conceals it from Liz, she is unaware of it) have been addressed by a number of contemporary Anglophone philosophers, who have developed accounts of the ways in which we may be held responsible for our attitudes. Iris Murdoch's attack, in her influential paper in *The Sovereignty of Good* (Murdoch 1970), was an early formulation of this line of thought; for Murdoch, the narrow concern with voluntary *actions* in the moral philosophy of her day (she cites Hare and Sartre) overlooked the moral relevance of the inner life, as she demonstrated with her famous example of a woman's inward reconsideration of her initially contemptuous attitude toward her daughter-in-law. Murdoch is also important for her defense of the moral significance of *attention* (which the same example also illustrates). For Murdoch, attention is central to the attitude of interpersonal love (which therefore involves an appreciation of the particularity of the loved person), an attitude which she places at the center of morality, in opposition to Kant.[36]

More recently, some more Kantian defenses of the idea that we can be morally answerable for our attitudes, including our "patterns of awareness," have been developed. Angela M. Smith, for example, argues that these phenomena, regardless of their nonvoluntary character, are morally assessable insofar as they reveal a person's underlying evaluative judgments and commitments. In agreement with Murdoch, Smith rejects a volitional account of responsibility and argues that our everyday attributions do not support it. Smith offers the example of forgetting the birthday of a close friend, realizing one has done so, and judging oneself in consequence to be morally at fault (Smith 2005, 236). Note that both Murdoch's and Smith's accounts focus especially on our answerability to people with whom we have close, personal relations for our attitudes, which makes them entirely suitable tools for the analysis of marital regret.

This answerability may depend, of course, on the expectations (often tacit) of the participants in the relationship in question, and so far, we lack the relevant information about Keith's marriage to Liz. In contemporary Western society, there is no single model of marriage; for the most part a "contractual" understanding of marriage prevails, in which the partners set their own terms (although sexual exclusivity, e.g., is often assumed to be part of the contract, some couples explicitly reject that clause). But this variation in the terms usually exists alongside an expectation of psychological *reciprocity*, an expectation that distinguishes personal relationships such as friendship and marriage from business relationships.[37] The symmetry in the marriage vows set out in the Book of Common Prayer (and quoted in my epigraph) testifies to this assumption of psychological reciprocity, of a mutual "loving" and "cherishing."[38]

Unpacking this norm of psychological reciprocity is a task in itself, for which there is insufficient space. It does not necessarily require each partner to make the *same* psychological contribution; partners usually differ in their temperaments or strengths, and it is often understood that they will not, in consequence, "love and cherish" each other in exactly the same ways. Nonetheless, at least in contemporary Western culture, it is common—and, I think, not unreasonable—for each partner in a marriage to aspire to occupy a space in the other's consciousness, which is at least as central and as large as the space occupied by the other in *their* own thoughts, and so, *if* Liz's thoughts and concerns are frequently benevolently focused on Keith, and do not engage with counterfactual marital imaginings, I think there are grounds for regarding Keith's marital regret as ethically defective, in relation to Liz. This Murdochian point applies, of course, even though Keith's behavior toward Liz is fine.

There is a further point, which a narrativist outlook can handle well, once we reject the narrowly individualist version of it. In getting married, the partners are normally understood to be expressing an intention to *share* their lives. (This is why preliminary conversations, about how each partner envisages the enterprise, may be wise. What time will we eat dinner?) Each person undertakes to coauthor the unfolding narrative *of the marriage*, in which this particular couple has the central role and in which the crucial pronoun is "we." That is why, beyond a certain point, Keith may need, ethically as well as prudentially, to restrain his regretful fantasy about Carey: it is at odds with, and arguably undermines, the narrative he has signed up to tell.

As for explanation, I suggested at the beginning of this chapter that, because of the impact on one's life of one's choice of spouse, the frequent occurrence of marital regret (at least in a transient form) should not surprise us. In addition, it is a familiar fact that contemporary Western capitalist culture hypes and sentimentalizes romantic love and weddings in a way that is bound to foster disappointment.

Many other sociological factors (e.g., the burden placed on marriage by our increasing longevity) could be relevantly cited. But, compatibly with these, it is worth mentioning the resources of psychoanalytical theory, which are deployed at a more fundamental, but less obvious, level of explanation.

Especially pertinent to our case, of course, is the Oedipus complex (called after the Greek myth narrated in Sophocles' tragedy, *Oedipus Rex*), first formulated by Freud and retained, although with important modifications, by his psychoanalytic successors. If the Oedipal hypothesis is correct, we do not only carry internalized versions of our earliest interpersonal relations throughout the rest of our lives, but we are also challenged in our earliest attachments by an intense love triangle that is not of our making and which introduces a painful and unavoidable ambivalence into our later attachments. Perhaps no other theory can offer a better, or more basic, explanation of marital regret. But that will have to wait for another time.[39]

NOTES

1. Landman and Manis (1992) provide some indicative data. They asked participants from three different samples of the population about what things they would do differently, in a range of domains, if they could have their lives over again. The most commonly expressed marriage-related counterfactual wish by the adult respondents was to have *timed* things differently: the majority in this group would have liked to have married later, after they had advanced their education or careers. The authors report that "Less than 10 percent . . . went so far as to say they would not marry the same person" (Landman and Manis 1992, 475). One wonders, however, whether those respondents who wished they had timed marriage differently were thinking (but not saying) that marrying at a different time would have meant marrying someone else? Today, the difference between marrying and cohabiting with a partner is often insignificant but, for the sake of simplicity, I will stipulate that the relation we are considering is legal "marriage," and I will refer to the two parties involved as "spouses." Although my example is heterosexual, I see no reason why a similar situation could not involve same-sex spouses.

2. In these novels, the regret is often to be *inferred* in circumstances when it is not explicitly voiced: it structures a character's mental life and is essential to the reader's grasp of the significance of the story. In Henry James' *Portrait of a Lady* (first published in 1881), Isabel Archer is unwilling to broadcast her marital unhappiness but the reader knows of it and the unvoiced supposition that she regrets marrying Osmond seems inescapable.

3. Connie Rosati argues that our nature as autonomous beings, who have to choose between various conceptions of the good, suggests that well-grounded regrets about our life choices may be unavoidable (Rosati 2007).

4. Arguably, Williams' distinction is *too* broad, if it cannot distinguish regret from wishful fantasy. See Scarre (2017) for a defense of Williams' formulation.

5. The distinction between rationality and functionality is not necessary for my purposes here.

6. Moreover, even the *attempt* at such a strategy would strike most people as ridiculous. That is not how we "fall in love," and our sense of the uniqueness of persons

makes us regard each one as "more than the sum of her parts." Furthermore, Keith does not necessarily believe that *only* someone like Carey would be a suitable spouse.

7. The most commonly regretted "inaction" was education, that is, a failure to undertake or to complete studies in college.

8. It is worth noting that the word "regret" wasn't actually used in the Terman study, but Gilovich and Medvec undertook a substantial amount of further research, where that word *was* used, to support their hypothesis. A 1984 survey of "ordinary conversation" in the United States looked at the frequency with which names of emotions appeared and found that "regret" was the second most frequently mentioned. "Love" came first (Shimanoff 1984).

9. But of course, we can, and often do, *also* remedy some kinds of inaction. For example, we may realize that we never thanked someone who helped us long ago and make this omission good. Perhaps, then, the inactions that cause us most regret are the ones that we cannot (straightforwardly) "undo."

10. Within this "indeterminate" category, fourteen respondents focused on their choice of spouse: "Should have chosen different mate; chose badly; poor marriage" (Gilovic and Medvec 1995, 382).

11. Note that thirteen of the respondents mentioned a "missed romantic opportunity" (Gilovich and Medvec 1995, 384).

12. Of course, there is also plenty of room for doubt about the coherence of regrets about one's past *actions* (in ways, e.g., discussed by Wallace), but this specific problem about finitude seems to apply especially to regrets about *not* having done various things or not having done more of them.

13. In fact, in his 1995 paper, Kahneman is not responding to the research by Gilovich and Medvec I have just discussed but that does not matter, since the difference of opinion is the same. The 1998 paper cowritten by all three researchers does take that Gilovich and Medvec research into account. In it, the three authors set out their difference in opinion once again and attempt a "partial resolution."

14. Although, interestingly, Williams' "constitutive thought" does still apply. One simply thinks that things would have been "better otherwise" in a wistful or enjoyable way. See Scarre (2017) for discussion of yet another putative type of "regret" (found in Descartes' writings), which, Scarre claims, is in fact a quite different phenomenon and therefore misleadingly named.

15. Note also that the adjective used by Kahneman—"wistful"—is more often associated with desire than with regret. According to the Merriam-Webster dictionary (accessed online), its primary definition is "full of yearning or desire tinged with melancholy."

16. Note, however, that the attribution of "full-blown" *beliefs* to Keith could be contested, and some of the sentences in this paragraph avoid this commitment. I do not have space to pursue this question, which belongs to the philosophy of emotion, but we can, at least, attribute Williams' "constitutive thought" to Keith.

17. Historical novels blend fact and imagination in a similar way such that the fact often strengthens the fiction.

18. According to the Merriam-Webster dictionary (accessed online), "fantasy" is "a creation of the imaginative faculty whether expressed or merely conceived."

19. Although I focus here on the Anglophone literature, there are also many important contributions to the theory of narrative by philosophers in continental Europe (see especially Ricoeur 1984).
20. The only *obvious* home for the concept of Narrative within philosophy is, I think, within aesthetics: film, drama, literature, and so on.
21. In a frequently cited sentence, MacIntyre claims, "The unity of a human life is the unity of a narrative quest" (MacIntyre 2007, 219). See Williams (2009) for harsh criticism.
22. As this remark in a footnote shows, Velleman thinks that the "added value" provided by narrative relations will be a feature of almost all cases of human lives. The exception, he suggests, would be a life: "with virtually no narrative structure at all—say, the life of someone who is maintained, from birth to death, in a state of semi-consciousness and inactivity" (Velleman 1991: 72).
23. As Anna Gotlib points out, power differentials may also play a role in determining which narratives "secure uptake." See her entry on "Feminist Ethics and Narrative Ethics" in the *Internet Encyclopedia of Philosophy*.
24. I think Velleman might find it hard to address this issue, because he seeks to resist the conclusion that the narrative-based evaluations made by people of their lives are determined by those people's individual, contingent desires (Velleman 1991, 75, footnote 23). If we admit the existence of "narrative desires," then their satisfaction is arguably no different from the satisfaction of the other desires we have in our lives, and it no longer adds to our well-being in a distinctive way.
25. For a pessimistic take on retrospection, see the last lines of Larkin's 1964 poem "Reference Back." The poem suggests that "linkage" to our past can only make us unhappy:

> Truly, though our element is time,
> We are not suited to the long perspectives
> Open at each instant of our lives.
> They link us to our losses: worse,
> They show us what we have as it once was,
> Blindingly undiminished, just as though
> By acting differently, we could have kept it so.

26. Alasdair MacIntyre claims that *social* obstacles, in the post-Industrial West, make it difficult for individuals to achieve narrative unity in their lives: "The social obstacles derive from the way in which modernity partitions each human life into a variety of segments, each with its own norms and modes of behavior. So work is divided from leisure, private life from public, the corporate from the personal. So both childhood and old age have been wrenched away from the rest of human life and made over into distinct realms. And all these separations have been achieved so that it is the distinctiveness of each and not the unity of the life of the individual who passes through those parts in terms of which we are taught to think and to feel" (MacIntyre 2007, 204).
27. Note that the sentence beginning "Rather . . ." marks an important divergence from Velleman, for whom the value-adding feature is the narrative structure itself, not the "recounting" of the narrative.

28. The central example in Rosati (2013) is borrowed from John Williams' (2003) novel *Stoner*, a novel that is very clearly the story of *one* life (Stoner's life), from beginning to end, and told from his perspective.

29. The clinical literature also recognizes more limitations to our *autonomy* as authors of the narratives of our lives. See Bruner (1987) for an illustration of the ways in which a collective family narrative can shape, and complicate, the identities of the family members. Psychoanalytical theory has much to offer on "narratives" of regret. Against Bittner (1992), I find the idea that healthy regret is a form of *mourning* extremely compelling. From this perspective, Larkin's attitude is dysfunctional precisely because of his inability to mourn the past.

30. Wollheim's psychoanalytically influenced philosophy addresses this lacuna. Examples of mental activity, he tells us, "are thinking a thought, volition or trying to perform an action, attention, repression, introjection" (Wollheim 1984, 34).

31. Martha Nussbaum is a prominent exponent of this view.

32. "Most people" is supposed to exclude philosophers who work on counterfactual statements. I do not mean to imply that there are *no* cases of regret where representational adequacy is central, and it certainly plays a role in beliefs (e.g., about causal consequences of an action) that are *associated* with regret.

33. A modal constraint is also often imposed in a different way, which can help to distinguish regrets from wishes. A friend has told me he sometimes wishes he were gay, but that he cannot *regret* not being gay, because he is never sexually attracted by other men.

34. This situation raises the issues—about luck in the way things turn out—discussed in Williams' presentation of "moral luck" (Williams 1976).

35. People also often quote the "Serenity prayer," written by the American theologian Reinhold Niebuhr: "God grant me the serenity to accept the things I cannot change; courage to change the things I can; and the wisdom to know the difference."

36. See Bagnoli (2003) for critical discussion of the contrast Murdoch draws between her views and Kant's.

37. Sartre and de Beauvoir, for example, famously did not demand sexual exclusivity of each other but—in a much-cited distinction—they saw their love affairs with others as "contingent" and their love for each other as "essential."

38. Until I checked its origins, I thought that "to hold," in the vow "to have and to hold," might refer to this sort of holding, that is, a "holding in mind." In fact, it is simply a variant of "to have": one is promising to hold one's spouse as one might hold a plot of land.

39. I would like to thank Sebastian Gardner, Richard Holton, Gabriele Taylor, Neil Vickers, and John Vorhaus for their helpful comments on the topic of regret and on an early draft of this chapter. Thanks also to Anna Gotlib for inviting me to write this chapter and for helpful comments at a late stage.

REFERENCES

Bagnoli, Carla. 2003. "Respect and Loving Attention." *Canadian Journal of Philosophy* 33 (4): 483–51.

Bittner, Rüdiger. 1992, "Is It Reasonable to Regret Things One Did?" *Journal of Philosophy* 89: 262–73.
Bruner, Jerome. 1987. "Life as Narrative." *Social Research* 54 (1): 11–32.
Byng-Hall, John. 1986. "Family Scripts: A Concept Which Can Bridge Child Psychotherapy and Family Therapy Thinking." *Journal of Child Psychotherapy* 12 (1): 3–13.
Dennett, Daniel C. 1992. "The Self as a Center of Narrative Gravity." In *Self and Consciousness: Multiple Perspectives*, eds., F. Kessel, P. Cole and D. Johnson. Hillsdale, NJ: Erlbaum.
Gilovich, T., and V. H. Medvec. 1995. "The Experience of Regret: What, When, and Why." *Psychological Review* 102 (2): 379–95.
Gilovich, T., V. H. Medvec, and D. Kahneman. 1998. "Varieties of Regret: A Debate and Partial Resolution." *Psychological Review* 105 (3): 602–5.
Gotlib, Anna. 2015. Feminist Ethics and Narrative Ethics. *Internet Encyclopedia of Philosophy*. http://www.iep.utm.edu/fem-e-n/.
Hurka, Thomas. 1996. "Monism, Pluralism, and Rational Regret." *Ethics* 106 (3): 555–75.
Inman, J., and Leigh McAlister. 1994. "Do Coupon Expiration Dates Affect Consumer Behavior?" *Journal of Marketing Research* 31: 423.
Kahneman, D., and A. Tversky. 1982. "The Psychology of Preferences." *Scientific American* 246: 160–73.
Kahneman, D. 1995. "Varieties of Counterfactual Thinking." In *What Might Have Been: The Social Psychology of Counterfactual Thinking*, ed. N. J. Roese and J. M. Olson, 375–396. Hillsdale, NJ: Lawrence Erlbaum.
Landman, J. 1987. "Regret and Elation Following Action and Inaction: Affective Responses to Positive Versus Negative Outcomes." *Personality and Social Psychology Bulletin* 13 (4): 524–36.
Landman, J., and J. D. Manis. 1992. "What Might Have Been: Counter-Factual Thought Concerning Personal Decisions." *British Journal of Psychology* 83: 473–77.
Landman, Janet. 1995. "Through a Glass Darkly: Worldviews, Counter-Factual Thought, and Emotion." In *What Might Have Been: The Social Psychology of Counterfactual Thinking*, ed. N. J. Roese and J. M. Olson, 233–58. Hillsdale, NJ: Erlbaum.
Lindemann, Hilde. 2014. *Holding and Letting Go: The Social Practice of Personal Identities*. New York: Oxford University Press.
MacIntyre, Alasdair. 2007. *After Virtue*, 3rd ed. London: Duckworth.
Murdoch, Iris. 1970. *The Sovereignty of Good*. London: Routledge.
Murdoch, Iris. 1998. *Existentialists and Mystics: Writings on Philosophy and Literature*, ed. Peter Conradi. New York: Allen Lane.
Ricoeur, Paul. 1984. *Time and Narrative*. Chicago, IL: University of Chicago Press.
Roese, N.J., and J. M. Olson, eds. 1995. *What Might Have Been. The Social Psychology of Counterfactual Thinking*. New Jersey: Lawrence Erblum.
Rosati, Connie S. 2007. "Mortality, Agency, and Regret." In *Moral Psychology*, ed. Sergio Tenenbaum, 231–60. New York: Rodopi.
Rosati, Connie S. 2013. "The Story of a Life." *Social Philosophy and Policy* 30 (1–2): 21–50.
Scarre, Geoffrey. 2017. "The 'Constitutive Thought' of Regret." *International Journal of Philosophical Studies* 5 (5): 569–85.

Shimanoff, Susan. 1984. "Commonly Named Emotions in Everyday Conversations." *Perceptual and Motor Skills* 58: 514–514.
Simonson, I. 1992. "The Influence of Anticipating Regret and Responsibility on Purchase Decisions." *Journal of Consumer Research* 19 (1): 105–18.
Smith, Angela M. 2005. "Responsibility for Attitudes: Activity and Passivity in Mental Life." *Ethics* 115 (2): 236–71.
Tenenbaum, Sergio, ed. 2007. *Moral Psychology (Poznan Studies in the Philosophy of the Sciences and the Humanities*, vol. 94). New York: Rodopi.
Velleman, David. 1991. "Well-Being and Time." *Pacific Philosophical Quarterly* 12: 48–77.
Velleman, David. 2003. "Narrative Explanation." *Philosophical Review* 112 (1): 1–25.
Wallace, R. Jay. 2013. *The View from Here: On Affirmation, Attachment, and the Limits of Regret*. Oxford: Oxford University Press.
Williams, Bernard. 1973. "Ethical Consistency." In *Problems of the Self*, 166–86. Cambridge: Cambridge University Press.
Williams, Bernard. 1981. "Moral Luck." In *Moral Luck*, 20–39. Cambridge: Cambridge University Press.
Williams, John. 2003. *Stoner*. New York: New York Review.
Williams, Bernard. 2009. "Life as Narrative." *European Journal of Philosophy* 17 (2): 305–14.
Wollheim, Richard. 1984. *The Thread of Life*. Cambridge, MA: Harvard University Press.
Zeelenberg, M. 1999. "The Use of Crying Over Spilled Milk: A Note on the Rationality and Functionality of Regret." *Philosophical Psychology* 12 (3): 325–40.
Zeelenberg, M., and J. Beattie. 1997. "Consequences of Regret Aversion: 2. Additional Evidence for Effects of Feedback on Decision Making." *Organizational Behavior and Human Decision Processes* 72 (1): 63–78.

Chapter 7

Regret, Responsibility, and the Brain

Ben Timberlake, Giorgio Coricelli,
and Nadège Bault

Regret describes an emotion that arises from a variety of circumstances. We focus here on a particular type of regret, decision regret, which comes to the study of decision making by way of traditional economics, along with insights from psychology. This is clearly not the only formal description of regret, but it bears resemblance to variations studied in other fields. The benefits of this regret definition are its formalization, its operationalized measurability, and its attendant body of literature in neuroimaging, which is especially critical for comparison to the neural bases of other phenomena.

Regret refers to a specific set of conditions and responses, which include learning from an imagined alternative outcome that could have been reached through different action by the person feeling the emotion. This arises after an actor or agent has made a choice, sees its outcome, and then realizes that another outcome—the result of a different choice—is more desirable. Decision-based regret, or "decision regret," is proportional to the magnitude of the difference between the obtained and missed outcome. These elements are the definitive components of decision regret: learning, responsibility, and counterfactual information. Other emotions may arise from any one or two of these elements, but all three must be present for regret. These situational requirements have long guided the psychological description of regret (Zeelenberg et al. 1996; Zeelenberg and Pieters 2007), and they persist in the economic definition of decision regret (Loomes and Sudgen 1982). Decision-making studies operationalize this description, using both behavior and a modified utility function to quantify the effects of the emotional experience (Bell 1982; Loomes and Sudgen 1982).

Like most decision processes, moral decision making pits multiple options against one another in an effort to arrive at the most desirable outcome. Moral norms are personal convictions reflecting rules of conduct one ought to adopt in a given situation. They represent socially derived, internalized values attributed to a pattern of behavior thought to be appropriate (Manstead 2000). Moral norms play an important role in decision making because internalized values attributed to a particular course of action are likely to guide behavior. Consequently, behaving in contradiction to one's own moral norms is likely to elicit strong negative emotions. In such a situation, regret is likely to arise, especially if the norm violation results in a negative outcome. Some studies suggest that feelings of regret are anticipated at the prospect of violating one's moral norms (Parker, Manstead, and Stradling 1995). Other studies have shown that anticipated regret and moral norms are confounded in explaining choices, especially those with moral implications (Newton et al. 2013; Rivis, Sheeran, and Armitage 2009). Despite preliminary evidence from social psychology of a possible overlap between anticipated regret and moral norms, the cognitive mechanisms linking the two concepts have not yet been deeply investigated. Evidence from neuropsychology, however, suggests that the brain mechanisms underlying regret anticipation and the implementation of moral norms might involve similar neural circuits.

By tracing the brain activity associated with moral decision making and decision regret behaviors, it becomes clear that some of the same brain areas are similarly implicated in both processes, suggesting that some connections between the two categories of choice may be identified. Here, we explore this potential connection between moral- and regret-based decisions by reviewing their features and neural bases.

COUNTERFACTUAL INFORMATION

Regret arises from comparison to an alternative result: one that has not actually occurred. It requires the imagination of an alternative reality that results from a different choice than the one made. The process of deconstructing the present to imagine a different reality, called counterfactual thinking, is at the core of regret. Counterfactual thoughts are often generated after goal failure (Byrne 2002). The functional role of upward counterfactual thinking, and thus of associated regret, is to learn from mistakes, to generate variant courses of action suspected to prove more successful when similar situations are encountered in the future.

In a simple illustration of the definition and measurement of decision regret, imagine a game of chance: a slot machine. A gambler can pull the lever in exactly one way and take whatever result comes. Win or lose, his actions make no difference (other than the choice to play the game in the first place). Nature, wearing the guise of probability, determines the outcome every time. If he loses, the gambler by definition feels disappointment (and if he wins, satisfaction) but not regret. Now imagine two slot machines next to each other. The gambler must choose one on which to stake his fortunes, yet when he pulls the lever, the wheels spin on both machines, and he can see both outcomes. Now he sees both his actual winnings or losses on the machine he chose as well as what he would have won or lost had he selected the other machine. If his slot machine loses while the other wins, he can imagine a world in which he made a different, winning, choice. This identification of the counterfactual precipitates regret. Simulations of this situation have been used in various experimental settings to measure and compare regret to disappointment (Camille et al. 2004; Gillan et al. 2014; Nicolle et al. 2011).

Regret is further characterized by a negative-valence error, which differentiates it from relief. The error is the difference between the obtained outcome and the imagined counterfactual outcome. This is an important distinction in regret: that the error must have negative valence rather than the obtained outcome itself. This underscores the idea that regret is the negative result of comparison between outcomes, which may give rise to changes in behavior. In the slot machine study, even when subjects won with a certain choice but saw that they could have won more had they made a different choice, the net emotional sensation was negative (Camille et al. 2004). People describe their emotions as more negative with a better foregone choice, even when the obtained outcome is the same. This comparison is so clear that the emotion following a good outcome of a choice made (winning $50) compared to a very good outcome of a foregone choice ($200) can be rated even lower than that following a bad obtained outcome (−$50) compared to a very bad outcome avoided (−$200) (Camille et al. 2004). That is, despite winning more money, people said they felt worse—because they compared their winnings with what they could have won had they made a different choice. This ability to imagine an alternative reality after the fact informs decision problems not yet encountered. In fact, after experiencing regret, subjects made choices in subsequent tasks that were consistent with trying to minimize that feeling of regret (Coricelli, Dolan, and Sirigu 2007).

LEARNING VALUE

In a more complex scenario that employs regret in learning, we might assign the two machines different probabilities of paying out. We could task the decision maker with earning the most money and therefore the goal of choosing the right (i.e., more likely) machine to play more often over the course of a number of opportunities. Such a sequential task (as employed in Daw et al. 2006) allows the exploration of learning and the comparison of various models, which can include those that incorporate regret learning. Lohrenz and colleagues adopt the regret-learning model and rename it "fictive learning" to discard emotional connotations and to maintain only the error signal of an unobtained outcome (Lohrenz et al. 2007). Subjects played an investment game, in which the researchers saw that incorporating fictive error (the difference between chosen-obtained and foregone-obtained) over gains better predicted the subject's subsequent bet than simple reward prediction error: the difference between what the subject thought she would win/lose and what she actually won/lost.

In the scenario of sequential choices of two different gambles, the difference between the results of the choice the gambler made and those of the one he did not—precisely the measure we call decision regret—can be described as a signal enlisted to learn to make better choices. That ability depends on computing that difference, then employing it to foresee a possible recurrence before the next choice is made, and finally making a different, presumably better choice (Coricelli et al. 2005). Anticipation of regret induces a disposition to change behavioral strategies (Ritov 1996) and characterizes an emotion-motivated learning process in decision making (Zeelenberg et al. 1996). In theories of adaptive learning driven by regret-based feedback (Foster and Vohra 1999; Foster and Young 2003; Hart 2005; Hart and Mas-Colell 2000; Megiddo 1980), learning occurs by adjusting the propensity to choose an action according to the difference between the total rewards that could have been obtained with the choice of that action and the realized total rewards. That is, the tendency of choosing machine A depends on how much would have been won by choosing that machine all along compared to how much the gambler has actually won. As gamblers, humans tend to be pretty good at this. Following regret-based learning models, decision makers converge to optimal choices (Coricelli and Rustichini 2010).

RESPONSIBILITY

People show strong regularities in the nature of the event they "undo" when reflecting on a bad situation. One of these regularities, the agency effect, is particularly at stake in the experience of regret: people more often generate counterfactuals that undo some undertaken action rather than inaction (Byrne 2002). Thus, people have greater regret for actions they have taken, more so than for those they failed to take—at least in the short term. When no action could have been taken to prevent a bad outcome, and in the absence of agency, people report feeling disappointment rather than regret. Disappointment is also elicited by counterfactual thought, though the critical outcome must be due to circumstances beyond the agent's control, absolving him of responsibility. The key distinction is this: Disappointment arises from recognizing that a better outcome might have come given the same choice; regret, from identifying a better outcome given a different choice (Zeelenberg et al. 1998). Both emotions come from examining outcomes and seeing that a better one could have been obtained, but regret is associated with the responsibility of having caused the suboptimal outcome by taking a specific action. Because regret comes with the outcome of a forgone choice, it does bring with it greater information, but its effect on subsequent decisions amounts to more than simply the addition of that data. Rather, the increased information allows for the recognition of agency, along with counterfactual comparison.

Zeelenberg and colleagues sought to differentiate regret from both disappointment and a general sense of happiness by repeating and expanding on studies by Connolly, Ordoñez, and Coughlan (1997). They asked college students to consider scenarios in which fictional college students changed their class assignments—either by their own choice or by computer fiat. The results of these changes for the fictional students range from improvement to neutral to downgrade. The subjects rated how the fictional students would feel along scales measuring happiness, regret, and disappointment as well as to what extent students in the stories were responsible for their outcomes. The researchers found that happiness tracked outcome but not responsibility, while disappointment and regret were assessed inversely depending on level of responsibility: that is, the more responsibility subjects perceived, the greater the amount of regret they believed the character would feel in downgrade outcomes.

Children as young as five seem to have some grasp of their agency. In a choice task involving two boxes containing different amounts of stickers, children reported greater happiness or unhappiness when they chose which box to open than when the choice was determined by an experimenter or a roll of dice (Weisberg and Beck 2012). Though it was long unclear at what age the notion of personal responsibility in choices emerges, recent research suggests that agency does not influence the emotional response to outcomes in children younger than six (Guerini, FitzGibbon, and Coricelli 2018). Using a modified wheels of fortune task (with stickers rather than money as the winnings) on children between ages three and ten, Guerini and colleagues found that children were more sensitive to the outcomes of the choice they made than those the computer made for them—but only in trials with complete feedback and only significantly for children ages six and older. That is, both counterfactual outcome and responsibility were required in order for the child to feel the outcome with greater magnitude. In trials with just partial feedback, the children's sensitivity to outcomes was similar when they made the choice and when the computer made the choice—situations that generate disappointment rather than regret. This evidence of differentiation at young ages further supports the necessary role of agency in regret.

NEURAL CIRCUITS OF REGRET

The comparison between the outcome of a choice and the foregone outcome of an alternative option triggers specific brain responses. The ventromedial prefrontal cortex (vmPFC) encodes the difference between what has been obtained and the outcome of the nonchosen option (Coricelli et al. 2005). The vmPFC is a functional area that includes the anatomical medial orbitofrontal cortex (mOFC), an area that encompasses the most central parts of both hemispheres at the very front of the brain. The vmPFC is believed to hold on to reward value over time, possibly through tonic activity, then to send that signal to other areas involved in choice, like the dorsolateral prefrontal cortex (dlPFC) and the medial caudate (Behrens et al. 2008; Hampton, Bossaerts, and O'Doherty 2006). Findings from neuroimaging studies support the understanding that responsibility is a necessary component of experiencing regret. Indeed, during the lottery task, activity of the OFC in response to a gain or a loss was modulated by the outcome of the nonchosen lottery (Coricelli, Dolan, and Sirigu 2007). However, when the outcome of the nonchosen lottery remained unknown, the counterfactual process between losses (or wins) and any missed outcome of the chosen lottery was accompanied by a weaker effect in OFC activity. Thus, the OFC appears to encode the counterfactual comparison between obtained and unobtained outcomes but only when the result comes from a choice rather than misfortune. vmPFC signals the value of the obtained outcome compared to that of the nonobtained outcome, suggesting that these regret signals are related to the way the brain evaluates choices and their consequences. It exhibits activity that correlates with regret at all stages of the choice process: preference, expectation, and reward (Montague, King-Casas, and Cohen 2006).

Correlates of regret have also been measured in parts of the brain considered to have key roles in assessing and communicating the value of choice (Nicolle et al. 2011). In neuroimaging studies, the anterior cingulate cortex (ACC) and hippocampus have also shown increased activity correlated with regret during choice tasks (Coricelli et al. 2005). The hippocampus, a cortical folding below the cerebral cortex, is implicated in consciously accessible declarative memory, which is important for making future decisions based on past events (Coricelli et al. 2007), such as trying to avoid previously encountered suboptimal outcomes. This ability to guide future actions is a key component in anticipating regret based on experience.

The vmPFC increased activity during the reported experience of regret reoccurs in the period just before making subsequent choices—the period leading up to a decision in which regret would be anticipated (Coricelli et al. 2007). Because the signal measured in the vmPFC appears in other areas, this reoccurrence suggests that the measurement is not merely of happiness nor simply an outcome value (Coricelli et al. 2005; Van Hoeck, Watson, and Barbey 2015). It suggests that regret is computed by one brain area and then conveyed to others that modulate and implement it in subsequent decisions. Critically, the differentiation of experience and anticipation is clear, though they both involve the vmPFC/mOFC (Coricelli et al. 2005). Thanks to that error signal, along with the opportunity to make a different choice, modeling regret anticipation is a reliable predictor of choice probability in certain sequential decision tasks (Coricelli et al. 2005; Marchiori and Warglien 2008). Marchiori and Warglien found that incorporating a regret signal into even a simple learning neural network better predicted human behavior than long-employed models like reinforcement learning and a hybrid model that combines reinforcement learning with a player's beliefs about other players. Coricelli and colleagues observed that, as players experienced more regret in complete-feedback trials of a sequential wheels of fortune task, they decreasingly chose options more likely to lead to regret. They also saw that the more a given choice had led to regret before, the less likely the subject was to choose it again (Coricelli et al. 2005). Regret, then, is not merely a negative emotion, but a calculated signal that guides agents away from choices that could reproduce that signal. This effort to minimize regret is a key differentiator in its role as a learning mechanism: the emotional experience alone would have little meaning beyond sensation, were it not to guide future behavior.

The examination of choice behavior of patients with lesions in the vmPFC reveals insightful to understand the causal link between regret-related brain activity and behavior. vmPFC patients are typically described as making disastrous life decisions despite apparently intact cognitive abilities. Experimentally, they are known to display abnormal emotions elicited by reward and punishment (Bechara, Tranel, and Damasio 2000; Bechara et al. 1996). Careful investigation of the underlying computational deficits has revealed a general deficit in integrating values attributed to various actions with the current goals (Camille et al. 2011), function that has been assigned to the vmPFC in brain imaging studies. Patients are able to assign a subjective value to options; however, they will not commit to the option with the highest value. Additionally, vmPFC lesions result in an inability to feel regret after a bad choice and consequently in anticipating future regret during the decision process (Camille et al., 2004). Both reported subjective ratings of the outcome of their choices and the associated skin conductance responses of vmPFC patients were different from that of controls. They failed to reflect a modulation by the outcome of the alternative option, which is the signature of regret. While controls learned to avoid potential regret during the course of the task, vmPFC patients did not.

While the fMRI and lesion studies mentioned above have identified common neural mechanisms for experienced and anticipated regret, more recent findings suggest that people with psychiatric and neurological dysfunction can exhibit one stage of the process but not another (Gillan et al. 2014; Levens et al. 2014). Although brain areas associated with the several stages of processing and anticipating regret overlap, they are not coextensive. Damage to the vmPFC may allow the recognition and experience of regret but not its application to future decisions (Levens et al. 2014). Various dysfunctions of this regret mechanism offer at least partial explanations of the behavior of people with evidence of neurological disorders. Both obsessive-compulsive disorder patients and people with high indications of psychopathy report feeling regret more keenly but do not avoid it in future choices to the same extent as healthy subjects (Gillan et al. 2014; Hughes, Dolan, and Stout 2013).

MORAL DECISION MAKING

The vmPFC, which represents a crucial portion of a proposed regret circuit, also plays a key role in some emotional components of moral decisions (Blair 2007; Koenigs et al. 2007; Moll et al. 2002). Brain imaging studies of moral decision making have implicated some of the same areas and networks in the frontal cortex that are associated with emotion and deliberation—often finding these regions to be in competition during difficult choices. A study of moral judgment (without any decision component) implicated the mOFC as part of a neural circuit that showed higher activity when subjects read sentences with a moral component. The same areas, which also included the temporal pole and the superior temporal sulcus, did not show higher activation when subjects read statements with emotional components but no moral element (Moll et al. 2002). Researchers have developed a range of these problems to probe the spectrum of moral decision making, and this has yielded distinct differences in choice and brain activity. Among the most well-known set of dilemmas is the family that arises from the trolley problem. Subjects read about a hypothetical situation in which they are standing next to a set of railroad tracks, while some distance away, a group of workers is standing on the track. The subjects are told that they see a streetcar coming down the tracks with no chance of stopping before striking and killing the five workers. The subjects are told they are standing next to a lever, which, if they pull it, will switch the car and send the train onto a side track, where there is a lone worker who will be struck and killed. Though this would be a difficult situation in real life, in the hypothetical, it is characterized as easy and impersonal—because the subject's level of involvement from the consequences is distant and most people presented with the question answer quickly and in the same manner (Greene et al. 2004). Most people choose to pull the lever, making a simple utility calculation (Greene et al. 2001). A variant of this dilemma that brings the decision closer to the subject, however, is the footbridge problem. Now, the subject is on a bridge over the railroad tracks. He can still see the workers, and there is still a street car barreling toward them, but instead of a switch, the subject has the opportunity to save the workers by pushing a large person, who is also on the bridge, off the bridge and into the path of the street car, saving the five workers but killing the innocent person. Given simple calculation of number of people saved versus killed, these situations are identical. Yet according to Greene (2007), the closeness of the action brings the emotional salience of the problem into conflict with the pure utilitarian calculation. This antagonism seems to be carried out in the brain in both processes and areas that bear resemblance to the experience of regret (Koenigs et al. 2007).

Another family of moral decisions brings an even sharper contrast. It starts with the easily solved infanticide dilemma, which poses the question of whether or not a teenage mother should kill her unwanted newborn baby. The prospect of killing a baby in service of discomfort is easily rejected, and subjects respond quickly and uniformly in the negative. Brain imaging during this decision showed lower levels of activity in the ACC and the dlPFC, suggesting little conflict between the overwhelming emotional aversion to the choice to kill the baby and the low level of utility. Subjects also consider a more difficult analogue of this problem: the crying baby dilemma, in which subjects are asked to imagine a group of people hiding from a group of outlaws. Among the people hiding are a mother and her newborn baby who begins to cry. This could alert the outlaws to the presence of those hiding, resulting in their deaths, including the baby. Subjects are asked if it is morally permissible for the mother to smother her baby to death, saving the people but killing her own baby. Here, the calculation leads to a simple utilitarian conclusion that more people are saved by killing the baby. Yet, this stands in conflict with the stark emotional opposition to killing a baby.

Notably, both types of moral dilemma—personal and impersonal—incorporate degrees of action, though Greene et al. (2004) differentiate between the greater agency of "authoring" and the impersonal deflection of a threat, described as "editing." Regret similarly requires a personal agency—that responsibility attenuated only if the choice giving rise to the emotion is shared with others (Nicolle et al. 2011). The role of responsibility links the two considerations and carries the question of decision-making regret to a moral level. The more a person gauges himself responsible for an outcome, the more keenly he feels regret (Frijda, Kuipers, and ter Schure 1989).

Both ranges of moral decision—those that favor utilitarian decisions and those with a greater emotional component—employ brain areas that compose part of the regret circuit. Greene and colleagues observed increased activity in the ACC and the dlPFC during more difficult dilemmas like the crying baby and the footbridge problems compared to easier dilemmas. They argue that this indicates that the ACC detects these conflicts and that the dlPFC then deliberates and resolves them. Supporting this framework, the dlPFC shows even greater activity when the problem results in a utilitarian judgment that violates personal morality. But it is also possible that the dlPFC instigates a period of cognitive control, delaying the decision to allow the ACC enough time to employ a utilitarian cognitive response, thus overriding a more immediate affective response (Greene et al. 2004). If the ACC is a general arbiter of antagonism, then it is no surprise that it would be more active both in cases of difficult moral dilemmas and for discrepancies between predictions and realities, as in experiences of regret. This shared step in decision making connects the two processes and suggests that cognitive resolution of conflicts of any type may be handled with some similarity.

OFC LESIONS MODULATE REGRET AND MORALITY

Patients with vmPFC lesions, like those who demonstrated difficulty with applying anticipated regret, also exhibit trouble in following social norms. Presented with the footbridge problem, which demands proximate action, most healthy people cannot overcome the emotional aversion of the proposition. Conversely, vmPFC patients exhibited utilitarian behavior, choosing to sacrifice one life in favor of five, a decision that appears to consider only the final tally of the choice and to ignore the emotional aspects (Koenigs et al. 2007). In a battery of hypothetical situations, these patients were presented with choices of sacrificing one life to save multiple other lives. Among the best-known nonemotionally salient dilemmas is the trolley problem, in which the trolley is diverted by a lever onto a track with one person, avoiding the death of five. In this dilemma, vmPFC lesion patients make the choice to pull the lever about as often as healthy controls do, making a pure calculation about the impersonal action of pulling a lever. Given that these patients had impaired autonomic activity in response to emotionally charged pictures, the authors conclude that the problem in generating "normal" moral judgments come from impaired emotional processing. This was supported by two other studies showing that vmPFC patients do not experience aversive emotional responses to moral violations (Ciaramelli and di Pellegrino 2011; Gu et al. 2015). When a personal element is involved, healthy people choose to intervene much less frequently (Greene et al. 2001). Not so lesion patients, who continue to make the utilitarian choice at about the same rate as they did in the less-emotional impersonal scenario (Koenigs et al. 2007).

Importantly, vmPFC lesions also impair the experience of self-conscious emotions such as shame or embarrassment (Beer et al. 2003). Moreover, the social behavior of lesion patients in social norms reinforcing games has been compared to that of psychopaths (Koenigs, Kruepke, and Newman 2010). It should also be noted that we do not suggest that the moral dilemmas described elicit regret. Rather, because the outcome of the choice has consequences for other people, the anticipated negative counterfactual emotion involved in these situations would better be described as remorse or guilt: cognitively distinct from regret (Baskin-Sommers, Stuppy-Sullivan, and Buckholtz 2016). Nonetheless, the results from the vmPFC patient studies mentioned here suggest that taking responsibility for one's own actions, questioning oneself, feeling regret, and reinforcing social norms rely on the same neural circuitry.

PSYCHOPATHY

Psychopathy is characterized by diminished inhibitory control, impulsive behavior, and violence. Notably, the psychiatric condition is also attended by unusual morality judgment, including the conflation of conventional and moral violations (Blair 1995). While healthy people see great differences in a conventional violation such as wearing inappropriate clothes in public and a moral violation such as hitting another person, psychopaths see less difference between the two types of transgression. Psychopaths are also more tolerant of moral transgressions against other people, which may stem from a lack of sufficient aversion to distress in others (Blair 2007). They display a similar deficiency for aversion in cost-benefit choice series.

The impaired decision making by people with psychopathic tendencies has long been attributed to their curtailed experience of emotions involving responsibility (Koenigs et al. 2012), but recent studies suggest that the breakdown in learning via regret happens further downstream, at the point of employing regret values in subsequent choices (Baskin-Sommers et al. 2016; Gillan et al. 2014; Hughes et al. 2013). This may well stem from a diminished vmPFC, which in psychopathic individuals, has been shown to be reduced in every dimension: volume, thickness, and surface area (Baskin-Sommers et al. 2016; Yang et al. 2005). If other considerations are equal, healthy people make the choice that carries the least expected regret, sometimes even at the cost of profit. Yet the higher people scored on a psychopathy scale, the less likely they were to avoid regret in a repeated wheels of fortune task (Baskin-Sommers et al. 2016). That behavior could not be explained by a lower negative reaction to a more desirable counterfactual outcome—in fact, high-psychopathy-scoring subjects had negative affects similar or exceeding controls. Those who scored highest on a psychopathy self-report scale experienced negative affects after a bad choice but seemed to ignore the signals warning them away from those choices with high possible regret. Their behavior was only driven by the expected value of the options. Another study failed to find a clear link between regret avoidance and psychopathic traits in criminal offenders (Hughes et al. 2013).

People with psychopathic indications are thus apparently capable of imagining alternative realities and generating and experiencing the negative emotion associated with the comparison to actual reality, suggesting that psychopathy is characterized not by a deficit of emotion but by weakened general cognitive processes like feed-forward counterfactual representation. So if these people were experiencing the emotion but apparently not employing it in choice tasks immediately following arousal, it raised the possibility that the information was not being applied to guide future choices in the manner of predictive models.

The understanding of moral processing in psychopaths is not well understood. Though people with psychopathy have long been observed to engage in amoral behavior, the mechanism of that deficiency has only recently been explored. Psychopathy has been ascribed to a depleted ability to empathize with a person being harmed as well as to a deficient mechanism that inhibits violence (Blair 1995). In that study, in which criminal offenders considered several scenarios of moral and conventional violations set in a school, Blair found that psychopaths significantly did not differentiate permissibility between the two types of violations, while nonpsychopaths did. Blair rejects several models in which psychopaths experience moral emotions but do not employ them in mentalization or fail to take perspectives of others. Rather, he proposes a fault in a separate system, a "violence inhibition mechanism." Cima Tonnaer, and Hauser (2010), by contrast, argue that while people with psychopathic traits may have some emotional deficits, enough emotion is preserved (or in fact may be unnecessary) to make similar moral judgments to healthy controls. The fact that they can identify the rightness or wrongness of moral actions, but then by definition act in contrivance, indicates that they may simply not care about morality, the study suggests. Whatever emotional component that is lacking in people with psychopathy may be the element responsible for the application of the moral understanding toward future decisions.

Yet by refining groups of people by placement on the psychopathy scale and with greater precision in the moral dilemmas presented, Koenigs and colleagues find that a counterfactual mechanism may indeed be at fault for some abnormal moral choices by people with psychopathy (2012). Using inmates from a Wisconsin prison, the study considered only those participants who scored in the highest and lowest portions of psychopathy indications. So doing further refined the high scorers in terms of their assessed anxiety as a part of a working theory that psychopathy is too broad a term for several possible conditions. Using the same situations as in the Greene study, both high-anxious psychopaths and nonpsychopaths endorsed the utilitarian outcome of personal dilemmas with approximately the same lower frequency. But low-anxious psychopaths judged the utilitarian choice acceptable more often than either of the other groups. The finding suggests that some subtypes of people with psychopathic indications resolve the emotion-utility conflict in a similarly unusual manner to that with which psychopathic people eschew regret.

A SOCIAL DIMENSION OF REGRET AND AGENCY

The consideration of others connects with regret not only in representing levels of responsibility. The regret circuit colocates with neurological phenomena that involve consideration of others via social versus private situations (Bault et al. 2011; Zhu, Mathewson, and Hsu 2012). Studies on levels of strategic thinking have shown higher levels associated with the same areas as counterfactual emotions like regret (Bault et al. 2011). In an experimental game called the "beauty contest" or "guessing game," the choices a player makes indicate the extent to which he is thinking about other players and how much he thinks they are thinking about him. Increased amounts of this recursive thinking are associated with higher levels of brain activity in the mOFC (Coricelli and Nagel 2009), the location of most of the vmPFC—a key component of the regret circuit. As with so many colocated brain activities, however, it is necessary to note that anatomical proximity does not necessarily indicate a functional relationship. Nevertheless, the notion of thinking about the activity in other brains (in the case of the recursive thinking demanded in the beauty contest) is different from other types of input in a similar way that the calculation and experience of counterfactual-based emotions (as in the case of regret) varies from other input—that is, it is largely internal.

Studies have associated the vmPFC/mOFC with thoughts about others (Frith and Frith 1999; Gallagher and Frith 2003; Hampton et al. 2006; Suzuki et al. 2016). These areas become active not only when thinking about others—when evaluating violations of social norms, for example—but also when it comes to representing our own mental state, including emotion (Gallagher and Frith 2003). When subjects were directed to think about a friend or someone who was similar to them, the vmPFC showed stronger activations (Mitchell, Macrae, and Banaji 2006). Given the vmPFC/mOFC association with processing information relevant to the self, Mitchell and colleagues suggest that thinking about related others may depend on self-evaluations in the vmPFC. This introduces the possibility of a connection between internal and external considerations: between regret's internally oriented self-evaluation and thoughts about others.

In fact, despite regret's essential interior aspect, it has been shown to be modulated by the actions of others. If an individual experiences regret that comes as the partial result of the actions of others, the brain appears to shift some of the blame for the less-then-optimal outcome to these others—thus reducing at least the anticipation of regret (Nicolle et al. 2011). As described above, measurable regret is defined by the notion of agency. It is usually addressed in a polar manner, however: with agency, the negative feeling associated with a different outcome is regret; and in its absence, disappointment (Zeelenberg et al. 1998). But within those categorizations, there appears to be room for gradation. Nicolle et al. had participants complete a task in which they made similar gambling choices as in standard regret tasks, but in some trials, the choice was determined not by the participant alone but by vote (they were told) of a group of which they were a member, ranging from two to eight people in all. In this case, the participant's action alone did not determine the choice and its attendant result. The measured effect saw reduced activity in the amygdala, compared to trials in which the participant was solely responsible for choices. The amygdala, implicated in emotional memory, is associated with activity involving personally relevant information. It is also known to integrate the relationship between stimulus and reward and to send it on to the vmPFC, where the information is used in subsequent choices (Coricelli et al. 2005). So increased activity during instances of regret in which the participant is the only decision maker suggests a kind of "self-blame regret," Nicolle and colleagues argue. The diminished sense of responsibility attenuates the negative feeling of regret, and that consequently appears also to dampen the learning effect. A better response in an alternative reality becomes clearer in the amygdala with greater individual responsibility. A related question, unexplored to this point, is how, if at all, shared responsibility for positive outcomes might modulate brain activity compared to that of negative outcomes or for positive outcomes that result from solo choices.

CONCLUSION

The goal of any decision process is to arrive at the optimal outcome, given the conditions. But when several important factors come into conflict in a decision, the brain must mediate among them. Separately, the processes for moral decision making and choices involving decision regret have been further explored via brain imaging and lesion studies. These have shown segments of these processes to share some anatomy and even similar dysfunction among people with psychopathy or lesions to the vmPFC. Our understanding of both systems still needs clarity before they can be considered to play any part in each other. But some recent research proposes frameworks that hint at how they might be joined. Blair argues that the learning systems in the vmPFC are the foundations of moral decisions that concern harm to other people (2007). These same systems undergird error signals that include decision regret. The work by Greene and colleagues suggested that the vmPFC might serve in a regulatory role, delaying decisions during high-conflict or difficult dilemmas—especially those involving competition between emotional and utilitarian outcomes. Moll and de Oliveira-Souza push back on Greene's model, saying this conflict framework is too complex. They hold instead that the lesions attenuate the prosocial influence of the vmPFC, thus allowing utilitarian decisions without the interference of emotion. Those who see the most connection between learning signals and moral decisions include Thomas and colleagues, who argue that the vmPFC's role is similar across reasoning processes, including moral and complex decision making. The vmPFC appears to integrate emotion into judgments of complicated decisions, acting as adjudicator when considering future consequences (Thomas, Croft, and Tranel 2011).

Moral decisions play serious emotional consequences in preserving the lives (or limbs) of others, while decision regret concerns the possible emotional pain of making a choice that results in something less than another known, better outcome. Though the implications of these decisions are of different magnitudes, the human brain appears to process similarly some of these difficult moral dilemmas and the effort required to avoid regret. These complex decisions require the ability to consider the impact of the choice before it is taken. They demand the ability to assess realities both encountered and imagined and to place them in conflict with each other while judging one to be the best.

AUTHOR NOTE

This work was supported by a European Research Council Consolidator Grant "Transfer Learning within and between brains" (TRANSFER-LEARNING; agreement No. 617629).

REFERENCES

Baskin-Sommers, Arielle R., Craig S. Neumann, Lora M. Cope, and Kent A. Kiehl. 2016. "Latent-Variable Modeling of Brain Gray-Matter Volume and Psychopathy in Incarcerated Offenders." *Journal of Abnormal Psychology* 125 (6): 811–817.
Baskin-Sommers, Arielle, Allison M. Stuppy-Sullivan, and Joshua W. Buckholtz. 2016. "Psychopathic Individuals Exhibit but Do Not Avoid Regret during Counterfactual

Decision-Making." *Proceedings of the National Academy of Sciences* 113 (50): 14438–43. doi: 10.1073/pnas.1609985113.

Bault, Nadège, Mateus Joffily, Aldo Rustichini, and Giorgio Coricelli. 2011. "Medial Prefrontal Cortex and Striatum Mediate the Influence of Social Comparison on the Decision Process." *Proceedings of the National Academy of Sciences* 108 (38): 16044–49. doi: 10.1073/pnas.1100892108.

Beer, Jennifer S., Erin A. Heerey, Dacher Keltner, Donatella Scabini, and Robert T. Knight. 2003. "The Regulatory Function of Self-Conscious Emotion: Insights from Patients with Orbitofrontal Damage." *Journal of Personality and Social Psychology* 85 (4): 594–604. doi: 10.1037/0022-3514.85.4.594.

Behrens, Timothy E. J., Laurence T. Hunt, Mark W. Woolrich, and Matthew F. S. Rushworth. 2008. "Associative Learning of Social Value." *Nature* 456 (7219): 245–9. doi: 10.1038/nature07538.

Bell, David E. 1982. "Regret in Decision Making under Uncertainty." *Operations Research* 30 (5): 961–81. doi: 10.1287/opre.30.5.961.

Blair, R. J. 1995. "A Cognitive Developmental Approach to Mortality: Investigating the Psychopath." *Cognition* 57 (1): 1–29. doi: 10.1016/0010-0277(95)00676-P.

Blair, R. J. R. 2007. "The Amygdala and Ventromedial Prefrontal Cortex in Morality and Psychopathy." *Trends in Cognitive Sciences* 11 (9): 387–92. doi: 10.1016/j.tics.2007.07.003.

Byrne, Ruth M. J. 2002. "Mental Models and Counterfactual Thoughts about What Might Have Been." *Trends in Cognitive Sciences* 6 (10): 426–31. doi: 10.1016/S1364-6613(02)01974-5.

Camille, Nathalie, Giorgio Coricelli, Jerome Sallet, Pascale Pradat-Diehl, Jean-René Duhamel, and Angela Sirigu. 2004. "The Involvement of the Orbitofrontal Cortex in the Experience of Regret." *Science (New York, N.Y.)* 304 (ii): 1167–70. doi: 10.1126/science.1094550.

Ciaramelli, Elisa, and Giuseppe di Pellegrino. 2011. "Ventromedial Prefrontal Cortex and the Future of Morality." *Emotion Review* 3 (3): 308–9. doi: 10.1177/1754073911402381.

Cima, Maaike, Franca Tonnaer, and Marc D. Hauser. 2010. "Psychopaths Know Right from Wrong but Don't Care." *Social Cognitive and Affective Neuroscience* 5 (1): 59–67. doi: 10.1093/scan/nsp051.

Connolly, Terry, Lisa D. Ordóñez, and Richard Coughlan. 1997. "Regret and Responsibility in the Evaluation of Decision Outcomes." *Organizational Behavior and Human Decision Processes* 70 (1): 73–85. doi: 10.1006/obhd.1997.2695.

Coricelli, G., and R. Nagel. 2009. "Neural Correlates of Depth of Strategic Reasoning in Medial Prefrontal Cortex." *Proceedings of the National Academy of Sciences* 106 (23): 9163–68. doi: 10.1073/pnas.0807721106.

Coricelli, Giorgio, Hugo D. Critchley, Mateus Joffily, John P. O'Doherty, Angela Sirigu, and Raymond J. Dolan. 2005. "Regret and Its Avoidance: A Neuroimaging Study of Choice Behavior." *Nature neuroscience* 8 (9): 1255–62. doi: 10.1038/nn1514.

Coricelli, Giorgio, Raymond J. Dolan, and Angela Sirigu. 2007. "Brain, Emotion and Decision Making: The Paradigmatic Example of Regret." *Trends in Cognitive Sciences* 11 (6): 258–65. doi: 10.1016/j.tics.2007.04.003.

Coricelli, Giorgio, and Aldo Rustichini. 2010. "Counterfactual Thinking and Emotions: Regret and Envy Learning." *Philosophical Transactions of the Royal Society of London. Series B, Biological sciences* 365: 241–7. doi: 10.1098/rstb.2009.0159.

Daw, Nathaniel D., John P. O'Doherty, Peter Dayan, Ben Seymour, and Raymond J. Dolan. 2006. "Cortical Substrates for Exploratory Decisions in Humans." *Nature* 441 (7095): 876–9. doi: 10.1038/nature04766.

Foster, Dean P., and Rakesh Vohra. 1999. "Regret in the On-Line Decision Problem." *Games and Economic Behavior* 29 (1–2): 7–35. doi: 10.1006/game.1999.0740.

Foster, Dean P., and H. Peyton Young. 2003. "Learning, Hypothesis Testing, and Nash Equilibrium." *Games and Economic Behavior* 45 (1): 73–96. doi: 10.1016/S0899-8256(03)00025-3.

Frijda, Nico H., Peter Kuipers, and Elisabeth ter Schure. 1989. "Relations among Emotion, Appraisal, and Emotional Action Readiness." *Journal of Personality and Social Psychology* 57 (2): 212–28. doi: 10.1037//0022-3514.57.2.212.

Frith, Chris D., and Uta Frith. "Interacting Minds—a Biological Basis." *Science* 286 (5445). doi: 10.1126/science.286.5445.1692.

Gallagher, Helen L., and Christopher D. Frith. 2003. "Functional Imaging of 'Theory of Mind.'" *Trends in Cognitive Sciences* 7 (2): 77–83. doi: 10.1016/S1364-6613 (02)00025-6.

Gillan, Claire M., Sharon Morein-Zamir, Muzaffer Kaser, Naomi A. Fineberg, Akeem Sule, Barbara J. Sahakian, Rudolf N. Cardinal, and Trevor W. Robbins. 2014. "Counterfactual Processing of Economic Action-Outcome Alternatives in Obsessive-Compulsive Disorder: Further Evidence of Impaired Goal-Directed Behavior." *Biological Psychiatry* 75 (8): 639–46. doi: 10.1016/j.biopsych.2013.01.018.

Greene, J. D., R. B. Sommerville, L. E. Nystrom, J. M. Darley, and J. D. Cohen. 2001. "An fMRI Investigation of Emotional Engagement in Moral Judgment." *Science (New York, N.Y.)* 293 (5537): 2105–8. doi: 10.1126/science.1062872.

Greene, Joshua D. 2007. "Why Are VMPFC Patients More Utilitarian? A Dual-Process Theory of Moral Judgment Explains." *Trends in Cognitive Sciences* 11 (8): 322–3. doi: 10.1016/j.tics.2007.06.004.

Greene, Joshua D., Leigh E. Nystrom, Andrew D. Engell, John M. Darley, and Jonathan D. Cohen. 2004. "The Neural Bases of Cognitive Conflict and Control in Moral Judgment." *Neuron* 44 (2): 389–400. doi: 10.1016/j.neuron.2004.09.027.

Gu, Xiaosi, Xingchao Wang, Andreas Hula, Shiwei Wang, Shuai Xu, Terry M. Lohrenz, Robert T. Knight, Zhixian Gao, Peter Dayan, and P. Read Montague. 2015. "Necessary, Yet Dissociable Contributions of the Insular and Ventromedial Prefrontal Cortices to Norm Adaptation: Computational and Lesion Evidence in Humans." *Journal of Neuroscience* 35 (2): 467–73. doi: 10.1523/JNEUROSCI. 2906-14.2015.

Guerini, Rossella, FitzGibbon, Lily, and Coricelli, Giorgio. 2018. "The Role of Agency in Regret and Relief in 3- to 10-Year-Old Children." *Journal of Cognitive Neuroscience:* 1–18. doi: 10.1162/jocn_a_01372 (in press).

Hampton, Alan N., Peter Bossaerts, and John P. O'Doherty. 2006. "The Role of the Ventromedial Prefrontal Cortex in Abstract State-Based Inference during Decision Making in Humans." *Journal of Neuroscience* 26 (32): 8360–7. doi: 10.1523/ JNEUROSCI.1010-06.2006.

Hart, Sergiu. 2005. "Adaptive Heuristics." *Econometrica* 73 (5): 1401–30. doi: 10.1111/j.1468–0262.2005.00625.x.

Hart, Sergiu, and Andreu Mas-Colell. 2000. "A Simple Adaptive Procedure Leading to Correlated Equilibrium." *Econometrica* 68 (5): 1127–50. doi: 10.1111/1468–0262.00153.

Hughes, Melissa A., Mairead C. Dolan, and Julie C. Stout. 2013. "Regret in the Context of Unobtained Rewards in Criminal Offenders." *Cognition and Emotion* 28 (5): 913–25. doi: 10.1080/02699931.2013.860370.

Koenigs, Michael. 2012. "The Role of Prefrontal Cortex in Psychopathy." *Reviews in the Neurosciences* 23 (3): 253–62. doi: 10.1515/revneuro-2012–0036.

Koenigs, Michael, Michael Kruepke, and Joseph P. Newman. 2010. "Economic Decision-Making in Psychopathy: A Comparison with Ventromedial Prefrontal Lesion Patients." *Neuropsychologia* 48 (7): 2198–2204. doi: 10.1016/j.neuropsychologia.2010.04.012.

Koenigs, Michael, Michael Kruepke, Joshua Zeier, and Joseph P. Newman. 2012. "Utilitarian Moral Judgment in Psychopathy." *Social Cognitive and Affective Neuroscience* 7 (6): 708–14. doi: 10.1093/scan/nsr048.

Koenigs, Michael, Liane Young, Ralph Adolphs, Daniel Tranel, Fiery Cushman, Marc Hauser, and Antonio Damasio. 2007. "Damage to the Prefrontal Cortex Increases Utilitarian Moral Judgements." *Nature* 446 (7138): 908–11. doi: 10.1038/nature05631.

Larquet, Marion, Giorgio Coricelli, Gaëlle Opolczynski, and Florence Thibaut. 2014. "Impaired Decision Making in Schizophrenia and Orbitofrontal Cortex Lesion Patients." *Schizophrenia Research* 116 (2–3). doi: 10.1016/j.schres.2009.11.010.

Levens, Sara M., Jeff T. Larsen, Joel Bruss, Daniel Tranel, Antoine Bechara, and Barbara A. Mellers. 2015. "What Might Have Been? The Role of the Ventromedial Prefrontal Cortex and Lateral Orbitofrontal Cortex in Counterfactual Emotions and Choice." *Neuropsychologia* 54: 77–86. doi: 10.1016/j.neuropsychologia.2013.10.026.

Lohrenz, T., Kevin McCabe, Colin F. Camerer, and P. Read Montague. 2007. "Neural Signature of Fictive Learning Signals in a sequential investment task." *Proceedings of the National Academy of Sciences of the United States of America* 104 (22): 9493–8. doi: 10.1073/pnas.0608842104.

Loomes, Graham, and Robert Sugden. 1982. "Regret Theory: An Alternative Theory of Rational Choice under Uncertainty." *Economic Journal* 92 (368): 805–824.

S R Manstead, Antony. (2000). The Role of Moral Norm in the Attitude-Behavior Relation: The Role of Norms and Group Membership. pp. 11-30 10.4324/9781410603210-2.

Marchiori, Davide, and Massimo Warglien. 2008. "Predicting Human Interactive Learning by Regret-Driven Neural Networks." *Science* 319 (2001): 1111–3. doi: 10.1126/science.1151185.

Megiddo, N. 1980. "On Repeated Games with Incomplete Information Played by Non-Bayesian Players." *International Journal of Game Theory* 9 (3): 157–67. doi: 10.1007/BF01781370.

Mitchell, Jason P., C. N. Macrae, and Mahzarin R. Banaji. 2006. "Dissociable Medial Prefrontal Contributions to Judgments of Similar and Dissimilar Others." *Neuron* 50 (4): 655–63. doi: 10.1016/j.neuron.2006.03.040.

Moll, Jorge, Ricardo de Oliveira-Souza, Ivanei E. Bramati, and Jordan Grafman. 2002. "Functional Networks in Emotional Moral and Nonmoral Social Judgments." *NeuroImage* 16 (3): 696–703. doi: 10.1006/nimg.2002.1118.

Montague, P. Read, Brooks King-Casas, and Jonathan D. Cohen. 2006. "Imaging Valuation Models in Human Choice." *Annual Review of Neuroscience* 29: 417–48. doi: 10.1146/annurev.neuro.29.051605.112903.

Newton, Joshua D., Fiona J. Newton, Michael T. Ewing, Sue Burney, and Margaret Hay. 2013. "Conceptual Overlap between Moral Norms and Anticipated Regret in the Prediction of Intention: Implications for Theory of Planned Behaviour Research." *Psychology & Health* 28 (5): 495–513. doi: 10.1080/08870446.2012.745936.

Nicolle, Antoinette, Dominik R. Bach, Chris Frith, and Raymond J. Dolan. 2011. "Amygdala Involvement in Self-Blame Regret." *Social Neuroscience* 6 (2): 178–89. doi: 10.1080/17470919.2010.506128.

Parker, Dianne, Antony S. R. Manstead, and Stephen G. Stradling. 1995. "Extending the Theory of Planned Behaviour: The Role of Personal Norm." *British Journal of Social Psychology* 34 (2): 127–38. doi: 10.1111/j.2044-8309.1995.tb01053.x.

Ritov, Ilana. 1996. "Probability of Regret: Anticipation of Uncertainty Resolution in Choice." *Organizational Behavior and Human Decision Processes* 66 (2): 228–36. doi: 10.1006/obhd.1996.0051.

Rivis, Amanda, Paschal Sheeran, and Christopher J. Armitage. 2009. "Expanding the Affective and Normative Components of the Theory of Planned Behavior: A Meta-Analysis of Anticipated Affect and Moral Norms." *Journal of Applied Social Psychology* 39 (12): 2985–3019. doi: 10.1111/j.1559-1816.2009.00558.x.

Suzuki, Shinsuke, Emily L. S. Jensen, Peter Bossaerts, and John P. O. Doherty. 2016. "Behavioral Contagion during Learning about Another Agent's Risk-Preferences Acts on the Neural Representation of Decision-Risk." 113 (14). doi: 10.1073/pnas.1600092113.

Thomas, Bradley C., Katie E. Croft, and Daniel Tranel. 2011. "Harming Kin to Save Strangers: Further Evidence for Abnormally Utilitarian Moral Judgments after Ventromedial Prefrontal Damage." *Journal of Cognitive Neuroscience* 23 (9): 2186–96. doi: 10.1162/jocn.2010.21591.

Van Hoeck, Nicole, Patrick D. Watson, and Aron K. Barbey. July 2015. "Cognitive Neuroscience of Human Counterfactual Reasoning." *Frontiers in Human Neuroscience* 9: 1–18. doi: 10.3389/fnhum.2015.00420.

Weisberg, Daniel P., and Sarah R. Beck. 2012. "The Development of Children's Regret and Relief." *Cognition & Emotion* 26 (5): 820–35. doi: 10.1080/02699931.2011.621933.

Yang, Yaling, Adrian Raine, Todd Lencz, Susan Bihrle, Lori LaCasse, and Patrick Colletti. 2005. "Volume Reduction in Prefrontal Gray Matter in Unsuccessful Criminal Psychopaths." *Biological Psychiatry* 57 (10): 1103–8. doi: 10.1016/j.biopsych.2005.01.021.

Zeelenberg, M., and R. Pieters. 2007. "A Theory of Regret Regulation." *Journal of Consumer Psychology* 17 (1): 3–18. doi: 10.1207/s15327663jcp1701_3.

Zeelenberg, Marcel, Jane Beattie, Joop van der Pligt, and Nanne K. de Vries. 1996. "Consequences of Regret Aversion: Effects of Expected Feedback on Risky Decision Making." *Organizational Behavior and Human Decision Processes* 65 (2): 148–58. doi: 10.1006/obhd.1996.0013.

Zeelenberg, Marcel, Wilco W. van Dijk, Antony S. R. Manstead, and Joopvan der Pligt. 1998. "The Experience of Regret and Disappointment." *Cognition and Emotion* 12 (2): 221–30. doi: 10.1080/026999398379727.

Zhu, Lusha, Kyle E. Mathewson, and Ming Hsu. 2012. "Dissociable Neural Representations of Reinforcement and Belief Prediction Errors Underlie Strategic Learning." *Proceedings of the National Academy of Sciences* 109 (5): 1419–24. doi: 10.1073/pnas.1116783109.

Part III

WHETHER TO REGRET

Chapter 8

"Bury Me in a Free Land": Regret for Slavery in Nineteenth-Century African American Philosophical Literature[1]

Catherine Villanueva Gardner

Regret as a moral emotion is typically framed from the perspective of the individual agent: we feel remorse about actions we have done (or omitted) as individuals, even if we believe we had little choice in the matter. The key here is that moral agency is viewed from the perspective of the individual, and moral judgments are made about actions, rather than character or specific virtues. It is also possible to feel regret about events or circumstances in which we do not have a special role; for example, if we are witnesses to a fatal accident. Here we would most likely feel sadness and wish that the accident could have been avoided, but we would not feel morally responsible in any way.

According to Bernard Williams in his account of the concept of "moral luck," the post-Enlightenment system of morality (exemplified by the philosophies of Kant and Utilitarianism) can only encompass these two definitions; however, Williams further identifies a particular species of morally nuanced regret he calls *agent-regret* that does not fit into the standard "mere regret"/"full remorse" binary. This third form of regret can be "sensed only by a person toward his or her own past actions, and it has a particular kind of expression, that is, a desire to make some kind of reparation" (Statman 1993, 6). Even in the case of a moral dilemma, where one must choose between two evils, and thus the choice is not actively made, the agent, according to Williams, "*should* feel (agent-) regret, and a desire to make up in some way for the wrong action he or she committed" (Statman 1993, 7). Thus, to an extent, on Williams' account, regret, if truly felt, leads to some kind of moral development or moral renewal, as Henry David Thoreau said, "To regret deeply is to live afresh" (Thoreau 1839, 95).

Further, Williams also identifies the "constitutive thought of regret in general . . . [as] something like 'how much better if it had been otherwise,' " and the feeling can in principle apply to anything of which one can form some conception of how it might have been otherwise, together with consciousness of how things would have been better" (Statman 1993, 42). In this general sense of regret, as defined by Williams, "what are regretted are states of affairs, and they can be regretted in principle, by anyone who knows of them" (Statman 1993, 42).

However, are any of these accounts of regret, what could be defined as "individualistic" accounts of actions, a good fit for regret for actions done to a group by another group, specifically *to* Americans racialized-as-black under slavery *by* Americans racialized-as-white? In short, can any of these accounts fully elucidate regret for the existence of the system of slavery? I will show that none of them is a good fit. Moreover, we also need to ask whether regret as a moral emotion, on either the more "standard" accounts or Williams' more morally nuanced and humanistic account, was accessible for enslaved and recently freed peoples.

It would seem that none of these accounts can truly capture regret for the existence of slavery from the perspective of the enslaved, the recently freed, or their descendants, although these options may allow for regret by the dominant group of Americans racialized-as-white. My argument will be that these accounts miss important elements of regret for slavery from the perspective of Americans racialized-as-black, and a different account can be drawn from the philosophical novels of two African American women: Pauline Hopkins (1859–1930) and Frances Harper (1825–1911), one that is more appropriate for the particular case of regret for American slavery.

I will begin with an examination of a modern example of a typical discussion of regret for American slavery that focuses on reparations and formal declarations of regret by governing institutions, with the emotion of regret understood as feelings of sadness and remorse. However, this is regret issued on behalf of the *dominant group*, who historically controlled and benefited from the institution of slavery, so it would seem that Americans racialized-as-black are excluded from full participation in regret for slavery.

I will then look to the historical past to the philosophical literature of Harper and Hopkins to draw out a racialized perspective on regret for American slavery—a "black regret"—that is both politicized and empowering and—as such—is a better fit for the subordinated group under slavery and its aftermath. Harper and Hopkins describe ways in which nineteenth-century Americans racialized-as-black have a more active and empowering participation in regret for slavery, and their moral emotion of regret is an emotionally richer and finer-grained response.

There should be no need to rehearse the oppressions suffered historically by Americans racialized-as-black in their different variations from outright bondage through Jim Crow to present-day social, economic, and political inequalities, as these oppressions have been well documented and recognized. However, it is important to recognize how the institution of slavery benefited Americans racialized-as-white, even those who did not own slaves or who occupied the lowest rungs of the socioeconomic ladder; indeed, even in the twenty-first century, vestiges of these racial benefits remain.

One of the most recent resurfacings of the restitution discussion took place in 2016 and concerned the Jesuit priests of the college, now known as Georgetown University, who sold 272 enslaved human beings in 1838 in order to keep their academic institution financially viable.[2] This specific case is remarkable for the sheer number of people sold all at the same time, and for the close ties between scholarship and slavery, as Jesuit-owned plantations in Maryland financed the college. We should not forget the fact that these enslavers were devoutly religious men; however, they showed more concern that the enslaved would be allowed to continue to practice Catholicism (and thus support the institution of the Catholic Church) than the morality of enslaving other humans or splitting families.

So, what is owed to the descendants of these slaves? There seem to be two parallel—but potentially interconnected—responses that are suggested in the current news and academic discussions. The first is to trace the history of these slaves and memorialize them in some way. The goal with this approach seems to be that it will lead to more emphasis on the history of Americans racialized-as-black. The second goal—in this particular case—is to offer these descendants a "preferential look" at Georgetown in roughly the same way a "legacy" student is treated.[3] Both of these options seem to be viewed through a particularly white prism. Specifically, they reflect white privilege.

Simply put, African American history *is* American history, and thus the fate of these slaves is part of Georgetown's history: it should be axiomatic that it is the subject of research. The second option, offering a preferential look, seems to have potential initially, but "legacy" admissions tend to be the preserve of white upper-class privilege. In offering the supposed equivalent to the descendants of the Georgetown slaves, the gesture (and it *is* only a gesture) actually draws attention to their *lack* of social privilege, a lack that can be directly traced to the oppression of slavery and the other oppressions, such as Jim Crow, that have come out of it. As Peggy McIntosh (1989), among others, has shown us, one of many of the elements of white privilege is that whites can avoid thinking about racial privilege if they so choose.

In this way then, regret for slavery becomes racialized in that reparations are offered by the dominant social group in such a way that racial privilege is upheld. At the time of writing, Georgetown University has not offered scholarships to the very small handful of "slave legacy" students it has currently accepted, which should lead us to ask how genuine the expression of regret truly is. The failure of Georgetown's act of regret is best expressed by

Sandra Thomas, the mother of two of the attending students, who pointed out that her children had a family support system that enabled them to attend Georgetown but asked what another student who was not that lucky would do: "He'll never go to Georgetown or any other school on this planet beyond a certain level. Now, what you going to do for him? Did his ancestors suffer any less? No" (Mtshali, 2017).

While Williams' notion of regret is, as I have said, more morally nuanced and extends further than the standard binary of mere regret/full remorse, it also fails to account for regret for slavery from the perspective of the enslaved, the recently freed, or their descendants. Williams' notion of regret is agent/action-centered, and here lies the problem: regret is felt about actions we have done and choices we have made, and it is crucial to notice that the emotion of regret—on Williams' conceptualization—would be limited for the enslaved, as their decision making and actions were severely restricted. On Williams' constitutive thought of regret in general, nineteenth-century Americans racialized-as-black could most certainly regret the institution of slavery, but could this emotion *best* be framed as regretting a particular state of affairs and as conceiving of how things could have been better? Consider, for example, Pauline Hopkins, writing of her central character, Sappho, in *Contending Forces*: "She had suffered much in meekness, but now dumb rage awoke her passions. For a time the spirit of revenge held full sway in the outraged heart" (Hopkins 1900, 341). Sappho certainly has the intellectual capacity to view the institution of slavery in the objective manner required by Williams, but in order to do so, she must discount her own past and that of her race. Moreover, her personal emotions are not of epistemic import. In short, her experiences become flattened out on Williams' account of a general sense of regret. We need, therefore, to find a different conceptualization of regret as a moral emotion that can allow for Sappho's emotions and those of her fellow ex-slaves.

Examining written records of the voices of the enslaved can—perhaps surprisingly—be potentially problematic; however, this examination is the final step to prepare the ground for the use of the fiction of Harper and Hopkins. It is certainly possible to find interviews with ex-slaves where they express personal regret over the loss of the slave system. For example, Sarah Douglas interviewed for the *Slave Narratives of the Federal Writers' Project* actually expressed regret that slavery had ended[4]: "Slavery times wuz sho good times. We wuz fed and clothed. Now poar ole niggers go hungry." In the interview, the woman explained that the beatings she and her husband received made her a better person: "Sho we wuz whipped in slavery times. Mah ole man has stripes on his back now wha he wuz whipped an ah wuz whipped too but hit hoped me up till now. Coase hit did. Hit keeps me fun goin aroun here telling lies an stealin yo chickens" (*FWP* Volume II. Part 2. 1936–1938, 196).

The use of stereotypically racialized black dialect here is an issue discussed in relation to the project by Catherine Stewart in *Long Past Slavery: Representing Race in the Federal Writers' Project* (2016). Stewart reports that interviewers were asked to focus on "colorful" stories, and the result was that white interviewers often relied on stereotypical black dialect and minstrel tropes to make these stories fit white narratives of plantation life for the (mainly) white project leaders (in contrast to black interviewers, who rarely wrote using dialect).

Needless to say, the regret for the ending of slavery expressed by Sarah Douglas has to be taken in context. The enslaver provided food and shelter. Some were generous to a point, while others offered little, but their motivation was economic: to get as much work as possible from their "possessions." The Slave Narrative Collection is a vital trove of information about the past, but it should not be forgotten that these interviews happened approximately seventy years after Emancipation and thus memories could have faded; that the interviewees would have been children or adolescents when they were slaves; and that the interviewer was typically white and thus the ex-slaves may have said what they thought the interviewers wanted to hear (e.g., the husband of Sarah Douglas denied he had scars).[5] Indeed, Stewart suggests that these narratives could be coded for a nonwhite audience. The white audience would hear a story reinforcing stereotypical beliefs in the—lying, stealing—nature of Americans racialized-as-black, while, on the other hand, a black audience would be reminded of their brutal treatment under slavery. At this point, we are torn: we cannot simply dismiss Sarah Douglas' words because we find her attitude disconcerting; we must respect her autonomy, but we do not know how much these words have been filtered through a white perspective.

In sum, we need to look elsewhere for less ambiguous expressions of regret about the institution of slavery from Americans racialized-as-black. Almost paradoxically, we can find more truth in expressions of regret in nineteenth-century *fiction*. Even though Hopkins and Harper are writing after Emancipation, the institution of slavery continued to hold the country in its grip, from work discrimination to the problematic existence of children who were the products of white rape of slave women to lynching.

However, when we look at the fictional work of Harper and Hopkins, and I will show that literature can play an important role for moral philosophy, we will see that regret is not simply understood in terms of sadness for the past actions of individuals, individual remorse, or a general sense of regret for a state of affairs; rather, regret is a complex emotion that can be both politicized and empowering, one that is felt both by individuals and a community. If we do not allow this particular group of Americans participation in regret for slavery, then we have again consigned them to passivity and excluded them from moral and political citizenship. Most significantly, we need to understand that regret for slavery can be racialized. While both white and black Americans can call for reparations, there was also a racialized regret in nineteenth-century America, something that is best explicated through nineteenth-century literature—in particular, through the work of Harper and Hopkins. In addition, I shall explain how black regret is a racialized emotion that is connected to the concept of "black privilege" invoked by Harper.

Starting in the 1980s, the so-called literary turn offered an alternative perspective to mainstream moral philosophy. Recent work has shown that the intersections of philosophy and literature are varied and multiple; for example, literature can function to expand one's understanding of others and the world around us, as Martha Nussbaum claims, or to expand our imaginations, as Richard Rorty claims. For the purposes of this discussion, it is best to follow the relationship between literature and moral philosophy identified by D. D. Raphael. Raphael examines four propositions: a work of moral philosophy can also be a work of literature (e.g., Plato's *Phaedo*); a work of literature can also be a work of moral philosophy (a claim to be elaborated below, as it is the most significant for this discussion); moral philosophy can feed literature (e.g., Iris Murdoch's moral thinking feeds her novels); and literature can feed moral philosophy (e.g., a character in a novel can be used as evidence for an issue in moral philosophy (e.g., Lorraine Code's discussion of Gwendolen Harlech from George Eliot's *Daniel Deronda* for Code's account of the epistemology of ignorance).[6]

According to Raphael, the second claim—a work of literature can also be a work of moral philosophy—does not mean that the work moralizes; rather, "it is presented as the outcome of a new perspective, in a form of persuasion that can fairly be called rational although not reducible to rules of inference like logic" (Raphael 1983, 4). I hold that the two authors I focus on—Frances Harper and Pauline Hopkins—are writing works of moral philosophy in Raphael's sense. Admittedly, as Raphael acknowledges, the acceptance of this claim will depend on the definition of moral philosophy one holds. Central to Raphael's claim is that literature can bring a sharpened moral insight similar to that produced by excellent moral philosophy, and that—it seems to me—is one of the elements that has been missing from discussions of regret for American slavery. We—whoever that "we" may be—do not just need empirical knowledge but also moral knowledge or insight in order to gain a better understanding of regret for slavery.

Initially, it may seem that the works of Harper and Hopkins are best used to explore the issue of regret as exemplifying Raphael's fourth claim. But the difference between Raphael's two claims carries a political significance. On claim four, I, the author of this discussion, am philosophizing, using Harper and Hopkins as evidence. On claim two, Harper and Hopkins *themselves* are *actively* writing philosophy. *They* are participating with a rational, persuasive moral voice as *moral and political citizens*. Nathanial Tobias Coleman (2014) has argued that persons racialized-as-black rarely have counted as philosophers; indeed, according to Coleman, even Frederick Douglass was encouraged by his fellow abolitionists to stick to the facts and leave the philosophy to them.[7] Therefore, it is politically and morally important to recognize Harper and Hopkins as philosophers. To do so is not simply to help my particular argument but to help build an overall recognition that authors racialized-as-black are participants in the greater philosophical conversation.

It is important to recognize that even though they are writing fiction, both Harper and Hopkins are highly qualified to speak to the empirical realities of slavery in the American South. In his introduction to Harper's *Iola Leroy, or, Shadows Uplifted*, William Still writes of his initial concerns about whether Harper would offer a book of "lasting worth" (Harper 1893, 1). However, he says he came to realize that Harper was uniquely qualified to write a work on American slavery, and he states that, since Emancipation, Harper has worked in nearly every state in the South in schools, churches, and so on. Hopkins was in many ways more of an activist-intellectual than Harper. According to Hazel Carby, Hopkins hoped that her fiction would encourage a resurgence of the forms of "political agitation and resistance of the antislavery movement" (Carby 1987, 129). Lois Brown's study of Hopkins claims that she wrote and participated in plays that became public history lessons, rewriting accepted historical narratives. According to Brown in an October 14, 2008, interview for Mount Holyoke College, the audience came to see "real" African American lives under slavery—cotton picking and overseers—"but when they sat down to watch Hopkins' play, they saw cohesive African American families, agency in terms of self-emancipation, and assimilation into American culture."

In both Hopkins' *Contending Forces* and Harper's *Iola Leroy*, the central character is a biracial young woman (Sappho and Iola, respectively), who identifies as black while appearing outwardly as white. Typically, biracial individuals in this era were the result of the rape of black slave women by their (white) enslavers. Whether it was publicly admitted or not, the races had always mixed, even from the earliest colonization of North America. The lines drawn between black and white were a social construct: who was eligible to be enslaved and who was not. Children of black women—regardless of whether they were born of a relationship with a fellow slave or rape by a white man—took the legal/racial status of their mother (although they were given the last name of their enslaver). Individuals racialized-as-white born to white women took their legal/racial status from their (white) father. However, white men needed white women to help them reinforce those lines; for example, white wives were needed to produce heirs to legally inherit property. Thus, the institution of slavery required marriage for white people, and, in its turn, gave white people social and legal benefits.

Moreover, the institution of slavery also required that the protections, both legal and social, of the institution of marriage *be denied* to those in bondage. Slave families were often viewed by their enslavers as a way of producing future bodies to exploit; they could be split apart at the whim of enslavers; while even the problematic legal notion of "coverture" (the legal "ownership" of the wife by her husband) could not protect sexually vulnerable black women from their enslavers. Women racialized-as-black were not seen by white men as possessing virtue and thus were vulnerable to sexual assault. At best, the woman's "owner" or father would be offered financial compensation for an assault.

While literary critics have questioned the ways in which these biracial women are depicted by Hopkins and Harper, in particular their sentimentalized depiction using the trope of the so-called tragic mulatto, the presence of these women complicates regret for slavery. On the traditional binary of mere regret/full remorse, both Iola and Sappho *can* feel "mere" regret for the abuse their mothers suffered. Yet given that they themselves are the product of this abuse, how are they to feel about their own birth/existence? These emotions surely cannot be placed on the moral level of sadness felt by onlookers. Nor can Williams' account of regret in general—not surprisingly—allow for these individual cases.

Sappho herself has an illegitimate son, who is the product of rape by a white man, and social mores mean that she cannot publicly recognize him as her own. Initially, Sappho regrets the existence of the child and neglects him, not because of any lack of motherly feeling but because of her bitterness and guilt over the circumstances of the child's conception. This aspect of slavery means that women racialized-as-black become defined as lacking sexual/ moral virtue (and thus reinforcing the acceptability of their sexual assault). Sappho asks whether "God will hold us [women racialized-as-black] responsible for the illegitimacy with which our race has been obliged, as it were, to flood the world?" (Hopkins 1900, 149). Neither the traditional binary nor Williams' more nuanced account can allow for Sappho's life in which she loathes the institution of slavery, yet dearly loves its consequences (her son). Moreover, the institution of slavery, and its long tentacles, did not simply affect the actions or freedom of action of women racialized-as-black, but it affected the way their character was viewed, and this latter point is something that I will explore.

Both Harper and Hopkins examine the way that the institution of slavery after Emancipation still played out in the lives of Americans racialized-as-black. The main characters of their novels experience the gamut of emotions tied to regret from anger to sorrow. Central to their feelings of regret is regret for the loss of family. In Iola's case, she does not know her immediate family or their whereabouts, and her search for them forms a main part of the narrative of the novel. In Sappho's case, it is only late in the novel that she retrieves her son from his caretaker and lives as a family with him. What is important to see, however, is that this regret functions as a spur to action for both characters; the regret is both politicized and empowering. These novels show us that the enslaved and the recently freed were not emotionally or psychologically immobile, despite their material circumstances.

In *Contending Forces*, Sappho suffers mentally and emotionally due to her rape and forcible confinement in a brothel, and she initially resists the romantic advances of William Smith; however, she decides no longer to pay "penance for involuntary wrongs . . . and be as other women, who loved and were beloved" (Hopkins 1900, 205). Sappho's personal regret for her circumstances, the all-too familiar results of the control of the bodies of slave women by their white enslavers, also functions as a generalized regret for the American institutions of slavery of individuals racialized-as-black:

> Such incidents [illegitimacy] . . . are not uncommon in any community where slavery has cast its baleful shadow. Emancipation has done much, but time and moral training among the white men of the South are the only cures for concubinage . . . So with shoulders bent and misshapen with heavy burdens, the Negro plods along bearing his cross—carrying the sins of others. (Hopkins 1900, 332)

In essence, Hopkins is stating that Americans racialized-as-black continue to be the engine for white society. While the former may no longer perform the physical labor, they now perform the ethico-social labor of bearing responsibility for the sexual sins of white society. As Sappho's best friend, Dora says of this responsibility, "What a crucifixion for a proud spirit like hers! This terrible curse of slavery! shall we never lose the sting of degradation?" (Hopkins 1900, 330).

Hopkins' depiction of Sappho's suffering needs to be parsed carefully. Sappho has an exquisite moral sensibility in that she suffers needlessly for the wrongs done to her. It would appear that Hopkins is using the character of Sappho to respond to stereotypes of women racialized-as-black as oversexed and promiscuous: "the charges brought against us as to our moral irresponsibility, and the low moral standard maintained by us in comparison with other races" (Hopkins 1900, 148). Through the depiction of Sappho, we can see a politicized critique of the institution of slavery: it is the direct cause of the lack of sexual morality in white men, and these white men—not women racialized-as-black—are morally responsible for illegitimacy and moral laxity in society as a whole.

For Hopkins, therefore, regret for slavery is not simply a generalized regret—in other words, saying it would have been better if it had never happened—there is also a racialized and politicized element. Black regret is—in essence—a raced/gendered critique of white men under the institution of slavery. Black regret is also a critique of the continued moral failings of white men after slavery, which have their foundations in slavery, such as the mistreatment and sexual assault of women racialized-as-black and the use of lynching as a way of containing black men. While black regret does not mean regret for the existence of individual mixed-race children born due to rape or forced concubinage of enslaved women by white men, it does mean regret for the existence of the institution that allowed white men the freedoms to treat other human beings in such a barbaric and immoral manner. Despite the fact that Hopkins may seem rather quaint to modern eyes in her attitudes toward female morality, she is in many ways ahead of her time in identifying white men as the source of moral and social ills.

Hopkins is not simply locating a source of moral blame, she is also locating a source of black female empowerment. The character of Mrs. Willis is featured as having a role as a professional speaker in *Contending Forces*. She offers a talk on "the place which the virtuous woman occupies in upbuilding a race" (Hopkins 1900, 148). According to Mrs. Willis, and we can assume she is a mouthpiece for Hopkins, virtue

> is an essential attribute peculiar to us—a racial characteristic which is slumbering but not lost . . . let us not forget the definition of virtue—"Strength to do the right thing under all temptations." Our ideas of virtue are too narrow. We confine them to that conduct which is ruled by our animal passions alone. It goes deeper than that—general excellence in every duty of life is what we may call virtue. (Hopkins 1900, 149)

Here Mrs. Willis is rejecting how morality is defined by white society for women racialized-as-black: a definition only in terms of sexual morality. More importantly, Mrs. Willis offers a different definition of morality or virtue for women racialized-as-black, one that is peculiar to these women and that will help these women build their race.[8]

Leaving to one side what would appear to the modern reader to be questionable essentialist thinking, Hopkins is making a significant point. The woman racialized-as-black is no longer seen as a passive being, defined only in terms of her sexual morality, but as a fully fleshed-out moral agent, given a central task in building up her race. Ultimately then, Hopkins offers a racialized and gendered perspective on regret for slavery. Rather than conceptualizing regret *simply* in terms of *actions or states of affairs*, Hopkins conceptualizes regret in terms of character or virtues. Enslaved women were unable to exercise their "racial characteristic" of practicing daily virtue. Reading Hopkins, this makes perfect sense, yet there is no conceptual space on the traditional binary or Williams' accounts for restriction of virtue or character. There is also a sense in which women racialized-as-black are in a position of empowerment when it comes to building up their race. However, Hopkins' account of regret does not lead directly to empowerment. This lack is an interesting difference between Hopkins and Harper, as the latter makes a direct connection between regret and a notion of "black privilege," as we shall see.

In *Iola Leroy*, Frances Harper explores regret for slavery felt by those racialized-as-black from a different perspective. Even though Hopkins is dealing with the brutal realities of rape, and the lynching of black men accused of raping white women, she is in many ways more sentimental in her dealing with slavery and its aftermath in the novel. Harper, on the other hand, explores regret for slavery within a context of family and racial identity as well as black empowerment and privilege.

Iola Leroy is the daughter of a Southern plantation owner and a slave. Although the two live on equal and happy terms, Leroy did not formally free Iola's mother, so, when he dies unexpectedly, Iola finds herself designated a slave. Until that moment, Iola was not aware of her status; indeed, she supported the slave system in the South. During the war, Iola works as an army nurse, and she meets a white doctor: Dr. Gresham. He wishes to marry her but wants to keep her heritage a secret from his family and (white) community in New England. In response, Iola says she would not enter a family or a community where she would only be welcome if she concealed her heritage, as she knows New England is not free from racial prejudice. In addition, she asks the doctor how they would deal with a child in future that showed traces of its African heritage. Would the doctor, Iola asks, be happy to hold in his arms (and thus to claim) his *own* child, who was a child of color?

For Iola, Dr. Gresham is asking her to disown her racial heritage as well as to disown her mother; indeed, she is resolved to find her mother and form family ties that have been broken. After the war, Iola does not deny her heritage in order to keep employment. Similarly, Iola's brother requests to join what was called during this period a "colored" regiment, even though he passes for white and would miss out on opportunities for promotion. Harper makes it clear that black folks are never certain or feel safe. Even when freed, their history reaches forwards to affect their lives, whether it is through discrimination or the physical threat of lynching. Yet Iola and her brother reject the security of whiteness.

Iola meets her uncle (Robert Johnson) in the army hospital. He is intrigued by the fact that she sings one of his mother's favorite hymns, and they wonder if they are related. All that she knows about her family is that her mother had a brother who had a birthmark on his forehead. It turns out that Robert does, in fact, have just such a birthmark, so after the war they both search for her mother and his mother (Iola's grandmother), hoping that they will be able to reunite their family.[9] This reuniting of Iola's family is aimed at undoing what slavery did to break up a family. In *The Half Has Never Been Told*, Edward E. Baptist explains how the efficiency of labor organization under slavery meant that workers needed to have no attachments. According to Baptist, separating husbands and wives and parents from children was an intrinsic part of the capitalist slave trade, not—as most historians have argued—an unfortunate side effect. Baptist's examination of patterns of sales shows that such sales drew on reserves of human wealth, rather than the white-washed myth that plantation owners sold the enslaved—and thus broke up families—only during economic hard times.[10]

Harper is showing us that part of the concept of racial identity is familial. Unlike the (white) Western tradition of the individualized agent (humans are inherently presocial, rather than connected to and constituted by social context), Harper's characters' racial identity is bound up with their family identity. This flips white identification on its head. Whereas to be born of a black mother means that a child is identified as black in white American terms, black identity for Harper is to be able to care for your family, in particular your children, and to be part of a family group.[11] Here we can see that human freedom for Harper is not simply an abstract or constitutional right, but it also requires a life lived within a family and personal relationships. On being introduced to Iola's family, Dr. Gresham says, "It has been said that every cloud has its silver lining, and the silver lining of our war cloud is the redemption of a race and the reunion of severed hearts" (Harper 1893, 216).

Another central component of Harper's account is her answer to how America can recover from the institution of slavery. Iola says that the "only remedy" is to understand fully how to apply the teachings of the Gospel to "our national life" (Harper 1893, 216). Robert (Iola's uncle) agrees and says Jesus has already answered the politicians' question of what to do with emancipated African Americans "when he said, 'Whatsoever ye would that men should do to you, do ye even so to them'" (Harper 1893, 216–17).

The central concept of Harper's *Iola Leroy* that is most relevant to regret for slavery is her concept of black privilege and its connecting emotion of black regret. They are not the flip sides of the coin of white privilege and white regret, for white privilege is social advantage at the expense of another group. Despite the fact that she was writing in the nineteenth century, Harper understands what we currently call white privilege: "To be born white in this country is to be born to an inheritance of privileges, to hold in your hands the keys that open before you the doors of every occupation, advantage, opportunity, and achievement" (Harper 1893, 265–66).

Dr. Latimer, whom Iola eventually marries, is offered the opportunity to be recognized by his rich grandmother if he rejects his slave mother and passes as white, with its attendant racial advantages. Iola admires Dr. Latimer for his refusal to accept these white privileges. For Iola, Dr. Latimer would pay too high a price in terms of honor and self-respect. Here Dr. Latimer's choosing to be racialized as black, and thus to reject white privilege, is framed as a moral choice. Individuals who work for the black community and/or self-define as black by choice are framed by Harper as moral heroes.

White regret attempts to make reparations for social advantage without actually reversing that advantage and its long tentacles reaching forward through history to the current day. In addition, white privilege is often invisible, so it is hard to dismantle, whereas black privilege is actively and consciously shouldered, making it both visible and empowering. Harper frames black privilege as the privilege to serve "the race," and it is articulated for the reader by both Iola and her brother. Black privilege is both a politicized and a religious idea, and Iola explains this ideal in speaking to Doctor Gresham:

> "I do not think life's highest advantages are those that we can see with our eyes or grasp with our hands. To whom to-day is the world most indebted—to its millionaires or to its martyrs?" "Taking it from the ideal standpoint," replied the doctor, "I should say its martyrs." . . . "To be," continued Iola, "the leader of a race to higher planes of thought and action, to teach men clearer views of life and duty, and to inspire their souls with loftier aims, is a far greater privilege than it is to open the gates of material prosperity and fill every home with sensuous enjoyment." (Harper 1893, 219)

It may be tempting to see Harper's concept of black privilege as sentimentalized; however, when its articulation is examined within its racial and historical context, we can see it is both empowering and politicized: Iola and Dr. Latimer find it "a blessed privilege to stand on the threshold of a new era and labor for those who had passed from the old oligarchy of slavery into the new commonwealth of freedom" (Harper 1893, 271). Black regret is the founding emotion for black privilege in Harper's *Iola Leroy*, an emotion that is also empowering and politicized. Black regret is not simply wishing that the institution of slavery had never existed nor believing that reparations should be made—it is an emotion that can bind together families and communities and ultimately the black race. Black regret is not a soft emotion; for example, Iola has been invited to a party, and she comments on not being overly given to amusements; however, her uncle responds that "this is the first holiday we have had in two hundred and fifty years, and you shouldn't be too exacting" (Harper 1893, 244). Here, through the reference to two and a half centuries of oppression, we can see that regret does not entail forgiveness for enslavers.

In discussing lynching and Jim Crow laws, Iola's mother says, "Slavery . . . is dead, but the spirit which animated it still lives; and I think that a reckless disregard for human life is more the outgrowth of slavery than any actual hatred of the negro" (Harper 1893, 217). Here Harper is commenting on the moral consequences of slavery. The institution did not simply bring about mistreatment of one racial group; rather, it has served to produce its overall dehumanization. This quotation is significant for my discussion of regret. Iola's mother is clearly referring to Americans racialized-as-white. The "careless disregard" that exists would seem to mean that it *may be morally impossible* for Americans racialized-as-white to feel true regret for slavery, as slavery has produced a moral bluntness in its wake. Initially, it would only seem that Harper is referring to nineteenth-century white Americans (those who grew up during the era of slavery), but careful introspection would indicate that we should ask whether this moral bluntness still exists in various forms, although not in *every* individual American racialized-as-white, in contemporary America.

The task of this discussion has been to conceptualize the regret for slavery felt by nineteenth-century Americans racialized-as-black to ask whether this regret can fit our available models: mere regret, full remorse, agent-regret. In brief, the answer is no, but if we do not allow this particular group of Americans participation in regret for slavery, then we consign them to passivity and exclusion from moral and political citizenship. Even in the case of Williams' more general sense of regret—states of affairs are regretted, in that we wish things were otherwise—it cannot allow a strong enough emotion in response to suffering under the institution of slavery.

Using the literary work of Hopkins and Harper as moral philosophy allows us to understand that regret for slavery produces a more complex bundle of emotions, from anger and the desire for revenge to empowerment and politicization. Harper and Hopkins describe ways in which nineteenth-century Americans racialized-as-black have a more active and empowering participation in regret for slavery and an emotionally richer and finer-grained response. Our modern discussions of regret for American slavery typically focus on reparations and formal declarations of regret by governing institutions, with regret understood as feelings of sadness and remorse. Obviously, Americans racialized-as-black can participate in these calls for reparations, but this is still regret issued on behalf of the dominant group who historically controlled, and benefited from, the institution of slavery. So—again—it would seem that Americans racialized-as-black are excluded from full participation in regret for slavery.

However, we can find in Hopkins and Harper two versions of a racialized regret. Hopkins' racialized regret is—essentially—a raced/gendered critique of white men under slavery and after Emancipation. Identifying the source of the cause of moral and social ills also allows Hopkins to identify its accompanying cure for the black race: women. Harper's version of racialized regret is connected to what she identifies as black privilege: the privilege to serve her race. While Hopkins blames white men as the source of moral and social ills, Harper sees the institution of slavery as the cause of a white moral disregard for human life, to the point where Harper may be questioning whether Americans racialized-as-white can feel true regret for slavery. Certainly, even the "good" white character of Dr. Gresham, in wishing to deny Iola's history and heritage, shows that his regret for the institution is not through and through.

Thus, Harper and Hopkins can show us that regret for slavery could be a racialized emotion in the nineteenth century. This then directs us to consider whether regret for American slavery felt in the twenty-first century also needs a racialized perspective. I am very hesitant—and certainly not qualified— to speculate how that might look, but, in the light of the large amount of enslaved human beings sold in cold blood to save Georgetown University from debt, it is doubtful whether Harper and Hopkins would consider "preferential admission" and/or archival research (or any other institutional form of apology) a sufficient demonstration of regret.

NOTES

1. "Bury Me in a Free Land" is the title of a poem by Frances Harper from 1854.
2. Noted, for example, in Rachel Sterns' *New York Times* article on April 16, 2016.
3. Kathryn Vasel notes this option in a *CNN Money* article on September 1, 2016.
4. These narratives were collected in the 1930s as part of the Federal Writers' Project (FWP) of the Works Progress Administration, later renamed Work Projects Administration (WPA).
5. Edward E. Baptist points out that the set questions asked by the interviewers for the WPA were leading questions; for example, "Have you been happier in slavery or free?"
6. Raphael uses a fairly loose sense of moral philosophy here. Some philosophers want to distinguish this sense from a more formal second-order sense or meta-ethics. For the purposes of my discussion, Raphael's account is sufficient.
7. It is certainly true that there are few philosophers racialized-as-black taught in our philosophy curricula, but this is not the same as saying that such philosophers do not *exist*. What does and does not count as philosophy according to mainstream philosophy is formed by multiple overt and covert biases.
8. This moral role is ambiguous. On the one hand, it would seem that women are remaining confined to the private sphere, as that is typically the sphere of the moral, where women educate their children and provide a moral example for their families. Yet nothing is said by Hopkins about the role of men, although we can speculate that men will have roles in the public and political sphere. On the other hand, the fact that she is only focusing on women is intriguing.
9. Baptist offers the story of Pierre Aucoin, a story that appears in different variations in the Works Progress Administration interviews of a brother and sister who unknowingly marry each other.
10. Hopkins offers an acidic critique of the splitting of slave families in *Hagar*. A slave trader called Haskins achieves a religious conversion. The proof of his change of heart is that he will no longer split husbands and wives if he can persuade someone to buy them together. This supposed religious softening of his heart still has not prevented Haskins from being a trader.
11. Having a father racialized-as-black, whether free or enslaved, and a white mother was a complex issue during the era of slavery. The earliest attempt to control

interracial relationships was in 1664. Maryland, then a British colony, passed a law that stated a white woman marrying a man racialized-as-black would forfeit her freedom. Initially, the law did not differentiate between a freed and an enslaved man, but by 1692 the laws spelt out punishments for interracial relationships.

REFERENCES

Baptist, Edward E. 2014. *The Half Has Never Been Told: Slavery and the Making of American Capitalism*. New York: Basic.
Baptist, Edward E. *Born in Slavery: Slave Narratives from the Federal Writers' Project, 1936–1938*. Arkansas Narratives, Volume II, Part 2.
Brown, Lois. 2008. Interview. July 18, 2019. https://www.mtholyoke.edu/media/lois-brown-publishes-groundbreaking-biography.
Carby, Hazel V. 1987. *Reconstructing Womanhood: The Emergence of the Afro-American Woman Novelist*. Oxford: Oxford University Press
Code, Lorraine. 2004. "The Power of Ignorance." *Philosophical Papers* 33 (3): 291–308.
Coleman, Nathaniel Tobias. July 18, 2019. 2014. "Philosophy Is Dead White and Dead Wrong." *Times Higher Education*. https://www.timeshighereducation.co.uk/comment/opinion/philosophy-is-deadwhite-and-dead-wrong/2012122.article.
Harper, Frances E. W. 1893. *Iola Leroy, or, Shadows Uplifted*, 2nd ed. Philadelphia, PA: Garrigues.
Hopkins, Pauline. 1900. *Contending Forces: A Romance Illustrative of Negro Life North and South*. Boston, MA: Colored Co-operative.
McIntosh, Peggy. July/August 1989. "White Privilege: Unpacking the Invisible Knapsack (1989)." *Peace and Freedom Magazine*, July-August, 1989, 10–12, Philadelphia, PA: Women's International League for Peace and Freedom.
Mtshali, Lihle Z. June 22, 2017. "Descendants of Georgetown Slaves to Attend the Prestigious School." *Essence*. July 18, 2019. https://www.essence.com/news/georgtown-university-slave-descendants-admission.
Nussbaum, Martha. 1992. *Love's Knowledge*. Oxford: Oxford University Press.
Raphael, D. D. 1983. "Literature and/as Moral Philosophy." *New Literary History* 15 (1): 1–12.
Rorty, Richard. 1989. *Contingency, Irony, and Solidarity*. Cambridge: Cambridge University Press.
Statman, Daniel, ed. 1993. *Moral Luck*. New York: SUNY Press.
Stewart, Catherine. 2016. *Long Past Slavery: Representing Race in the Federal Writers' Project*. Chapel Hill: University of North Carolina Press.
Thoreau, Henry David. 1839. *Journals*. Entry for November 13, p. 95. The Thoreau Institute at Walden Woods: The Walden Woods Project. https://www.walden.org/log-page/1839/#1839-11.
Williams, Bernard. 1993. "Moral Luck." In *Moral Luck*, ed. Daniel Statman, 35–71. New York: SUNY Press. Originally published in Bernard Williams, *Moral Luck*. Cambridge: Cambridge University Press, 1981.

Chapter 9

Regret: Considerations of Disability

Teresa Blankmeyer Burke

The word for "sorry" in American Sign Language (ASL) involves moving your right fist in tight concentric circles over your heart. To change this sign to indicate "regret," the circling motion of "sorry" becomes a compound sign with the addition of a second movement of opening your closed fist and pulling it a few inches away from your body, then pressing the palm of your right hand hard over your heart to convey anguish. As your hand hits your chest, you simultaneously hunch your shoulders slightly forward in a movement that emphasizes humility and a willingness to claim ownership of this emotion. Sometimes, the second part of the sign is emphasized by placing the left hand over the right.

If one of the differences between an emotional expression of apology and an emotional expression of regret includes an agent's relevant involvement in the regrettable occurrence, this compound ASL sign of apology plus ownership is quite fitting. As I have thought about the notion of regret in disability contexts, I have paid particular attention to what distinguishes expressions of apology from expressions of regret. The bulk of the discussion about disability in the literature on regret, including memoir, focuses on two kinds of cases: the regret of the (presumably nondisabled) parent of a disabled child regarding their child's disability status and the regret felt by people who have become disabled. Jay Wallace's book, *The View from Here: On Affirmation, Attachment, and the Limits of Regret*, introduces the concept of "the attitude of disability affirmation" as an explanation for how the phenomenon of potential disability regret is negotiated when a disabled parent desires a child with the same disability as their own. The disabled parent's attachment to their disability identity and all it engenders is offered as partial explanation for the absence or mitigation of disability regret (Wallace 2013, 118–19). In the case of the disabled person who refuses to admit to feeling the emotional of disability regret, Wallace suggests that this may be due to a kind of confusion about the objective value (or disvalue) of disability with the affirmation of the person as the disabled individual she is (Wallace 2013, 122–5).

In this chapter, I use Wallace's account of disability regret as a starting point for thinking about regret and disability more broadly, including such topics as the possible regret of experiences that might have been, the notion that one might not regret one's disability and not be confused about what one is valuing, and what kinds of justification would be most cogent in such a move of disability affirmation, including the role of "transformative experience" and disability. I work through four cases to explicate my views: the case of parents considering a pediatric cochlear implant for their deaf child; the case of parents making genetic selection for deafness through preimplantation genetic diagnosis and in vitro fertilization; the case of the Deaf adult contemplating a cochlear implant for himself; and finally, the case of open future regret (hereinafter OFR) as expressed toward disabled people.[1]

REGRET AND LANGUAGE CHOICES

Hearing parents who learn that their infant child is deaf are faced with a unique choice regarding language. Since the deaf child is unable to acquire language in the manner of hearing children, which is through repeated environmental exposure, they must make a choice about how their deaf child will communicate with them—through a signed language such as American Sign Language or through a spoken language such as English. If the parent's or caregiver's preferred option is for their deaf child to use spoken English, a cochlear implant is recommended in most cases and pursued as a way to provide the deaf child with augmented auditory experience that will provide additional information as the child receives auditory-verbal training to learn to speak and hear with the cochlear implant.[2]

If the parent or caregiver opts to emphasize signed language as a first language, followed by the written form of the dominant spoken language of their community, the child and parent will both learn signed language. This typically occurs in an infant-toddler program in the child's home with visits from a specialist who works with the deaf child plus the hearing parent or caregiver, teaching them all signed language. Later, the deaf child is placed in a language immersion experience, usually a preschool setting, and as the child becomes older, they may be placed in a mainstream educational environment with a signed language interpreter or attend a residential or day school designed for deaf and hard-of-hearing children.

In *The View from Here: On Affirmation, Attachment, and the Limits of Regret*, Jay Wallace takes up the issue of Deaf parents who opt against providing their Deaf child with a cochlear implant as a point of confusion about the retrospective views of Deaf parents whose life projects are shaped by their deafness and the future potential of young children who are beginning their lives. His analysis, based on Elizabeth Harman's account of "I'll be glad I did it" reasoning, considers that people who have lived with significant disabilities have good reasons to affirm their disabilities, and this move of affirmation shapes the Deaf parents' reasoning about cochlear implants for their Deaf children in a way that is flawed (Wallace 2013, 125). By framing the issue as one of limiting their child's future opportunities, Wallace overlooks what I take to be the key issue from a signing Deaf perspective, which is that of full versus partial access to language. The signing Deaf parent knows that their child will have full access to language in the home; the question is whether to pursue a technology that will provide additional, though partial, access to the dominant spoken language of the family's home. Yet in considering the Deaf parent's decision about cochlear implant surgery, Wallace overlooks the impact of this choice on language acquisition and learning, namely that culturally Deaf parents may have similar reasons as culturally Hearing[3] parents around the choice of a cochlear implant for their child based on their concerns about their ability to provide what their child needs.

Not surprisingly, parents struggle over the choice of whether to choose to pursue a spoken language or a signed language and whether to provide their child with a cochlear implant or not. The choice of a signed or spoken language is often framed in the philosophical and bioethics literature as a dichotomy that will shape the child's future, either providing access to the dominant spoken language society or to the signed language community but not both. Yet, this characterization is not wholly accurate, for there are programs for children with cochlear implants that provide not only auditory-verbal instruction but also language immersion in a signed language.[4] Regret or the lack of regret expressed by parents (or caregivers) regarding surrogate decision-making choices about pediatric cochlear implants is potentially more problematic not just because of the high stakes of the decision, which has direct consequences for a deaf child's language acquisition or deprivation, but also because the choice is made for the child before they are able to consent or refuse to consent.

In an essay based on her memoir, Tamsin Coates writes of her challenges as a hearing parent over a decade ago regarding the decision-making process of whether to provide her two deaf sons with cochlear implants:

> When it came to deciding what was best for the boys' future, I faced difficult decisions. The hardest I have had to make so far was in choosing whether my boys should have cochlear implants. These devices are relatively rare. Not many people have them and people who can hear often mistake them for hearing aids.

The implant, which involves skull surgery, enables hearing by stimulating the hearing nerve directly via electrodes.

With my background as a speech and language therapist, I felt I should know what to do, but I found the conflict between wanting to follow my professional training and trusting my maternal instincts overwhelming. (Coates 2012, 29)

In this passage, Coates reveals the conflict between her professional training as a speech therapist and her maternal instincts. As a speech therapist, she is aware that the experience of hearing through cochlear implants will not be identical to that of a child with typical hearing.

As I have argued elsewhere, a deaf child raised in mainstream spoken language communities under the best circumstances will at times experience only partial access to language; a child who is fluent in a signed language will have the experience of full access to language (Burke 2017, 281). While Coates does not put her dilemma in these terms, she does acknowledge the potential psychological impact of her choice by articulating her concern about the message to implant her children that it sends to the signing Deaf community (and to her sons). The message is clear: something is wrong with them that needed to be fixed. She counters this message by describing her choice to affirm their culturally signing Deaf identity in addition to obtaining cochlear implants.

Nearly a decade on from Cameron and Campbell's diagnosis, there is a lot more understanding about cochlear implants that has reaffirmed my self-confidence as a mother. In making that choice I was not wishing for my boys not to be deaf. When equipment isn't worn, they still are. It is part of them and, while encouraging them to use their implants, I have also strived to promote their confidence in their identity as deaf youngsters. They appreciate contact with deaf peers and role models. They sign as well as speak. They are part of a new generation of deaf children who use fantastic technology but who are also secure in their deaf identity . . . I don't regret my decision to go ahead with the surgery it hasn't been an easy ride, but my children are both wonderful, talented boys who are living life to the full. (Coates 2012, 29)

Coates situates her cochlear implant decisions for her sons as one that she does not regret in the context of her choice to provide both signed language community and spoken language community for her sons. By choosing two language options rather than one, coupled with her assessment that they are well-adjusted individuals, she has provided justification for her choice while also hedging her bets.

The reasons for the hedging may have been due to limited empirical data on parental decisions regarding cochlear implants. One qualitative study of 439 responses of parents of children with cochlear implants indicates that the majority of parents did not regret their decision to implant their deaf child, though the authors of the study acknowledge that this is not surprising given the nature of their study, with parents of children who had successful cochlear implant outcomes being more likely to participate in this research (Christiansen and Leigh 2002, 204). Yet the authors also note, "We often saw expressions of regret for 'what might have been' among parents whose children experience very different degrees of success with the implant" (Christiansen and Leigh 2002, 204).

One concern that hearing parents or caregivers may have regarding language choices they have made for their deaf child is that the child may grow up to express discontent with the surrogate decision regarding the choice for or against a cochlear implant (Mauldin 2016, 51). Although this choice is typically made by a hearing parent or caregiver, there is another potential pool of influential surrogate decision makers in the mix who are often not considered in this calculus: signing Deaf adults. The signing Deaf adult has an insight into the richness and depth of the signing Deaf community, plus a firsthand experience with what it is like to be a deaf person living in a hearing society. The nonsigning Deaf child who grows up with a cochlear implant and spoken language may at some point become curious about the signing Deaf community and wish to enter it. Depending on when this response manifests, it may not only be potential fodder for parental regret but also for the deaf person's regret at not pursing the other language path earlier on. Conventional scientific wisdom has long held that the reason for encouraging early implantation in infants and toddlers is to take advantage of the young brain's plasticity to interpret signals from the cochlear implant into meaningful sound and language (Tomblin, Barker, and Hubbs 2007, 517). Yet, this propensity for language acquisition is not restricted to spoken language but also holds for signed languages (Petitto 1989, 9). If a deaf person is to acquire native or native-like fluency in a signed language, early language exposure is the best way to do so.

It is my anecdotal observation after fifteen years as a faculty member of Gallaudet University that a substantial number of young adults who received cochlear implants as young children have enrolled in Gallaudet University in part to learn American Sign Language and explore the signing Deaf community. One telltale indication of a student who has had cochlear implant surgery but does not always wear the cochlear implant is a C-shaped scar behind the implanted ear. In most cases, this is covered by hair that hides the scar, but a Gallaudet University first-year tradition known as BALD DAY (uppercase letters indicate ASL gloss) involves students first dyeing their hair various colors at the beginning of spring semester, followed by shaving the head completely. Once the bare head is exposed, the number of students with cochlear implants is easy to identify.

Students who are new signers are similarly easy to identify, since their modality accent gives them away. Just as a speaker of a spoken language can often be identified as non-native, a similar phenomenon occurs across language modalities, with non-native signers recognized as not just non-native speakers of a particular signed language but also non-native to the modality class of signed languages. These new signers with cochlear implants do pick up American Sign Language, but depending on their facility with language, including adeptness with the new modality, they may find themselves experiencing partial access to signed language that parallels their partial access to spoken language. This is due to the limitations of the relatively small number (e.g., twelve to twenty-two) of intracochlear electrodes of a multiple-channel cochlear implant, which is considerably less than the approximately 3,000 inner hair cells in a typical human cochlea (Tang, Benitez, and Zeng 2011). For this reason, despite their ability to function in a spoken language environment, the successful cochlear implant user does not possess the same quality of auditory experience as a person with species-typical hearing.

The young deaf adult who is a new signer may not have learned about the potential barriers to acquiring fluency in a signed language until she is placed in a signed language environment. Accordingly, a sense of regret about language choice may not occur to the new signer until she encounters these barriers and tries to acquire a signed language. Yet, is this a proper attribution of a sense of regret? The new signer likely did not have sufficient agency to pursue a signed language while living with adults who made language modality choices for her. Wallace's analysis of the Deaf parents who resist implanting their deaf child depicts their decision as attributable to "the affirmative attitude they have adopted toward their own lives which gives them a strong reason to embrace the disability when they look on it retrospectively." Yet Wallace elides the converse, which is that for hearing parents who choose the path of cochlear implantation with one language modality, a similar harm and potential locus of regret exists for the nonsigning deaf young adult with a cochlear implant (Wallace 2013, 126).

REGRET AND GENETIC SELECTION

Perhaps Wallace's analysis of the confusion between Deaf parents' retrospective life project analysis and the future potential of deaf children is better suited to the ethical question of whether to engage in genetic selection for deafness than cochlear implantation. Genetic selection involves decisions regarding genetic screening of genetically intact and unaltered fertilized eggs, zygotes, and embryos. There are two types of genetic screening: genetic screening of embryos, which occurs during pregnancy, and preimplantation genetic diagnosis (PGD) screening, which occurs prior to implanting a fertilized egg into the womb. Currently, genetic screening for deafness is possible for both prenatal and PGD types of screening; it is somewhat limited since not all genes associated with deafness have been identified. When requested, genetic screening is conducted for the GBJ2 gene (Connexin 26), which is one of the most common causes of genetic deafness in the United States (Norris et al. 2006, 732). Genetic *selection* of deafness does not involve any alteration of genetic material but only involves choosing unaltered but screened fertilized eggs.

Additionally, selection for deafness can only occur when the potential parents each possess compatible genetic material that in combination can result in fertilized eggs with the trait, which can then be implanted via PGD. One could imagine a case where each potential parent has a genetic basis for hearing loss, but these individual genes are not compatible in combination with the birth of a deaf child. Creation for deafness, on the other hand, occurs when the potential parents who wish to bear a deaf child do not have the genetic material necessary to bring this about. In fact, genetic selection for deafness is *impossible* when the potential parents do not have the genetic material necessary to bring about deafness. For these potential parents to bring about a deaf child, the genome of the embryo must be altered by gene insertion or deletion, such as that used with CRISPR technology. This section focuses on the case of genetic selection only.

One motivation for Deaf parents to use genetic selection in order to ensure deaf children could be that they hold (per Wallace's terminology) affirmative attitudes toward their disabilities and come to identify with them as part of what gives meaning to their lives. Having spent all or most of their lives as Deaf, it is not unreasonable to imagine such people as having led full and rich lives with life projects shaped by their identities as Deaf people. Wallace describes the connection between identity affirmation, project affirmation, and life affirmation of some disabled people as interconnected and dependent upon the ability to unconditionally affirm their lives, tied to the tendency to unconditionally affirm their projects and identities as disabled persons, including the affirmation of their disability (Wallace 2013, 124). I do not take issue with this account.

Wallace contrasts the above view of disabled people whose identities as disabled people inform their life projects and life affirmation with an account of a different group of disabled people. In this other account, Wallace describes individuals with disabilities who do *not* develop a disability identity that is intertwined with their life projects and affirmation. For this set of disabled people, what gives significant meaning to their lives are not activities that presuppose their disability experience or their disability identity but activities that are unrelated to their disability or only peripherally connected to it. Extrapolating from this, Wallace speculates that members of this group of disabled people "might well regret on balance the disabilities they have had to live with, even while they adopt an attitude of unconditional affirmation toward the life they have actually lived" (Wallace 2013, 125).

I find this acknowledgment of disability regret apart from the lived life as a disabled person troubling, in part because it raises for me an issue similar to that highlighted in Elizabeth Barnes' discussion of bad difference (Barnes 2016, 101–3). Barnes provides a value-neutral account of disability that allows conceptual space for the argument that some disabilities are bad difference rather than mere difference. This so far is consistent with the idea that an individual might suggest that his disability is a bad-difference disability rather than a mere-difference disability and, given the normative connotation, could move from bad disability to a claim of disability regret. My worry about this notion of disability regret put forth by Wallace is that it falls prey to a mistake of reasoning similar to that of the disability paradox, a phenomenon documented by empirical studies in which nondisabled persons' perceptions of disability well-being do not track the reports of disabled persons. For Wallace's purposes, he maintains that the important element of disability regret is that it can be imagined; that is, it is an attitude toward disability that is distinguished from the positive orientation of disability affirmation of people whose meaningful life projects at least in part rely on an association and connection of disability identity. Again, Wallace does not claim that such people are mistaken in their valuation of their lives and even identities—he just thinks that the move from valuing one's own disability is not the same as valuing disability simpliciter. I'm not wholly convinced that imagining disability regret is where the focus should be, preferring instead to think about how disabled people actually do reason about their disabilities. It may well be that some people with disabilities do exhibit disability regret; my concern is that such a claim ought to be grounded in something other than imagination.

So how does Wallace's discussion of disability affirmation and disability regret relate to the topic of genetic selection? If Wallace's account of disability valuation confusion is correct, this would suggest that Deaf parents who use genetic selection to bear a deaf child have made a mistake in reasoning by conflating the affirmation of their experience of being a Deaf person and how it has shaped them with the affirmation and valuation of their deaf child. In the first case, the valuation of deafness is instrumental—it is valued for the ways in which Deaf people's lives have been shaped by deafness, from the nature of language modality to the intimacy of eye contact (Burke 2014, 11). But it seems to me that Deaf people do not value being Deaf for merely instrumental reasons but for intrinsic reasons. They value being Deaf for its own sake. And if this is the case, it is harder to see how Wallace's argument for disability regret can challenge genetic selection for deafness.

COCHLEAR IMPLANTS, TRANSFORMATIVE EXPERIENCE, AND THE POTENTIAL FOR REGRET

The previous two cases have dealt with different aspects of surrogate decision making. In the pediatric cochlear implant case, the potential parents contend with concerns about making a choice that they or their deaf child may find cause to regret. In the genetic selection case, the discussion turns on the question of whether regret that one has a disability is sufficient to trump the desire of Deaf parents who want to use genetic screening to select a potentially deaf embryo over one that is not deaf. In this next case, I shift from surrogate decision making and regret to agential decision making and regret.

Imagine a middle-aged signing Deaf adult, Omar, who is fluent in the written form of English and also eloquent in ASL. Omar values his standing in the world as a signing Deaf person and does not wish to become a Hearing person in the sense of adopting all of the cultural mores of Hearing community, but he is curious about the experience of audition and hearing. Given this, he decides to undergo cochlear implant surgery. But before doing so, he reads L. A. Paul's philosophical analysis of the transformative elements of cochlear implant surgery. Unlike the case of pediatric cochlear implantation discussed by Paul, Omar, as a signing Deaf adult, is already formed and shaped by his experiences as a signing Deaf person fluent in two language modalities, written English and signed ASL. Yet he anticipates that the cochlear implant surgery has the potential to transform him in the two ways outlined by Paul: epistemically and personally (Paul 2014, 61). Epistemic transformation includes the experience of being able to access information and knowledge about something currently unavailable to him—the ability to hear sound.[5] For the purposes of this discussion, I will stipulate that the experience of sound uptake prior to implantation is significantly different from the experience of sound uptake after implantation. Unlike my earlier discussion of pediatric cochlear implantation, the key issue here is not language acquisition, but that preimplant and postimplant experiences are significantly different in terms of their epistemic content. Personal transformation, on the other hand, deals with what it is like to be a person with a cochlear implant—from preferences to experiences.

Paul's work on transformative experiences advances the argument that making a transformative life decision, such as whether or not to acquire a cochlear implant, is complicated by epistemic inaccessibility. Omar cannot know beforehand what it is like to be a person with a cochlear implant or, put another way, what it is like to be a person who hears through a cochlear implant. Additionally, Omar cannot know what the preferences of his future self will be once he acquires a cochlear implant, including whether or not he will regret this decision.

Paul's analysis focuses on the issue of epistemic inaccessibility and the challenges this presents to decision making. Omar could try to imagine what it is like to hear through a cochlear implant, or what it might be like to be a hearing person. He could even shadow a hearing person or person with a cochlear implant for a period of time to try to simulate this experience. Yet, imagination and simulation are, according to Paul, insufficiently robust to provide epistemically accessible content. When hearing parents consider a cochlear implant for their deaf child, they appeal to the kinds of experiences that are epistemically available to them, including what it is like to hear (sans cochlear implant) and project these experiences on to their child. In Omar's case, he has lived in the world as a signing Deaf person, and he knows that he will not lose his ability to sign once he acquires his cochlear implant. What he worries about is whether he will regret getting a cochlear implant.

Some of his regrets might be tied to physical sensation. He may have unrealistic expectations about the quality of sound he will experience (such as music) and his ability to appreciate or comprehend it. He may wonder if hearing with his cochlear implant will be physically uncomfortable in the way that he remembers from his childhood experience of wearing behind the ear hearing aids, which both felt awkward behind the ear and made unpleasant noise that was not helpful or informative. He may also wonder if the cochlear implant surgery will have a side effect of dizziness or vertigo and whether that will be temporary or long-lasting.

Omar may also wonder about regrets that are social in nature. He has confided to some of his closest friends about his decision to get a cochlear implant. Most of his friends are neutral or supportive, but one of his oldest friends, Elias, who harkens back to his elementary school days at the state residential deaf school, has reacted with anger and disgust. Omar is hopeful that time will mitigate Elias' reaction, but he is also concerned that his friendship with Elias may be beyond saving. Omar also wonders whether his relationships with his hearing family members who do not sign, including his parents, will improve, and whether having a cochlear implant will make communication easier at work during those times when he doesn't have access to an interpreter. He anticipates the cochlear implant may provide more communication options and thinks that this could make his life different in some ways, but he isn't able to predict how those differences will make him feel and possibly change who he is. He knows that each person's experience with a cochlear implant is unique and expects that his experience of encountering sound in different ways will transform him. Omar understands that best practice for cochlear implantation of adults is to implant the ear with more hearing capability. It is thought that the neural connections to this ear will be more responsive to noise. Omar also knows that the kind of cochlear implant he is about to receive will not preserve any residual hearing in that ear, and he is a little worried about the loss of hearing in that ear should the cochlear implant not be successful. Omar doesn't use his residual hearing for language comprehension, but he does rely on it for environmental information.

After Omar receives his cochlear implant, he goes through a year of learning how to listen and train his brain to recognize sound. Omar is very frustrated with what he hears, and finds it confusing and difficult to comprehend—he believes that he is worse off than he was before his implant. Yet he is committed to the process of auditory rehabilitation and understands that he must continue his auditory training if he is to realize the full potential of his cochlear implant. After a second year, Omar has acquired the ability to distinguish some environmental noises, but he is unable to understand speech without also relying on speechreading. When Omar thinks about his decision to get a cochlear implant, he is filled with regret.

In the case of Omar, he has made the decision to obtain a cochlear implant with considerable information. He has watched captioned videos about the procedure and rehabilitation, he has consulted with two different cochlear implant surgeons, and he has met and talked with several signing Deaf people who have received cochlear implants as adults. Prior to getting his cochlear implant, Omar believed that he has gathered enough information to make an informed decision. Omar also believed that he made the best decision possible based on the evidence at hand. Yet, Omar feels a sense of regret and chagrin about his decision; namely, he feels that he didn't understand how getting a cochlear implant would change him from someone who enjoyed being social and spending time outdoors to someone who found spoken conversation and being outdoors mentally fatiguing. Omar now preferred to reduce the stress he felt with his cochlear implant by isolating himself from the world.

Given that Omar made this decision himself, and that he has noted a change in the things he values postimplant, he satisfies the conditions of what Wallace describes as agent-regret, which is an attitude experienced by people who have been relevantly involved in the regrettable experience. While Omar acknowledges that he was indeed relevantly involved, he questions whether he truly understood what he valued prior to his cochlear implant surgery. The vulnerability he experiences from the change in how he interacts with the world as a person who hears somewhat has altered the way he is in the world from how he was prior to his implant surgery. One question here for those who favor an agential view of regret is about the elements of forward-looking information needed to qualify conditions of retrospective assessment as regret. If there are facts that are epistemically inaccessible, can Omar's decision count as one of agential-regret? Another question is whether decisions involving potentially transformative disability-related experiences have features that undercut the moral emotion of regret. In Omar's case, the personally transformative practice of modifying his sensory experience is not just a physical transformation. Yet, the physical changes may influence social aspects of transformation, calling new attention to the social construction of disability and perhaps inviting a reevaluation of affirmation and influence of one's disability identity. Finally, is there something about the nature of disability in conjunction with transformative experiences that shapes the character of regret? The paradigm case for most of the discussion around disability and transformative experience begins with moving from a disabled state to one that is "less" so. If one grants that a feature of regret tracks a neutral conception of what might have been—whether that is more desirable or less desirable—this neutrality seems at odds with the popular notion of longing as it relates to disability and what might have been. In this case, I would argue, the presumptive framing of disability in terms of loss or privation primes the pairing of disability transformative experiences and regret to move away from a state of disability to a state of less disability. How this is defined will depend on one's valuation of disability—I created the Deaf case of Omar partly as a challenge to popularized mainstream valuations of disability valences. I suspect that carefully considering the valence of disability, and asking whether disability transformative experience accounts accord with "bad disability" or "mere disability," will shed more insight on this question going forward.

"MISS DEAF AMERICA" AND OPEN FUTURE REGRET

Expressions of sorrow and sympathy are frequently proffered to people with disabilities, and deaf people are no different in this regard. The title of this section is taken from Brandi Rarus, a former Miss Deaf America, who described an encounter at a school assembly where a young deaf boy offered her a card he had made for her that included a drawing of her with crown and sash, plus the words, "Dear Miss Deaf America, I am sorry you are deaf" (Rarus and Harris 2014, 75). In her description, Rarus notes that this took place at a school with a mainstream education program for deaf children in a school with mostly hearing children and teachers, underscoring the nature of this deaf boy's educational environment. She recounts their brief conversation, first by clarifying with the boy in sign language that he understood what he had written on the card and then responding with, "You must not be sorry. I am not sorry. Look at me. I am doing well. I am in college. I am happy. I am Miss Deaf America. Being deaf is a great thing, and it's great for you, too. Do not be sorry!" (Rarus and Harris 2014, 76). That this exchange takes place in American Sign Language rather than a spoken language is somewhat unusual; that the expression of sympathy comes from a child who is also deaf is less so, given that the child has likely picked up on sentiments expressed by those in his environment. In this section, I shall take up the notions of sympathy and sorrow expressed in such comments and construct an analysis that clarifies what I refer to as OFR.

Dena Davis uses Joel Feinberg's conception of a child's right to an open future to critique using genetic technology to select for deafness, arguing that the deaf child will experience fewer opportunities due to being deaf rather than hearing (Davis 1997, 12). The more opportunities an individual has, the more open her future. Liberal societies stress the maximizing of opportunity and offsetting the negative effects of the "natural and social" lottery in order to promote individual autonomy and lifestyle choice. On this account, the state of deafness, whether chosen through selection or by happenstance, functions to restrict the deaf person's opportunities. I suspect that when people offer an expression of sorrow or sympathy to deaf persons about their status as deaf people, a plausible interpretation of this is to convey regret that their experience of being in the world (as deaf people) limits their opportunities. This expression of regret for limited opportunities is what I call OFR. A common experience shared by deaf people that elicits such OFR typically unfolds as follows. First, a hearing person invites a deaf person to engage in social interaction by making a comment or request to the deaf person, such as asking for directions or remarking on the weather. Following this, the deaf person does not understand what has been said but does have enough awareness to recognize that something has been said and that a response is expected. Next, the deaf person responds to the hearing person with a statement of deaf identity (e.g., "I'm deaf—I missed that. Can you please say it again?"). This statement may be spoken, mouthed, or even written. The hearing person frequently responds to the deaf identity claim with a simple apology (e.g., "I'm sorry"), opting to discontinue the conversation and instead following up with a statement of benediction or affirmation.

At first glance, it might seem the concluding conversational response in the example above is merely an apology for disturbing the deaf person. Yet I would classify this interaction as one of OFR in part due to the frequency of additional comments that single out the deaf person's status as a deaf person and acknowledge the difference in social standing of deaf persons. These comments may not be intended as patronizing, but for deaf people who have experienced this phenomenon repeatedly, it can be uncomfortable to be the object of this distinct combination of apology and compassionate affirmation based on the physical trait of disability. I contend that part of the deaf person's discombobulation is tied to the refusal of the hearing person to engage in social interaction with the deaf person as equal parties, which reinforces the sense that the apology is not about the hearing person's mistaken assumptions about communication but instead is offered on behalf of the deaf person's deafness.

Let's stipulate that the typical expression of OFR is not about an individual expressing regret for the agent's own actions—presumably, the person expressing regret to the deaf person has no causal or proximate role related to the deaf person's physical disability. (For the purposes of the open future analysis of regret, I'm setting aside the class of cases in which parents or others may bear culpability for causing deafness directly or indirectly.) These expressions of regret seem to capture a broader notion regarding the whole of constraints imposed by deafness, ranging from physical constraints of truncated auditory experiences to a lack of social opportunities due to limitations of public and private infrastructure. The OFR thus acknowledges that deafness is not just articulated in terms of bodily difference and variation but also in terms of the deaf person's capacity for inclusive interaction with the social environment (Padden and Humphries 2006, 131). But acknowledging the social component of disability adds a complication to the notion of agential responsibility and regret. While it is relatively easy to make a determination as to whether an individual bears responsibility for the physical or embodied characteristic of deafness via genetic material or some other means, attribution or recusal of responsibility-related social constraints related to deafness is not so simple. I suggest that these commonplace expressions of OFR for disability should be interpreted as indirectly acknowledging the role the agent and others in society have played in contributing to the social constraints on the disabled person's future.

Possible objections to my analysis of OFR include the following: persons offering OFR may have no awareness of the social aspects of disability discrimination constraints; persons offering OFR may acknowledge these social aspects of disability discrimination but reject responsibility for decisions made by others (whether before their time or currently); and that persons offering OFR have in mind a more restrictive scope that only includes regret for constraints imposed by the physical experience of deafness but not by the social experience.

A lack of explicit awareness about the social aspects of disability discrimination does not seem to be a sufficient objection to the concept of OFR, in part because of its broadness, which offers sympathy without constraint. The response of "I'm sorry" to a statement of deaf identity in a variety of contexts does not pick out a particular aspect of being deaf but responds to the whole of being deaf. Taking up the second objection, which emphasizes the role of particular agential blame and responsibility for the socially constrained futures of deaf people in a society that has been constructed over centuries, it might be useful to consider some features in reparations discussions related to the history of slavery in the United States. Among other things, reparations are a proposed solution to redressing initial harms done by slaveowners who are no longer living, with these harms having had lasting effects through generations. This temporal aspect of reparations for initial harms done in the past includes an awareness of the ways in which social capital privilege has been conferred on members of a number of communities—not just limited to those who are direct descendants of slaveowners but to those who have no direct connection to this history while still reaping its benefits. If reparations are to be considered from a Deaf (or disability) perspective, one step might be to engage in consciousness raising among hearing communities so that the social harms done via OFR (a version of pity) can be understood and attended to. Since social attitudes create social realities—or, put another way, since social narratives create social identities—what is needed are powerful counternarratives against the master narratives of OFR and their attendant pity. These new and disruptive stories must be taken up not just by the Deaf community but by everyone.[6]

CONCLUSION

This chapter has identified just a couple of the ways in which disability and regret can intersect using cases involving deaf lives to illuminate these very complex issues and questions. Disability is a multivocal phenomenon; my choice of cases of deafness and deaf lives only reflects the lived experience of disability with which I am most deeply familiar and does not begin to exhaust the topic of disability and regret. It is my hope that in analyzing a particular disability deeply (and I recognize that there are those in the signing Deaf community who reject the definition of Deaf lives as disabled lives), I have provided some guidance as to how one might proceed with other aspects of disability and regret. There is more to be excavated regarding questions of disability and the potential for regret in surrogate decision making about disability treatment, just as there is regarding surrogate decision making and the selection of potential disabled lives. The transformative nature of acquired disability is often the first thing people consider when asked about disability and regret. In flipping the script to explore the possibility of the loss of a particular kind of disability identity and the challenges in trying to determine whether one's future self might regret the loss of a disability identity, I hope to have provoked some reflection about the valence of disability as well as the valence of regret. Finally, in ending with a trope of disability pity that many, if not most people with disabilities, have encountered in our lives, I have attempted to push the imposition of regret back where I think it rightfully belongs—with a society that has tried to retrofit Deaf and disabled lives.

Would disability regret exist if society were structured in such a way that the futures of disabled lives were wide open? I can only speculate, but I suspect that the varieties of disability regret would be less reliant on conceptions of pity and more dependent on the lived experiences of disabled people as individuals who experience the same gamut of the moral emotions as nondisabled people do. I imagine a future in which disabled people would be thought of as experiencing the same varieties of regret as nondisabled people rather than be presumed to be filled with a singular regret about the content of our otherwise rich, complicated, and meaningful disabled lives.

NOTES

1. I follow the convention in deaf studies of using uppercase "Deaf" and lowercase "deaf" to make a distinction between two senses of the word. The uppercase "Deaf" represents people who identify as hard of hearing or deaf and who use a signed language as one of their primary languages. The lowercase "deaf" refers to the auditory status of hearing loss, with hard-of-hearing people typically classified as having mild to moderately severe hearing loss and deaf people classified as having severe or profound loss. Two points are important for this chapter: I take it that deaf children of hearing parents who have not acquired language (e.g., most pediatric candidates for cochlear implants) are auditorily deaf but due to their youth and lack of agency have not (yet?) affiliated with the signing Deaf community. For this reason, I will refer to members of this population using the lowercase "deaf," including paraphrases of arguments. In the case of quotations, such as those of Tamsin Coates, I preserve the original language. I also note that the field of Deaf Studies is considering recent challenges to this convention of upper- and lowercase D/deaf. For more information about this discussion, see Annelies Kusters, Maartje de Meulder and Dai O'Brien's chapter 1. "Innovations in Deaf Studies: Critically Mapping the Field," in *Innovations of Deaf Studies*, edited by Annelies Kusters, Maartje de Meulder and Dai O'Brien (Kusters, Meulder, and O'Brien 2017, 14).

2. Cochlear implants are prosthetic devices that provide auditory capabilities to the user when successful. The literature about the efficacy of these prosthetic devices is considerable and I will not engage in the merits or criticisms of this technology here. For the purposes of this article, I am simply stipulating that persons with this medical intervention have had a range of outcomes from highly successful listening experiences, including sophisticated levels of speech comprehension, to less successful outcomes.

3. I suggest that just as the distinction of uppercase "Deaf" and lowercase "deaf" denotes two different aspects of the experience of deafness, there is a parallel argument to be made for the experiences of hearing. The uppercase "Hearing" refers to the sociocultural and linguistic aspects of Hearing culture (including spoken language) and lowercase "hearing" refers to audiological classification. In the case of audiological deaf people who use a spoken language and not a signed language, their cultural orientation is Hearing (uppercase). For more on this, see "Armchairs and Stares: On the Privation of Hearing" (Burke 2014, 16–20).

4. The Laurent Clerc National Deaf Education Center on the Gallaudet University campus is one such place. See the following website for more details: https://www.

gallaudet.edu/kendall-demonstration-elementary-school/academics/early-childhood-education-program

5. Most deaf people have some residual hearing—it is rare to have no capacity for hearing at all.

6. I thank Anna Gotlib for conversation on this point.

REFERENCES

Barnes, Elizabeth. 2016. *The Minority Body: A Theory of Disability*. Oxford: Oxford University Press.

Burke, Teresa Blankmeyer. 2014. "Armchairs and Stares: On the Privation of Deafness." In *Deaf Gain: Raising the Stakes for Human Diversity*, ed. H-Dirksen Baumann and Joseph J. Murray, 3–22. Minneapolis: University of Minnesota Press.

Burke, Teresa Blankmeyer. 2017. "Choosing Accommodations: Signed Language Interpreting and the Absence of Choice." *Kennedy Institute of Ethics Journal* 27 (2): 267–300.

Christiansen, J. B., and I. Leigh. 2002. Cochlear Implants in Children: Ethics and Choices. Washington, DC: Gallaudet University Press.

Coates, Tamsin. 2012. "I Questioned Myself as a Mother; When Tamsin Coates Chose Surgery to Help Her Deaf Sons Hear, She Was Accused of Cruelty. But She Has No Regrets." *Daily Telegraph (London)*, November 26, 2012, Monday, 29. https://advance.lexis.com/api/document?collection=news&id=urn:contentItem:574H-MBD1-JBVM-Y210-00000-00&context=1516831.

Davis, Dena S. 1997. "Genetic Dilemmas and the Child's Right to an Open Future." *Hastings Center Report* 27 (2): 7–15.

Kusters, Annelies, Maartje De Meulder, and Dai O'Brien. 2017. "Innovations in Deaf Studies: Critically Mapping the Field." In *Innovations in Deaf Studies: The Role of Deaf Scholars*, ed. Annelies Kusters, Maartje De Meulder, and Dai O'Brien, 1–53. Oxford: Oxford University Press.

Mauldin, Laura. 2016. *Made to Hear: Cochlear Implants and Raising Deaf Children*. Minneapolis: University of Minnesota Press.

Norris, V. W., K. A. Arnos, W. D. Hanks, W. E. Nance, and A. Pandya. 2006. "Does Universal Newborn Hearing Screening Identify All Children with GJB2 (Connexin 26) Deafness? Penetrance of GJB2 Deafness." *Ear Hear* 27 (6): 732–41. doi: 10.1097/01.aud.0000240492.78561.d3.

Padden, Carol, and Tom Humphries. 2006. *Inside Deaf Culture*. Cambridge, MA: Harvard University Press.

Paul, L. A. 2014. *Transformative Experience*. Oxford: Oxford University Press.

Petitto, Laura Ann. 1989. "Knowledge of Language in Signed and Spoken Language acquisition." In *Language Development and Sign Language*, ed. B. Woll and J. Kyle, 1–9. Bristol: University of Bristol.

Rarus, Brandi, and Gail Harris. 2014. *Finding Zoe: A Deaf Woman's Story of Identity and Adoption*. Dallas, TX: Benbella.

Tang, Qing, Raul Benitez, and Fan-Gang Zeng. 2011. "Spatial Channel Interactions in Cochlear Implants." *Journal of Neural Engineering* 8 (4): 046029. doi: 10.1088/1741-2560/8/4/046029.

Tomblin, J. Bruce, Brittan A. Barker, and Sarah Hubbs. 2007. "Developmental Constraints on Language Development in Children with Cochlear Implants." *International Journal of Audiology* 46 (9): 512–23.

Wallace, R. Jay. 2013. *The View from Here: On Affirmation, Attachment, and the Limits of Regret*. Oxford: Oxford University Press.

Chapter 10

Regret Aversion in Riskless Choice Contexts: A Formal Model of Choice Behavior and Morally Problematic Choice Architectures

Caspar Chorus[1]

INTRODUCTION

The notion of regret aversion has a rich tradition in the economic sciences. Prominent examples of microeconomic models of regret-based decision making include the minimax regret framework (Savage 1951) and regret theory (Bell 1982; Loomes and Sugden 1982). What these frameworks and models have in common is that they postulate that when choosing between options, the decision maker aims to avoid the situation where a nonchosen option turns out to perform better than the chosen one. Indeed, there is ample empirical evidence from the field of psychology and the neurosciences that the phenomenon of regret aversion plays an important role in decision making (e.g., Coricelli et al. 2005; Zeelenberg and Pieters 2007). A commonality between the regret-based theories, frameworks, and models presented in economics, psychology, and other fields is that they refer to so-called risky decision making.[2] That is, the decision maker does not know in advance the performance of each of the options in her choice set. The classical example being that of a lottery: one does not know in advance if the lottery ticket is a winning one, and regret-based models assume that when considering buying a lottery ticket, the decision maker contemplates the anticipated regret that will be experienced when not winning.[3] It goes without saying that the scope of (regret-based models of) risky decision making is much broader than lotteries; regret-based models are routinely used to model decision making in all sorts of contexts including health, transportation, and financial decision making (insurance, investment decisions); see section 5 in Bleichrodt and Wakker (2015) for a recent review of applications of regret theory for risky decision making. Crucially, by design and by definition, regret-based models of economic decision making construe regret as resulting from—and inexorably bound to—imperfect knowledge; in a world of perfect information and optimal decision making, there would be no regret.

In this chapter, I will argue that this perspective on regret minimization is incomplete, and that regret aversion also plays a role in so-called riskless situations where the decision maker has full advance knowledge of the performance of all options in her choice set, in terms of all relevant criteria. First, I will present a formal model of regret-based decision making in riskless choice contexts. This so-called random regret minimization model (RRM model from here on) has been recently introduced in the domain of transportation (Chorus 2010, 2014a; Chorus, Arentze, and Timmermans, 2008; Jang, Rasouli and Timmermans, 2017; van Cranenburgh, Guevara and Chorus 2015) and has since been applied in a wide variety of decision-making contexts within and well beyond that domain.[4] Subsequently, I will use this model to explore why some choice sets (or choice architectures) are morally problematic as they generate high levels of—anticipated—regret on the side of the decision maker. By taking these steps, I connect the notion of regret aversion in riskless choice contexts to the literature on nudging and choice architectures,[5] which is rapidly gaining attention among researchers in marketing, health, transport and environment, behavioral economics, and ethics (e.g., Avineri 2012; Johnson et al. 2012; Selinger and Whyte 2011; Sunstein 2015; Thaler, Sunstein, and Balz 2014; Thorndike et al. 2012).

The next section presents the RRM model. A measure of "choice set regret" is derived in the section "A Measure of Choice Set Regret and Morally Problematic Choice Architectures," where it is also explained that choice set regret is a function of the specific composition (i.e., architecture) of the choice set; in that section, I will also argue why some choice set compositions or architectures may be considered morally problematic as they trigger disproportionally high regret levels among decision makers.

A RANDOM REGRET MINIMIZATION MODEL OF RISKLESS DECISION MAKING

Before presenting the RRM model in mathematical notation, I give a behavioral introduction and interpretation. Consider a choice situation where a decision maker makes a choice from a finite set of discrete and mutually exclusive options (called alternatives); each option being described in terms of a number of dimensions or criteria (called attributes). The RRM model postulates that a decision maker, when making a choice from this set, aims to minimize regret, by means of choosing the alternative from the set with minimum regret. From the analyst's perspective, a considered alternative's regret is composed out of a random part and a systematic part. The random part contains all factors unobservable by the analyst but relevant to the decision maker. The systematic part contains the influence of all observable factors (i.e., attributes of the alternative[6]). This *systematic regret* of a considered alternative is postulated to equal the sum of all so-called binary regrets that arise from bilaterally comparing the considered alternative with each competitor alternative. This *binary regret* in turn is specified as the sum of all so-called attribute regrets that arise from comparing the considered alternative with a particular competitor in terms of each attribute. This *attribute regret* is an increasing function of the product of the attribute difference and the taste parameter (decision weight) associated with the attribute. In other words, attribute regret increases (1) as the extent to which the competitor alternative outperforms the considered alternative in terms of a particular attribute increases and (2) as the importance, to the decision maker, of the attribute increases. Crucially, attribute regret is postulated to be a *convex* function of attribute differences and decision weights: the regret that is caused by a deterioration of a considered alternative's relative (i.e., compared to a competitor) performance on a particular attribute is larger than the reduction in regret, which is caused by an improvement of equal size.

To make this more concrete, I present a running example that will return in various shapes and forms in the remainder of this chapter. Consider the situation where the decision maker is moving to a new town for work and is considering a set of three residential alternatives (house A, B, and C) offered by her real estate agent. Each house is described in terms of a number of attributes, such as the size of the garden, number of rooms, commute time to work, price, and so on. The decision maker is assumed to compare house A with house B and with house C in terms of the size of the garden, number of rooms, and so on. Consider the comparison of A with B in terms of the attribute "size of garden": assume that the decision maker prefers a larger garden over a smaller one. Now, if house A has a smaller garden than house B, this generates attribute regret ("garden regret"). The more important the size of the garden is to her, and the bigger the difference between sizes of A's garden and B's garden (in favor of the latter), the larger the amount of generated "garden regret." If house A has a bigger garden than house B, the comparison of A with B in terms of the attribute "size of garden" generates "garden rejoice" (rejoice being the somewhat awkward term used by economists to describe the opposite of regret). Rejoice, just like regret, becomes larger when the attribute becomes more important and when the difference between the garden sizes increases (in favor of house A). Crucially however, the regret that is associated with a given difference in garden size in favor of house B is larger than the rejoice that would be associated with the same difference in garden size if it were in favor of house A. Likewise, A is compared to B, and with C, on all other attributes; all these resulting attribute regrets are summed to obtain the full systematic regret associated with house A. The same is done for house B and C to obtain systematic regrets for all three alternatives. Adding random errors to all three systematic regrets (in order to represent "noise" in the decision-making process and the presence of attributes that are omitted in the model) leads to so-called total regrets for all three houses. The decision maker is subsequently assumed to choose the house with lowest total regret.

In mathematical notation, in its most generic form, the total regret of a considered alternative is written as follows:

$$RR_i = R_i + \upsilon_i = \sum_{j \neq i} \sum_m \mu \cdot \left[\ln\left(1 + \exp\left[\frac{\beta m}{\mu} \cdot (x_{jm} - x_{im})\right]\right) - \ln(2) \right] + \upsilon_i \quad (10.1)$$

RR_i denotes the total regret associated with considered alternative i.
R_i denotes the systematic regret associated with i.
υ_i denotes the error terms associated with i; if it is assumed that its negative follows an i.i.d. Extreme Value Type I distribution, practical Logit type choice probabilities (P) are obtained:

$$P(i) = \frac{\exp(-R_i)}{\sum_{j=1..j} \exp(-Rj)}.$$

β_m denotes the taste parameter (decision weight) associated with attribute x_m.
x_{im}, x_{jm} denote the values associated with attribute m for, respectively, the considered alternative i and another alternative j.
μ is a regret aversion parameter. If μ approaches 0, only regret matters and its behavioral counterpart, "rejoice," is irrelevant. If $\mu \gg 0$, regret and rejoice are equally important. In that case, the RRM model reduces to a classical, linear in parameter multiattribute utility maximization rule. Although μ can be allowed to vary across attributes, in this chapter I will assume that it is generic.

Note that subtraction of the term ln(2) is merely cosmetic and is done for reasons of ease of exposition: it ensures that neither regret nor rejoice is generated by a comparison between two alternatives in terms of an attribute on which both alternatives have the same value, that is, where $(x_{im} - x_{jm}) = 0$. In other words, subtracting this term implies that attribute regret functions always go through the origin (see figure 10.1). From the perspective of the analyses performed in this chapter, this is inconsequential: it merely shifts the regret function downward without affecting its shape or regret differences

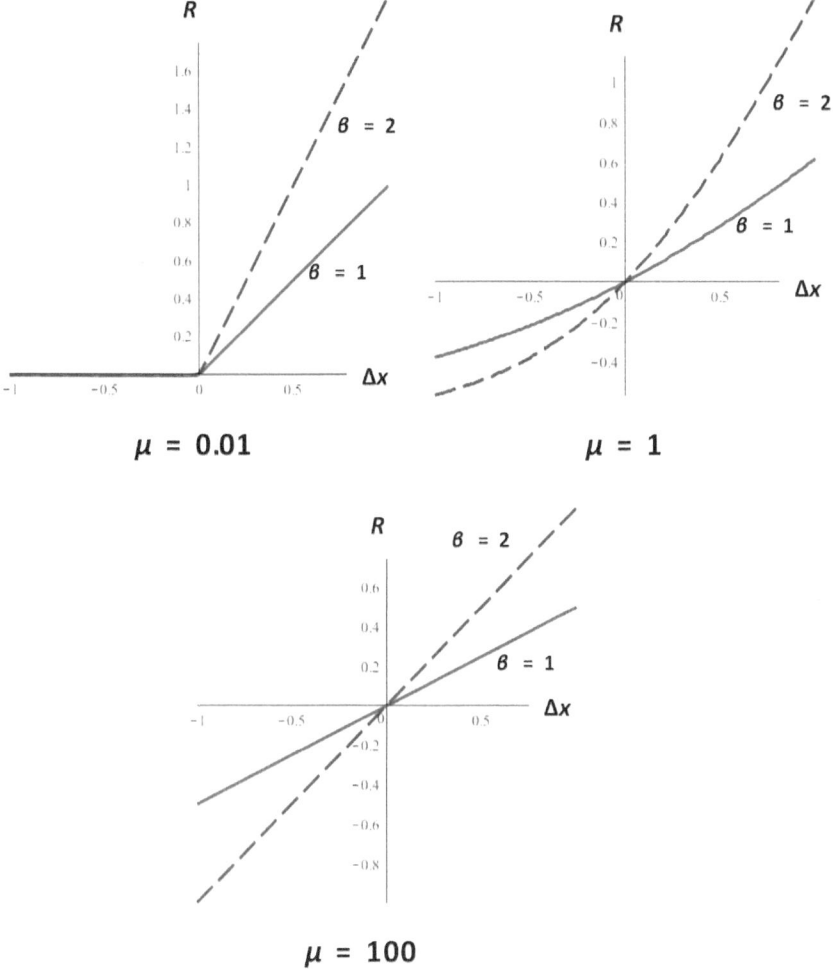

Figure 10.1. Attribute regret $\mu \cdot \left[ln\left(1 + exp\left[\frac{\beta_m}{\mu} \cdot \left(x_{jm} - x_{im} \right) \right] \right) - ln(2) \right]$, for different values of μ, β

between alternatives. As such, (not) subtracting the constant ln(2) does not affect choice behavior, as explained in more detail in Chorus (2014c) and in Chorus and van Cranenburgh (2018).

Figure 10.1 visualizes the shape of the attribute regret function, for different values of μ and β. The focus is on a comparison between a considered alternative i and one competitor alternative j in terms of attribute x. For simplicity of notation, I denote $x_j - x_i$ by Δx. Note that the right-hand side of each panel (i.e., the part of the domain where Δx is positive) represents the situation where the competitor alternative outperforms the considered alternative, leading to regret. The part of the domain where Δx is negative represents the situation where the considered alternative performs better than the competitor, leading to "rejoice" (or negative regret).

Figure 10.1 clearly illustrates the key behavioral properties of the attribute regret function, as presented at the beginning of this section. The left-hand-side panel represents extreme regret aversion. If a chosen alternative performs better than a competitor ("rejoice"), the extent to which it performs better is assumed to be irrelevant to the decision maker; the only thing that matters to her is to avoid the situation where the chosen alternative performs worse. In the context of our running example, if house A has a smaller garden than house B, comparing house A with B in terms of the size of their gardens will generate regret. The larger the difference in size (represented by Δx), and the more important the attribute (represented by β), the more "garden regret" is generated. However, if house A has a larger garden than house B, comparing house A with B in terms of the size of their gardens will not generate "garden rejoice," irrespective of the magnitude of the difference and the importance of the attribute.

The right-hand-side panel represents the behavioral complement of the regret-only model: performing better than a competitor (rejoice) is now equally important as avoiding a worse performance (regret). In the housing choice example, the regret associated with house A having a garden that is Δx units smaller than B's garden is equally large as the rejoice that would be associated with house A having a garden that is Δx units larger than B.

The middle panel represents the intermediate position where there is mild regret aversion, that is, a mild overweighting of regret relative to rejoice. This implies that while it is somewhat important to the decision maker that the considered alternative performs better than a competitor in terms of the attribute, it is considerably more important to her to avoid the situation where the chosen alternative performs worse than a competitor in terms of the attribute. Table 10.1 further illustrates this RRM model with moderate regret aversion (i.e., with $\mu = 1$) in the context of the running example of house A being compared to house B in terms of the size of their respective gardens (assuming that garden size is measured in acres). The values presented in table 10.1 may be directly compared to the plot (middle panel) presented in figure 10.1.

As postulated in the model, an increase in attribute importance (i.e., a shift from $\beta = 1$ to $\beta = 2$) results in an increase in regret and rejoice levels.

Table 10.1. Illustration of attribute regret ($\mu = 1$) in the context of the housing choice example $ln\left(1+ exp\left[\beta \cdot \left(x_{jm} - x_{im}\right)\right]\right) - ln(2)$

Values Correspond to the Middle Panel of Figure 1	$\beta = 1$ (per acre)	$\beta = 2$ (per acre)	Regret/Rejoice
Garden A is 1 acre smaller than Garden B	0.62	1.43	Regret
Garden A is 0.5 acre smaller than Garden B	0.28	0.62	
Garden A is 0.5 acre larger than Garden B	−0.22	−0.38	Negative regret,
Garden A is 1 acre larger than Garden B	−0.38	−0.57	i.e., rejoice

Furthermore, regret aversion (i.e., overweighting of regret compared to rejoice) is also clearly visible.

In the remainder of this chapter, I will focus on the RRM model where $\mu = 1$ (visualized in the middle panel of figure 10.1). This is done for reasons of ease of exposition and without loss of generic applicability of results. The resulting model specification is known as the conventional (or "classical") RRM model; this specification was introduced by Chorus (2010) and is currently the most widely used version of RRM. It has been incorporated in various Econometrics software packages (Greene 2012; Vermunt and Magidson 2014), is extensively covered in a recent Econometrics textbook (Hensher, Rose, and Greene 2015), and is taught in several choice modeling courses. As can be seen above, this RRM model specification postulates moderate levels of regret aversion.

A particularly important behavioral property of the RRM model is worth highlighting here: the RRM model implies *reference dependent* and *semi-compensatory* behavior. This is a direct result of the reference dependency and convexity of the attribute regret function that was introduced earlier: improving an alternative in terms of an attribute on which it already performs well (relative to a competitor alternative) generates only small decreases in regret, whereas deteriorating to a similar extent the performance on another equally important attribute on which the alternative has a poor performance (relative to a competitor alternative) generates more substantial increases in regret. This can be easily verified by looking at figure 10.1 (middle panel): when the initial situation is positioned more to the right of the vertical axis (i.e., more deeply in the regret domain), the additional regret of a further deterioration of the attribute generates more additional regret. As a result, the extent to which a strong performance on one attribute can compensate for a poor performance on another depends on the relative "position" (in terms of the performance with respect to relevant attributes) of each alternative in the set. When a choice alternative is deteriorated in terms of an attribute on which it already performs poorly, this deterioration is very difficult to compensate by improving another attribute of the alternative, especially when the alternative already performs well on the improved attribute.

It is instructive at this point to observe the relation between the behavior implied by the RRM model and the notion of Loss Aversion (LA) in riskless choice as was put forward by Tversky and Kahneman (1991). The two models (LA and RRM) both postulate that reference points matter for decision making, and that losses with respect to that reference point loom larger than gains of equal size. A crucial difference between the two models is the choice of reference point: whereas the LA model uses the status quo as a reference point, the RRM model uses the attributes of other alternatives in the choice set as reference points. Take again the situation where the decision maker is moving to a new town and is considering a set of houses offered by her real estate agent. The LA model postulates that she will compare each house *with her current house* (e.g., in terms of the size of the garden, commute time to work, mortgage payments); in contrast, the RRM model postulates that she will compare each house *with all other houses in the choice set* (in terms of all relevant attributes). Notwithstanding these differences in terms of reference point definitions, both the LA and RRM models have in common that they postulate that the decision maker will put a penalty on houses that perform worse than her reference point on a particular attribute, and that this penalty is larger than the reward associated with a house that performs better than her reference point on a particular attribute. The RRM model's premise that reference points consist of attributes of competing alternatives make that model particularly suitable for the analysis of choice architectures. That topic will be further explored in the next section.

But before I move on to the derivation of a measure of choice set regret, one final comment is in place. Up until this point, this chapter has presented the RRM model as a *theoretical* model of decision making; its properties have been illustrated with preset values for relevant parameters (i.e., regret aversion parameter μ and taste parameter β). However, the RRM model is above all an *empirical* model of choice behavior, designed for the econometric analysis of observed choices. That is, the model has been developed within the so-called discrete choice theory (DCT) tradition (Ben-Akiva and Lerman 1985; McFadden 1973; Train 2009). DCT aims to identify taste parameters in a maximum likelihood-based process of model estimation and subsequently aims to use the estimated choice model to forecast choice behaviors of individuals and market shares for products and services. DCT is nowadays routinely used in various subfields of the social sciences, earning its main developer the Nobel Prize in Economic Sciences (McFadden, 2001). Within the DCT framework, the RRM model is developed as a counterpart of the so-called linear in parameters random utility maximization (RUM) model that is the *de facto* model for the empirical analysis of choice behavior. Notwithstanding the immense popularity of linear in parameters RUM model, it is well known that its behavioral realism may in some situations be compromised by its implicit assumptions of (1) absence of reference point effects and (2) fully compensatory behavior. Inspired by the success of so-called Behavioral Economics research, various models have been proposed to overcome these potential behavioral limitations of RUM—see Leong and Hensher (2012) for an overview. In recent years the RRM model has become one of the most popular behavioral alternatives for RUM.[7] There is now a very considerable amount of evidence of a strong empirical performance (in terms of model fit and predictive ability) of RRM models, also when compared to conventional RUM models (although it should be noted that the relative performance of RUM and RRM models is highly data set specific). Comparisons have been documented in various applications including transport (e.g., Kaplan and Prato 2012), health (e.g., Chaugule et al. 2015), marketing (e.g., Lim and Hahn 2016), energy and environment (e.g., Thiene et al. 2012), tourism (e.g., Boeri et al. 2012), and anthropology (Nielsen et al. 2015). See also a relatively recent empirical overview paper (Chorus, van Cranenburgh, and Dekker et al. 2014), reviewing forty-three empirical comparisons reported in international peer-reviewed scholarly journals and a more recent overview (van Cranenburgh et al. 2015) focusing on the most generic RRM model as presented in equation (10.1). The remainder of this chapter will be based on the premise that while the RRM model may not necessarily be the best available choice model on each and every dataset, it does have a strong empirical performance in general, making it a viable and relevant framework from which to study choice behavior.

A MEASURE OF CHOICE SET REGRET AND MORALLY PROBLEMATIC CHOICE ARCHITECTURES[8]

A Measure of Choice Set Regret

Equation (10.1) serves to define the level of regret, which is associated with choosing a particular *alternative* from a choice set. In principle, by combining these equations with the minimization objective underlying the RRM models, one can derive the regret that is associated with a *choice set* itself, in a conceptually easy way: simply take the minimum (across alternatives) of regrets. However, note that—as mentioned earlier—the analyst has limited knowledge concerning the regret of alternatives; this is reflected by the error terms present in equation (10.1), which represent all sorts of factors that are unobserved by the analyst yet are important for the decision maker when she chooses from the set. The presence of error terms implies that the analyst cannot know for sure which alternative is chosen and what would be the total regret *(RR)* of that alternative, also once—after calibrating the models and obtaining estimates for βs—the systematic regret, denoted *R*, is fully known. As a consequence, the regret that is associated with a choice set has to be written in terms of an *expected* minimum (RRM). It has been shown (Chorus, 2012) that for RRM, and given the abovementioned i.i.d. Extreme Value Type I error term distributions, this expected minimum boils down to a convenient closed-form formulation (where *J* denotes the number alternatives in the choice set), which is called the LogSum:

$$LS_{RRM}^J = E\left[\min_{j=1..J}\{RR_j\}\right] = \int_{-\infty}^{+\infty}\left[\min_{j=1..J}\{RR_j\}\cdot f(\upsilon)\right]d\upsilon$$

$$= -\ln\left[\sum_{j=1..J}\exp(-R_j)\right] \quad (10.2)$$

There is one feature of the RRM-LogSum, which is of particular relevance to the analyses presented in the next section: *improving an alternative's attribute(s) does not necessarily cause a decrease in the expected regret of a choice set*. More specifically, the expected regret of a choice set may *increase* when an alternative with an initially poor performance on many of its attributes (and hence an initially low choice probability) is improved in terms of one of its attributes. It is easily verified that this particular type of nonmonotonicity of the RRM-LogSum follows directly from the behavioral premises underlying the RRM model that were described further above: improving an attribute of an alternative with an a priori low-choice probability will of course lead to a decrease in its own regret (i.e., the regret function of any alternative is monotonous in attribute changes). However, in line with the notion that regret arises from the *comparison* of alternatives, the attribute improvement will lead to increases in the regrets of competing alternatives. To the extent that these competing alternatives have higher-choice probabilities than the considered (i.e., the improved) alternative, these increases in regret receive more weight in the LogSum than does the decrease in regret of the improved alternative. Only when the attribute improvement is of such a magnitude that the improved alternative becomes a popular alternative itself (i.e., when its choice probability becomes high relative to the competition), does the expected regret of the choice set—as formalized through the RRM-LogSum—start to decrease.

Taking this reasoning one step further, the RRM model postulates that the level of expected regret of a choice set will be relatively high when the choice set is, put colloquially, "difficult to choose from" in the sense that every alternative is associated with a relatively high level of regret. This is, for example, the case when every alternative in the choice set has a poor (relative) performance on at least one attribute. In this situation, each alternative from the set is associated with nontrivial levels of regret. In contrast, when a choice set contains a "clear winner" in the form of an alternative that outperforms the competition on most attributes, and which does not have a very poor performance on any attribute (compared to the competition), the level of expected regret that is associated with the choice set is relatively low. As such, the RRM model predicts that a deterioration of an alternative's attribute may in fact result in a decrease in choice set regret when it helps identify a clear winner in that set. Likewise, the RRM model predicts that an improvement of an alternative's attribute may lead to an increase in choice set regret when it hampers the identification of a clear winner and as such makes the choice more difficult.[9]

For illustrative purposes, consider the following illustrative example (depicted in figure 10.2): suppose a decision maker faces a choice between three houses with two attributes each: attribute x represents the size of the

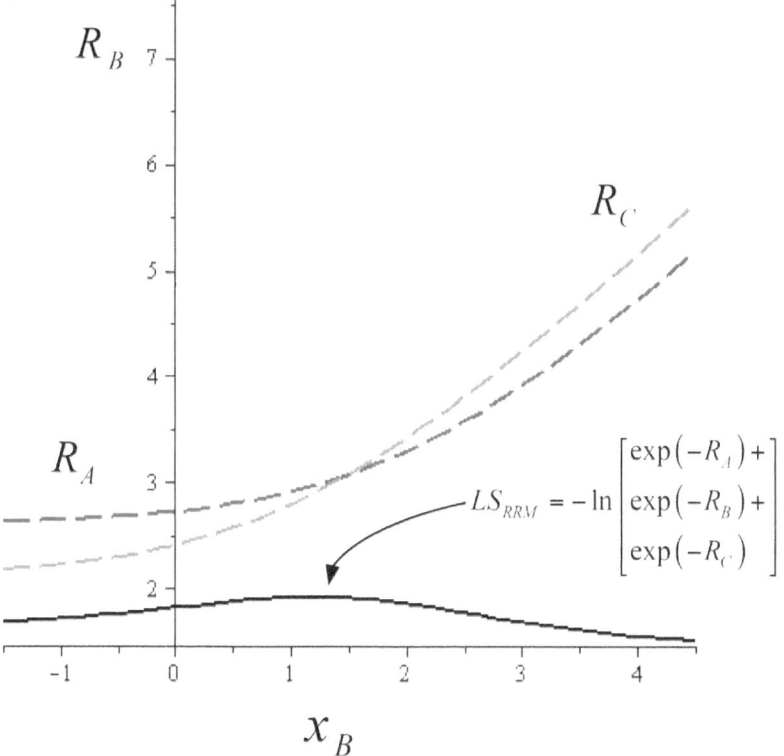

Figure 10.2. The RRM-LogSum—solid line—as a function of attribute performance.
Source: Chorus, 2012

garden, and attribute y represents some metric measuring neighborhood quality. Assume that the three houses have the following performance: $A = \{2,1\}$, $B = \{x_B, 1.5\}$, and $C = \{1,2\}$. That is, A performs well on garden size (x) but less well on neighborhood quality (y). The opposite is the case for alternative C, while B has an intermediate performance on neighborhood quality. I now vary the size of B's garden (x_B), and—assuming for ease of exposition that both attributes have unit weight—I plot the regrets of each house, as well as the total regret associated with the choice set, as a function of x_B. Figure 10.2 shows that regret is relatively low for very low values of x_B and that it reaches its lowest point for very high values of the attribute. For intermediate values of x_B, however, regret is relatively high. This implies that improving house B in terms of the attribute "garden size" when it initially performs (very) poorly in terms of that attribute only decreases the expected regret associated with the choice situation when the improvement is such that the attribute, after the improvement, attains a (very) high value.

The behavioral intuition behind this nonmonotonicity of the RRM-LogSum can be put as follows: when alternative B has a very poor performance on attribute x, this makes that there is a very high level of regret associated with that alternative. However, this very high level of regret for the alternative does not translate into a high level of expected regret for the choice situation, because there are alternatives with much lower regrets available (implying that B has only a very small chance to be chosen). Furthermore, the fact that B performs poorly on x implies that alternatives A and C have relatively low regrets (since their comparisons with B barely generate regret at all). When x_B attains an intermediate value, B's regret decreases but the regrets associated with the other two alternatives increase since now, comparisons with B does generate some regret. The result is a situation where all regrets are of about similar magnitude, and expected regret associated with the choice situation as a whole *increases*—because the regret associated with the alternative(s) with lowest regrets (A, C) increases. Only when x_B becomes very high, does the expected regret associated with the choice situation start to decline: in that situation, the regret associated with A and C grows, but since B's regret is now (much) lower than these two regrets this increase in A's and C's regret becomes more and more irrelevant (as their choice probability now becomes very low). The fact that B's regret declines now finally starts resulting in a lower level of expected regret associated with the choice situation as a whole. Only when x_B becomes very high, a lower level of expected regret is obtained than was associated with the situation when B performed very poorly on x.

It should be clear then that this non-monotonicity of the RRM-LogSum is not just a mathematical artifact: it is a direct result of the RRM model's underlying behavioral premises. Interestingly, this rather peculiar property of the RRM-LogSum is in line with recent empirical work in consumer psychology concerning decision makers' preferences for choice sets as a function of their size and composition (e.g., Schwartz et al. 2002).

Morally Problematic Choice Architectures

Consider a choice architect with the authority to determine the values of every attribute, for every alternative in a choice set.[10] The architect is faced with an initial choice situation, where alternatives—given their attributes—have a particular probability of being chosen by the decision maker; her goal is to change the attribute values of one or more alternatives in such a way that a particular change in choice probabilities is achieved. This architect may be—working for—a private sector party (e.g., a consumer products firm, in which case the decision maker is a consumer) or a government agency (e.g., a Ministry of Transport, in which case the decision maker is a citizen). For ease of exposition, I make a number of additional assumptions that do not affect the generic applicability of the argument being put forward further below:

- The initial choice set, faced by the decision maker, contains a fixed number of alternatives that are described in terms of a fixed number of attributes. These numbers cannot be altered by the choice architect. In the private sector party example, alternatives may refer to different consumer goods, for example, smartphones; attributes are then quality aspects, for example, design features of a smartphone. In the Ministry of Transport example, alternatives may refer to different courses of action taken by a citizen/traveler, for example, to work from home, carpool, or drive alone to work; in this case, attributes are policy dimensions, for example, tax incentives or rules to promote carpooling.
- The choice architect changes, at will, one or more attributes of one or more alternatives, with the aim of changing the probability that a randomly sampled decision maker chooses a particular alternative. That is, the choice architect aims to change the market shares of, or distribution of demand across, different alternatives.
- From the viewpoint of the decision maker, each attribute is formulated in such a way that increasing its value is beneficial to her. From the viewpoint of the choice architect, increasing an attribute's value is costly to her. For example, to increase the market share of a smartphone, a consumer firm may decide to increase its battery life or improve its camera. Doing so is costly for the firm. Or, to increase demand for carpooling, the Ministry of Transport may decide to introduce a tax incentive or to build carpool facilities; these are costly from the perspective of the ministry. I refer to these costs as "design costs."

Given these assumptions, it is not straightforward what makes a choice architecture morally problematic. As seen in the previous subsection, different choice tasks may impose different regret levels, but this in itself does not imply that every choice architecture that has a relatively high level of choice set regret felt by the decision maker is morally problematic. More specifically, consider the situation where a choice architect is able to achieve her goal of redistribution of market share across alternatives, at the cost of some increase in choice set regret. Would this have to be called a morally problematic choice architecture? Intuitively, one might be tempted to let the answer depend on the proportionality of the change (i.e., increase) in regret levels, compared to the achieved redistribution of market share: a substantial modal shift to the carpool alternative may justify a small increase in choice set regret among commuters, but a marginal increase in market share for a particular smartphone that comes at the cost of a large increase in choice set regret among consumers may be considered unjustifiable. However, comparing the size of regret increases faced by decision makers with the size of market share redistribution achieved by the choice architect is fraught with difficulty, in light of the fact that these are noncommensurable entities; see Radin (1993) and Harel and Porat (2011) for more about noncommensurability. Hence, it is very difficult, if possible at all, to establish a rigorous notion of what would constitute proportionality in this context. As such, I choose to formulate—inspired by the notion of Pareto optimality—a narrower definition of morally problematic choice architectures, which circumvents explicitly comparing regret levels and market share redistribution:

A choice architecture is considered morally problematic, when there is another choice architecture which generates the same choice probabilities (market shares), at the same design costs, but resulting in lower choice set regret.

In the following, this definition of morally problematic choice architectures is illustrated using a very simple and stylized example: the initial choice set from which the decision maker has to choose contains three alternatives, each described in terms of four attributes. All attributes are formulated in such a way that their associated taste parameter (attribute weight, or β) equals 1 (which implies that higher attribute values are preferred over lower ones by the decision maker), and that the associated design cost faced by the choice architect equals 1 unit per unit increase in an attribute's value. The initial choice set is depicted in figure 10.3. Clearly, in this initial choice set, alternative B is superior in terms of every attribute; plugging the attribute values and the associated taste parameters in the RRM model (i.e., equation 10.1 with $\mu = 1$) results in a choice probability of 1 (market share of 100 percent) for alternative B and a choice set regret of 0.5. The design cost of this choice set, which by definition equals the sum of all attribute values in the set, equals 24.

Initial Choice Set	Alternative A	Alternative B	Alternative C
Attribute 1	2.0	4.7	0.5
Attribute 2	1.5	4.2	2.1
Attribute 3	1.6	3.9	0.1
Attribute 4	0.5	2.8	0.1
Choice probability	0	1	0
Design cost of choice set	24		
Choice set regret	$-\ln\left[\sum_{j=1..J} exp(-R_j)\right] = 0.5$		

Figure 10.3. Initial choice set

The aim of the choice architect is to redistribute choice probabilities (market shares) such that half of the demand for alternative B is transferred to alternative C, which may be a more sustainable travel mode (Ministry of Transport example) or a smartphone with a higher profit margin (consumer firm example). The choice architect considers two interventions that may do the job. The first-choice architecture is depicted in figure 10.4, the second in figure 10.5. Both choice sets achieve the aim of redistributed market shares (again note that choice probabilities are computed by plugging attribute values and associated taste parameters into the RRM model discussed in the section "A Random Regret Minimization Model of Riskless Decision Making"). Furthermore, both come at the same design cost, which is obtained by summing up all attribute values in the choice set; more specifically, the aimed for redistribution of demand comes at an increase of 50 percent in design costs. However, whereas the first architecture imposes on decision makers a choice set regret of 3.3 units, the second architecture imposes a choice set regret of 8.3 units.

The reason why the second "architectured" choice set (figure 10.5) generates so much more regret than the first one (figure 10.4) is that in the first choice set the two popular alternatives are very similar in every attribute and as such, choosing one of them generates hardly any regret. In the second set, however, there is much difference between the two popular alternatives in terms of three out of four attributes; that is, alternative B performs poorly on attributes 1 and 4 (compared to C), and alternative C performs poorly on attribute 3. As a result, a choice for either one of the two popular alternatives (B and C) still generates considerable attribute regret.

In other words, although the two architectures are exactly the same in terms of the resulting distribution of demand across alternatives, and in terms of design costs, the second architecture imposes much more regret on the decision maker and as such constitutes a morally problematic choice architecture. When considering an intervention in an existing choice set, a choice architect

Architecture (I)	Alternative A	Alternative B	Alternative C
Attribute 1	3.1	3.8	3.6
Attribute 2	0.4	3.5	3.2
Attribute 3	1.5	3.7	4.1
Attribute 4	3.0	3.1	3.1
Choice probability	0	0.5	0.5
Design cost of choice set	36		
Choice set regret	$-\ln\left[\sum_{j=1..J} \exp(-R_j)\right] = 3.3$		

Figure 10.4. A choice architecture

Architecture (II)	Alternative A	Alternative B	Alternative C
Attribute 1	0.8	1.9	4.4
Attribute 2	0.5	4.1	4.1
Attribute 3	4.0	4.0	0.5
Attribute 4	5.0	2.5	4.6
Choice probability	0	0.5	0.5
Design cost of choice set	36		
Choice set regret	$-\ln\left[\sum_{j=1..J} \exp(-R_j)\right] = 8.3$		

Figure 10.5. A morally problematic choice architecture

is recommended to explore different choice sets capable of achieving his design goals and choose the one with minimal choice set regret.

ACKNOWLEDGMENT

The author would like to acknowledge funding from the European Research Council (ERC) under the European Union's Horizon 2020 research and innovation programme (grant agreement No. 724431).

NOTES

1. Professor of Choice behavior modeling; c.g.chorus@tudelft.nl; +31-15-2788546; Jaffalaan 5, Delft, the Netherlands.
2. Strictly speaking, Savage's Minimax Regret framework refers to decision under uncertainty, as opposed to risk, in the sense that it does not presume that the

decision making holds particular perceptions regarding probability distributions (Knight 1921).

3. In fact, some lotteries are specifically designed to trigger regret aversion associated with *not* buying a lottery ticket (Zeelenberg and Pieters 2004).

4. Note also that the RRM model be can easily extended to cover risky decision making as well (Chorus 2014b; Chorus et al. 2008); in this chapter, I will focus on riskless choice contexts.

5. A definition of the notion of choice architecture presented on Wikipedia (Lemma "Choice architecture," accessed July 18, 2016) reads as follows: "Choice architecture is the design of different ways in which choices can be presented to consumers, and the impact of that presentation on consumer decision-making. For example, the number of choices presented, the manner in which attributes are described, and the presence of a 'default' can all influence consumer choice."

6. It could also include characteristics of the decision maker; for ease of exposition, I ignore this extension in the remainder of this chapter.

7. This does not imply that I here present the RRM model as a "better" or "more realistic" choice model than linear in parameter RUM models. Rather, in our view, choice behavior is a subtle and multifaceted phenomenon (with great levels of heterogeneity across individuals and contexts); this makes it important that there are multiple models available to study choice behavior. The RRM model has been developed to form an addition to the choice modeler's toolbox, certainly not as a potential replacement of other models.

8. The first part of this section draws extensively from Chorus (2012, 2014c).

9. It may be noted that, in addition to this property, the RRM-LogSum differs from the RUM-LogSum in another fundamental way: whereas the latter will always increase if one attribute is improved for all alternatives to a similar extent, this is not the case for the RRM-LogSum. Since regret is a function of *relative* performance, improving all alternatives along the same attribute and to the same extent (e.g., by making all alternatives five dollars cheaper) will leave the expected regret associated with the choice situation unchanged.

10. The realism of this assumption can be debated, as in some instances a choice architect will only have the authority to determine some attributes of some alternatives in the set, for example, in the situation where a consumer goods firm introduces a new product in a choice set partly shaped by competitor firms. However, for reasons of clarity of exposition, I here choose to maintain this assumption.

REFERENCES

Avineri, E. 2012. "On the Use and Potential of Behavioural Economics from the Perspective of Transport and Climate Change." *Journal of Transport Geography* 24: 512–21.
Bell, D. E. 1982. "Regret in Decision Making under Uncertainty." *Operations Research* 30 (5): 961–81.
Ben-Akiva, M. E., and S. R. Lerman. 1985. *Discrete Choice Analysis: Theory and Application to Travel Demand*, vol. 9. Cambridge: MIT press.

Bleichrodt, H., and P. P. Wakker. 2015. "Regret Theory: A Bold Alternative to the Alternatives." *The Economic Journal* 125 (583): 493–532.
Chaugule, S., J. W. Hay, G. Young, O. A. Martin, and E. F. Drabo. 2015. "Does Differential Framing of Opt-Out Alternatives in Discrete Choice Experiments (Dces) Matter? Comparison of Random Utility Maximization (rum) and Random Regret Minimization (rrm) Models." *Value in Health* 18 (3): A24–A25.
Chorus, C. G. 2010. "A New Model of Random Regret Minimization." *European Journal of Transport and Infrastructure Research* 10 (2): 181–96.
Chorus, C. G. 2012. "Logsums for Utility-Maximizers and Regret-Minimizers, and Their Relation with Desirability and Satisfaction." *Transportation Research Part A: Policy and Practice* 46 (7): 1003–12.
Chorus, C. G. 2014a. "A Generalized Random Regret Minimization Model." *Transportation Research Part B: Methodological* 68: 224–38.
Chorus, C. G. 2014b. "Acquisition of Ex-Post Travel Information: A Matter of Balancing Regrets." *Transportation Science* 48 (2): 243–55.
Chorus, C. G. 2014c. "Benefit of Adding an Alternative to One's Choice Set: A Regret Minimization Perspective." *Journal of choice modelling* 13: 49–59.
Chorus, C. G., and S. van Cranenburgh. 2018. "Specification of Regret-Based Models of Choice Behaviour: Formal Analyses and Experimental Design-Based Evidence—Commentary." *Transportation* 45 (1): 247–56.
Chorus, C., S. van Cranenburgh, and T. Dekker. 2014. "Random Regret Minimization for Consumer Choice Modeling: Assessment of Empirical Evidence." *Journal of Business Research* 67 (11): 2428–36.
Chorus, C. G., T. A. Arentze, and H. J. Timmermans. 2008. "A Random Regret-Minimization Model of Travel Choice." *Transportation Research Part B: Methodological* 42 (1): 1–18.
Coricelli, G., H. D. Critchley, M. Joffily, J. P. O'Doherty, A. Sirigu, and R. J. Dolan. 2005. "Regret and Its Avoidance: A Neuroimaging Study of Choice Behavior." *Nature Neuroscience* 8 (9): 1255–62.
Greene, W. H. 2012. *NLOGIT: Version 5: Reference Guide*. Econometric Software, Inc.
Harel, A., and A. Porat. 2011. "Commensurability and Agency: Two Yet-to-Be-Met Challenges for Law and Economics." *Cornell Law Review* 96: 749.
Hensher, D. A., J. M. Rose, and W. H. Greene. 2015. *Applied Choice Analysis*. Cambridge: Cambridge University Press.
Jang, S., S. Rasouli, and H. Timmermans. 2017. "Incorporating Psycho-Physical Mapping into Random Regret Choice Models: Model Specifications and Empirical Performance Assessments." *Transportation* 44 (5): 999–1019.
Johnson, E. J., S. B. Shu, B. G. Dellaert, C. Fox, D. G. Goldstein, G. Häubl, . . . and B. Wansink. 2012. "Beyond Nudges: Tools of a Choice Architecture." *Marketing Letters* 23 (2): 487–504.
Kaplan, S., and C. G. Prato. 2012. "The Application of the Random Regret Minimization Model to Drivers' Choice of Crash Avoidance Maneuvers." *Transportation Research Part F: Traffic Psychology and Behaviour* 15 (6): 699–709.
Knight, F. H. 1921. *Risk, Uncertainty and Profit*. New York: Hart, Schaffner and Marx.
Leong, W., and D. A. Hensher. 2012. "Embedding Decision Heuristics in Discrete Choice Models: A Review." *Transport Reviews* 32 (3): 313–31.

Lim, J., and M. Hahn. 2016. "Random Regret Minimization Model Versus Random Utility Maximization Model: When to Use What in Marketing." *INFORMS Marketing Science Conference*, Shanghai, China
Loomes, G., and R. Sugden. 1982. "Regret Theory: An Alternative Theory of Rational Choice under Uncertainty." *The Economic Journal* 92 (368): 805–24.
McFadden, D. 1973. "Conditional Logit Analysis of Qualitative Choice Behavior." Chapter 4 in *Frontiers in Econometrics*, ed. P. Zarembka, 105–42. New York: Academic Press.
McFadden, D. 2001. "Economic Choices." *American Economic Review* 91 (3): 351–78.
Nielsen, Martin Reinhardt, Jette Bredahl Jacobsen, Bo Jellesmark Thorsen. 2015. Decision Rules for Hunting and Trading Bushmeat: Maximising Utility or Minimising regret? *Paper presented at the International Choice Modeling Conference*, Austin, TX.
Radin, M. J. 1993. "Compensation and Commensurability." *Duke Law Journal* 43 (1): 56–86.
Savage, L. J. 1951. "The Theory of Statistical Decision." *Journal of the American Statistical Association* 46 (253): 55–67.
Schwartz, B., A. Ward, J. Monterosso, S. Lyubomirsky, K. White, and D. R. Lehman. 2002. "Maximizing versus Satisficing: Happiness Is a Matter of Choice." *Journal of personality and social psychology* 83 (5): 1178.
Selinger, E., and K. Whyte. 2011. "Is There a Right Way to Nudge? The Practice and Ethics of Choice Architecture." *Sociology Compass* 5 (10): 923–35.
Sunstein, C. R. (2015). "Nudging and Choice Architecture: Ethical Considerations." *Yale Journal on Regulation*, Forthcoming.
Thaler, R. H., C. R. Sunstein, and J. P. Balz, J., Sunstein, C., & Thaler, R. (2014). Choice architecture. E. Shafir, The Behavioral Foundations of Public Policy, 428–439.
Thorndike, A. N., L. Sonnenberg, J. Riis, S. Barraclough, and D. E. Levy. 2012. "A 2-Phase Labeling and Choice Architecture Intervention to Improve Healthy Food and Beverage Choices." *American Journal of Public Health* 102 (3): 527–33.
Train, K. E. 2009. *Discrete Choice Methods with Simulation*. Cambridge: Cambridge university press.
Tversky, A., and D. Kahneman. 1991. "Loss Aversion in Riskless Choice: A Reference-Dependent Model." *Quarterly Journal of Economics* 106 (4): 1039–61.
van Cranenburgh, S., C. A. Guevara, and C. G. Chorus. 2015. "New Insights on Random Regret Minimization Models." *Transportation Research Part A: Policy and Practice* 74: 91–109.
Vermunt, J. K., and J. Magidson. 2014. *Upgrade Manual for Latent GOLD Choice 5.0*. Belmont, MA: Statistical Innovations.
Zeelenberg, M., and R. Pieters. 2004. "Consequences of Regret Aversion in Real Life: The Case of the Dutch Postcode Lottery." *Organizational Behavior and Human Decision Processes* 93 (2): 155–68.
Zeelenberg, M., and R. Pieters. 2007. "A Theory of Regret Regulation 1.0." *Journal of Consumer psychology* 17 (1): 3–18.

Chapter 11
Long-Term Regret, Perspective, and Fate
Christopher Cowley

Regret seems to be a familiar enough word in many different contexts. I want to focus on regret that is "long-term" and "momentous." By this I mean the regret of a decision made many years ago, where such a decision had a big impact on one's life. Let me introduce two examples:

- A twenty-one-year-old woman enrolls to study medicine and eventually becomes a surgeon. At the age of forty-one, she is burnt out, fed up by the institutional bureaucracy and the sexism, by the exhausting workload, irritated by the "whiners" and the "hypochondriacs" among her patients. She can still do the job well enough, but her heart is not in it, and she is dismayed by the thought of spending the rest of her working life in it. She considers withdrawing from medicine and surveys her options. She declares that she regrets having enrolled in medicine twenty years previously.[1]
- A man and a woman get married (but do not have children). Twenty years later, they have an ugly divorce. The man declares that he regrets having married the woman twenty years previously, that he "wasted the best years of his life" with her.[2]

First, a definitional stipulation. For the purposes of this chapter, I will take regret to be *propositional* (I regret the fact that "I did X"), *first-personal* (I regret something about me and my life, rather than wishing that something else had happened), and something only appropriate to a *free choice* on a matter under personal control (I regret choosing X when I was free to choose Y). In other words, it is a judgment about a past choice (or series of choices that launch and develop a single project) which the protagonist now considers to have been mistaken. Regret is not a mood or a feeling of disappointment;[3] it is not nostalgia or a sense of being stuck or of not feeling at home.

And I am interested in momentous choices. Clearly, the choice of marital partner and career probably had a big impact on these two people, not just on their lives (the options available at a given moment) but also on them as individuals and on their understanding of themselves. They each enjoyed their marriage and their career in the minimal sense that they did not leave earlier. I want to ask: is regret only about the mistaken choice, or is it also about the "road not travelled by," the counterfactual life path running parallel to the true life path? Does it involve an implicit (or maybe explicit) comparison to what I might have become by now if I had married this other person or chosen that other career? And in addition to these questions about the past and the counterfactual present, what do such regrets entail for the future?

Finally, let me distinguish regret (the mental state) from expressions of regret. We all hear expressions of regret all the time, whereas I am more interested in the mental state that the expressions purport to express.

In exploring these questions, I am aiming at the following conclusion: when it comes to expressions of long-term regret about meaningful choices, I do not think such expressions can correspond to a *coherent* mental state. That is, I am not sure whether it is possible to *be* regretful (in the judgment sense) about long-ago events that had a deep impact on one's life. Instead, expressions of regret express something else, something I tentatively want to call a *mode of being*, a kind of stance or orientation on one's life. This positive proposal will be little more than a proposal, for I do not have the space to work it out properly; but I think it is robust enough to set up some useful work for the future.[4]

SETTING THE SCENE

Since regret is such a familiar word, it is worth spelling out some further assumptions that need to be made in order to narrow the philosophical questions into something manageable.

1. I will be speaking about *regret* and not about *remorse*. Remorse is when I regret doing something morally wrong.[5] For my purposes, this would be an extra layer of complication, and so I am only discussing regret informed by the protagonist's understanding of her own self-interest. Self-interest I interpret in the broad sense: not just health and wealth and pleasure but also things like the richness or meaningfulness of one's life. In taking this broader sense, however, I want to avoid the philosophically thorny concept of authenticity (of being "true to oneself"), as in "I regret choosing X because it was not the authentic choice."
2. I shall be relying on a key distinction between *regret* and *lament*. Under my "propositional" conception of regret, I regret a choice that was within

my control. Whereas I lament a situation that was or is outside of my control. I lament the earthquake that killed so many people; I lament that I am not taller. Whereas I regret betting on the horse Albert because I could have bet on any number of horses.[6]
3. When I regret a choice, I presuppose that I was free to have chosen differently, and I explicitly wish that I could "undo" the choice. In contrast, Taylor (1985, 99) gives the example of an employer "regretting" the decision to sack an inefficient employee, even though she continues to consider the sacking to be "necessary and beneficial" and does not want to undo it. I would call this "lament" or "feeling bad" not regret. Similarly, when a politician makes an unpopular budget decision to spend on X rather than Y, she might say that she "regrets" the fact that she "had to" make that decision. But if she does not want to undo the decision, then she cannot really regret it.
4. My understanding of "freedom to decide" is fairly abstract, and I do not want to go too deep into questions of positive freedom and autonomy. So in my examples, I am taking the protagonist as being aware that she really could choose X or Y, even if she is strongly attracted to X and not at all to Y. In real life, the first protagonist might not have "chosen" medicine; she might have simply drifted into it as the obvious thing to do; and the second protagonist might not have "chosen" but seen herself as acting under a necessity of love.
5. There are a number of borderline phenomena that are *partly* in my control and therefore a matter partly of regret, partly of lament. I have in mind things like character traits ("I regret not having been courageous enough to challenge him") or self-deception ("I had a sense that something was wrong, and I regret not facing it"). For the sake of simplicity, I will start by ignoring such cases, but they will become relevant later on.
6. I am interested in protagonists who are *in the middle of their lives*. That is, they not only have to make sense of the past but also of their future; and this prompts the question of the best way to use the past to make decisions about the future. One obvious example of long-term regret is Tolstoy's Ivan Illyich, but I will not discuss him because in one sense he gets off too easy. If I may put the point rather brutally: sure, he regrets his career choices, but, knowing that he is dying, it is enough for him to say "OK, I was wrong"—and then to die. He does not need to do anything with his regret. Whereas my protagonists face an indefinite future where they have to deal with their regret in one way or another.[7]
7. I do not want to broach the normative question of whether a person *should* regret a past decision. I want to start with an example of someone who *does* regret their decision or who is wrestling with the temptation to regret the decision. It is perfectly coherent for someone to *refuse* to regret a

decision, especially a decision that ended up annoying or disappointing a lot of people, where such refusal could be a matter of Edith Piaf-style defiance and bare assertion of authenticity.[8] (There is a separate question about whether people who take up this defiant stance do so as part of an elaborate self-deception or as part of an immature reluctance to understand their life, but I won't consider these possibilities here.) Alternatively, there are some who do not want to regret, who see no point to regret, but they nevertheless find that they are *assailed* by their regrets.[9]

A First Paradigm: Short-Term Trivial Regret

Given my understanding of regret, I now want to examine what I mean by "long term" and "momentous." Let me approach these questions negatively, by way of a comparison with the regret one might feel over a "short-term" and "trivial" decision, such as a horse bet. Earlier today, I went to the bookies and put money on Albert for the 3.45 at Cheltenham; here I am at Cheltenham, the race has just finished, and—damn!—Barbie won. I know I could have bet on Barbie, I was free, but I chose not to. I know a bit about horses, I know Albert's track record is pretty good, but I now regret my decision because Albert lost and I'm out of pocket. If I had bet on Barbie, I know exactly by how much I would be richer than I am now. I wish I could undo my decision: I can easily imagine myself, that morning, placing the bet the other way. My frustration arises from just how "close" Barbie, and the extra winning stakes, were to me at the time.

Even with this simple and familiar example, we face two interrelated problems that incline one to skepticism about the coherence of the mental experience of regret, regardless of the verbal expression. The first problem has to do with the fact that the *past is the past*, what's done cannot be undone,[10] no good crying over spilt milk, and so on. The second problem has to do with my understanding of the situation *at the time* (this morning at the bookies'). Yes, I was physically able to bet on Barbie, but I didn't because the situation appeared to me as such and such, and I approached the situation with this and that mental state (what I knew and believed as well as what I didn't know and didn't believe), and *given all these facts* about the interaction between me and the situation, then I *had to* bet on Albert. (If I went back in time, I would go back to that same situation and that same set of mental states, and I would bet on Albert all over again.) This second problem was famously summarized by Sartre when he said "when I deliberate, the game's up."[11] When one deliberates, one has the illusion of freedom; instead, one's deliberation and decision will be determined by what reasons present themselves to one, with what relative salience, and how such reasons "fit" with the rest of one's being. This could be used to mount a challenge to free will, but I don't want to go down that road.

However, even if I assume I was free back then, we're still left with a problem about the meaning of my regret in the horse-betting scenario. One answer to this problem is to say that regret is not really about wanting to *change* (undo) the past but about *learning* from the past in order to choose better in the future. Call this the "instrumental" conception of propositional regret. I lost money on Albert this time, but at least I know to keep away from Albert the next time. The skilled horse better plays the long game and gets to know the horses and the jockeys and the tracks. Maybe she still wins some and loses some, but her bets get more informed and less risky, and after several dozen bets, she comes off richer.

A Second Paradigm: Long-Term Trivial Regret

Let's say I am now forty years old. When I was twenty years old, I bought a bunch of IBM shares. I could have bought Apple shares, but I didn't, and now (at age forty) I regret that, considering what the shares of Apple and IBM are now worth. This would be the same as the horse bet except for the time span, which adds a further reason for skepticism about the coherence of regret; for here we might be tempted to say that my twenty-year-old self was a *different person*.

I hasten to emphasize: I'm not advocating a radical metaphysical claim here. Obviously, my twenty-year-old self is me-at-forty in virtue of tracing out a single path through time and space without splitting or merging, in virtue of my experiential memories of doing what that twenty-year-old self did, in virtue of the banks holding me to the thirty-five-year mortgage contract I signed when I was twenty, and so on—in virtue of leading a single life. But we might be tempted to say that the twenty-year-old is a (somewhat) different person in the sense of my present *bewilderment* in understanding how "he" could so frivolously invest in IBM shares when it was already clear back then that Apple was on the rise. "What the hell was I thinking?" I now ask rhetorically. (The same bewilderment might assail me when I read the diary written by my twenty-year-old self.) We might be tempted to put it in terms of maturation and authenticity. Back then I was young and ignorant, I was distracted by surfaces, I hadn't found my core values. Now, at forty, I know who I am and no longer have to search or pretend.

In this "bewilderment" sense of personal *dis*continuity, I could then conclude that I *cannot* regret buying the IBM shares then because I cannot sufficiently identify with the person who bought those shares in the first place. Someone else bought the shares, and I am stuck with the consequences. All I can do is *lament* the fact that I am not as wealthy today as I would have been if I/he had done my/his due diligence back then. (But I/he was lazy and ignorant, etc. etc.)

There are deeper questions of identity here, of course. Although I am accepting metaphysical continuity that would be sufficient for me (now, at forty) to agree without hesitation to pay the mortgage payments, I might still have a *choice* about how much to identify with my twenty-year-old self in *narrative* terms: I may choose to reject that individual, or I may choose to embrace him as the person living out an earlier chapter in a single life story, where there is real narrative coherence from chapter to chapter, right through to my present self-conception. I will return to this choice later on, as my examples get more complicated. For the moment, I am still talking about a *trivial* project, by which I am referring to the question of mere wealth—I do not mean "trivial" in reference to the questions of identity, which are not trivial at all. I am assuming that I am otherwise comfortably off, and that if I were a little wealthier in virtue of owning profitable Apple shares now, this would not make a serious difference to my life.[12]

LONG-TERM MOMENTOUS DECISIONS

Now I want to move to the central class of cases: I regret a *momentous* choice of many years ago, something that had a deep impact on my life and on me. My opening examples were about regretting one's choice of career and one's choice of spouse.[13]

As part of my definition of "momentous," let me spell out three important ways in which momentous choices differ from trivial choices. First, the resulting commitments are highly time-consuming and highly ramified. They have an impact on many different parts of my life, and are unpredictable over the longer term precisely because of this variegated impact. To put it another way: if I choose to study medicine (rather than law) at twenty-one, then this choice will open up new options that I did not have before, and each chosen option will open up further options, to the point where, once I am forty-one, I have rejected not just a lot of options but also a lot of alternative life paths.

(Throughout I am counting as an "option" something that is genuinely open to me, in the abstract sense of freedom and autonomy described among my opening assumptions, i.e., the options available to me given my particular knowledge, abilities, character, connections, and so on, at the moment of choice. If I lack/lacked the 20–20 vision required to be a fighter pilot, then being a fighter pilot is not/was not an option for me. And so I therefore claim that I can lament but I cannot regret, later, not having become a fighter pilot when I was younger.)

Second, momentous choices (or series of choices[14]) do not just change my options; they change *me* in unpredictable ways as well. They are not a separate discrete project; instead, I am invested in them to such a degree that it is hard to say where "I" end and the project begins. With horses or IBM shares, I can contemplate them from a distance: I would almost certainly still be me whether or not I had invested in IBM. After twenty-years years of *working* as a doctor, however, I can't help *becoming* a doctor to a certain extent, identifying with the job, with the health service, with the profession.

This means, however, that the past person, the nondoctor who made the initial momentous choice to go into medicine at age twenty-one, is *even more* different from me (the doctor) now at forty-one, and this would seem to justify even more skepticism about the coherence of regretting such long-ago choices. I would be even more inclined to lament rather than regret the "other" person's decision to study medicine, landing me with the consequences twenty years later.

Third, one's present regret about past momentous choices requires a certain *context of present anxiety*. Before one can articulate present regret, one first has to reach an appropriate position of disharmony in relation to one's present career (or spouse). Obviously, if everything's going well and the future is golden, one won't be regretting anything! I won't try to specify the requisite disharmony in greater detail, because it can be any number of different phenomena: it is enough if I take examples of people who already regret.

In addition to the disharmony and the apparently closed future as a doctor, the anxiously regretful protagonist finds she is unable to console herself with the thought that "that was all right for a bit, but now I'm bored and it's time to move on." She finds herself unable to "close" the medicine "chapter" and to start a new chapter without regret. For when she faces the future, the regrets assail her, not only because of her sense of being stuck because of the past but also because of her pained awareness of the opportunity costs of her career (or marriage) over such a long period. Of course, Edith Piaf will tell her not to regret, but the doctor can't help it. And so she turns to the philosopher to help her make sense of that regret in a spirit of self-discovery.[15]

COUNTERFACTUALS AND PERSPECTIVE

I'm still working with the doctor example, but let me switch into the first person. I am now forty-one, and I regret choosing at twenty-one to study medicine. My regret entails that I should have chosen a different subject at university and pursued the different career that would have resulted from that study. But such counterfactual speculation is risky. It is already difficult enough for me, at forty-one, to reimagine myself back into my twenty-one-year-old self, with my beliefs and hopes and desires of the time, applying to study medicine at university. But to go back to my twenty-one-year-old self, and then choose a *different* subject (say, law), and then to imagine myself forward from there, along a separate life path all the way to the age of forty-one, accumulating twenty years of law and legal career behind me, this is surely little more than a useless fantasy, bearing the most tenuous connection to *my life*, that is, the determinate life that I have lived through, the life that has produced *me*, a doctor, here and now at forty-one years of age.

The idleness of such counterfactual speculation would seem to drain all meaning from my long-term regret. Perhaps all there is left to say with confidence is: I don't *like* being a doctor at forty-one, and I'm *curious* about what "I" would have been like, at forty-one, as a lawyer with twenty years of legal training and legal career behind me. If I speak of not liking the present, then I am only lamenting. It is perfectly coherent to lament my present situation and to use that lament to start planning a new career into the future. However, the protagonists in my examples are careful to use the word "regret," and I want to see if I can take the word seriously in those contexts.

I want to introduce the metaphor of a *perspective*. In its original "geometric" use, the idea is that what I can see of the world will depend on where I am located and on what direction I'm facing. From this perspective I can see the sea, but if I take two steps to the right I cannot because there's a building in the way. By analogy, at any one moment in my life, I look out on the world (and on myself in that world) from within a determinate perspective (or orientation or stance): given various things about me, about my life hitherto, and about my antecedent understanding of the world, I *notice* certain things and do not notice other things; and among the things I notice, I am *bothered* by certain things and not by other things, based on something that could be loosely called my "values."[16] I cannot look at the world "cold," I have to look at it from within the perspective. There are certain characteristic (for me) ways of thinking, of feeling, of remembering, of hoping, of fearing, certain spontaneous inclinations, and so on. To a certain extent, I can perceive some elements of my perspective and sometimes correct for them: to take a banal example, the tofu on my plate does not look or taste good, but I force it down in the knowledge that it's good for me. Sometimes my perspective will change, and I do not notice the change: but as a result of the change in perspective I may come to notice different things in the world.

Note that the metaphor of perspective implies a way of seeing; but I stress that I am taking it in a wider sense to include all aspects of experience, including the value-laden: the aversions and longings, the ways of remembering and hoping (fondly or desperately), and including character dispositions. And while I cannot directly choose my perspective, I can make certain momentous choices in the knowledge that my perspective will be affected in the future, perhaps in unpredictable ways. The eighteen-year-old army cadet is offered a place at officer school and told he has a promising future but refuses because he fears (perhaps quite reasonably) being brutalized by army life and combat experience.

Back to the forty-one-year-old doctor, and here's the point: a good deal of my present perspective has been shaped by my momentous commitments in the past. Many elements of my perspective might not be surprising to others, as when they chide me: "You would say that, you're a doctor!" As a result, I find myself, at this age, with this professional background, looking at and thinking about the world from within *this* perspective. Importantly, it is *from within this perspective* that I also remember my past, that I evaluate my past momentous choices as mistaken, and that I imagine the counterfactual life paths I might have chosen. In other words, my regret necessarily expresses the values that partly constitute the perspective from within which I look at the world and at my own life. As such, when I try to imagine *another* life path in another career, I cannot reliably predict what sort of perspective I would have ended up in, what sort of values I would have had, and therefore what sorts of regret judgments about the past I would have been inclined to make as a forty-one-year-old lawyer. This is yet another reason for skepticism about any robust coherence of regret beyond idle daydreaming.

And because of the problems of identity across time, and of perspective, I will probably find that I have very little to *learn* from the past, in the way that I learned from the mistaken bet on Albert the horse. Now that I am forty-one, I will never again face the same momentous choice that my twenty-one-year-old self faced. Any decisions I face now, at forty-one, have an entirely different significance because they are "located" at a different position in my life and understood from within a different perspective.

Let me qualify that; I will learn *some* "life lessons" from a bad marriage. Maybe I married more out of greed than out of love, and, twenty years later, I now regret that; and I *use* that regret instrumentally to help me to make choices henceforward. But how much can I use, really? It will be like a taxi driver who moves from Paris to Rome, intent on doing the same job. Certainly, there are some mistakes she made in Paris that she will be careful not to repeat in Rome: very drunk customers often throw up. But all of her determinate knowledge of the Paris *terrain* is useless in Rome. Insofar as I can learn from a bad marriage based on greed, such learning invokes a very thin notion of regret, and I have been exploring a deeper notion. Who is to say whether the marriage failed *because of* the greed? Who is to say whether a counterfactual marriage based on love, at twenty-one, would have been better or worse than the marriage I had? Indeed, who is to say whether a marriage based on greed, but to someone *else*, at twenty-one, would have been better or worse? As such I'm not sure I can learn anything from my marital decision at twenty-one: even if that had been the same person as me now, he was in a different perspective.

And yes, maybe I can conclude, at forty-one, that medicine is not (or no longer) for me, and I can launch a career in law. But the options available to me, and my understanding of those options, will be very different to the options and understandings available to the twenty-one-year-old. Even at a crude practical level, it will be much more difficult, after completing law school, now aged forty-four, to find a legal traineeship, when competing against all these twenty-four-year-old law graduates, and that's not only because of their superior confidence and diligence and lack of commitments. It's also because they are stepping forward into the big adventure of their life.

PERSPECTIVE, FATE, AND CHARACTER

So far, my position remains one of skepticism about the coherence of the mental state of propositional regret over long-ago momentous choices. I introduced the metaphor of a perspective to add meat to the skepticism. In this section, I want to explore the metaphor a bit further by bringing in the concepts of fate and character.

Fate is a bit of a dirty word in philosophy, I realize.[17] On the one hand, it has connotations of metaphysical or social determinism—neither of which I would accept: part of the distinctive experience of regret, I have been claiming, is precisely that there was a choice, that I made it, and that I was sufficiently free to have chosen something else. If a natural disaster had befallen me, entirely determined by the laws of nature, that would be unpleasant, but there would be no sense that it was my fault, and that I ought to regret a decision. On the other hand, fate has connotations of divine meddling, and my account has been strictly secular up until now. I am interested in people making decisions in their lives, consulting their friends and family, seeking more or less information, and then deciding. (Perhaps some of the more religiously inclined might consult a priest for advice, but I have been assuming that the final decision rests very much with the individual.)

But I think the concept might help us develop this concept of a perspective. Robert Solomon, one of the few philosophers who has written about the concept, offers (2003, 440) the example of a man and a woman married to one another for many years. Let's align the example with the ages of my other examples. It will be natural to speak of their first encounter, both aged twenty-one, as a matter of fate, Solomon says. Of course, the husband and wife both appreciate the massive undetermined contingencies of that first encounter as well as the contingencies of attraction and logistics that allowed their relationship to lead to a wedding and then to survive the kids and the seven-year itch and the myriad other stressors, up to the point now, at forty-one, when they are both looking back at their first encounter from the vantage point of a long a successful marriage. And Solomon claims that there is no contradiction in appreciating the massive contingency *and* seeing the first encounter as fated, precisely because the husband and the wife look back on the encounter, at forty-one, from within a perspective that has been heavily shaped by the series of events launched by that first encounter;[18] just like there is no contradiction to see the original decision to wed as entirely free but nevertheless fated. The fact that he has already made it through many years of marriage to reach this point means that they are, as it were, implicated in the marriage, implicated to a degree of not being able to imagine themselves out of the marriage. This kind of imaginative inability is what makes the first encounter fated, not in some objective deterministic sense but fated within the perspective from which the enquirers contemplate—and must contemplate—the past.[19]

Perhaps a better way to understand this sense of necessity that grounds the origin of a perspective is to consider the hot-housed prodigy in sport or music. Spotted at six with unusual talent and determination (and blessed/cursed with ambitious parents), she is intensely coached through to international success at eighteen. A key component of the perspective with which she looks out on the world, at eighteen, is precisely her highly developed talent. But for her to achieve international success at eighteen, it was necessary that she be hot-housed from an early age, without it of course being necessary *simpliciter* that the parents chose to hot-house her. (In contrast, it would have been impossible for her to choose at seventeen to achieve international success a year later.) And because her talent and success are such major parts of her life and perspective, she cannot coherently imagine what her life would have been like without the hot-housing childhood.[20]

Another important component of perspective is character. I have in mind the minimal sense in which the generous person tends to notice opportunities for generosity and tends to respond appropriately and unreflectively to such opportunities. The stingy person does not notice the opportunities *as* opportunities; and when such opportunities are pointed out to her, the stingy person will ignore them or rationalize her nonresponse.[21]

Character is tricky because it is not under one's direct control, but it is partly under a long-term control. The promising eighteen-year-old army cadet chose not to go to officer school because he did not want to risk the brutalization that he reasonably believed would accompany both the army career and the combat experience. This part control raises questions about whether one can regret one's character or whether one can only lament it.

I think one can distinguish at least two kinds of character regret, with two quite different objects. The first is when the forty-one-year-old doctor (1) laments some of the character trait she has now, for she thinks of herself as brusque and unsympathetic with her patients; while at the same time (2) she regrets the decision to become a doctor at twenty-one, partly because, that decision *causally contributed* to the development of that present lamentable character trait. The second form of character regret is when the forty-one-year-old doctor looks back on her decision as a twenty-one-year-old to study medicine and now believes that she was too cowardly in succumbing to pressure from her parents: she regrets having chosen not to put up more of a fight in order to study something else. (Again, because I understand regret in volitional terms, then I cannot regret what I am or was, I can only regret what I chose to *do*.)

However, there are important limits in regretting not having done something long ago in the past, because it comes too close to *making excuses* for present lamentable traits. The best response to such a temptation is Sartre (1946):

> For many have but one resource to sustain them in their misery, and that is to think, "Circumstances have been against me, I was worthy to be something much better than I have been. I admit I have never had a great love or a great friendship; but that is because I never met a man or a woman who were worthy of it; if I have not written any very good books, it is because I had not the leisure to do so; or, if I have had no children to whom I could devote myself it is because I did not find the man I could have lived with. So there remains within me a wide range of abilities, inclinations and potentialities, unused but perfectly viable, which endow me with a worthiness that could never be inferred from the mere history of my actions." But in reality and for the existentialist, there is no love apart from the deeds of love; no potentiality of love other than that which is manifested in loving; there is no genius other than that which is expressed in works of art. [. . .] In life, a man commits himself, draws his own portrait and there is nothing but that portrait. (Sartre 1946)[22]

So, I remain with my skepticism about whether long-term regret about past momentous decisions is sufficiently coherent to take seriously, however tempting it is as a response to leading a human life. The only way to "save" regret, I will argue, is to reinterpret it as something very different; something that I can only adumbrate for reasons of space.

REGRET AS A "MODE OF BEING"

"Mode of being" is a loosely Heideggerian notion[23] and starts with an extension of the metaphor of perspective. In the above, I was already stretching the metaphor beyond the perceptual to encompass all aspects of experience, but this left intact the distinction between the experiencer and the experience. "Mode of being" continues the development even further, to speak not just of experiencing but of being, about one's place in the world, one's relationships with significant others, and one's relations to the past and future (i.e., more than just one's *beliefs* about one's place in the world, about one's relationships with others, and about one's relations to the past and future). In addition, I want to call regret a "bidirectional" aspect of being, by which I mean: regret not only *reveals* one's mode of being to others and to oneself, but it also partly *constitutes* one's being in the world. To experience deep regrets about momentous decision, to take such regrets seriously, is to *be* a certain sort of person.

For most of this chapter, I have been speaking of regret as a kind of personal problem, something that imposes itself oppressively on the protagonist (as if from outside) and which the protagonist has to solve or at least neutralize. Indeed, perhaps the protagonist would go to therapy to seek help in dealing with her regret, perhaps by ignoring it, perhaps by reinterpreting it, perhaps by defying it, perhaps by atoning for it. However, to see regret as a mode of one's being is to lose this sense of a problem that needs to be solved and to accept it as something importantly *primordial*, in the sense of something that underlies and organizes all of one's experiences. Precisely because regret is essentially backward-looking and personal, it reveals one's identity across time, the very identity one must presuppose in order to live coherently *as* an agent, and *as* a particular agent, from one part of one's life through to another. I am not merely the sum of my present properties and relationships; I am also the sum of my ideals about the future that guide my present, and I am also the sum of my past accomplishments—and of my regrets about past failures. My regrets partly express my essentially diachronic existence across time.

At the beginning of the piece, I distinguished regret from nostalgia, but in the context of this section, there are useful similarities between the two. For nostalgia is something that one can feel keenly, but it is not merely a feeling, for it has a clear object. And yet it is not entirely about that object; it is also part of the protagonist's mode of being. In the simple sense, to ask someone about their nostalgia is to ask about the object and to expect an answer of the form "I miss X because of A, B, C." However, it might also be quite inappropriate to then ask the protagonist why she does not *pursue* or *return to* X if she is so nostalgic about it. Indeed, it could be the height of insensitivity to suggest that in not pursuing or returning to X they have demonstrated that they are not truly nostalgic for X after all. My point is that genuine nostalgia need not be linked to or validated by any future action.[24]

By way of an *indirect* attempt to define regret as a mode of being, let me ask: what does it mean for one person to get to know another person, a stranger? I meet her at a party, I make (fallible, of course) judgments about her appearance, her age, her clothing, her accent. Initial conversation reveals something about her employment and hobbies and favorite films, where she comes from, where she's lived. As I get to know her better through the weeks and months that follow, I learn more about her tastes, her character, her fears, her ambitions and ideals—and her regrets. She might not articulate the regrets as such, I might have to infer it, more or less reliably. Indeed, she might not want to disclose something so personal to me. And she might not even have admitted such regrets to herself. If she does articulate the regret, the important thing is that she is *not* asking me for advice on how to deal with it, or even how to learn from it, or atone for it. She may not even be asking me for sympathy or reassurance. Rather, she is describing a very personal aspect of her life, of her perspective, of her being, of her understanding of fate in her unique life.

As I say, this is far from a complete account. By way of conclusion, let me mention the example of Stevens the butler in Ishiguro's *The Remains of the Day* (1989). Stevens has been an unmarried butler in a fine English mansion for about forty years. At one point during that time, he developed a conversational intimacy with a housekeeper named Miss Kenton. As the story opens, Stevens is in his sixties and is visiting Miss Kenton, now Mrs. Benn, whom he has not seen since she left the mansion twenty years previously to get married. Ishiguro uses the device of the unreliable narrator to split the story into Stevens' own recollections, on the one hand, and the story that we are meant to understand from between the lines, on the other. It is clear to us that Miss Kenton was fond of Stevens, and made her fondness and availability known to him, but without understanding her he rejected her without admitting to himself, either then—or now—that she was fond, and that he too was fond. During the final pages of the book, the two meet up. She eventually admits that her marriage has not been as good as she had imagined *her marriage to Stevens* might have been. It is only then that Stevens discovers that his "heart was breaking" (239) and he understands what he has missed. He does not go so far as articulating regret for his earlier blindness. Rather, he has developed a sadder but deeper understanding of who he is now, as a product of his past. He certainly is not seeking to "solve" the problem of his regret, to do anything about it, since he is clear about how to spend his remaining years, employed in the same house as he has always been.

One last thought. Is Stevens' understanding necessarily sadder? In one sense, of course it is. But if we take regret as a mode of being, then there might be just a bit more to it than that. Consider Tiffany Watt Smith:

> More often than not, what at the time seems an inconsolable loss is not the end of the story. Perhaps we'll adjust ourselves to our regrets. Perhaps we'll learn from them. But unlike resignation or acceptance, regret is ultimately a kind of desire for something different to have happened. It makes the mind waver, it gnaws. And by allowing us to imagine the possibility of things ending differently, it contains, rather peculiarly, a little germ of hope. (2015, 209)[25]

NOTES

1. I will be making some general points about careers, so I do not want to be too specific. However, one classic example is that of the 1954 film *On The Waterfront*. Terry Malloy (played by Marlon Brando) was a promising young boxer who deliberately lost a fight so that his brother could win a lucrative bet. Eventually his boxing career failed, and the film opens with him, several years later, now working as a bodyguard among the corrupt longshoremen of New Jersey. In a famous scene, Malloy expresses his regret thus: "I coulda had class. I coulda been a contender, I coulda been someone. Instead of a bum, which is what I am—let's face it."

2. The website Coaching for Divorced Women has a section responding to the claim that "I wasted the best years of my life on that man": http://www.coachingfordivorcedwomen.com/wasted-years-life-man/ (accessed August 2016).

3. Regret is sometimes confused with disappointment. For my purposes, the distinction hinges on control. I am disappointed when my expectations are frustrated, and that is typically out of my control. As Landman (1993, 47) puts it, "The child is *disappointed* when the Tooth Fairy forgets his third lost tooth. The child's parents *regret* the lapse." The distinction is fuzzier in the case of being disappointed with oneself: "I regret not trying harder" comes close to "I am disappointed with myself for not trying harder"—but in the latter case there is a sense of detachment, watching an event take place.

4. This chapter has been strongly influenced by David Velleman's paper "Persons in prospect" (2015) and especially its first section, "The identity problem," where he explores certain themes about personal identity first introduced by Derek Parfit in his *Reasons and Persons* (1984).

An important recent book about regret was Jay Wallace's *The View from Here: On Affirmation, Attachment, and the Limits of Regret* (2013). However, Wallace has a fundamentally different starting point than I, and so I do not discuss him further. He takes two central examples of what I would call "costly *success*," one of which is Bernard Williams' (1981) semi-fictional Gauguin, who feels he "had to" abandon his family in order to paint: *ex hypothesi*, there is no sense that Gauguin would not choose the painting life path, now that he knows how successful he has become. In contrast, I begin with examples of *failure*, people who feel trapped in their life as a result of a decision long ago.

5. The best discussion of remorse is from chapter 4 in Raimond Gaita (2004). A lot of what I will be saying is inspired by Gaita, although my ambitions are more modest than his. Discussions of remorse also raise questions of whether it is possible or admirable to *forgive oneself*; I will not discuss this possibility (partly because I am skeptical about whether it could ever be more than self-serving), and I will be more interested in the broader option of somehow "dealing with" or "accepting" the regret.

6. One the most famous discussions of regret in the literature is from Bernard Williams in "Moral luck" (1981), which is the starting point for Wallace' (2015) book. I want to distinguish my terminology from Williams's on two counts. First, when Williams writes, "The constitutive thought of regret in general is something like 'how much better if it had been otherwise,'" I would say that such a wish constitutes

a lament, whereas I am taking regret to be about my own free decision. Second, one type of regret, for Williams, is "agent-regret": "which a person can feel only toward his own past actions" (27). However, Williams uses this conception to capture a different phenomenon and describes a lorry driver (28) who, without a trace of negligence or culpability, kills a child through sheer bad luck. Williams says the driver feels agent-regret because he caused the death, whereas I would not call this regret at all since the accident was not in the driver's control.

7. A striking example of regret soon before death is the song "Hurt," written by Trent Reznor, but sung by Johnny Cash, with a moving video directed by Mark Romanek. The video was made in 2003, when the seventy-one-year-old Cash already had visible health problems, and he died seven months later. In the song, Cash asks, "What have I become?" Where Illyich explicitly regretted his career choices and the neglect of his family, Cash is not specific about particular life choices but only regrets having become a certain kind of person here and now. Insofar as one's character is only partially under one's control, this will be an expression of part lament, part regret. It is a fascinating and poignant example but one I cannot pursue in any detail here.

8. In 1959, Edith Piaf made famous the song written by Charles Dumont: "Non, je ne regrette rien."

9. Rudiger Bittner (1992) asks whether it is *reasonable* to regret. Whatever the answer is, I am not sure this is a very interesting question. I think it is far more interesting to take people who *do* regret and to explore what such regret amounts to.

10. Lady Macbeth, in the sleepwalking scene (Act V, scene i), says, "What's done cannot be undone." She is referring to all the murders that have been necessary for her husband to ascend and retain the throne. There is always a challenge for the actor about how to say these words, whether they are words of past-oriented regret or whether they are words of future-oriented pragmatism.

11. Sartre, J. P. (2003/1943), *Being and Nothingness*, trans. Barnes, Routledge Classics, p. 473.

12. Again, strictly speaking, there was not a single choice to buy IBM when I was twenty. There was an initial choice to buy them, there was a second and a third and a fourth choice, and so forth, to keep them, all the way down to the present. But it still makes sense to say that I regret having undergone the "project" of owning the IBM shares for so long: things would have been much better if I had bought Apple twenty years ago, it would have been clear year by year that I should keep Apple, and I would be better off today.

13. I borrow the word "momentous" from William James, although I am not using his discussion at all. One could also include as momentous those choices about *where to live*. Perhaps I move to an unfamiliar town or country (perhaps with an unfamiliar accent or language) because of a job or a marriage, and over the years I settle into the place (learn the language) to the point where it has become very familiar. And yet, even when the job or the marriage continue to go well, I might come to a conclusion that I do not and never will feel at home in this place, and that I regret leaving the place or the country where I grew up. Such a judgment is particularly relevant as one reaches "a certain age" and starts to think of where one would like to retire, grow old, and die.

14. Even when I make an explicit lifelong commitment, for example, to be a spouse or a priest, I know that any number of things could induce me to leave the marriage or the priesthood. This does not mean that I contemplate such eventualities explicitly, of course, during the early stages!

15. I deliberately chose *medicine* as the career of my regretful protagonist, because I wanted to avoid the particular kind of regret that arises from the discovery of the *moral frivolity* of certain careers. Certainly, I could join the bank at twenty-one because I want the money, and then at forty-one, I come to regret the choice since I now wish I had spent my time and talent on something of greater moral value, for example, of greater direct public service. But I want to include regret over careers with clear independent value, such as medicine. After all, one could take the line that *nobody* can regret a career in medicine since nobody can regret doing good. However, I am more interested in people who admit that "of course medicine, in the abstract, is a good thing, it's just that it wasn't the right thing *for me*."

16. The word "value" is importantly ambivalent here between the experiencing subject and the object experienced. Some values are "in" me so that "based on my values I notice X" refers to my system of priorities, preferences, ideals, cares, projects, and so on. Other values are "in" the world so that I notice something *because* it is valuable: there is then the question of whether the object is valuable *simpliciter* (so that we all should experience it as valuable) or whether it is valuable *for me*, given who I am and given "my" values (the question of "fit"). There are then the meta-questions of whether I have the "correct" values and of whether a particular object "merits" so much attention (or whether, e.g., a friend might judge that it is "beneath me" to pay attention to that object). I am trying hard to avoid getting embroiled in these meta-questions and am mainly interested in the questions of fit that contribute to the metaphor of perspective.

17. I recall meeting another philosopher and telling her that I was interested in fate. She snorted, "Call yourself a philosopher?" And at that moment, we had revealed ourselves to one another: I saw her as an unimaginative technician; she saw me as a touchy-feely fantasist.

18. In the beginning, I was speaking about an unsuccessful marriage, someone who regretted wasting their life with this other person. What is interesting about the successful marriage is that there are actually three overlapping entities: the husband, the wife, and the marriage. Each entity has its own perspective

19. This has the interesting corollary that the events of one's recalled life become less fated as one moves closer and closer to the present, because they are less and less influential in shaping the perspective. This "waning influence" conception of fate is to be contrasted with the "waxing influence" conception that structures many biographies: the youngster experimenting, distracted this way and that, until she finds a job she likes, where she excels and rises and grows, and it becomes more and more clear that she is fulfilling her destiny.

20. Note that I am introducing the hot-housing example to illustrate an extreme form of this kind of necessity—the example is less useful to understand regret since, as I have been understanding the term, the eighteen-year-old prodigy cannot coherently regret the hot-housing because she herself was too young to choose it in a

sufficiently autonomous sense. She "lands" in her perspective at the beginning of her adult life. Needless to say, she is not stuck there. While she may lament her restrictions in the present and lost opportunities in the past, she faces an open future and sufficient freedom to choose her next momentous commitment.

21. There is a philosophical debate about self-ascription of virtue terms, that is, whether the genuinely generous person can sincerely describe herself *as* generous or whether such self-ascription automatically undermines itself. I am remaining agnostic on this question. Generosity is certainly a component of perspective, but I am taking an agent who reliably and spontaneously reacts to the world in a way that would be considered generous by most unbiased onlookers.

22. I have not supplied pagination because I have drawn from an online source.

23. But I am emphatically not relying on the authority of a Heideggerian text here, for I am no expert. I have no clue of whether Heidegger would approve of my use of the term.

24. Another related phenomenon is the loss of innocence. I do not mean the mere loss of sexual virginity. I mean, for example, the loss of idealism in a politician, the loss of ambition in a bureaucrat, the loss of patriotism in a soldier. In each case, the loss is felt as a loss of something good, something that can no longer be retrieved, and something that cannot be compensated for by the acquisition of experience and wisdom.

25. I am grateful to Carolyn Wilde and Paddy McQueen for discussion of this topic as well as to Anna Gotlib for very helpful comments on a first draft.

REFERENCES

Bittner, R. 1992. "Is It reasonable to Regret Things One Did." *Journal of Philosophy* 89 (5): 262–73.
Dostoyevsky, F. (1864/1981). *Notes from the Underground*, trans. Ginsburg. New York: Bantam Books.
Gaita, R. 2004. *Good and Evil: An Absolute Conception*. London: Routledge.
Ishiguro, K. 1989. *The Remains of the Day*. New York, New York: Penguin.
Landman, J. 1993. *Regret: The Persistence of the Possible*. Oxford: Oxford University Press.
Sartre, J. P. 1946. "Existentialism is a Humanism," trans. Mairet, online version available at: https://www.marxists.org/reference/archive/sartre/works/exist/sartre.htm (accessed August 2016).
Solomon, R. 2003. 'On Fate and Fatalism." *Philosophy East and West* 53 (4): 435–54.
Taylor, G. 1985. *Pride, Shame and Guilt: Emotions of Self-Assessment*. Oxford: Oxford University Press.
Velleman, D. 2015. "Persons in Prospect." In *Beyond Price: Essays on Birth and Death*. Cambridge, UK: Open Book.
Wallace, J. 2013. *The View from Here: On Affirmation, Attachment, and the Limits of Regret*. Oxford: Oxford University Press.
Watt, Smith T. 2015. *The Book of Human Emotions*. London: Profile Books.
Williams, B. 1981. "Moral Luck." In *Moral Luck*. Cambridge: Cambridge University Press.

Index

actions, 2, 4, 5, 6, 7, 10–14, 17, 19, 21, 22, 24, 29, 31, 33, 34, 38, 41, 48, 53, 59, 61, 70, 77, 79, 84–92, 100, 103, 107, 108, 110–14, 121, 122, 124, 125, 127, 129, 138, 139, 145–49, 157, 166, 168, 170, 171, 175, 176, 178, 187, 188, 190, 191, 194, 196, 216, 251, 255; agential 10; incompatible 33; involuntary 70n11; less-than-admirable 29; regrettable 12, 14, 22, 91, 92, 112, 113, 148; thoughtless and careless 5; voluntary 157
actor effect, 147
affect-colored attitudes, 29
After Virtue, 151
agent regret, 1, 5, 9, 10, 11, 20, 31, 77, 78, 82, 87, 88, 103, 187, 200, 213
Age of Innocence, The, 21, 144
alienation, 92–93, 134
American Sign Language (ASL), 203, 204, 207, 208, 214
anger, 29, 45, 55, 59, 61, 68, 101, 121, 155, 194, 200, 214; OED definition of, 55
Anglo-American philosophy, 76
Anglophone philosophy, 124, 145, 146, 151–54
anterior cingulate cortex (ACC), 170, 173, 174
apology, 39, 114, 201, 203, 215
Aristotle, 83, 105
arousal, 29, 176
ashamed person, 33, 34, 45
attribute regrets, 223, 225–27, 235
Austen, Jane, 17
Aviv, Rachel, 39

Bach, Dominik R., 65
backward-looking pain, 2, 3, 15, 16, 252
Bagnoli, Carla, 51–53, 56, 62, 63
BALD DAY, 207
Baptist, Edward E., 197, 198
Barnes, Elizabeth, 210
Baskin-Sommers, Arielle, 106
Bennett, Jonathan, 35, 56
Ben-Ze'ev, Aaron, 4, 80
Bernstein, J. M., 37
binary regrets, 223
Blair, R. J., 176
bourgeois predicament, 13
Bovary, Emma, 151
Breugelmans, Seger M., 6
Brown, Lois, 193
Buckholtz, Joshua W., 106
Bush, George W., 16

Cairns, Douglas, 121
Camille, Nathalie, 65–68, 102, 107
Carby, Hazel, 193
character regret, 77, 82, 88, 251
Chorus, C. G., 225, 227
Cima, Maaike, 176
Coates, Tamsin, 205, 206
cochlear implants, 206, 207, 211–14
cognitive emotion, 20, 77
cognitive psychology, 146–51
Coleman, Nathanial Tobias, 193
Coleridge, Samuel Taylor, 126
collective identity, 92–93, 112
Confessions, 128, 129, 134
Connolly, Terry, 169

259

Contending Forces, 190, 193, 195, 196
Coricelli, Giorgio, 19, 21, 65, 72n56, 165–79, 221
cost-benefit analyses, 16
Coughlan, Richard, 72n48, 169
counterfactuals, 246–49; inference, 6; information, 166–67; memories, 82; thinking, 6; thoughts, 166
Cowie, Roddy, 80, 81

Davis, Dena, 215
decision maker, 224, 226
decision-making, 8, 18
decision regret, 165, 168
decision theory, 9, 16, 146
de facto model, 229
Dennett, D. C., 83, 86–88
Descartes, René, 77, 83, 85, 160n14
desires, 8, 9, 32, 33, 58, 68, 87, 161n24, 203, 246
De Sousa, Ronald, 61
Dilman, Ilham, 30
disability affirmation, 203, 204, 210
disability regret, 203, 204, 210, 217
disappointment, 63–65
discrete choice theory (DCT) tradition, 228
displeasure, OED definition of, 56
disrespect, 108
Dolan, Raymond J., 65
dorsolateral prefrontal cortex (dlPFC), 170, 173, 174
Douglas, Sarah, 190, 191
Douglass, Frederick, 193
Duhamel, Jean-René, 65

Eaton, Marcia, 91
Ekman, Paul, 81
Emma, 17
emotion, 3, 54, 61; retrospective moral self-condemnation, 39
emotional attachments, 77, 79
emotional intelligence, 5
emotional response, 2, 68, 169, 174
emotion literature, philosophy of, 51–53
emotions, 32, 34, 40, 81; classifying, 29–30; and thoughts, 30–32
established emotion, 80
excitement, 29, 102
experienced regret, 146

false remorse, 39–41
fate, 249–50

Faulkner, William, 2, 15
Feinberg, Joel, 215
fictive learning, 168
Financial Times, 122
Flaubert, Gustave, 144
Frankfurt, H. G., 79, 86–88
Freud, 159
Friedman, M., 83, 88
Frith, Chris, 65
Fulkerson, Laurel, 126

Gaita, Raimond, 123–28, 130, 134, 139
Gendler, Tamar, 34
general reactive attitudes, 46, 60
genetic selection, 208–10
Gibert, Martin, 34
Gilovich, Thomas, 101, 104, 147–50
Goldie, Peter, 31, 88
Good and Evil: An Absolute Conception, 124
Greene, Joshua D., 173
Greenspan, Patricia, 31
grief, 55–56, 104; definition of, 55
Guerini, Rossella, 169
guilt-feeling agent, 5

Half Has Never Been Told, The, 197
Hare, Caspar, 52
Harel, A., 234
Harman, Elizabeth, 205
Harper, Frances, 188, 191–94, 197–201
Harris, Paul, 34
Haufniensis, Vigilius, 126
Hauser, Marc D., 176
Hitler, Adolph, 59
Hobbes, T., 85
Holocaust, 59, 60
Hopkins, Pauline, 188, 190–94, 196, 197, 200, 201
Huck Finn, 41
Hurka, Thomas, 155, 156
Hurlburt, Russ, 81

identification, 92–93
immoral action, 99, 107
immoral regret, 29, 109, 110
impossible regret, 103–4
inactions, 88, 145, 147–50, 168
interpersonal regret, 100, 108, 110, 112–14
Iola Leroy, or, Shadows Uplifted, 193, 197, 199

Ishiguro, K., 253
Ivan the Terrible and His Son Ivan, 126

"James-Lange" theory, 80
Jankélévitch, Vladimir, 126, 131, 132, 136
Joyce, J. M., 52, 76

Kahneman, Daniel, 147, 149, 150, 228
Kant, Immanuel, 85
Kashdana, Todd, 37
Ketcham, Katherine, 39
Kierkegaard, Soren, 87, 137–39
King Lear, 17
Klassen, Johann A., 51
Knowles, John, 17
Korsgaard, Christine, 89, 90

lament, 59, 241, 242, 244, 245, 246, 247, 250, 255, 257
Landman, Janet, 4, 7, 16, 17, 51, 52, 53, 56, 64, 76, 77, 81, 150
learning value, 167–68
Lickel, Brian, 111–13, 116n17
Locke, John, 77, 83, 85, 86, 89, 90
Loftus, Elizabeth, 39
Lohrenz, T., 167
Long Past Slavery: Representing Race in the Federal Writers' Project, 191
long-term momentous decisions, 245–46
long-term trivial regret, 244–45
Loss Aversion (LA) model, 228

MacIntyre, Alasdair, 151, 161n21, 161n26
Madame Bovary, 144
Magna Carta, 84
Maibom, Heidi, 30
Marchiori, Davide, 66, 171
marital regret, 145, 154–59
McIntosh, Peggy, 189
measure of choice set regret, 229–33
medial orbitofrontal cortex (mOFC), 170, 172
Medvec, Victoria Husted, 101, 104, 147–50
membership regret, 100, 111–12
memory, 90–92
Midgley, Mary, 90
Miss Deaf America, 214–17
Mitchell, Jason P., 177
moral action, 99, 107, 176
moral attitude, 32, 45, 48, 49, 69n5
moral decision making, 172–74

moral differences, 4
moral distress, 62
moral emotions, 1, 7, 18, 29, 33, 109
moral epistemology, 34
moral geographies, 5, 11
morality, 98, 174–75
moral judgment, 20, 30, 33, 172, 174, 176, 187
morally problematic choice architectures, 233–36
moral myopia, 2, 3
moral norms, 114, 165, 166
moral psychology, 109, 115n11, 138, 141n11
moral reasonableness, 110
moral regret, 107, 109, 110
moral responsibility, 10, 46, 47, 69n4, 84
moral selfhood, 84
moral sentiment, 35, 122
moral value, 10, 256
Morton, Adam, 30, 32, 34, 38, 41
Mrs. Dalloway, 17
Murdoch, Iris, 157

Nahmias, Eddy, 84
narcissism, 2, 3
narrative, 90–92; in Anglophone philosophy, 151–54
narrative unity, 151, 161
negative emotional attitude, 83
neural circuits, regret, 170–72
Nichols, Shaun, 34, 84, 90
Nicolle, Antinette, 65, 68, 178
nonagential regret, 3–5
nonmoral normativity, 49
nonmoral "obligations," 49
non-narrative people, 153
normative attitudes, 48, 49
Nussbaum, Martha, 31, 192

Oedipus complex, 159
Olson, Eric, 84, 89
open future regret (OFR), 215–17
orbitofrontal cortex (OFC), 67, 68
Ordóñez, Lisa D., 72n48, 169
Orth, U., 37

palliative consolation, 137–39
pareto optimality, 234
participant reactive attitudes, 45, 46
Paul, L. A., 211, 212
personal reactive attitudes, 45, 60

personal regret, 77, 92, 93, 103
personal responsibility, 21, 22, 64, 110, 169
personal transformation, 211
personal well-being, 152
person concept: contemporary accounts of, 86–92; early development, 84
personhood, 82–84; animalist accounts of, 84; emotions and, 79–80
person-making, 93; narratives, 88–89
phony regret, 77, 81
pity, OED definition of, 55
Plato, 83, 192
Porat, A., 234
Pradat-diehl, Pascale, 65
preimplantation genetic diagnosis (PGD), 208, 209
Prinz, Jesse, 30
pseudo-regret, 98, 103, 104
psychological damage, 37–39
psychological reciprocity, 158
psychopaths, 106, 175–77
psychopathy, 106, 175–77

R4, agent-related emotion, 59, 61, 63
Radin, M. J., 234
rage, 29, 80, 126
random regret minimization (RRM) model, 23, 222–29, 234, 235
random utility maximization (RUM), 228, 229
Raphael, D. D., 192, 201n6
Rarus, Brandi, 214
reactive attitude, 45–73; and normativity, 45–51; responsibility and standard-based value, 50; Strawson's view, expanding, 46–47
reasonable action, 99
reasonable regret, 98–116; moral regret, easy case of, 105–8
regretful person, 33
regrets, 1–25, 32, 38, 47–48, 50, 51, 59, 61, 63–65, 86, 90–92; and agency, 177–78; aversion, 221; brain and, 165–79; as cluster concept, 100; cognitive content of, 82; as condition for personhood, 76–94; cousins of, 29–42; defined, 6; defining, 100–103; definition of, 54, 77–80; disability considerations, 203–19; as emotion, 80–82; emotional experience of, 107; emotional phenomenology, 101; future of, 24–25; and genetic selection, 208–10; guilt *versus*, 3–7, 104–5; as human predicament, 9–15; hyperbolic and metaphorical uses of, 60; impossible, 103–4; and language choices, 204–8; memory and imagination, 82; minimization, riskless decision making, 221–37; mode of being, 251–53; neural circuits of, 170–72; OFC lesions, 174–75; person-making, 76; persons and, 77–79; perspective and fate, 240–57; perspective and transformation, 144–62; philosophers on, 9–15; rational content, 102; reactive attitude, 45–73; reasonable, 105–10; regretting, 15–18; responsibility and, 165–79; and self-knowledge, 121–42; shape of, 3–18; for slavery in nineteenth-century African American philosophical literature, 187–202; social dimension of, 177–78; valuing, 7–9; via proxy, 110–11
Regret: The Persistence of the Possible (1993), 16
Remains of the Day, The, 253
remorse, 35–38, 47–48, 121–24, 128, 132, 134, 135–37, 145, 241
Remorse and Reparation, 121
remorseful person, 33, 127, 131, 140
reparation, 22, 121–24, 135–37, 139, 187, 188, 189, 192, 199, 200, 216, 217
Repin, Ilya, 126
responsibility, 47–48, 56–57, 168–69; negative emotion, 57–58
responsibility studies, 65–66
retrospection, 14, 37–39
retrospective emotions, 19, 30, 32–34, 36, 40, 41, 42
retrospective thought, 2
revision criterion, 66–68
Rime of the Ancient Mariner, 126
riskless decision making, 222–29
risky decision making, 221, 237n4
Robins, R., 37
Roese, Neal J., 65
Rorty, Amélie, 51–53, 82, 101
Rorty, Richard, 192
Rosati, Connie, 152–54
Rossi-Keen, Daniel E., 46
Rosthal, Robert, 136
RRM-LogSum, 230, 231, 233
ruination, 131–35

Sallet, Jerome, 65
Sartre, J. P., 251
Schechtman, M., 77, 83, 88, 89, 90, 91, 151

Scheler, Max, 127, 131–33
Schopenhauer, 127, 132, 133
Schwitzgebel, Eric, 81
scientific confirmation, 63–68; regret and disappointment, 63–65; responsibility studies, 65–66; revision criterion, 66–68
self-accusatory retrospection, 38, 41
self-agency, 64
self-blame regret, 65, 178
self-deception, 242, 243
self-defining stories, 78
self-directed regret, 7
self-involved emotion, 5
self-knowledge, 121–42
self-narrative, 88, 91
self-reactive attitudes, 46, 67, 69
self-reflexive reactive attitudes, 46
Sense and Sensibility, 1
sense of regret, 188, 190, 191, 200, 208, 213
Separate Peace, A, 17
Shakespeare, 17
shame, 31, 34, 36, 38, 45
shared identity, 112
short-term trivial regret, 243–44
Sirigu, Angela, 65, 167, 170
slave legacy, 189
Slave Narratives of the Federal Writers' Project, 190
Small House at Allington, The, 144
Smith, Adam, 122, 123, 127
Smith, Angela M., 157
Smith, Tiffany Watt, 253
Smith, William, 195
social psychology, 112, 146–51, 166
sociopaths, 83
Solomon, Robert, 31, 249
Sophie's Choice, 63, 125
Sources of the Self, 151
Sovereignty of Good, The, 157
St. Augustine, 128–31, 134
Stewart, Catherine, 191
Still, William, 193
Strasser, Mark, 62
Strawson, Galen, 2, 90, 153
Strawson, P. F., 45–47
Strohminger, N., 84, 90
Stuppy-Sullivan, Allison M., 106
Styron, William, 125
Sugden, Robert, 53
Summerville, Amy, 65
systematic regret, 223, 224, 230

Tappolet, Christine, 31, 33
Taylor, Charles, 88, 151
Taylor, Gabriele, 30, 53, 242
Terman, Lewis, 148
Tessman, Lisa, 14, 30
Thoreau, Henry David, 187
Tonnaer, Franca, 176
transformative experience, 23, 204, 211–14
Trollope, Anthony, 144
Truman, Harry, 17, 25n3
Tversky, A., 147, 228
Twain, Mark, 35, 36

unconditional affirmation, 13, 210
undermined regret, 37
undermined shame, 37, 40
unpleasant emotion, 4, 101, 107
unreasonable action, 99
unreasonable regret, 109, 110

van Cranenburgh, S., 225
Velleman, David, 141n10, 152, 153, 154, 161n22, 161n24, 161n27, 254n4
ventromedial prefrontal cortex (vmPFC), 170–72, 174, 175, 179
View from Here: On Affirmation, Attachment, and the Limits of Regret, The, 2, 12, 203, 204
violence inhibition mechanism, 176

Wallace, R. Jay, 2, 12–15, 88, 89, 146, 203, 204, 208–10
wantons, 79
Warglien, Massimo, 66, 171
well-being, 2, 5, 9, 152–54
Wharton, Edith, 144
whole moral personhood, 88
Williams, Bernard, 10, 11, 30–32, 48, 81, 103, 145, 146, 187, 188, 190
Williston, Byron, 121, 135
Wollheim, Richard, 151
Woolf, Virginia, 17
World at War, The, 124

Zagzebski, Linda, 30
Zawistowska, Sophie, 125
Zeelenberg, Marcel, 6, 51, 64, 72n48, 105, 107, 115n5, 115n9, 116n13, 150, 169

About the Contributors

Audrey L. Anton is associate professor of philosophy at Western Kentucky University. Her research interests include ancient philosophy (especially Aristotle's ethics), moral psychology (especially moral responsibility), ethics (especially virtue ethics), and philosophical gerontology. She is the author of *Moral Responsibility and Desert of Praise and Blame* (Lexington, 2015), the editor of *The Bright and the Good: The Connection between Intellectual and Moral Virtues* (Rowman & Littlefield International, 2018), and over a dozen articles. Anton is currently the Philip L. Quinn Fellow at the National Humanities Center (2018–2019), a recipient of a Thyssen Junior Fellowship (Institute for Advanced Studies, Central European University, deferred to 2020), a former recipient of a Loeb Classical Library Foundation Fellowship (2017), and an Enduring Questions grant from the National Endowment for the Humanities (2013–2015).

David Batho is associate fellow at the University of Essex. He has published in phenomenology and the medical humanities.

Nadège Bault obtained a PhD in cognitive neuroscience from the University of Lyon. Her research focuses on decision making and learning processes in social environments.

Teresa Blankmeyer Burke is associate professor of philosophy at Gallaudet University, a bilingual university that uses American Sign Language and English to serve deaf, hard of hearing, and hearing students in Washington, DC. She is the only signing Deaf philosopher in the world with a doctorate in philosophy. Her publications cover a wide range of genres, including peer-reviewed scholarship in philosophy, bioethics, policy, and interpreting ethics.

She has also written for the general public, including mainstream media publications, creative nonfiction, and poetry in both American Sign Language and English. Dr. Burke has served on a number of national and international committees for a variety of organizations, including the World Federation of the Deaf, the American Philosophical Association, the Hearing Loss Association of America, and the National Association of the Deaf (United States). Burke divides her time between Washington, DC, and the historic neighborhood of Barelas in Albuquerque, New Mexico, and is currently working on a philosophical memoir about grief and resilience about her experience as a young widow and single mother in Cody, Wyoming.

Caspar Chorus is professor of choice behavior modeling at Delft University of Technology and head of its department of Engineering Systems and Services. Trained as an engineer and econometrician, Chorus's aim is to develop and empirically validate mathematical models of human decision making. He has developed models of bounded rationality, such as the random regret minimization model that is used worldwide and embedded in various software packages. Currently, sponsored by a two-million-euro consolidator grant from the European Research Council, he and his team are developing models of moral decision making, which describe how humans behave in moral decision-making contexts. This work opens up the possibility to equip artificial intelligence with a moral compass inspired by human morality. Chorus's work has received various international awards and recognitions as well as funding from highly competitive grant schemes. His main area of application is transport; Chorus is steering committee member of the European Association for Research in Transportation, and he is editor-in-chief of the *European Journal of Transport and Infrastructure Research* (open-access, ISI-listed). In addition to his work in choice modeling and transport, Chorus develops advanced choice models for various other fields, such as sociology, health, marketing, and environment and energy.

Giorgio Coricelli is professor of economics and psychology at the University of Southern California. He studies human behaviors emerging from the interplay of cognitive and emotional systems.

Christopher Cowley works on ethics and agency at University College Dublin. He is the author of *Moral Responsibility* (Routledge, 2013) and has edited a volume on the *Philosophy of Autobiography* (Chicago, 2015). He is currently working on a book on the philosophy of criminal law.

James DiGiovanna is assistant professor of philosophy at John Jay College CUNY. He works on personal identity, robots as persons, and human enhancement. Recent publications include "Literally Like a Different Person" in *Southern Journal of Philosophy* and "Artificial Identity and Robot Ethics" in *Robot Ethics 2.0*. He is currently working on a book on artificial personhood. His feature film, *A Forked World*, has been shown at underground film festivals around the United States. He was formerly a film reviewer for alternative weeklies and an editor for Marvel Comics.

Catherine Villanueva Gardner is professor of philosophy and women's and gender studies at the University of Massachusetts, Dartmouth. She is the author of two monographs: *Empowerment and Interconnectivity: Toward a Feminist History of Utilitarian Philosophy* (Pennsylvania State University Press, 2013) and *Women Philosophers: Genre and the Boundaries of Philosophy* (Westview Press, 2003/1999). In addition, she has also written articles in the feminist history of philosophy, aimed at recapturing forgotten women philosophers and reinterpreting canonical philosophers, such as Plato and David Hume, through the lens of gender. She is a coeditor and cofounder of the online *Journal of Feminist Scholarship*. Gardner is currently working on a third monograph exploring nineteenth-century African American philosophy.

Anna Gotlib is associate professor of philosophy at Brooklyn College CUNY. Her areas of research and teaching include normative and applied ethics (especially bioethics/medical ethics), moral psychology, philosophy of law, and feminist philosophy. Her work has appeared in *Hypatia*, *The International Journal of Feminist Approaches to Bioethics*, *Journal of Bioethical Inquiry*, *The Kennedy Institute of Ethics Journal*, and a number of edited volumes. She is a coeditor of *IJFAB* (*International Journal of Feminist Approaches to Bioethics*) and is the editor of a volume entitled *The Moral Psychology of Sadness* (Rowman & Littlefield International, 2017). She is currently working on a monograph on memory, identity, and trauma.

Adam Morton is a philosophical generalist working mostly in epistemology and the philosophy of the emotions, with excursions into ethics and the philosophy of language. Signs of overambition are that his two most recent books are *Emotion and Imagination* and *Should We Colonize Other Planets?*

Maura Priest is assistant professor and bioethicist in the Department of Philosophy in the School of Historical, Philosophical, and Religious Studies at Arizona State University. She has a doctorate and master's in philosophy from University of California-Irvine, a master's in bioethics from Columbia University, and a certificate in pediatric bioethics from Children's Mercy Hospital. Priest has published more than twenty peer-reviewed articles in ethics, epistemology, political philosophy, and bioethics.

Sarah Richmond is senior lecturer in the Department of Philosophy on the Faculty of Arts & Humanities at University College London. Her philosophical interests lie at the "Humanities" end of the subject.

Ben Timberlake is a doctoral candidate in cognitive and brain sciences at the University of Trento, Italy. His research concerns the transfer of regret across decision making and learning contexts. His thesis investigates this phenomenon specifically in conditions of aging and emotional priming.

www.ingramcontent.com/pod-product-compliance
Lightning Source LLC
Chambersburg PA
CBHW022010300426
44117CB00005B/119